SCOTTISH AND ENGLISH SCHOOLS

Scottish and English Schools

A comparative survey of the past fifty years

G. S. OSBORNE

LONGMANS

LONGMANS GREEN & CO LTD
48 Grosvenor Street, London W1

Associated companies, branches and representatives
throughout the world

Printed in Great Britain by
The Bowering Press Plymouth

Contents

PART III: THE FORMATIVE YEARS

PART IV: THE ACADEMIC TRADITION

PART V: THE DEMOCRATIC TRADITION

PART VI: SPECIALIZATION

PART VII: THE TEACHERS

23 A GRADUATE PROFESSION?

24 NON-GRADUATE COURSES

25 QUALIFICATIONS AND SALARIES

PART VIII: SOME CONCLUSIONS

26 MORAL TRAINING

27 TEACHER AND TAUGHT

28 THE TRANSMISSION OF CULTURE

Preface

H.M. Inspectors! Twa o' them, fegs!
H.M. Inspectors! Twa orra glegs!
Come to inspect and examine the skweel!
Hinner the wark and speir like the deil!

The chief purpose of this book is to compare the 'state systems' of education: what, in England, are known as 'maintained schools' and, in Scotland, as 'public schools'. Independent schools, the universities, technical colleges and, of course, teacher-training colleges have been considered too, because a country's education must be looked at as a whole. But, if references to these other institutions appear unsystematic, it is because my main interest has been in the schools. Similarly, historical accounts are given, but these are selective, mentioning only what appeared to be significant for an understanding of present day primary and secondary schools.

Differences in the scale of provision, and in the organization, of full-time school education are instructive in themselves. Admittedly in both England and Scotland the state now compels all children between the ages of about five and about fifteen, and enables children of other ages, to spend approximately forty weeks in the year in a group, in a classroom, with a teacher, though there is some variation in the extent to which children are also expected to study outside the classroom. Admittedly, too, the number of teachers, the total number and ages of the children, the number and size of groups, which go to make up a school are all very much governed by external factors which could easily obscure the basic assumptions (if any) behind school planning. Yet there are elements in the pattern of school organization which seem to point quite clearly to differences in educational ideas.

To discover whether the actual practice of the schools points in the same way by trying to observe them at work would have been impossible. Nevertheless there did seem to be a way of comparing the climate of educational thought in England and Scotland. One could take the annual reports of the Government Departments of Education, the various official Handbooks of Suggestions for Teachers which they have published, and the reports of advisory councils, *ad hoc* working parties and the like, and see what had been said about education in each country by the people actually in charge of it. These official documents ought to provide a straightforward means of comparing the schools as seen through the eyes of those who are responsible for their control. Departmental publications are anonymous but they can be assumed to draw their facts from their own statistical returns and – more particularly – their impressions from the reports submitted by H.M. Inspectors. Departmental advice to teachers must be assumed to accord with that given by the Inspectorate. There could be no better source of knowledge about the schools than the observations of several hundred men and women engaged full time on seeing them at work, and no better indication of the trend of ideas in education than the suggestions offered to the schools by those whose job it is to ensure that their standards are at least maintained and, if possible, improved. Official descriptions of what is going on might occasionally be coloured by assumptions about what ought to be. So much the better: this might involve an unconscious revelation of what those assumptions are. The annual reports might partly have been written with an eye to the Minister earning some political credit: this could be equally revealing. Advisory councils usually consider evidence from every possible section of the educational world before making their recommendations. It is sometimes a criticism of their reports that they lack imagination and merely reflect the general consensus of educational opinion. For our present purpose this, if it is true, would be their greatest merit.

This approach seemed to offer possibilities. An Englishman who writes about Scottish education does so at his own risk. His personal observations of the schools would certainly be suspect. This method would mean that, if Scottish educators were to be criticized at all, they would be condemned out of their own mouths. It would, of course, mean suppressing one's own views. For example, the Advisory Council on Education in Scotland made a devastating criticism of the ordinary M.A. course at the Scottish universities when they mentioned that a student will frequently take some subjects 'not because he is interested in them, but because they are necessary to conform to the degree regulations, or, in some cases, because they are considered to be soft options' – not, the Council commented, the best preparation for a future teacher who should inspire his pupils with a love of learning. That is not, however, the main criticism which I myself would have wished to make of the Scottish ordinary degree course.

But the approach adopted turned out to have an unexpected drawback. It proved to be all too easy to condemn Scottish education by quoting the Scottish Education Department. To the outside world Scots maintain an attitude of conviction that Scottish education is superior to any in the world. But, in publications intended to be read by Scottish teachers, the accent is on self criticism. This would not have mattered quite so much if the tone of the English publications had not been so apparently complacent. This does not mean that the English are self-satisfied (though it will confirm Scottish beliefs in that). It is simply that there is a difference in technique.

Statements made by the Ministry of Education can never be taken at their face value. They may be not so much statements of bare fact, as of expectation. By declaring enthusiastically that it is so, it is hoped to cajole teachers into making it so. The annual report for 1962 says: 'What one Inspector reports of one school is now typical of many', and one can feel the implication that it ought to be typical of many more. The impression given is that England has the best of all imaginable schools – and that, given enough encouragement, they will rapidly improve out of all recognition. It could be misleading to compare this kind of wishful thinking with the Scottish reports which are usually hortatory in tone and sometimes downright hectoring.

Compare, for example, the following descriptions of primary schools:

Ministry of Education Annual Report 1962[1]

'During recent years junior education has earned for itself widespread recognition and respect. The majority of junior schools now reflect the nature of the children for whose sake they exist; they are friendly, lively and industrious places where relationships between staff and children are natural and unstrained, where teachers acknowledge the importance of the children's individuality and are willing to adapt their methods to encourage its growth. There is evidence of independent, progressive thought and practice in an increasing number of schools . . .

'Where the able and the slow now work together there is likely to be less class teaching, more individual and group work, more flexible arrangement of time-tables and, it is hoped, more detailed record keeping . . .

'Original writing is one of the most striking features of good junior schools . . .

'Many teachers now recognise the value of first hand experience both in and out of school as an aid to learning. . . . Oral discussion is encouraged as a means for children to begin to clarify their ideas and set them into coherent patterns and it frequently happens that they discover for themselves that real learning requires work in many subjects; for example, what began as history may well include literature, mathematics and science before the matter under investigation is brought to a satisfying conclusion. . . .

'Notable advances are being made in the learning of mathematics . . .'

Scottish Education Department Annual Report 1960[2]

'In the majority of schools, earnest teaching has secured a satisfactory standard of work in all subjects. This is particularly true of schools where the staffing position has been reasonably stable. In those which have been less fortunate and where, for lengthy periods, some of the instruction has been in the hands of less competent teachers, the maintenance of normal standards has, however, not been possible . . .

'County schemes of work have proved a steadying influence in providing a standard and an aim, as well as giving guidance in details of method. Most teachers realise that these schemes are based on the requirements of pupils of average ability and must be modified to meet the needs of the less able. Fewer seem, however, to recognise the need to extend their scope for the benefit of the ablest pupils. Not all are successful, moreover, in avoiding the pitfall of too rigid an adherence to the accepted scheme. This may stifle initiative that might otherwise have resulted in a widening of the pupils' interests . . .

'Group methods have long been successfully practised in infant classes and

[1] Cmnd. 1990, p. 19.   [2] Cmnd. 1359, p. 14.

the small but steady increases in their use in the upper classes of the primary
school reported in recent years has continued. Young teachers are usually willing
to adopt these methods but sometimes need skilled guidance to enable them to
avoid the initial pitfalls. Admittedly, some of the less competent teachers can
manage little beyond class teaching; but many could do more to cater for the
differing abilities within their classes than their present rather limited efforts to
help the slowest pupils with reading and arithmetic . . .

'The "free" composition of the infant room is beginning to appear in classes
PIII to PIV. Its encouragement may do something to counteract the present
lack of vitality in the written exercise of many schools where excessive attention
to form has often resulted in correct but dull writing . . .

'Arithmetic, with emphasis on the use of number in practical situations, is
generally on satisfactory lines in infant classes. In the later stages of the primary
school, however, there are still many classes where the aim of proficiency in
mechanical arithmetic leads to neglect of practical work in the use of weights
and measures and of problems in familiar contexts. This neglect hinders rather
than helps mechanical proficiency because the realities of the subject are lost.
Interest in the Cuisenaire method of teaching arithmetic has continued to develop.
Few attempts, however, have been made so far to use the child's exploration of
his environment as a means of introducing some mathematical ideas.'

The aspects of primary school practice of which the two Departments appear
to approve are similar: it would not be fair to assume from these quotations that
the schools in England have been more successful in adopting them than the
primary schools of Scotland. The difference in style of the official publications
may in itself be significant: but it makes comparisons more difficult.

Terminology causes a certain amount of difficulty: many of the terms used are
explained in the text and there is a glossary. Occasionally there are references to
'the Ministry' when it might have been more accurate to refer to the Department
of Education and Science, but this is a convenient way of distinguishing the
English government department from the Scottish Education Department
which has for many years been known in educational circles as 'the Department'.
Similarly the English Colleges of Education are occasionally described as
'training colleges' even though they have now adopted the title in use in Scotland
since 1958. 'Secondary', with a capital, is used of Secondary (grammar) schools
before, in England, the 1944 Act reclassified all schools for pupils over eleven,
and, in Scotland, the 1939 Code similarly brought all post-primary education
under the same regulations: 'secondary', with a small letter, is used in the sense
which it has acquired after these dates. 'Public School', with capitals, means a
school in membership of the Headmasters' Conference: 'public school', a maintained school in Scotland.

The verses at the head of each Part are taken from a collection of poems by
J. C. Milne. They are written in the Buchan dialect of north-east Scotland. If

this dialect is strange to English readers – and even to those who are familiar with the Scots of Burns – the career of the man who wrote them was no less soundly within the Scottish tradition and yet unusual to the English view. J. C. Milne was a 'lad o' pairts': brought up on an Aberdeenshire farm, he took three first class honours degrees at Aberdeen University: in English and moral philosophy, mental philosophy and geography. He was in turn a lecturer in logic at the University, the headmaster of a primary school and principal master of method at Aberdeen College of Education.

If Aberdeen and north-east Scotland receive more than their fair share of mention, there is no need for apology: the education provided in that area is commonly regarded as the quintessence of Scottish education.

The comparison is between Scotland and England. Wales has been excluded. But, in some of the tables, it has been impossible to separate the figures for England and Wales.

Acknowledgements

We are grateful to the following for permission to reproduce copyright material: The Aberdeen University Press Ltd for 'Discipline', 'The Lad O' Pairts', 'Teachin'', and lines from 'Twa Young Inspectors', 'A Dominie's Say', 'To a Young Dominie', 'Dominie Dandie (1)', 'Dominie Dandie (2)', 'Graduation for All?' and 'Divine Purpose' from *Poems of J. C. Milne*; George Allen & Unwin Ltd for material from *The Poor Student and the University* by L. D. Whiteley; The Association of Commonwealth Universities for material from *Applications for Admission to Universities* by R. K. Kelsall; The Clarendon Press for material from *The Educational Systems of Great Britain* by G. Balfour; University of Durham for material from *Elementary School Work 1900–1925* by R. D. Bramwell; Edinburgh University Press for material from *The Democratic Intellect* by G. E. Davie; The Controller of Her Majesty's Stationery Office for material from various Departmental reports, etc. and from Command Paper 1359 (1960–61) *Education in Scotland in 1960* and Command Paper 1990 (1962–63) *Education in 1962* (Report of the Ministry of Education for England and Wales); Longmans, Green & Co. Ltd for material from *English Social History* by G. M. Trevelyan; National Union of Teachers for material from *The Training of Teachers and Grants to Intending Teachers* (1936–1938); Oliver & Boyd Ltd for material from *250 Years of Scottish Education* by H. M. Knox, *The Rise and Progress of Scottish Education* by A. Morgan, and *Scottish Democracy 1815–1840* by L. J. Saunders; The Scottish Educational Journal for material from articles entitled 'Applications for admission to Universities' by R. K. Kelsall, and 'The Home Background of Student Teachers' and 'The Quality of Student Teachers' by J. Scotland, published in *Scottish Educational Journal* Vols. 46 and 47, and The University of London Press Ltd for material from *A History of English Education from 1760* by H. C. Barnard, *Education in Ayrshire through Seven Centuries* by W. Boyd, and *Post Primary Education in Scotland* by N. A. Wade.

PART I

Historical Background

Till Fiersday last, as far's I min'
I thocht my skweel wis daeing fine.
Till Fiersday last, fin, dyod, there cam'
Twa young Inspectors fae the Cam!

They speirt gin I'd a gweed degree.
Says I, 'Fae twixt the Don and Dee.'
Says t'ane te t'ither, 'Och ay, och hon!
Cam's sweeter far than Dee or Don!'

CHAPTER ONE

Church, State and School

BEFORE THE UNION OF 1707

'Order on the petition of Fitzpayne Fisher, referred by Council stating his pains in finishing a treatise which will be of great use in all schools for youths, and intending a journey to Scotland, desires money for it, and a pass, to request Council to order him the pass and £100, to be paid by Mr Frost, for his encouragement to perfect the work.'[1]

This quotation from the Calendar of State Papers for 13 August 1652, is as good a starting point as any for a comparison between English and Scottish education. The Long Parliament wanted a report on Scottish education from Fitzpayne Fisher to help in the drawing up of plans for reform in England. The head which had worn the crown of both kingdoms was severed. Charles II had been crowned King of Scotland, but not of England. Commissioners had arrived in Dalkeith to declare invalid any authority in Scotland purporting to be derived 'otherwise than from the Parliament of the Commonwealth of England'. But, though the English parliamentarians had defeated the Scots in battle, when they wanted to work out a comprehensive scheme for education in England, they turned to Scotland for an example. They did so because Scottish education was reputed to be better and also because similar impulses towards reform had been at work north of the border, and to rather more effect. This antithesis of national differences and common influences, of English dominance in political affairs and Scottish superiority in education, is a feature of the history of education in Britain.

In the year 1600 there had been eight universities in Britain: two in England and six in Scotland – of which three were in the county of Aberdeen. This, however, is too simple a measure of the extent of the lead which Scotland (and north-east Scotland in particular) had over England. Even now in the mid-twentieth century, it is difficult to compare the provision of university places because Scottish universities undertake work which, in England, is done in the grammar schools. In the sixteenth century the difference between school and university studies was even more blurred. The Scottish universities included Edinburgh, founded by the Town Council in 1582 on the model of Calvin's Academy in Geneva; Marischal College, Aberdeen, dating from 1593; and a short-lived establishment in Fraserburgh which had been started in 1592. In England six of the nine 'great' Public Schools were founded between 1550 and 1612, including Gresham College ('which is an epitome of an University by it

[1] See W. A. L. Vincent, *The State and School Education 1640–1660*, 1950, p. 81.

selfe') with its seven Professors of divinity, civil law, medicine, rhetoric, astronomy, geometry and music.[1]

In the early years of the Reformation the policy of the Crown in England had been to try to ensure that existing church schools should continue to be maintained and, even – but with limited success – to divert additional church revenues to the establishment of free grammar schools. In the more settled conditions of the second half of the sixteenth century, however, many new schools were founded. In the seventeenth century Parliament was equally determined that the constitutional struggle and reform of the church alike should not reduce the country's educational provision, and even more determined that some of the church's wealth should be used for educational purposes. In 1649 this principle was slightly extended. Not only were the first fruits and tenths (which since the reign of Henry VIII had been payable to the Crown) to be devoted to the maintenance of ministers and schoolmasters, but, in so far as the revenue from this source did not amount to £20,000, the balance was to be made up by the Exchequer.

The Scottish Parliament went further. In 1616 the Privy Council decreed that a school should be established in every parish. This was ratified by Parliament in 1633 and a further Act for Founding Schools was passed in 1646. Though similar proposals[2] were made in England, they never reached the statute book.

But, though there was much that was common to the two countries in the impulses towards educational development at this period, the difference between them was soon to become apparent again:

'The Reformation broke down the barriers between England and Scotland in one way only to re-establish them in another. Between the sixteenth century and the eighteenth, two kingdoms are drifting towards a "personal" and then a "real" union. But two churches are drifting into discord and antagonism.'[3]

After the Restoration the legislation which has been mentioned was promptly repealed in both Scotland and England. But in Scotland one of the last achievements of the independent Scottish Parliament was to re-enact the statutes of 1633 and 1646 in an Act for Settling Schools of 1696. England had to wait for two hundred years before the schools should receive from the Government a grant of £20,000 – the exact amount that had been diverted to education by the Long Parliament. Calvinistic Scotland adopted (or, rather, continued) a policy of cooperation between church and state which was made practicable by the adherence of the overwhelming majority of its people to the Church of Scotland. South of the border the Universities of Oxford and Cambridge were closed to nonconformists and Roman Catholics. The rise of Methodism was to reinforce a situation in which the established church served only half the nation.[4] The state

---

[1] See J. W. Adamson, *A Short History of Education*, 1922, p. 151.

[2] See Vincent, op. cit., p. 89 ff.

[3] F. W. Maitland, quoted in G. E. Davie, *The Democratic Intellect*, 1961, p. xi.

[4] The Church of Scotland at present claims 1,281,000 communicant members compared with only two million for the Church of England.

itself played no part in the provision of education. Not that the religious divergence was the only factor:

'While it is right to bring into prominence this Heraclitean rhythm of a simultaneous drawing towards and away from England, it is probably misleading to identify the differentiating factor with religion, and to imply the absence of a serious secular division between North and South. On the contrary, the Great Britain of the 1707 Union is surely best regarded, not as an arrangement of two state churches in one state, but rather as a unity in politics combined with diversity in what may be termed social ethics. The principle of centralisation was confined to the parliamentary and fiscal spheres, and local autonomy remained intact not only in the church, but also in the judicature, and, what is equally important, in certain fundamental institutions in which legal and clerical interests met, such as, above all, the educational system. Hence from the beginning of the eighteenth century to the end of the nineteenth, the distinctive code regulating the Scottish way of life was based not simply on a religious separation, but on a distinctive blend of the secular and of the sacred.'[1]

SCOTLAND BEFORE 1872

It was, and still is, an essential ingredient of the distinctive Scottish attitude that to make the schools freely available to the whole population is to benefit the state as well as the individual. This is based on sound economics – that the best use should be made of the nation's talent: on a sense of duty – that to develop the talents given to man is a moral obligation. But it is above all based on a belief that sound education will foster good government and the true religion. The boy of humble background who can clear all the academic hurdles to advancement is just the type of recruit whom the learned professions, and the country, need. The lad o' pairts is distinguished not only by his intellectual ability but by the moral qualities which have enabled him to persevere with his studies.

Long before the Reformation, Scotland had enjoyed the kind of cooperation between the church, the state and the schools which was to become such a feature of her educational system. An Act of 1494 (or perhaps 1496) requiring all barons and freeholders to put their eldest sons to school from the age of eight or nine 'until thai be competentlie foundit and have perfit Latyne,' though it was never enforced, has been claimed as the first statute imposing compulsory education anywhere in the world. And

'though the management of the grammar schools originally belonged to the church yet the burghs as early as the fifteenth century claimed . . . a voice in appointing the schoolmaster. From the beginning of the sixteenth century the Church was becoming less and less influential in the management and maintenance of these schools, and the town councils were taking their control and support more and more into their own hands. The Reformation merely com-

[1] G. E. Davie, *The Democratic Intellect*, 1961, p. xi.

pleted the transference of the patronage of the grammar schools from the Church to the Burgh. Similar schools of subsequent date originated in some cases in private endowments but mainly in the action of the burghs themselves. This was purely voluntary on the part of the latter, for there was no statutory obligation on the burgh to establish and support these schools.'[1]

One example may be quoted of the way in which the interests of the municipality preserved the continuity of a school through the upheaval of the Reformation. 'The change-over in Ayr was easily effected. The Council continued to manage the burgh school as it had been doing for some time before, and it ensured the financial help required when the funds necessary for the upkeep of the school were no longer forthcoming from church sources. Actually some of these funds came into the town's possession.'[2] The hope of the Scottish Reformers was that this kind of financial arrangement would be much more common than in the event it proved to be. Their proposals for a national system of education went far beyond the resources of any government authority at the time. The English Parliament might well look north of the border for an example. So comprehensive were the Scottish plans that Morgan, writing in 1927, could say without exaggeration that 'most of the progress in Scottish education since Knox's day has consisted in advancing towards his ideals. The great education Acts of 1872 and 1918 are but modern expressions of some of his ideals, others having still to be fulfilled'.[3] Even the legislation of 1945 falls short of John Knox's scheme in at least one respect. There have been suggestions (on both sides of the border) that the problem of premature leaving from grammar schools might be countered by compulsion, but the government have not been willing to impose a different measure of compulsion on selected children. The *First Book of Discipline* had no such scruples:

'The children of the poor must be supported and sustained at the charge of the Church until trial be taken whether the spirit of docility be found in them or not. If they be found apt to letters and learning then may they not – neither the sons of the rich nor the sons of the poor – be permitted to reject learning. They must be charged to continue their study, so that the Commonwealth may have some comfort of them.'

Like the much less ambitious schemes in England, these plans depended for finance on a diversion to educational purposes of the church revenues, but most of the money found its way into other pockets. Nevertheless something was saved. The burghs continued their voluntary support of the schools. Outside the burghs the Act for Settling Schools, 1696, provided that a school should be established in every parish not already possessing one: it prescribed the salary that the schoolmaster was to receive, and directed that the cost of maintaining the school should be borne by the 'heritors' (landowners). They were to con-

[1] A. Morgan, *The Rise and Progress of Scottish Education*, 1927, p. 76.
[2] W. Boyd, *Education in Ayrshire through Seven Centuries*, 1961, p. 14.
[3] Morgan, op. cit., p. 53.

tribute in proportion to the valued rent of their properties, and might pass on not more than half the cost to their tenants. The appointment of the schoolmaster was made by the heritors subject to the approval of the presbytery. In other words there was to be a uniform system of parish schools, supported out of rates but subject to some surveillance by the church. Possibly the fact that education thereby became a local, and not a central, government service helped it to continue undisturbed after the Union. The principle of local autonomy might not after 1707 have extended to Treasury expenditure on a service for only one area of the Kingdom.

Too much should not be made of this early statute. It has been said of it: 'Never was there a wiser law, and never was a law more studiously disregarded.'[1] The machinery for seeing that the heritors carried out their duties was ineffective. But it is as much of an overstatement to suggest that the Act was inoperative as to suppose that it resulted in a completely adequate national system of schools. The significant fact is that by the middle of the nineteenth century Scotland had over a thousand 'public elementary schools', and this is over a thousand more than England had at the same date. The actual number does not matter. The Scots had grown accustomed to the idea of a statutory educational system during the two centuries before the legislation of 1870–72.

During the eighteenth century a considerable number of 'private adventure' schools had been founded, and, by the beginning of the nineteenth, the parish system had shown its inability to keep up with modern developments. The parochial schools were neither the only schools nor the most numerous. The rapid growth of population in the industrial areas had meant that only one school to each parish was quite inadequate. Even in the rural areas (and even supposing that the heritors carried out their responsibilities) some parishes were so large in extent that they had been divided for ecclesiastic, though not for educational, purposes. The Church of Scotland had, however, often provided a school in the new parishes. Voluntary societies had been almost as active as in England. After the Disruption of the Church of Scotland in 1843 the 'break-away' Free Church had been particularly active in building new schools. At first sight therefore the situation was not so very different from that in England. There were those thousand-odd parochial schools, but they were outnumbered three to one by voluntary schools. The actual number of schools in 1864 was:

TABLE 1. *Status of schools: Scotland* 1864

Parochial, etc.	1,133
Burgh, etc.	87
Church of Scotland	519
Free Church	617
Other Presbyterian	45
Episcopal	74
Roman Catholic	16
Undenominational	1,084
Private adventure	910

[1] H. G. Graham, quoted in H. M. Knox, *250 Years of Scottish Education*, 1953, p. 6.

The Church of Scotland, however, exercised varying measures of control over a large proportion of the schools, whether the financial backing came from the rates or from other sources. Some of the church schools had been provided by the kirk session and some directly by the general assembly, whereas the presbytery had been specifically charged with the surveillance of the parochial schools: these were but different organs of the same church. Moreover some kirk sessions had claimed a right of supervision over private schools in their parish similar to that exercised by the presbyteries under the Act of 1696, and indeed some private schools had been established, if not at the instigation, at least with the connivance, of the kirk sessions in order to supplement the educational provision of their area. It should be added, too, that the dispute leading to the Disruption was more over matters of church government than over fundamental doctrinal differences. The distinction between statutory and voluntary or private schools had never been important:

'All these schools were equally "Presbyterian" in tradition and objectives and in the methods and content of instruction. The parish school had the advantage of legal continuity and support, a local prestige and a recognised connection with church and state, but it was arguable that the provision of education was at least partly a matter of supply and demand. The parent paid for what his children got, even in the established schools, and if private schools could provide a better article at a cheaper rate, the public system could not but be stimulated by a healthy competition.'[1]

That was in the eighteenth century, but in 1878 one of Her Majesty's Inspectors of Schools could still write that 'Public and Presbyterian are practically interchangeable terms'.[2]

ENGLAND BEFORE 1870

In England up to the Restoration the endowed grammar schools had been open to the children of poor parents, and the Reformers, such as Sir William Petty, had wished none to be excluded from the schools 'by reason of the poverty or inability of their parents: for hereby it hath come to pass that many are now holding the plough that might have been fit to steer the state'.[3] But within a few years of the Restoration, Wase described the prevailing attitude to free education as a belief (which he himself did not share) that it was dangerous to government, 'as diverting those whom Nature and Fortune had determin'd to the Plough, the Oar or other Handicrafts from their proper design'.[4] The grammar schools and the universities were reserved for those who could be relied upon to support the 'establishment'. The dissenting academies were later tolerated and between 1778 and 1791 dissenters and Catholics became legally

---

[1] L. J. Saunders, *Scottish Democracy 1815–1840*, 1950, p. 244.
[2] Scottish Education Department, *Annual Report 1878–9*, p. 173.
[3] *The Advice of W.P. to Mr. Samuel Hartlib for the Advancement of some particular Parts of Learning*, 1684.
[4] *Considerations concerning Free Schools, as settled in England*, 1678.

free to teach. Some rudimentary instruction was offered to the children of the poor by way of charity – mainly under the aegis of the Church of England – but it was different in kind from that offered to the children of 'established' parents.

The prospect that the monitorial system, introduced at the beginning of the nineteenth century, might make available education which was both cheap and efficient disturbed (as increasing industrialisation was also bound to disturb) the comfortable situation which had obtained for more than a hundred years. Anglican reaction to the activities of the Quaker, Lancaster, and the Benthamites was varied. Some hoped simply to suppress the new movement. Others looked to the government to intervene. In the event the church was forced to expand its own schools in competition. Whitbread's Bill of 1807 was modelled on the Scottish system of one school to each parish, and its author relied on the monitorial system to keep the cost to the ratepayers down to an acceptable level. But the Archbishop of Canterbury said that 'it would go to subvert the first principles of education in this country, which had hitherto been, and he trusted would continue to be, under the control and auspices of the Establishment',[1] and the House of Lords rejected the Bill. The failure of this and other measures left the way open for elementary education to become the monopoly of the two great voluntary bodies, the British and Foreign Bible Society and the National Society for Promoting the Education of the Poor in the Principles of the Established Church (to give it its full title). It proved easier for the state to subsidise the two societies than to exercise control over them. The grant-in-aid of £20,000 had been voted in 1833 by a mere fifty members of the House of Commons (but only twenty-six had troubled to turn up to vote against it.) The establishment of a Committee of Council to supervise the disbursement of the money attracted much more political interest: it was only achieved by a constitutional sleight of hand and, even then, barely survived a vote of 280 to 275 in the Commons and overwhelming opposition from the Lords.

When, finally, the Elementary Education Act, 1870, found its way on to the statute book, it was very much a compromise. As its promoter explained, it was intended 'to complete the present voluntary system, to fill up gaps, sparing the public money where it can be done without, procuring as much as we can the assistance of the parents, and welcoming as much as we rightly can the cooperation and aid of those benevolent men who desire to assist their neighbours'.[2]

Areas which were adequately served by voluntary schools remained without a school board with power to establish or maintain schools until 1902.

THE RELIGIOUS QUESTION: 1833 TO 1944

In spite of national differences in the relationship between the churches, the state and the schools, there were, in the mid-nineteenth century, superficial resemblances between the range of voluntary schools on both sides of the border.

[1] *Hansard*, IX, p. 1178 (11.8.1807).
[2] *Hansard*, CXCIX, p. 444 (17.2.1870).

Whether because they were misled by this or because they were indifferent to 'regional peculiarities', the United Kingdom government, when at last they took a hand in the provision of popular education, paid no attention whatever to the special traditions of Scotland. The 1833 grant in aid was not available to Scottish schools; the following year a separate sum was allocated to Scotland; but in 1839 the Committee of Council was established to supervise the spending of a consolidated sum for the whole of Britain, and the disbursement of government grants rapidly became a means of introducing a considerable measure of uniformity, since acceptance of a grant would involve acceptance of the conditions laid down in the Code. Most of the parochial schools in Scotland, and some of the voluntary schools, reacted by simply refusing to apply for grant. (In this they were not completely alone. In England, too, 'many country schools were maintained by the local squire, whose pride in his estates often led him to decline government aid'.[1] But if the English squire was prepared to dip into his pocket to retain his school's independence, the Scottish ratepayer was much more frequently prepared to pay increased rates.) Only one parochial school in three drew on the Privy Council grants. But the attitude of some of the voluntary schools was very different: two-thirds of the Roman Catholic schools, and every single Episcopal school, claimed grant. This can be interpreted either as showing that some much needed help was given to minority religious groups, or that the policy administered from London was tending to produce the kind of 'dual system' with which England was to become only too familiar.

By 1870, however, the lesson had been learned. England had its Elementary Education Act and, two years later, the Education (Scotland) Act was designed to meet Scottish conditions. As regards the religious question the Scottish Act differed from the English in three respects. Firstly, the preamble recited that it had been the custom in public schools to give religious instruction to children whose parents raised no objection, but with liberty to parents who did object to withdraw their children from religious instruction without forfeiting any of the other advantages of the schools, and declared that it was expedient that the schools should continue this practice. There was no provision, as there was in the English Act, forbidding the teaching of any religious catechism or formulary distinctive of a particular denomination in a rate-aided school. Secondly, the voluntary schools were given the opportunity of transferring their properties to the school boards and in fact most of them, with the main exception of the Episcopal and Roman Catholic schools, did so.

Thirdly, the two Acts made opposite provision for tackling the deficiencies in school provision. In England the voluntary bodies were given a period of grace in which to 'fill up gaps' before the new school boards were allowed to establish schools. The strength (as well as the past weaknesses) of the voluntary system is shown by the numbers of new church schools which were provided. In Scotland it was the school boards which were given a period of grace in which to 'fill up gaps'. This, on top of their ability to accept the transfer of voluntary schools, created a very different situation:

[1] Hadow Report, *The Education of the Adolescent*, 1926, p. 12.

TABLE 2. *Board and Voluntary Schools*

	Board schools	Voluntary schools
England		
1870	—	8,978
1880	3,433	14,181
1901	5,878	14,275
Scotland		
1901	2,788	353

The Act of 1872 had pointed the way. The 1918 Act solved the religious question in Scotland. It repeated the opportunity for voluntary schools to be transferred, and gave warning that grants would no longer be payable to voluntary schools which did not comply within two years. The time previously devoted to religious instruction in the transferred schools was not to be reduced: the teachers were to be appointed and dismissed by the education authority, but any teacher appointed to a transferred school was to be approved as regards religious beliefs and character by representatives of the church in whose interests the school was conducted. No objection seems to have been raised by ratepayers that the transfer of these denominational schools would involve a subsidy of denominational teaching,[1] or by the teachers' organizations that it would submit some of their members to a religious test.

In England, in spite of, or perhaps because of, the 1870 compromise, the religious question led to at least two crises. The transfer of responsibility from the central government to the local authorities for the maintenance of voluntary schools was the occasion for a threat by nonconformists to boycott the 1902 Act because of the subsidy to voluntary schools from the rates. Most of the voluntary schools were those provided by the Church of England. (Indeed three out of four voluntary schools are still Church of England schools.) In 1908 the teachers resisted successfully a move to give clergymen a right of entry into, and to permit denominational teaching in, council schools.

Some of the fire died out of these disputes as time went on. Nevertheless every attempt to extend the educational system raised some of the old controversies and involved difficult financial negotiations with the churches. They had much less stake in Secondary schools than in the primary schools, and perhaps have not received from the government enough financial assistance to hold that position in the secondary field which they had in elementary education. (At present some forty per cent of maintained primary schools are voluntary schools compared with only fifteen per cent of secondary schools.) But they fought hard to get some help from the state for the new schools they had to build for 're-organisation' and for the extra places needed for the raising of the school leaving age. The 1918 Act had allowed the raising of the school leaving age to fifteen by local bye-law, but nothing had been done about this until the Labour government came to power in 1924. The Board of Education then announced their

[1] But there have been one or two murmurings during 1966 against the subsidy of denominational schools.

willingness to consider proposals and four education authorities had had their bye-laws approved before the government went out of office. On their return to power in 1929 Labour gave notice of their intention to raise the school leaving age on 1 April 1931; they introduced a short Bill to give effect to this and to provide for maintenance allowances for the children affected. 'There can be little doubt that, had it not been for the "dual system" by which Church schools and Council schools exist side by side but on a different footing, the school leaving age would have been raised as planned.'[1] But the churches felt that they could not find the money necessary to extend the voluntary schools and, after a conference with them and with the teachers and education authorities, the government withdrew the Bill and introduced a revised one which would have permitted the local education authorities to give financial aid to voluntary schools for the purpose of reorganization in exchange for an extension of public control over the appointment of teachers in the schools. The Bill had not been passed by the end of the parliamentary session and in the following session the government reverted to their original scheme; but in the committee stage in the Commons they accepted an amendment from a Roman Catholic member that the Bill should not come into operation until a separate Act had been passed authorising building grants to voluntary schools. 'The Bill being now a mere pious aspiration, the Lords rejected it.'[2] Eventually the 1936 Act provided for the raising of the school leaving age to fifteen, for the financing of new voluntary secondary schools and for both denominational and 'agreed syllabus' religious instruction in such schools. The date fixed for the Act to come into force was 1 September 1939. Most of the war years were taken up with further negotiations with the churches. It was in January 1941 that the President of the Board of Education announced that comprehensive plans for educational reconstruction were being drawn up, in August of the same year that the Archbishop of Canterbury led a deputation, including the free churches, to see the President, and in 1943 that the Roman Catholic and High Churches tried to get the government to accept 'the Scottish solution', whereby teachers in voluntary schools would be appointed by the education authorities subject to approval on religious grounds by the church concerned. But the teachers rejected that suggestion. It was not until August 1944 that the new legislation received the royal assent. The compromise that was eventually reached was a most complex one. Voluntary schools are divided into two categories ('aided' and 'controlled') according to the amount of control over denominational teaching by the church authorities and the financial responsibilities of the church and the education authority respectively. But even the 'voluntary controlled' schools, for whose maintenance the education authorities are now completely responsible, remain the property of the trustees, whereas the transferred schools in Scotland were either sold or leased to the education authorities.

The apportionment of responsibility for the upkeep, improvement and, if necessary, extension of voluntary schools is a most complex one. It means that

---

[1] J. Graves, *Policy and Progress in Secondary Education 1902–1942*, 1943, p. 130.
[2] Graves, op. cit. p. 131.

local education authorities are sometimes inhibited from reorganizing the schools in their area as they would like. The financial settlement has from time to time been reopened by the churches – most recently as a consequence of the government's instructions that secondary schools should be reorganized on comprehensive lines.

CHAPTER TWO

The State and Education

STATE INTERVENTION IN SCOTLAND

We have seen that, after 1833, most Scottish (as well as some English) schools refused to apply for the Privy Council grants.

Passive resistance in Scotland might perhaps have died out as financial necessity forced schools to submit to the Code. But in 1862 the Revised Code provoked an active revolt. The often quoted justification of the system of payment by results – that 'if the new system will not be cheap it will be efficient, and if it will not be efficient it will be cheap'[1] – is remembered as the most notorious example among many of the British government's penny-pinching attitude to education, and it is true that Gladstone, as Chancellor of the Exchequer, wanted to keep expenditure down. But it was also based on the findings of the Newcastle Commission that the schools were too interested in the work of their senior classes and that the teaching of more elementary work was grossly inefficient. This criticism was later claimed to be just as true of Scottish schools, but Scottish schoolmasters were violently opposed to having their attention forced away from the lad of o'pairts. They could at the time deny accusations of neglecting their lower classes because the Newcastle Commission's investigations had not extended to Scotland. The Revised Code also repeated the rubric, to which Scots had already taken exception, that the purpose of government grants was to 'promote the education of the children belonging to the classes who support themselves by manual labour'. The democratic as well as the academic tradition was offended. There were, of course, protests against the Revised Code on both sides of the border, but in England they did not prevent it from being administered – with diminishing severity – for the next thirty years or so. Scottish protests brought about a suspension, from 1864 onwards, of the financial provisions of the Code. The examinations of school work continued to be held, but the amount of grant was not dependent on the results. The Committee on Education claimed that the examinations proved the strictures of the Newcastle Commission to have been equally applicable to Scottish schools, but by then the Scots had won their point.

The objections to the Revised Code also led to the appointment of the Argyll Commission to undertake for Scotland the sort of survey which had been started in England by the Newcastle Commission and was followed up by the Clarendon and Taunton Commissions. The Committee of Council continued to be responsible for the education of both countries up to the passing of the 1870–72 legisla-

[1] *Hansard*, CLXV, p. 229, 13 Feb. 1862.

tion but the Education (Scotland) Act, 1872, was framed on the basis of the Argyll Commission's investigations. The Act was not only, in important aspects, different from the English Elementary Education Act, 1870, it also set up a separate Scotch Education Department. But the new Department continued to share the same President, the same Vice-President and the same Permanent Secretary: headquarters remained in London, although an Advisory Board, sitting in Edinburgh, assisted for some six years with the introduction of the new legislation. Its establishment was in fact seen by some patriots, not as an improvement on the former Committee of Council but as a shift of effective power from local government in Scotland to a central government agency in London. The new act gave much greater powers of direction.

'There can be no doubt that this period of tutelage to England resulted in grave educational loss to Scotland. In 1872, England was at least a generation behind Scotland in its educational ideals and practice. Yet it was English ideals, English standards, English classification, which ruled Scotland for more than a decade ... the true aims of instruction were forgotten, and the formative value of education was sacrificed to the informative.'[1]

In 1885 the Scotch Education Department was finally separated from the English department, given its own Permanent Secretary, and made responsible to the Secretary for Scotland, whose office was revived after a lapse of a century and a half. Educational administration was in the van of the modern move towards greater devolution of government for Scotland. Even so, headquarters remained in London until 1922 when the (renamed) Scottish Education Department started a removal to Edinburgh, which was only completed in 1939.

Whether the Department was too much influenced by English ideas must be a matter of controversy, though its expenditure was certainly controlled under a financial settlement which, though generous, nevertheless tied the amount made available by the Treasury for education in Scotland to the amount (or, rather, to any increases in the amount) spent in England and Wales. Whether the Department's policies were misguided or enlightened, it is not to be denied that they were clearly stated and vigorously prosecuted. Whether or not they can claim full credit for the undoubted advances that were made it is a fact that the Department was called upon to administer and develop a system of education which, for a century and more, had not only maintained but increased its lead over England. Many of the innovations in education during the nineteenth century can be claimed as having been initiated in Scotland. The claim is in some cases a marginal one because England was in an expansionist mood too, and ideas were travelling more quickly than in the past. But Scotland can point, to give only three examples, to the first infants schools (founded by a Welshman), the first technical college (which was to become the first technological university) and the first permanent university chair in education. The variety of these examples is sufficient to suggest that Scotland was in a position to expand her

[1] Burnet, Grierson and others, *Problems of National Education*, 1919, pp. 8, 15, (quoted in Davie, op. cit.).

educational system at a time when England was still, to a large extent, pre-occupied with problems of building the essential framework of hers. The statistics which began to be available as a result of the work of the various commissions of enquiry in the middle of the nineteenth century proved with rough figures the superiority of Scottish education which had hitherto had to be taken largely on trust. It was reckoned, for example, that Scotland had one university place for every 1,000 of the population. This compared with 1:2,600 in Germany and 1:5,800 in England. It may be objected that the Scottish universities included provision for some instruction that elsewhere was under-taken in the Secondary schools[1], but the comparable figures for Secondary school places were: Scotland 1:140, Prussia 1:249, France 1:570 and England 1:1,300.[2] Even more convincing evidence of the soundness of the Scottish system is provided by the Registrar General's figures of the proportion of people who were unable to write their names and had to sign the marriage register by making their mark:

TABLE 3. *Persons signing marriage register by mark. Percentages.*

	England and Wales		Scotland	
	Men	*Women*	*Men*	*Women*
1861	24.6	34.7	10.6	21.3
1871	19.4	26.8	10.0	19.6
1881	13.5	17.7	7.1	13.9
1891	6.4	7.3	3.4	5.3
1901	2.8	3.2	—	—

At the parliamentary level the Scottish system was helped by the fact that the precedent of 1870–72 established a habit of legislating for education in the two countries at more or less the same intervals of time, but allowing considerable variations to meet their different conditions:

'The general Acts of 1872, 1908, 1918 and 1945 may be said to correspond roughly with those of 1870, 1902, 1918 and 1944, but, while seemingly parallel, the Scottish acts introduced important points of principle only subsequently adopted in England. Similarly, the special measures relating to school attendance passed in 1883, 1901 and 1936 generally implied a higher leaving age or more effective attendance at school than the English Acts of 1876–80, 1900 and 1936. As specific examples we may mention that in primary education the principle of compulsion was accepted in Scotland in 1872 and in England not fully till 1880, the principle of free education in Scotland in 1889 and in England in 1891, and the school leaving age of fourteen in Scotland in 1901 and in England not universally until 1918. In secondary education the right to free schooling was recognised in Scotland in 1918 and in England in 1944 and the reorganisation of

---

[1] 38 per cent of the university students were under the age of eighteen.
[2] Argyll Commission: see H. M. Knox, *Two Hundred and Fifty Years of Scottish Education,* 1953, p. 72.

all post-primary education as secondary in Scotland in 1936 and in England only in 1944.'[1]

The differences in the enactments concerning the upper limit of compulsory schooling probably had the most profound effect on the spirit in which the central authority tackled the task of encouraging developments in the field of post-primary education. The principle in the English Acts was to empower the local authorities to make bye-laws. Such delegation of the decision to make education compulsory in limited areas was probably unavoidable in 1870 when the country was so far from having sufficient schools as to make it impracticable to contemplate the introducing of universal compulsion. But the same principle of local action by bye-laws to raise the age from fourteen to fifteen was incorporated in the English Act of 1918. In Scotland the 1872 Act and all subsequent Acts made uniform provision for the whole country. In particular the 1918 Act contained power to raise the school leaving age to fifteen for the whole of Scotland. This inspired the Scottish Education Department to such efforts to co-ordinate and develop all post-primary education that a delay of thirty years in actually putting the provision into effect was to some degree offset.

SECONDARY EDUCATION, CHARITABLE ENDOWMENTS AND LOCAL ADMINISTRATION

But, although the principle was established in 1870–72 of separate legislation for Scotland, the 1872 Act itself was not particularly felicitous in the provision it made for secondary education. It is true that, unlike the English Elementary Education Act it was a measure to amend and extend the existing law 'in such manner that the means of procuring efficient education for their children may be furnished and made available to the whole people of Scotland'. As such it could not avoid dealing with secondary as well as primary education. The two main types of school then existing were to be distinguished more by their different provenance than by the type of education provided. There was a burgh school in almost every town of consequence and these schools have been regarded as more or less the equivalent of Secondary schools because they were usually larger, better able to provide for senior children than the parochial schools and sent their pupils on to the universities at a more advanced stage. But most of them also provided elementary education. The parochial schools, on the other hand, were by no means purely elementary schools. The link between the village school and the university was cherished. The secondary instruction given even in the smallest school was to be safeguarded by section 67 of the Act which required the Scotch Education Department, when framing their minutes, to take due care that the standard of education previously existing in the schools should not be lowered but as far as possible maintained. The 1872 Act actually set up a uniform system of school boards for the whole country, and parochial and burgh schools alike came under the jurisdiction of the new boards.

[1] H. M. Knox, op. cit., p. 241.

But an exception was introduced into an otherwise simple pattern of school organization. The Act listed eleven (ineptly named) 'higher class schools'. The school boards were supposed to take steps to relieve the burgh schools of their elementary work and any former burgh school, or indeed any former parochial school, which was engaged predominantly in 'higher' education, might by resolution of the school board, become a higher class school. The only attraction of such a course was that the school would thereby be free from inspection by the Department and its staff need not have the qualifications required of teachers in other schools. There were to be no financial grants: in fact the schools would not only have to continue to obtain their revenue from fees, from endowments and from the 'common good' (a fund of public endowments held in trust by most burgh councils in Scotland), they were explicitly debarred from receiving any assistance from the rates. This was clearly a move to put Secondary schools in Scotland on something like the same footing as the endowed grammar schools in England. But apart altogether from the fact that the Scots were not content with the meagre provision of secondary education which satisfied the English, it ignored the extent to which Scotland was less well provided with educational endowments. In their third report the Colebrooke Commission of 1872 complained that

'Provision of the amplest kind has been made by law for elementary instruction. By means of rates, parliamentary grants and fees, elementary schools have been, or are in the course of being, established and supported throughout Scotland. The universities are aided from year to year with Imperial money. . . . But while the elementary schools and the universities are thus fostered by the State, and enriched by individuals, the secondary schools which ought to fill the gap between these institutions are left to starve. Parliament has not granted them any aid, and private benefactors, who deal liberally with the universities, forget the source that supplies the objects of their liberality.'[1]

In the year 1864 the endowments for Eton alone were greater than those enjoyed by all the burgh schools and all the universities in Scotland put together. Of a total of £175,000 annual endowments for schools in 1872, £112,000 was for schools in the four cities of Glasgow, Edinburgh, Dundee and Aberdeen – 'not that these centres of population are over-endowed, but some of the smaller burghs, and indeed the greater part of the country generally suffered from lack of the assistance and stimulus which come from such endowments'.[2] The charitably minded in England had, by and large, directed their generosity towards individual institutions, but in Scotland the practice has usually been to set up funds for more general purposes. The burghs have long enjoyed the use of the 'common good' funds devoted to general charitable purposes, of which education is only one, for the inhabitants of the town. The most influential educational trusts have been such as the Milne and Dick bequests in north-east Scotland

---

[1] Royal Commission appointed to inquire into the Endowed Schools and Hospitals (Scotland), *Third Report*, 1875, p. 109.
[2] Morgan, op. cit., p. 100.

which have been used to supplement the work (originally by the payment of a supplementary salary to the schoolmaster) of parochial and burgh schools in an area covering three or four counties. The trusts of most of the hospitals (which might perhaps have become the Scottish equivalent of the English Public Schools, have been so broadened in scope as to include the provision of technical and further education and the award of bursaries.

The provision for the designation of 'higher class schools' had little immediate effect. Within ten years of the 1872 Act and its attempt to persuade the burgh schools to slough off their elementary work, the Moncrieff Commission expressed the opinion that 'it is not only possible to combine thorough elementary teaching with instruction in the higher branches, but that any separation is detrimental to the tone of the school and dispiriting to the master'.[1] Nevertheless the higher class schools were the precursors of the Secondary schools.

Very soon, however, the adventitious way in which financial assistance had been made available to secondary schools in both England and Scotland had led to a considerable degree of confusion. In Scotland the school boards had statutory authority to provide secondary education but were explicitly forbidden to support it out of the rates. Some English school boards did in fact support 'higher' education out of the rates until it was made clear to them by the Cockerton judgment that they had no power to do so. Various *ad hoc* measures were taken to develop secondary and technical education: Scotland was a year ahead of England with a Technical Schools (Scotland) Act in 1887, but only one school board took any action under it. The Science and Art Department was, however, disbursing grants quite independently of the educational departments, and Scotland was drawing rather more than a proportionate share of these (£67,000 out of a total of £470,000 for the whole of the United Kingdom by the time that the grants came to an end). The first central government grants towards secondary education in England, other than those of the Science and Art Department, were made by the Local Government Act of 1888, which provided for grants to the newly created local councils for certain specific purposes, including grants to the county and county borough councils to develop technical education, the balance being available for the relief of rates. The Local Government (Scotland) Act of the following year allotted to Scottish authorities a sum equal to eleven-hundredths of the amount paid out in England and for the same sort of purposes, but – as another example of the greater willingness of the Scots to pay for public education – the balance was used, not to relieve the rates, but for the partial abolition of school fees. The following year the so-called 'Whisky money' was also used, south of the border, in part, to relieve the rates, but north of it for the reduction of school fees. When, in 1891, school fees in England were also reduced or abolished, it was felt only fair that Scottish authorities should be given an 'equivalent grant' to match the sums paid out to the English school boards in compensation for the loss of school fees. This was worth £60,000 and it was decided to use it for the development of secondary education.

But these various and uncoordinated boosts for secondary schools naturally

[1] *Report of the Commissions on Endowed Institutions in Scotland, 1880–81*, p. vii.

resulted in an administrative muddle. In England the Bryce Commission suggested that the way out of the muddle was to establish secondary education committees for each area, with equal representation from the county councils and the school boards, to coordinate the provision of education other than elementary. This would have left the school boards to continue their existing functions. The recommendation was not accepted. The solution adopted in the 1902 Act was a much more radical one. The school boards were abolished. In their place the counties and county boroughs were created local education authorities for all purposes. The only concession to some former school boards was that non-county boroughs with a population of more than 10,000 and urban districts of more than 20,000 might become education authorities for elementary education only (Part III authorities). England was thus given a reasonably unified system of local administration.

On the other hand the 1902 Act was more tentative in the powers it gave to the new authorities. They were enabled to 'supply or aid the supply' of Secondary education. In effect this meant that they could for the first time offer financial assistance from the rates to the endowed grammar schools, and could also for the first time provide Secondary schools on their own initiative. But, in a sense this meant that, just as in 1872 the school boards had only been able to 'fill up gaps' in elementary education, in 1902 the authorities could only fill up gaps in Secondary provision. They had to start from the basis of the schools already existing. Or, as Barnard puts it:

'In the field of secondary education the Act of 1902 perpetuated the "dual system" as well as in that of elementary education; but it was of a different kind. On the one hand were the old endowed grammar schools, which had hitherto received no assistance from public funds, but were now aided by local education authorities. After 1902 there also came into existence a number of municipal or county secondary schools, founded and maintained by the councils.'[1]

This arrangement continued virtually unchanged until the 1944 Act made much the same provision for dealing with this dual system as with that in the elementary school field. The former endowed grammar schools could become either 'aided' or 'controlled' voluntary schools.

In Scotland the anomalous position of the higher class schools was rectified to the extent that those which were publicly administered could be supported from the rates and those which were independent received direct grants from the Department. But the grants were administered under a separate Code, thus perpetuating a distinction between Secondary and elementary schools which need never have existed. But on the administrative front Scotland failed to find a way through the muddle for some time. Knox explains that

'It was generally expected that the English Act of 1902 . . . would be followed by a parallel measure, but, in spite of a number of attempts, nothing was actually effected for several years afterwards. . . . Eventually, in 1908, a full-scale Educa-

[1] H. C. Barnard, *A History of English Education from 1760*, 1961, p. 203.

tion Act was passed, but the Scottish parochial tradition of two hundred years proved more resistant than its counterpart in England which had only lasted thirty. In consequence, the parish continued as the educational administrative area for most purposes, and school boards were retained, but their powers were considerably extended.'[1]

What in fact happened was that something very like the Bryce Commission's recommendation was adopted in Scotland. The secondary education committees were also kept in existence with powers which overlapped those of the school boards. The Scottish parochial tradition had, in fact, been strong enough to give a pretty vigorous dying kick.

In 1918 the school boards finally disappeared. The counties, together with the four cities (Glasgow, Edinburgh, Dundee and Aberdeen – and also Leith, which was very soon afterwards amalgamated with Edinburgh) became the area of educational administration. The school board tradition lingered on after death, in that the education authorities were divorced from the general structure of local government. The school boards had of course been *ad hoc* authorities, but in England from 1902 onwards the all-purpose local authorities took over responsibility for education. In Scotland the new education authorities were single-purpose, separately administered and separately elected. So strict was the separation from other local government services that the minor local authorities were not even represented on the school management committees, and therefore the parishes ceased to be connected in any way with the schools which they had fostered since the seventeenth century. Finally in 1929 the parish was abolished in Scotland altogether. The English Local Government Act of that year considerably strengthened the county and county borough councils at the expense of the minor local authorities, and at the same time transferred to them the powers of the remaining *ad hoc* poor law authorities in England. The Scottish Local Government Act followed much the same principles by transferring to the all-purpose authorities the functions of both the poor law and the education authorities. But, in the general reform of the smaller local authorities, the parish disappeared.

THE STATE AND SCOTTISH UNIVERSITIES

It might have been thought that the battle for Scottish autonomy in education had long since been won. But the report of the Robbins Committee on Higher Education at the end of 1963 started a new debate about the organization of the central government's machinery for the administration of education. The one recommendation in the report which caused more controversy than all the others was the suggestion that the universities and other institutions of higher education should receive their funds from a reconstituted University Grants Committee which would be responsible to a Minister for Arts and Science. This would had been a tidy solution in so far as all higher education for the whole of Britain

[1] H. M. Knox, op. cit., p. 175.

would have been under the control of one minister, and the remainder of education in England under the existing Minister of Education, but in Scotland under the Secretary of State. Objections were, however, raised to the separation of administrative responsibility for higher education from that for other kinds of education. The very strong body of opinion in England which supported these objections found it impossible to devise an alternative scheme which would take account of the special position of Scotland. In the event some unity has been achieved in English administration at the expense of an anomaly whereby institutions of higher education in Scotland are subject to the ultimate control of a Secretary of State who has oversight of both higher education in Britain and of schools in England and Wales, but the remainder of the educational system in Scotland is administered by the Secretary of State for Scotland.

So far as the Scottish universities are concerned this does not in fact mark any change from the previous position. Indeed it was widely believed at the time of the debate over the Robbins proposals that the Scottish universities would object very strongly to being put under the jurisdiction of a Scottish minister. They have always received what government assistance they have had from United Kingdom funds. They did successfully resist the move, initiated by Gladstone, to make the Scottish universities into four colleges of a federal University of Scotland on lines similar to the University of Wales, but have nevertheless been encumbered with a joint consultative machine which the Robbins Report now wishes to see abolished. But in all other administrative respects they have been aligned with the other British universities.

The debate over the status and functions of the Scottish universities covered most of the nineteenth century and has been described in terms of a drawn out battle between anglicizing and traditional forces.[1] Official investigations into university affairs were first prompted by a quarrel between the Senate of Edinburgh University and the town council, but Scottish opinion was rather surprised when, in 1826, the government appointed a Commission to investigate all four universities. That this was felt to be an intrusion into Scottish affairs is evidenced by the objections raised north of the border – particularly by the general assembly of the Church of Scotland. That the United Kingdom government was using the power of the purse to force Scotland to come into line with England was widely believed. 'The best part of the patriotic case is furnished by the contrast between the large sums given not merely to England but to thankless and rebellious Ireland for literature and science and the shabby allowances to Scotland for similar objects', wrote Lord Cockburn in 1852. No immediate action was taken, however, on the recommendations of the 1826 Commissioners, and a Bill introduced into Parliament in 1836 was withdrawn in the face of opposition from Scotland. In 1857 a further commission was appointed, partly, perhaps, because both Oxford and Cambridge had been the subject of royal commission reports and partly because Scottish feelings had received a nasty jolt with the introduction of competitive examination for entry into the Indian Civil Service.

[1] See Davie, op. cit.

'The Indian Civil Service was thrown open to competition, and, at the very first trial, those candidates who had been educated in Scotland failed egregiously. Of the many benefits, which, now admittedly, the Union of the Kingdoms had conferred on Scotsmen, the connection which it opened to them with the East India Company had been the most unquestionable. . . . Small wonder then that the alternative which was placed before the people of Scotland either of renouncing for their children the highest and most lucrative branch of this coveted service, or of improving their educational institutions, should have given little cause for hesitation.'[1]

The recommendations of this commission were given effect by the Universities (Scotland) Act 1858, the provisions of which were welcomed by the traditionalists (who claimed that it was unsatisfactory only in that it did not go far enough) and criticized by those who thought that it was misconceived.

The debate centred on two points which are interconnected. First on the philosophic and non-specialized nature of the Scottish university course, and secondly on the age of admission to the universities. For long the Scottish universities had been seen, not as a third stage of education following on the primary and secondary stages, but as rivals of the secondary schools. The rural lad o' pairts proceeded direct from his parochial school to the university, and could there receive elementary instruction in subjects which were beyond the scope of the village dominie. It was accepted that the university junior classes in Greek, for example, would be attended by students who had no previous knowledge of the language. The usual age of admission from the parochial schools was fourteen or fifteen: pupils from the burgh schools were usually about two years older. The general arts course at the universities was intended to provide a broad basis of four years' study up to the age of about nineteen or twenty, which was then followed by specialized training for the church, for the law, or for teaching. Medicine was organized slightly differently but still required attendance at some classes in arts as well as in the medical faculty. The 1826 Commission had proposed the abolition of the university junior classes. The 1858 proposals were more in the nature of a compromise in that the general arts course was to be of four years' duration but might be reduced to three for students who could reach a certain standard of attainment in a preliminary examination. The traditionalists had scored a victory in that the general course was a central part of university studies: they felt only that the 1858 settlement did not go far enough since insufficient new chairs were founded to take care of the work leading to a second degree (the LL.B. the B.D., or the honours M.A. to be awarded after one further year's work in a narrower field following on the ordinary M.A.). The school of thought which wished to see the Scottish universities adopting something more like the English pattern, on the other hand, considered that the general arts course postponed too long the opportunity for specialization. The main difficulty in their case was that any more radical alteration of the university course, and in particular the imposition of

[1] *Edinburgh Review*, Vol. 107, pp. 99, 100.

higher standards for entrance, implied a complete reorganization of the whole educational system, the widespread provision of secondary schools intermediate between the parochial school and the university, and the provision of general education in the secondary schools to a much higher standard than had previously been attempted.

The new Education Act, with its provisions for higher class schools, had been passed in 1872. Oxford and Cambridge had again been the subject of a royal commission and of fresh legislation in 1877. In 1876, too, the Scottish universities found another royal commission being appointed to examine their affairs. It reported in 1878 in favour of rather more specialized courses. No legislative action was taken until 1889. The Universities (Scotland) Act of that year is one of those curious compromises which would appear to be designed to satisfy no one, yet it was not only accepted but has persisted ever since. The age of admission to the universities was rapidly forced up by about two years (though it is still not as high as in England: even at present some twenty-one per cent of students entering degree courses at Scottish universities have not reached their eighteenth birthdays, compared with only four per cent south of the border). The universities soon abandoned their junior classes. The Preliminary Examination was applied to all. The ordinary arts degree was to be awarded after a three-year course but was no longer a necessary preliminary to the honours course, merely an alternative to it. The honours course was to be spread over four years and honours students were required to take three courses outside their main field of study (since reduced to two. This requirement did not, however, involve such a breadth of study as was required for the ordinary degree with its compulsory logic or philosophy, its languages and scientific subjects: the outside subjects could be taken in fields related to the main honours course). Such a compromise could well have resulted in the ordinary course becoming a mere fossilized vestige of the old arts course. Although it has, in the event, shown some capacity for modification and development, it is nevertheless true that the ordinary degree has increasingly come to be regarded as very much a second best to a good honours degree; its comparative value may perhaps be judged by the fact that a student of average ability is probably better advised to make sure of a 'good' ordinary degree than to risk coming away with a 'third' in the honours course.

The compromise worked. The Scottish universities have received financial assistance from the Universities Grants Committee since it was set up in 1919. There have since been no complaints that government policy towards the universities has been unfair to Scotland. Nor has the settlement which was reached prevented the Scottish universities from prospering. They could not hope to maintain the same pace of expansion as the universities in England because the number of places available in England was so very inadequate. Nevertheless Scotland still has more university places in proportion to her population in spite of the rapid expansion in England:

TABLE 4. *University places*

	1830	1900	1938	1950	1962
England	3,000	13,200	56,000	63,600	85,400
Scotland	4,400	6,000	10,000	15,000	19,500

But the main result of the settlement of the university question was that it clarified the need for an adequate system of Secondary schools and, by imposing university entrance qualifications, gave the Secondary schools a definite goal to aim for.

SOME CONTEMPORARY COMPARISONS

Over the last fifty years education in England has made rapid strides to catch up on Scotland's lead. Back in the nineteen-twenties the Hadow Committee could still look to Scotland for an example. After describing some of the features of secondary education in the United States, France and Germany they wrote: 'The most systematic attempt to develop post-primary education, pursued with much care, practical insight and popular support over many years, is to be found, however, nearer home. It is supplied by Scotland.' On the other hand people in Scotland itself could entertain an occasional doubt about the superiority of their educational system over that south of the border. One of H.M. Chief Inspectors of Schools admitted that the claim of Scottish superiority was not quite so incontrovertible as it had been, but then comforted himself by referring to the one feature of the Scottish system which is still much more rigidly controlled than in England:

'Whatever may be thought [he wrote in his report for 1921] of the claim that continues to be made that Scotland is far ahead of England in educational efficiency, it can at least be said that in the matter of the supply of certificated teachers there still seems to be ground for the claim. While in Scotland the un-certificated teachers come to less than one per cent of all the teachers employed, the uncertificated teachers in England seem to number about twenty-nine per cent, and most of them appear to have broken off their school education at a much earlier age than did their Scottish equivalents. In other matters the contrast is less convincing. England had a larger task and took it up later.'[1]
The number of unqualified teachers in English schools has, by 1962, been reduced to one in forty, but the number who would not be regarded as certificated under the Scottish system is at least one in three, even if one ignores the fact that non-graduate women completing training before 1963 have only had a two-year course of training whereas the Scottish non-graduate course was extended to three years as long ago as 1931. All men in Scotland, other than teachers of practical subjects, must have taken a course of four years or more leading to a

---

[1] General Reports for the Year 1921 by His Majesty's Chief Inspector of Schools, 1922, p. 32.

university degree, as well as professional training, and all graduates must take a course of professional training: neither of these measures has yet been taken in England. The position in Scotland is so carefully guarded that English teachers must apply for 'exceptional recognition' before being allowed to teach in a certificated capacity in Scotland. Like Fitzpayne Fisher in 1652 they still need a 'pass'.

In other matters the contrast is less convincing. At one stride in 1944 the legislative basis of the English system was put on a par with that of the Scottish. There is now no essential power available to Scottish education authorities which is not also enjoyed by those in England, nor any right conferred on Scottish parents which may not also be exercised by English parents. The stimulus which this gave to English education immediately after the war had to some extent been forfeited by Scotland by the simple fact that Scottish plans were so advanced before the war. In particular the raising of the school leaving age to fifteen in 1947 was felt in England to inaugurate a new era of secondary education for all. In Scotland it merely meant that rather more children might now be expected to complete the three-year secondary course which had been established in the nineteen-twenties.

To attempt to compare post-war developments in the two countries in simple terms is, however, impossible. Obviously it is no longer enough to make the simple quantitative comparisons which, up to fifty years ago, were so much to Scotland's advantage. Virtually all children between the ages of five and fifteen are now in school. The fact that in England some six per cent of them are in independent schools as against barely two per cent in Scotland is the least of the obstacles to making accurate statistical comparisons between the two state systems. Below the age of five England at first glance appears to have a slight edge. The percentage of the three to five age groups in attendance at schools of all types in January 1962 was:

TABLE 5. *Percentage of age group attending schools*

	3 +	4 +	5 +
England	3.3	29.8	99.0
Scotland	2.2	6.1	86.6

But, though this probably reflects some slightly more extensive provision of nursery schools and classes in England, a far more important factor is the detailed difference between the statutory provisions for the commencement of compulsory schooling which probably accounts for most of the discrepancy between the figures for the five year age group when taken at a particular date in the year. Beyond the age of compulsory schooling comparisons become even more difficult because of the different organization of the schools and in particular of the different relationships between the schools and institutions of higher education. The actual percentages of each age group still in attendance at schools of all types (including independent schools) in January 1962 were:

TABLE 6. *Percentage of age groups attending schools*

	15+	16+	17+	18+	19+
England	42.2	22.4	12.0	4.1	0.4
Scotland	33.0	19.5	12.4	3.0	—

The difference in the fifteen-plus age group represents an admitted short-coming of the Scottish system compared with the English. The junior secondary schools have scarcely begun to develop the type of advanced course which is becoming a common feature of the English secondary modern school. A recent working party in Scotland considered the possibility of introducing a Certificate of Secondary Education:

'We have taken cognizance [they wrote] of the recommendation of the Secondary School Examinations Council that a national examination at age sixteen at a level below that of the General Certificate of Education should be introduced in England. Conditions in Scotland are however very different from those in England. The proportion of children who remain at school until the age of sixteen in courses below the level of the Scottish Certificate of Education is as yet relatively small.'[1]

On the other hand the figures for seventeen-year-olds at school, close as the percentages are, point to a very interesting fact. Ten years ago the percentage of all seventeen-year-olds who were in attendance at school in England and Wales had overtaken the figure for Scotland. It is during these last ten years that there has been such a spectacular increase in the number of pupils staying on in the grammar and senior secondary schools. The average annual increment during that period south of the border has been at the rate of 0.51 per cent, but in Scotland it has been 0.7 per cent.

As regards higher education Scotland would appear still to be in the lead with full-time courses, especially with university courses. In spite of the fact that no new university was founded in Scotland between 1593 and 1963, whereas no fewer than two dozen universities had been established in England in the hundred years before the Robbins Report, it is still a fact that there are more university places in Scotland in proportion to the population. The following percentages of students entering full-time higher education are expressed as a percentage of weighted age groups for England and Wales to take account of the different ages of entry, but for Scotland they are expressed as a simple percentage of the seventeen-year age group:

TABLE 7. *Percentage of age group in full-time higher education*

	Universities	Teacher Training	Further Education	All Full-time
England & Wales	3.9	2.5	1.9	8.4
Scotland	5.1	2.4	2.4	9.9

[1] Brunton Report, *From School to Further Education*, 1963, p. 50.

If, however, *part-time* higher education is also taken into account the honours are more or less even because 3.5 per cent of the relevant age groups in England follow part-time day courses at an advanced level against only 1.5 per cent in Scotland, and 2.4 per cent take evening classes against only 1.3 per cent. The initiatives leading to the Robbins Report came equally from both sides of the border. If competition for university places in England was leading to intolerable pressures in the schools, there had also been a campaign to found a new university in Scotland. If the report recommended that the colleges of advanced technology (which had been so designated in 1956) should be given university status, the decision that one of the central institutions in Scotland (which had been so designated in 1899) should become a university had already been taken before the report was published. If the assimilation of the teacher training colleges in England into university schools of education seems a rather more logical development from their existing position than the proposals for degree courses in the Scottish colleges of education, at least the latter have, since 1958, enjoyed an independent status undreamt of in England, and the Robbins Committee suggested that the Scottish title should be adopted south of the border. Throughout the report, too, there is recognition of the special position of Scottish institutions, indeed a rather tentative attitude towards the recommendations for Scotland. And, if the nineteenth century had seen a move to anglicize the Scottish universities, the wheel sometimes comes full circle. 'We think', says Robbins, 'it is no accident that the Scottish system has often served as a model for higher education in the English-speaking world.'[1]

Perhaps, when all is said and done, the main difference at present is simply this: the English are hardly aware of what is happening north of the border, but in Scotland several current controversies are conducted with that added passion which comes from the emotions roused by comparison with England. Whatever developments are taking place in England are happening in a mood of sublime indifference to the educational system of Scotland, if not of the rest of the world. The Crowther Report, for example, acknowledges that the English sixth form with its 'system of specialization for young people while they are still at school is singular. Neither in Western Europe nor in North America is there anything of the sort.'[2] Yet the report goes on to justify specialization by saying that 'subject mindedness' is not only one of the marks of the sixth form, it is one of the natural phenomena of adolescence; 'It is there whether we use it or not.'[3] The English tend to regard the distinctive features of the Scottish system – if they regard them at all – as a regional peculiarity. It might be more accurate to regard them as being at least part way towards the continental way of doing things. Nationalistic to a fault, however, the Scots value what is typically Scottish without going out of their way to show that it is founded on a broader tradition. Their situation inevitably leads them occasionally to emphasize the peculiarly Scottish element in their education by pointing out simply that it is un-English.

[1] Robbins Report, *Higher Education* (Cmnd. 2154), 1963, p. 97
[2] Crowther Report, *15 to 18: A Report of the Central Advisory Council for Education (England)*, 1959, p. 258   [3] Ibid, p. 262.

Political and economic subordination to England produces some of the tensions which are to be observed in Scottish education today. Yet Scottish education is not only based on a broader tradition: its influence has spread. While the English deplore the 'brain drain' of graduates who take posts abroad, university graduates have for long been Scotland's main export. It is, truly, 'no accident' that the Scottish system has often served as a model in the English-speaking world.

PART II

The Voice of Authority

O dinna tak' te teachin,
Ye clivver loons and quines!
Ye'll only haud the ploo-stilts,
While Directors grip the rines!

CHAPTER THREE

The Control of Education

THE CHAIN OF COMMAND

'One of the remarkable features – and one of the real problems – about the promotion of public education in this country is that the great majority of us who have direct responsibility for the educational service did not in fact come up through the public educational system ourselves.' This was admitted by Sir Edward Boyle speaking, as Minister of Education, to the annual conference of the National Union of Teachers in 1962. Two years later he found himself one of a team of three ministers charged with responsibility for the educational system of England and Wales (and part of the educational system of Scotland too) who had all been educated at Eton and Oxford. Not that the educational system of Scotland as a whole was in a very different position. The Secretary of State for Scotland at the time was also a product of Eton and Oxford. One of the remarkable features of the public education of both countries has in fact been that, for so much of their recent history, they have been administered by politicians to whom the systems have been foreign.

The complaint of Scottish patriots has, however, not been that they have suffered from the ministrations of English politicians, but that the educational system has been too much under the control of anglicized Scots. From Stanley Baldwin ('When the call came to me to form a government, one of my first thoughts was that it should be a government of which Harrow should not be ashamed') to Harold Macmillan ('Mr Attlee had three old Etonians in his cabinet. I have six. Things are twice as good under the Conservatives'), British Prime Ministers have been in the habit of boasting in jocular terms of the Public School background of their ministerial colleagues. They have also shown a tendency to favour Scots with an English education. Harold Macmillan's government re-shuffle of July 1962 increased the number of ministers of cabinet rank who had been to Eton and Oxford to ten, of whom three (not counting Macmillan himself) were Scots. The remaining Scottish members of his government had been to school at Winchester, Cheltenham, Ampleforth and Fettes respectively: all had graduated at either Oxford or Cambridge.

Even in the Labour government formed immediately after the 1964 general election the Secretary of State for Education and Science was educated at a Public School and Oxford University and, of his two Ministers of State, one had been to a Public School and the other to Cambridge. As for Scotland, the Secretary of State himself had attended Ayr Academy and the University of Glasgow, but the Parliamentary Secretary at the Scottish Office specifically

D

charged with control of education had been educated at an English Grammar School and the University of London.

The influence of politicians on the schools must, however, not be overrated. From the very beginning (by which one means since 1833) the policy of the British government in education has been one of indirect rule. To start with it was merely a question of a grant-in-aid to bodies which were already providing schools. Reluctantly, the government came to supervise the work of these bodies. Since the beginning of the present century, the secular agencies of local government, the school boards and the local educational authorities, have replaced the voluntary societies. But Whitehall has continued its policy of indirect rule. The central government may be said to have administered popular education with the benevolence due to a reasonably well-behaved colony, which, though not worthy of more than a modest financial investment, can be relied upon to cause no embarrassment and, with a little encouragement, will progress steadily towards self-government. The Scottish sector of the colony has been slightly more troublesome than the English. It has shown an absurd unwillingness to adopt the 'British way of life'. But on the whole it has been left to work out its own salvation.

But, like other colonies with their own strong traditions, Scotland has not found this situation altogether easy to accept. Some of her leaders have been under suspicion for being too sympathetic to the English ideals they have picked up at their Public Schools, or at English universities. And this suspicion has fallen on civil servants as well as on ministers. The Scottish Office is in a peculiar position: seen from Whitehall it is a local administrative agency which, in accordance with the general policy of delegation, can be allowed a fairly free hand. Seen from Scotland itself the Office is both an agent of the central government in distant London and, at the same time, the country's own government department, which ought to be responsive to local opinion. If there is any suspicion that a particular policy had its origins in London, Scottish sensibilities are quickly aroused. Yet simultaneously there is a willingness to allow a far greater measure of authority to be centralized in the hands of the Department than would be tolerated in England. Influences from south of the border must be resisted: yet it is only by maintaining some kind of national cohesion that Scotland can preserve her separate identity and her traditions.

Historically, the Scotch Education Department came into being nearly thirty years earlier and in very different circumstances from the Board of Education. It was set up in 1872 with the express task of putting the new legislation into effect. It had to bring under its influence not only the large number of independent schools but also the equally large number of parochial schools which, far from being used to the idea of government control, had up to then mostly ignored the existence of the Committee of Council. All these schools were rapidly welded into a coherent system. In the primary field the number of independent schools dwindled to insignificant proportions. In the secondary field even those schools which remained independent – and even those which it was the policy of the 1872 Act to encourage to be independent – came under the Department's supervision in a matter far more important than administrative control: the Department introduced the Leaving Certificate, and any school which wanted to present its pupils for the examination had to be open to inspection and to have its curricula approved.

For the first forty-six years of its existence the Department's views carried the greatest possible weight. It was the only effective administrative body in Scottish education. Local administration was carried out by nearly a thousand school boards and by county education committees whose powers overlapped those of the school boards. It was not until 1918 that local education authorities covering reasonably large areas were established and not until 1929 that the education authorities in their present form came into being.

The Board of Education on the other hand, was not set up until thirty years after the passing of the Elementary Education Act, 1870. By the time it came into being, the period of grace allowed by the Act to the voluntary bodies had expired, and some of the larger school boards had seized the initiative. Within two years the local education authorities took over from the school boards. In the large towns they took over the same areas and continued the same policies. Elsewhere the county councils were far more effective than the school boards had been, and some of the larger counties too, soon took the initiative. Inevitably, therefore, the local authorities in England have always been in a much stronger position *vis-à-vis* the Board than have the education authorities in Scotland.

The Board of Education was established after the Bryce Commission had recommended that the administrative muddle in secondary education should be countered by the establishment of some unified authority to supervise the secondary schools. This, in their view, 'ought to consist of a department of the Executive Government presided over by a Minister responsible to Parliament, who would obviously be the same Minister as the one to whom the charge of elementary education is entrusted'. Its function would be 'not to control, but rather to *supervise* the secondary education of the country, not to override or supersede local action but to endeavour to bring about among the various agencies which provide that education a harmony and a cooperation which are now wanting'.[1] In spite of the cautious wording of this recommendation, a Bill to set up the Board of Education in 1898 was rejected, mainly because it made inspection by officers of the proposed Board compulsory for all schools within the scope of the Charity Commissioners and the Endowed Schools Acts. A revised Bill the following year merely permitted the new Board of Education to inspect any school which invited them to do so, and provision was also made for the recognition of other inspecting agencies (in practice the universities).

In the year the new Board took over there were 5,700 elementary schools maintained by the local school boards: there were 14,500 'direct grant' schools (i.e. the voluntary schools which drew grants under the Code from the central government). But the effective task of integrating all these schools fell on the

[1] *Report of the Royal Commission on Secondary Education,* 1895, p. 257.

local education authorities to which the responsibility for maintaining both types of school was transferred in 1902. A survey carried out in 1897 had shown that there were also about 6,200 independent schools. They ranged from the well-established Public Schools, through the endowed grammar schools to numerous small (and probably inefficient) private schools. To the new local education authorities also fell the task of giving financial assistance to such of these independent schools as made a contribution to the supply of secondary education in their area, and of developing a coordinated system of secondary education.

Everything favoured the local education authorities for the counties and county boroughs even though the system was not a completely tidy one and they had no powers over elementary education within those boroughs and urban districts which were large enough to claim 'Part III' status. (It perhaps brings home the difference in density of population to note that five of the Scottish counties had a population less than the minimum stipulated for an urban district in England to exercise its own powers over elementary education.) The Part III authorities were given slightly more extended powers in 1918 and it transpired that some of them developed a more vigorous administration than the surrounding county. But the 1902 system of local administration in education went a long way towards, if it did not completely reach, the pattern which has been adopted in local government generally since 1944, in which each county and county borough is recognized as the main unit for local administration even though there may be further delegation within the county. The 1944 Act provided for a two-tier system within the counties, under which some areas might be administered by excepted districts (which might claim delegated powers as of right), and some others by divisional executives (set up by the county council, but with representation from the minor local authorities). At yet more local level the 'dual system' had an incidental effect in the sphere of school management. The buildings of the voluntary schools in England have remained the legal property of the trustees, and it was part of the religious settlement that the provisions of the trust deed governing religious instruction should be observed. This made it more or less essential that each voluntary school should have its own body of managers including, in addition to representatives of the local education authority, the 'foundation' managers or governors. The pattern which has evolved for the management of both voluntary and county schools has considerable similarity. For voluntary schools which have kept 'aided' status, one-third of the members are appointed to represent the authority and the remaining two-thirds are 'foundation' members. For 'controlled' schools two-thirds represent the authority and one-third are 'foundation' members. By an obvious analogy the constitution of the management committees of county primary schools (though not of the governing bodies of county secondary schools) provides for two-thirds of the members to be appointed by the local education authority and for the remaining one-third to be appointed by the 'minor' local authority – the borough or urban district or the parish council. The absence in Scotland of any similar type of dual system has meant that there has not been the same need for a separate management committee for each school. In practice, between 1918 and 1947 Scotland did have management committees responsible for either one school or a group of schools but the minor local authorities were not represented on them.

In England, therefore, managerial control of the schools may operate at four different levels: the Minister and the Department; the local education authority and its director of education; the divisional executive or excepted district; the managers or governors working in cooperation with the head teacher. In any administrative system which rests on such a complex division of responsibility as this, power is likely to concentrate at certain points in the hierarchy. The policy-making, or directive, power has tended to cluster around the local education authorities: the representation of local interests around the individual school. In the simpler Scottish system the directive agency is the Department: local interest tends to be represented by the education authority rather than the school.

AMATEURISM AND PROFESSIONALISM IN ADMINISTRATION

The existence of a strong body of independent schools must also have been a very important factor in the development of an administrative system for state education in England. It was the independent schools' suspicion of government interference which served to clip the wings of the Board of Education before it was even established. The delegation of authority to the individual maintained school seems to have been modelled on the independent schools. One of the outstanding features of education in England is the prestige of the Public Schools, and the main distinguishing feature of the independent schools is, precisely, their independence.

It is a commonplace that the Public Schools and the Universities of Oxford and Cambridge have had an influence on the educational system of England far beyond the teaching of future cabinet ministers. The maintained schools have copied them, have tried to compete with them for university places for their pupils, and have tried to attract Oxford and Cambridge graduates on to their own staffs.

The independent schools have formed a steadily decreasing proportion of the total educational provision of the country. Their numbers have fallen from just over 6,000 (out of a total of 26,000 schools in all) in 1897 to just over 4,000 (out of 35,000) at present. At the same time the importance of the best of them has increased. The nine 'great' Public Schools of Victorian days have their current equivalent in the two hundred schools in membership of the Headmasters' Conference and/or the Governing Bodies Association – which is the usual definition of a Public School.

Similarly, the two ancient Universities of Oxford and Cambridge provide a steadily diminishing proportion of the total number of university places in England:

TABLE 8. *University places*

	1830	1900	1938	1950	1962	1980[1]
Oxford and Cambridge	3,000	6,800	11,000	15,000	17,800	?20,000
London University	—	2,200	13,000	18,300	22,600 }	
Other English	—				}	?250,000
Universities	—	4,200	16,000	30,300	46,000 }	

But this comparative decline in the number of places at Oxford and Cambridge has merely intensified the competition for them. The Robbins Report described it as a 'very deep rooted problem', and recommended that the government should attempt to solve it by 'the deliberate development of other universities in such a way that the relative attraction of Oxford and Cambridge is no longer so great'.[2]

The two ancient universities have been under fire in the past for preferring pupils from independent schools. They have been able to show recently that they have accepted exactly the same proportion of applicants from each type of school – but they receive many fewer applications from pupils of maintained schools in relation to the total output of such schools than they do from the independent and direct grant schools. Nobody seems to know precisely what it is that inhibits maintained school pupils from trying: the suggested explanations include the possibility that the pupils themselves judge their chances of success to be so small that they do not even make the attempt, that the schools feel unable to compete with the independent schools in terms of their staffing, buildings and equipment, or that the differences of organization make it difficult to offer a third year in the sixth form and special tuition for open scholarships. But the assumption behind these suggestions is that the maintained schools should compete, and would compete more effectively if it were possible for them to do so. The accession of Oxford and Cambridge to the Universities Central Council on Admissions may widen their field of recruitment. Meantime, however, the grammar school boy who wins one of the coveted places is seen both as triumphing over others more privileged than himself and, when he reaches the banks of Isis or Cam, of joining the privileged classes.

There are signs that among the politicians of both parties the possession of an Oxford or Cambridge degree is becoming more important than to have attended the right school. Certainly among civil servants this is so. Between 1948 and 1965 the percentage of Oxbridge graduates among recruits to the administrative class increased from seventy-eight to eighty-five.[3] Given that the graduate of Oxford and Cambridge shows a marked disinclination to enter the teaching pro-

[1] The figure of 20,000 for Oxford and Cambridge is simply assumed from the Robbins recommendation that 10,000 should be regarded as about the maximum size for a university, but the Franks Report has suggested a higher figure for Oxford.
[2] Robbins Report, p. 79.
[3] See the Sixth Report of the Estimates Committee, *Recruitment to the Civil Service,* (H. of C. 308, 1965.)

fession, this sets the educational administrator apart from the teachers in the schools he is administering almost as much as if he had attended an independent school. Yet, at the same time, he has the comfortable feeling that many of his basic assumptions are shared. Generally speaking the cleavage between the central administration on the one hand and the local education authorities and teachers on the other has not led to bad feeling. There was, of course, the famous Holmes-Morant circular which deplored the fact that local education authorities had appointed 123 inspectors of their own, of whom 'not more than two or three have had the antecedents which were usually looked for in candidates for Junior Inspectorships – namely that they had been educated first at a public school, and then at Oxford or Cambridge'. These local inspectors were drawn from the ranks of elementary school teachers who were 'as a rule uncultured and imperfectly educated', 'creatures of tradition and routine'; they compared unfavourably with H.M. Inspectors 'of the 'Varsity type who had the advantage of being able to look at elementary education from a point of view of complete detachment, and therefore of being able to handle its problems with freshness and originality'.[1] But, though there was inevitably resentment at such an outspoken statement, teachers in the maintained schools, members of the education committees which maintain them, and the parents of children who attend them, have generally given tacit agreement to the assumption of superiority by the Public Schools and ancient universities, and have tried to copy their ways of doing things.

Thus the government in England has been able to govern with a light hand. They have, once or twice, been prepared to intervene with some decisiveness when the situation seemed to call for it. The Revised Code of 1862 was one such example. Another was Morant's Secondary School Regulations of 1904. (These, incidentally, not only set a rigid pattern for the development of the new municipal Secondary schools but also restored to the Board of Education some of the power that had been denied to it by the opposition to the first Board of Education Bill. Although in the second Bill, which became law, the Board had only been empowered to inspect Secondary schools by invitation, the Regulations provided that inspection of a school by any agency other than the Board would not be regarded as sufficient for the purpose of grant.) But the Revised Code and Morant's Regulations are the two instances of government action which have been most criticized both by contemporary commentators and by historians of English education. Most of the criticism has been on the matter of principle, but there is also the implication that the government should not behave so forcefully. Not only have politicians and civil servants governed with a light hand, there has been a strong expectation that they should do so.

The situation in Scotland is rather more complex. The Secretary of State has usually had the same educational background as his government colleagues but has had to be deeply involved in Scottish affairs. The administrators in the Scottish Education Department have increasingly been Scottish born and Scottish educated, though they are nevertheless members of the home civil service. H.M.

[1] For a copy of the circular see A. Tropp, *The School Teachers*, Heinemann, 1957.

Inspectors of Schools have at times been criticized[1] because most of them have had a background of teaching in senior secondary schools and have had little practical experience of primary or of junior secondary schools: nevertheless they have invariably been qualified to teach in Scotland and have usually had experience of teaching in maintained schools. In part the Scottish Education Department has played a more active role for historical reasons, and in part because Scotland is a relatively small country. In part it may be that those administrators and inspectors who have themselves been educated in Scotland have been tempted to control more effectively what they know more intimately. They share a common background, if not with the pupils in maintained schools, at least with a majority of the teachers. But in part the Department has governed the schools with a heavier hand because it has been expected to do so.

The ideal in England in spite of increasing professionalism is still of the amateur. In Scotland respect is reserved for the expert. In his lonely outpost of Empire the product of the English Public Schools needed to be extremely versatile: he acted as local magistrate, political adviser and administrator. At home, the politician might find himself Minister of Education one day and President of the Board of Trade the next. In the civil service the way to advancement often is to move from one department to another. In the democratic control of education the lay member of the education committee plays his part, but the teachers who serve on the committee contribute their views on matters which fall outside, as well as on those strictly within, their professional competence.

In Scotland the tendency is towards specialization of function. The job of the teacher is to teach, and until recently teachers have not sat on education committees at all. The job of administrators is to administer, and an education department which does not get down to the task allotted to it is an anomaly. To an English observer this looks like authoritarianism. It is merely a different way of doing things. One obvious piece of evidence for this belief in specialization of function is that the *ad hoc* local authorities for education were kept in existence for twice as long as in England. The idea of a single-purpose authority for education has remained in favour. The Scottish Local Government Act, 1929, when it transferred the education service to the all-purpose local authorities, copied the English Education Acts from 1902 onwards in providing that the local authorities should appoint an education committee to which all matters connected with education must be referred, and *might* be delegated. But the Local Government (Scotland) Act, 1947, slightly strengthened the position of the education committees in requiring that powers under the Education Acts (with the usual exception of the power to raise a rate) *must* be delegated to the committee. The Educational Institute of Scotland has recently declared that its policy is the ultimate restoration of the *ad hoc* authorities.

[1] e.g. in the *Report of the Scottish Advisory Council on Secondary Education*, (Cmnd. 7005) 1947, p. 139.

CONSULTATION WITH TEACHERS

This has its effect on the part played by teachers in the educational system. To the English teacher the Scottish headmaster appears as something of an autocrat within his own school: the differentiation of function between head and assistant means that the head feels himself to be the organizer of the school: he feels entitled to tell his teachers what they should do, and they expect to be told. But, equally, to the Scottish teacher the English headmaster appears as something of an autocrat because he has a much larger voice in the general management of the school. Whereas the Scottish head will only expect to be consulted by the director of education on strictly professional matters, the English head, at the expense of having to explain his point of view to a body of lay managers or governors, participates as of right in the discussion of all matters affecting his school.

The existence of a separate body of managers or governors for each school serves in practice to increase the influence of the head teacher. A head will sometimes refer to them as 'his' managers or 'his' governors. He is regularly present at their meetings, frequently as the only professional teacher: this is very different from being present at a committee meeting which may be attended by a number of head teachers and by the director of education in addition. The position of a headmaster at governors' meetings is very similar to that of the head of an independent school who acknowledges no professional superior. The most obvious sphere in which the position of the headteacher is affected by the existence of bodies of managers and governors is in the appointment of teaching staff. In England, the appointment is usually recommended, after interview, by the managers or governors, the headteacher being, of course, present at the interview and his opinions carrying by far the greatest weight. In Scotland, teaching appointments are made after interviews before a subcommittee, or before the full education committee. A Working Party on Relations between Education Authorities and Teachers, which reported in 1962[1], mentioned that a previous advisory council had recommended in 1959 that the headteacher of every secondary school (but not of primary schools) should be consulted when appointments were made to the staff of his school, and should be present at the interviews. But they recorded that, although the Secretary of State had endorsed this recommendation, it had not been fully adopted in all areas. Even where it had, the director or his representative would usually be present too.

This is the most obvious example, but not perhaps the best because, in a system which attaches as much importance to 'personality' as does the English, the right to select one's assistants is regarded as fundamental. It is a matter in which the personal views of each head are likely to be decisive. The Scottish working party, however, came to the conclusion that teachers should play a bigger part in the selection of candidates for appointment in the schools, and recommended that education committees should set up special interviewing panels which might consist of five members of the education committee and

[1] *Report*, p. 6.

three teachers from the area: each headteacher would 'be invited to attend during consideration of the filling of any vacancy in his school'.[1] The selection of teachers to serve on these panels was to be left to each authority, but it was suggested that one method might be for the teachers in an area to elect, or their associations to nominate, those from whom members of the panels would be drawn. The participation of other teachers is bound to dilute the influence of a headmaster over the selection of members of his staff.

A second working party reported in 1962 on the question of appointing teachers to serve on education committees in Scotland. They recalled that the English Education Acts from 1902 onwards had provided that, although persons in the paid employment of local authorities are normally disqualified from membership of the council and its committees, there should be a specific exemption from this rule to make it possible for teachers in maintained schools to serve on the education committee or its subcommittees. There has been no such provision in Scotland where the normal disqualification has up to now applied to teachers as to other employees. The only exception has been in the constitution of local subcommittees for the management of educational establishments or groups of establishments. The composition of these subcommittees provides for the representation on them of, *inter alios*, parents or pupils of schools under their management (a relic of the days of the *ad hoc* education authorities) and for the inclusion in their membership of teachers serving in the establishments for which they have responsibility. The working party came to the conclusion that it should also be made possible for education authorities if they wished, but not mandatory upon them, to co-opt serving teachers on to their main education committees. They rehearsed the arguments both for and against this move. One of the strongest arguments against it, in their view, was that since the days when the English first decided to include teachers as co-opted members:

'Directors of education have come to occupy a position of importance in the educational system. They combine in themselves the professional knowledge and experience of educators on the one hand with the qualities of judgement and practical experience of the administrator on the other. It is their duty to be the link between the education committees as the lay body controlling the local educational system and the teachers as the professional experts responsible for carrying out the actual educational process.'[2]

The Education (Scotland) Act, 1963, made it possible for authorities to co-opt teachers on to their education committees. By the end of 1964 twenty-four of the thirty-five authorities had decided to do so, and eight had definitely decided not to.[3]

At national level the arrangements for the negotiation of teachers' salaries reflect the different attitudes to the government departments. In England, so much are teachers regarded as the employees of the local education authorities, that the Burnham structure left the burden of salary negotiations to the two

---

[1] Ibid., p. 25.   [2] *Report of a Working Party*, 1962, p. 9.
[3] See *The Times Educational Supplement*, 6 Nov. 1964.

sides, and the Minister of Education has hitherto only had the power either to approve or to reject the settlements they reached. In Scotland the joint negotiating committee has only proffered advice to the Secretary of State who has had power to fix salaries by regulation.

Salaries apart, Scottish teachers have gained a much more powerful voice in the control of their own profession than English teachers enjoy. They have been helped by the fact that, whether or not the profession is any more united (secondary school and primary school teachers have their points of difference), at least the teaching profession in Scotland is identifiable. In England, as long as untrained graduates are accorded 'qualified status' it will always be difficult to define precisely what a teacher is. In Scotland the teachers' associations played no small part in making professional training a prerequisite for recognition. Since 1958 teachers have had some voice in the control of training for future members of the profession in that the governing bodies of the colleges of education include teacher representatives who are elected every three years by ballot among their colleagues in the schools. Similarly the teachers have representation on the Scottish Council for the Training of Teachers (which is an executive as well as an advisory body.) The Wheatley Report[1] recommended the setting up of a Teachers' General Council to control membership of the profession in much the same way as the General Medical Council does for doctors. Legislation has been passed to give effect to this. A register of teachers will be maintained and the Council will decide both who may be admitted to and who should, if necessary, be struck off, the register: it will appoint visitors to satisfy the Council that the work of the colleges of education is being carried out satisfactorily.

[1] *The Teaching Profession in Scotland*, Cmnd. 2066, 1963.

CHAPTER FOUR

Some Examples

The previous chapter dealt with the part played by different agencies in the administrative control of education. In this chapter brief surveys of the development of post-primary education other than in the traditional academic Secondary schools will suggest that the Scottish Education Department were far more decisive in their policy-making than the Board of Education in the nineteen-twenties and thirties. (These surveys incidentally fill in a little more of the historical background to a more detailed study of secondary education later in the book.) Then a discussion of the administration of the School and Leaving Certificate examinations and the control of the curriculum in primary schools will suggest that, in these fields too, the voice of authority speaks in firmer accents north of the border, although there have been recent changes. Finally an examination of the function of headteachers points some of the differences in attitude in the two countries.

POST-PRIMARY SCHOOLS: SCOTLAND

It could be that the Scotch Education Department had to take a more positive line than did the Board of Education because the Scottish system at the beginning of the present century was more developed than the English. Whereas the Board could leave it to the schools and the new local education authorities to work out their own ways of providing universal education virtually from scratch, the Department felt called upon to combat the firmly established academic tradition in Scotland in an attempt to make suitable provision to meet the needs of children of average ability who were now to form the majority of the school population. Certainly one of the problems which the Scotch Education Department had to face, both in the organization of leaving certificate courses in Secondary schools and in their attempt to encourage post-primary courses other than those preparatory to university entrance, was the extent to which the public elementary schools attempted to carry on the tradition of the parochial schools by seeking to prepare their best pupils for the universities in spite of the changed conditions consequent on the abandonment by the universities of their junior classes and the introduction of the Leaving Certificate. The Act of 1872 had attempted to set up a distinct type of school (the higher class school) which would carry the main burden of providing an academic type of Secondary education. But there was no financial advantage to a school in becoming recognized as a higher class school. In 1892, when some exchequer money became available for the subsidy of secondary education, the county committees were set up to distribute the funds. They showed themselves much too ready to allocate small sums to a large number of schools. In 1897 the Department told them that, while they were in favour of a certain amount of Secondary education being given in the elementary schools, there should be careful selection of the schools in which facilities for this were to be provided, and every effort should be made to see that such schools did not compete with any established higher class school. The following year the Department reported that their intervention had checked to some extent the dissipation of the grants for secondary education over a large number of schools.

One way in which the higher class schools might have achieved a stronger position than they did was that, when it was first introduced in 1888, the Leaving Certificate could only be taken by pupils of these schools. Four years later, however, public elementary schools were allowed to present candidates in the examination and within ten years no less than seventy per cent of all candidates for the examination were pupils of 'elementary' schools. The Department's views on this were expressed in no uncertain terms: 'In the case of many of these schools the candidates are few and they make a very poor appearance, and it is impossible not to doubt the expediency of such schools attempting such work for a handful of scholars who gain little by it. The effort is laudable, but it scarcely repays the time and labour spent upon it.'[1] The effort also, of course, had its effect on the development of other types of post-primary courses.

The development of these other types of post-primary courses can be traced back to the provision in the Code of 1867, in which, in order to 'encourage instruction beyond the elementary subjects' grants were introduced for certain 'specific subjects' which might be taken in Standards IV, V and VI. In their Code of 1873, the first for which they were responsible, the Scotch Education Department, against advice to the contrary, extended the number of specific subjects to include a wide range of subjects (the total eventually grew to thirteen). This 'met with a withering fire of criticism, much of which continued as long as the scheme was in operation. It was charged that the Department had not been guided by the spirit of the 1872 Act because the scheme included science and other non-university subjects'.[2] For the next ten years Latin was the most popular of the optional specific subjects: it was then overtaken by French, which remained the most popular subject until the scheme was abandoned. In 1898 post-primary education was reorganized: 'advanced departments' were to provide courses up to the school leaving age, based largely on the work formerly done under the table of specific subjects. In addition a new type of school, the higher grade school, was to offer courses of a predominantly scientific, technical or commercial nature to pupils who were prepared to take a three-year post-primary course. This new scheme had to be radically reshaped when, only three years later, the Act of 1901 raised the leaving age to fourteen. The advanced

[1] *Education (Scotland) Reports, 1897–98*, p. 183.
[2] N. A. Wade, *Post-Primary Education in the Primary Schools of Scotland 1872–1936*, 1939, p. 45.

departments were replaced by 'supplementary courses' for the majority group
of pupils who would leave school at fourteen. This again raised a storm of
criticism. As regards the higher grade schools,

'too much time had been devoted to specialized courses to conform to the Scottish tradition of a general secondary education course which capable pupils
between twelve and sixteen years of age might take in the State-aided elementary
school to prepare for direct university entrance. The Code for 1903 contained a
new clause which permitted higher grade schools, with the sanction of the
Department to offer a general uniform course in preparation for the Intermediate Certificate as a substitute for the specialised courses.'[1]

In 1907 the Secondary (higher class) schools were required to adopt the intermediate curriculum for the first three years of their course and possession of the
Intermediate Certificate became the prerequisite for entering the final two years
of the leaving certificate course. The higher grade schools thereafter became
virtually 'three year' Secondary schools and some developed five year courses.
But it remained the intention of the Department that a variety of post-primary
provision should be offered, and in particular that the supplementary courses
should have a quite independent existence. Circular 374, issued in 1903, said:

'My Lords are of opinion, from a careful consideration of the facts, that the
tendency – not confined to any one class of school – to make one and the same
school with one and the same staff serve many different functions is the weak
point of educational organisation in Scotland as compared with that of other
countries, with which, in other respects, Scotland might justly challenge comparison, and they are satisfied that increasing division of function as between
different types of schools is an essential condition of further educational progress. This division of function . . . does not necessarily imply a distinction of
higher and lower, but simply a difference of aim and purpose with a corresponding difference in the subjects of instruction.'

The Department's policy, however, met with only moderate success in two
ways: firstly the extent to which the supplementary courses were centralized was
very limited indeed. Twenty years later, even in the four cities, no less than 172
out of a total of 293 elementary schools were providing supplementary courses
as a 'top' to the school. Secondly, where centralization was effected, the supplementary courses were often provided within a higher grade or Secondary school.
Admittedly this was only being done in three such schools in the cities, but,
outside, nearly half the higher grade and Secondary schools were providing
supplementary courses in addition to the intermediate or leaving certificate
courses or both.

The next big step in the development of post-primary education came in 1921.
Circular 44 was issued in that year to outline the Department's proposals 'in
face of the contemplated extension of the school age' up to fifteen. Authorities
were advised to concentrate their attention on two main groups of children:

[1] ibid., p. 106.

those who were likely to complete a full course of secondary education; and those who would leave school at the age of fifteen or thereby.

'So far as the former group is concerned but little difficulty is likely to be encountered. Despite defects and imperfections which experience is gradually remedying, the present organization of secondary education in Scotland may be regarded as fairly satisfactory. Moreover the force of public opinion is strong enough to ensure the maintenance of the immemorial Scottish tradition that, subject to the overriding condition of intellectual fitness, no child, whatever his home circumstances, shall be debarred access to the secondary school and university by lack of opportunity. There is abundant evidence that, so far as this particular obligation is concerned, the liberality of education authorities has brought Scotland nearer to the ideal than she has been at any previous period in her educational history. Indeed the only point as to which doubt arises is whether due attention is always paid to the overriding condition.'

So far as the second group, the majority, was concerned the Department referred to their circular 374 of 1903, and said that the principles then laid down for the supplementary courses still held good for the framing of courses in the 'advanced divisions' (as they were henceforth to be called). 'Up till now, however, it can hardly be said that they have been translated very effectively into practice.' In considering proposals the Department would look for 'evidence of a determination to secure for the non-secondary pupil the full share of attention to which he is entitled. This implies, wherever practicable, an entirely separate organization even in subjects which are common to the secondary and the non-secondary pupil.' Like the proposals both for the specific subjects and for the supplementary courses, the circular met with a barrage of criticism. The Educational Institute of Scotland made counterproposals for a New Intermediate course for all pupils between the ages of twelve and fifteen. The subjects to be included in the course of any particular pupil would differ according to whether he proposed to continue his education to the age of seventeen or eighteen, or to be finished with it at about the age of fifteen, but there would not be a separate organization for the subjects which were common to all types of course and the common subjects would outnumber the differentiating courses by three to two or by four to one. An advisory council report commissioned by the Department and published in January 1923 made proposals very similar to those of the E.I.S. and met with general approval from education authorities and the teachers' organizations. But the Department were convinced of the correctness of their own policy. In May they issued a draft of two new Codes based completely on the principles of circular 44: one for Secondary schools and the other for the elementary schools including the advanced divisions. There were, of course, further strenuous objections. The leader writer in the *Scottish Educational Journal* (the official organ of the E.I.S.) said:

'The unity of the educational system is entirely lost by any such division as that of non-secondary and secondary, inasmuch as the very terms imply the one group is in the mind of the author or authors of Circular 44 exclusive of the other group. This exclusiveness will be strenuously opposed by teachers, Education Authorities, and without doubt ultimately in the House of Commons, when the draft Regulations are being discussed. . . . What the country requires and demands is a national system, which involves the complete coordination and articulation of the various parts, and offers to the pupils the fullest advance according to their talents. . . . We desire to have a system linked up into one homogeneous whole, and embracing all stages of education, from the primary school to the university. No other system can be considered satisfactory, or meet with the approval of the teaching profession of Scotland. The policy of the Institute has for many years been a full secondary education for all pupils. The Advanced Divisions, whatever may be said to the contrary, are palpably intended to furnish certain pupils with an inferior type of education. Unless and until the curriculum of all post-qualifying pupils is the same and carries with it the same privileges and is not separated even in name, the opposition to the Codes will be continued. All post-qualifying education must be the same for all pupils.'[1]

Nevertheless, the Codes did come into force, and the leader writer of the *Scottish Educational Journal* was over-optimistic in thinking that opposition in the House of Commons would be sufficient to prevent them. Those higher grade schools which had developed five-year courses were upgraded into Secondary schools; the intermediate examination was abandoned so that the leaving certificate course became a simple five year course with no kind of break at the end of the third year. The alternatives to the leaving certificate course were the three-year advanced division course leading to a new Day School Certificate (Higher) at the age of about fifteen, and the two-year advanced division course leading to the Day School Certificate (Lower).

The fate of the Department's renewed attempt to foster courses other than the traditional academic secondary course was very quickly made clear. In their Report for 1922–23 the Department had admitted that 'Thus far the practical outcome of the Circular has been comparatively small'. The picture of the advanced division courses which emerged was that 'the curriculum in many cases tends to be of the familiar "Intermediate" type. Not a few of the schools were staffed and equipped for that curriculum, and they have just carried on. But the instances of variation are fairly numerous and they will become more common as new schools come into the system. Where a new curriculum is offered it reproduces the main features of the Intermediate course but contains a new group of subjects which gives it its distinctive character.' With that kind of modification the Department seemed to be satisfied.

Again, as with previous attempts, the process of reorganization and centralization continued but slowly: indeed the Department themselves were now preaching caution and advised that every scheme of centralization should be considered very carefully on its merits before being adopted. H.M. Inspectors are occasionally to be found suggesting that some authorities were perhaps

[1] *Scottish Educational Journal*, Vol. 6, 25 May 1923, p. 375.

going rather too far in their reorganization schemes. By 1939 the number of schools which provided advanced division courses only, and had no primary department, had reached fifty, but outside the large towns the all-age school with an advanced division 'top' was still the most common type: forty-four per cent of all primary schools had such a 'top'. The proportion of Secondary schools which provided advanced division as well as leaving certificate courses had dropped from just under one-half to about one-third.

The Education (Scotland) Act 1936 finally gave promise that the raising of the school age, which had been on the statute book since 1918, would at last be brought into effect, and in circular 103 the Department called on education authorities to submit schemes outlining their proposals for school organization. This time they were less categoric about questions of organization and left the authorities to take local conditions into account.

'It is anticipated [said the Department] that Authorities will propose to continue the five-year secondary courses generally on their present lines for pupils for whom they are the most suitable form of secondary education. But if these courses do not already include a due measure of the non-academic and practical subjects, the desirability of including such subjects in suitable circumstances should receive careful and sympathetic consideration; and wherever possible an endeavour should be made to provide courses of the various types accepted by the Department for the purpose of the Leaving Certificate. . . . The three-year course (at present known as three-year advanced division courses) will become of greatly increased importance. . . . For many pupils courses based entirely on academic subjects will not be educationally appropriate. Suitable provision should be made for their instruction in courses having a commercial, technical, domestic or rural bias in accordance with the indications given in the Day School Code, 1923.'

A new Code was put into force in 1939 in spite of the fact that the raising of the school leaving age to fifteen on which it was based had been postponed at the outbreak of war. This Code met one of the main criticisms which had been levelled against the Department in that it was a single set of regulations governing all types of school. The 'parity of esteem' between certificate and non-certificate courses for which the Department itself had been pleading in its own way since 1903 (but which the teachers had accused the Department of denying by the formal separation of the two types of post-primary course) was now given explicit recognition by putting all kinds of post-primary course under the single heading of 'secondary'. Courses of secondary education were henceforth to be distinguished only by their length. The five-year course – the successor of the full Secondary course up to the Leaving Certificate – would lead to the examination for the (renamed) Senior Leaving Certificate and the three-year course would lead, for the best pupils, to the Junior Leaving Certificate, to be awarded on the same basis as the former Day School Certificate (Higher). The Department were now at pains to urge the necessity for a diversity of provision, not by emphasizing the difference between the two broad categories of academic

E

and less academic children, but by insisting that the variety of courses offered, both of five years and three years duration, should be wide enough and flexible enough to cater for individual needs. The three-year course would not normally be predominantly academic, but the five-year courses should by no means be confined to pupils whose aptitudes were primarily of a literary nature: they should include scientific, practical and technical courses. On the other hand it was clearly assumed that pupils allocated to five-year courses would, at least for the first two or three years, study a language other than English, whilst the three-year courses, in order to avoid the pitfall of being merely abbreviated versions of the longer courses would have 'a definite character' of their own.[1]

POST-PRIMARY SCHOOLS: ENGLAND

The growth of post-primary courses in England can, as in Scotland, be traced from the provisions of the 1867 Code governing 'specific subjects'. At first confined to the introduction of rather more advanced teaching to pupils in Standards IV to VI, the specific subjects led to the development of suitable courses for children who stayed at school long enough (or were promoted through the school rapidly enough) to spend some time in the seventh standard when that was added, and later in the 'ex-standard classes'. Some urban authorities found it convenient to draft the children from these top classes of the elementary schools into one central school. There were various different arrangements, and transfer to the central school might take place at different ages in different areas. The schools themselves might variously be known as central schools, higher grade schools or higher elementary schools. They differed from the higher grade schools in Scotland in being the result of local growth and not a separate category of school established by the regulations of the government department. Like the Scottish higher grade school as originally conceived, however (and not as it soon developed), the schools tended to offer a curriculum for children who were intending to seek employment in industry. The Cross Commission in their final report of 1888 were divided in their views about the administration and financing of these schools, but neither section of the Commission was anxious to assimilate the higher elementary schools into the Secondary school sphere.[2]

The Bryce Commission, on the other hand, thought that the higher grade or higher elementary schools should be treated as secondary schools and placed under the jurisdiction of the authorities for Secondary education, the establishment of which they recommended. Even so, they were insistent that these schools should be coordinated with other Secondary schools in the area, and brought into a definite and organic relationship with them in such a way as to cooperate and not compete with the existing Secondary schools. The local education authorities, which were set up by the 1902 Act, started their work, however, in circumstances which were hardly favourable to the further development of the

[1] *Memorandum explanatory of the Day Schools (Scotland) Code*, 1939.
[2] *Report of the Commissioners appointed to inquire into the Elementary Education Acts*, 1888, pp. 239 and 248.

higher elementary schools. The fact that the Cockerton judgment ruled that expenditure on them had been *ultra vires* need not necessarily have been a great blow because the Board of Education hastened to repair the damage and the higher elementary schools were at last given official recognition and covered by their own code of regulations. The fact is that these schools had developed not merely without official directive or encouragement; they had, it was revealed, no legal justification for existing at all.

But the authorities were preoccupied with their new powers to establish, maintain and assist Secondary (grammar) schools. Morant's regulations made for a distinctively academic curriculum in the Secondary schools and the Board of Education was, for about a decade, rather obviously indifferent to the progress of other types of post-primary education. In fact, if it is a criticism of the Scottish Education Department that, in the first twenty or thirty years of the present century, they attempted to push the schools too far and too fast along a road they were reluctant to take, it is an equally valid criticism of the Board of Education that they played altogether too passive a role in the fostering of new developments. Nearly all the experiments and progress in the field of post-primary education outside the Secondary schools were undertaken by the schools themselves or by the local education authorities. The more successful innovations became an accepted part of the country's educational provision mainly by a process of ratification – often reluctant ratification – by the Board of Education of steps which had already been taken. To a far greater extent than even the Scottish Education Department's most outspoken critics could claim, the attitude in England was governed by a firm determination that post-primary courses, other than in the Secondary schools, should be seen as an appendage of the elementary school system. With far less justification than in Scotland, there was fear lest other types of course should in any way compete with, or overlap, the work of the Secondary schools. Nevertheless this determination was not so firm as to lead to any prohibition. The Board's attitude was completely permissive. Whereas the Scottish Education Department retained a measure of financial control over the situation by keeping a differential rate of grant for post-primary courses up to 1924, the Board of Education themselves were proud of the fact that 'the introduction of the "Block Grant" in 1900 marked the end of the system in force since 1862 by which the choice of subjects in Elementary schools had been controlled by monetary consideration'.

The 1918 Act gave local education authorities power to provide 'advanced instruction' in the elementary schools, but the Board refrained from trying to define what was meant by this or giving any guidance. In their Report for 1924–25 the Board boasted that 'No attempt has been made to suggest, still less prescribe, the lines upon which courses of advanced instruction should be organized'. The Hadow Committee in their 1926 Report had to refer to the parliamentary debates when the 1918 Bill was being considered before deducing that what had been in mind was instruction of a general practical nature and not specific training for particular industries, that it was to be provided for children who stayed on at school beyond the age of fourteen, as well as those who, by rapid progress through the earlier stages had reached the top class before the age of fourteen. When, in 1925, the Board of Education had sought to discover the extent to which 'advanced instruction' was in fact being provided in the schools, many local education authorities found some difficulty in answering the questionnaire which they sent out, and the Board had to call upon H.M. Inspectors of Schools to help to interpret the answers. The result of such a permissive attitude, of course, was considerable variety in the arrangements made in different areas. The Hadow Report distinguished eight broad headings under which to group the differing policies of the local education authorities (or nine if one includes the category of 'Authorities which are adopting several of these arrangements simultaneously'). The main differences were:

(a) Selection of pupils: admission to the advanced courses might be dependent on a qualifying (or even a competitive) examination; it might be dependent on the pupil having reached a given stage in the elementary school course, or simply on having reached a stipulated age. Admission to the courses at some fixed age was in fact comparatively rare: the other criteria for admission were more or less equally adopted by different authorities.

(b) Organisation: 420 out of a total of 550 schools or departments providing advanced instruction were central schools drawing pupils from several other schools in the area. Only 130 drew their pupils exclusively from one primary department.

(c) Usual age on entry: an average age of about eleven plus was by far the most usual on entry to the advanced course, though ten plus and twelve plus were quite common, and a few departments admitted children at about the age of thirteen.

(d) Length of course: 300 of the schools had a four-year course; 185 had a three-year course and most of the remainder offered a two-year course.[1]

The total number of children taking an advanced course at the time of the enquiry was 98,459, or about five per cent of all children in the elementary schools over the age of eleven (this compares with 71,816 enrolled in the advanced divisions of the primary schools in Scotland at the same date serving a school population of about one-tenth the size of England's).

A definite break between primary and secondary education was probably an essential prerequisite to the establishment of a satisfactory organization of secondary courses. Such a break had been implicit in the Scottish system from 1903, backed as it was by an examination to be taken at the age of about twelve, which was administered by the Department itself. A similar break between stages had been hinted at in England too before the beginning of the century, but the Board showed a tendency to change its mind about the most suitable age for it. England had to wait for the Hadow Report before an accepted policy was put into effect. Once they had the backing of a widely acclaimed report, the Board carried forward with 'reorganization' with as much speed as circumstances permitted. But between the publication of the report and the outbreak of war

[1] Hadow Report, p. 57.

the provision of 'advanced courses' in the new secondary modern schools made no headway at all. The schools were reorganized, and in some cases given handsome new buildings, but they had no success in lengthening the average length of the secondary course for their pupils.

The Hadow Report had, with some hesitation, come down in favour of a school leaving examination to be taken at the age of fifteen plus, and specially designed for the pupils of secondary modern schools. The hope was that this might offer an incentive for some pupils to remain voluntarily at school. But the Board of Education did not follow up the suggestion.

Nevertheless the idea of the 'rising tide in the veins of youth' at the age of eleven plus caught the imagination. The motto of 'secondary education for all' provided a slogan for reconstruction plans. Efforts were made to lengthen the period of compulsory schooling, even though the obstacles were so great that it took ten years to get the necessary measure onto the statute book. The obstacles, however, were those of economic difficulties, of the religious question, of politics and organization rather than of educational controversy. The history of English education at this time does not leave the impression of disagreement between the department and the teachers which one gets from Scottish education. Perhaps it was that the Board had no very clear policy of its own. Perhaps its techniques of persuasion were more subtle. Or perhaps its methods of consultation were more highly developed. There is an element of truth in all these. The Spens Report in 1938 came out strongly in favour of developing the work of the junior technical schools: the Board had published the year before a *Review of Junior Technical Schools in England.* The Norwood Report felt 'that full treatment of Sixth Form work in general is not here necessary, for it has been well undertaken in the pamphlet on Sixth Form work published for the Board of Education; to it we would draw attention'.[1] At the same time the Spens and Norwood reports continued where Hadow had shown the way. Based on wide-ranging evidence from every corner of the educational world, they gave point and publicity to the next moves. In 1943 a government White Paper on Educational Reconstruction recommended 'three main types of secondary school to be known as grammar, modern and technical schools'. A few days later the publication of the Norwood Report 'transformed tri-partitism from a proposal into a doctrine'.[2] The Board, or rather their successors, the Ministry of Education, were soon to be found talking of tri-partitism as if it were a fact of nature, and not something which had only recently been imposed on English education for a deliberate purpose. The impression that is left is that important developments in policy are not to be found in the memoranda and pamphlets of the government department, still less in statutory rules and orders, but in the reports of the Consultative Committee and the Secondary School Examinations Council.

[1] *Curriculum and Examinations in Secondary Schools,* 1943, p. 75.
[2] H. C. Dent, *Secondary Education for All,* 1949, p. 137.

SECONDARY SCHOOL EXAMINATIONS

The Scottish universities were opposed to a matriculation test. But they had been conducting local examinations on the lines of the Oxford and Cambridge 'locals' for some years – Edinburgh and St Andrews since 1865, Glasgow since 1877, and Aberdeen since 1880. Few candidates had, however, been presented for them. The Scottish Education Department had also been conducting experiments in the examination of the 'higher branches of knowledge' during the eighteen-eighties, and in 1888 called a conference of headmasters and the universities as a result of which they instituted the Leaving Certificate. This was confined at first to the higher class schools, but in 1892 it was thrown open to the pupils of any recognized school.

It was their powers of inspection of the schools which the Department used to justify their proposal to examine the pupils, and a feature of the Scottish Leaving Certificate has always been that, although it is intended to test the candidates' knowledge at the end of a secondary school course, success in the examination papers has not been regarded as a sufficient guarantee in itself that the course has been properly followed. Schools were required to submit their curricula for approval, together with a scheme of study in each of the subjects offered. The final award of the certificate was 'determined by the School record of the pupil and such written, oral and practical examination as the Department may from time to time decide to hold in the last session of the course'. Considerable weight was attached to the teachers' estimates, which were required to be submitted for each examination candidate. A heavy load fell on the inspectorate not only in setting and marking the papers, but in visiting the schools, conducting local tests and discussing the pupils' performance with their teachers. The examinations were held in March in order to leave the summer term available for this consultation. The result was not only that the teachers played an important part in the conduct of these examinations, but also that the Department were in a strong position, through the inspectorate, to influence the work of the schools in detail.

In England, Oxford and Cambridge had, apart from the College of Preceptors, been first in the field of school examinations in 1858, and it is from their early work that the School Certificate eventually developed. As other universities also took a hand in the examination of secondary school pupils each university attracted a following of schools, open to their inspection and presenting candidates for their examinations. An attempt was made to conduct the examinations in very much the same way as the Scottish Leaving Certificate. 'To complain, therefore of the influence of University Examining Bodies on the work of the schools is, historically, irrelevant. Those Bodies came into existence with the very intention of influencing the schools.'[1] The Oxford and Cambridge 'locals' had been purely external examinations and had been criticized by the Taunton Commission in 1868 as being too difficult to test the work of the majority of

[1] N. Morris, 'An Historian's View of Examinations', in *Examinations and English Education*, ed. S. Wiseman, 1961, p. 11.

secondary school pupils. The Oxford and Cambridge Joint Board examinations, introduced in 1874, were intended mainly for the Public Schools: at first a 'higher certificate' it was open only to candidates aged at least eighteen, but in 1884 a lower certificate was also introduced for fifteen- and sixteen-year-olds. The London University Matriculation Examination had been designed purely as a university admission test, but in 1902 the London University Extension Board was established for the specific purpose of examining and inspecting secondary schools. Its School Certificate was open only to pupils of schools which had been inspected by the University Board. The Oxford and Cambridge Joint Board made similar arrangements for their new School Certificate from 1905, and the Northern Universities Joint Matriculation Board, founded in 1903, introduced a system of inspection of secondary schools in 1910. With the growth of the secondary school system any adequate inspection however was likely to outgrow the resources of the universities. Morant's Regulations in 1904 had, moreover, rendered inspection by the universities supererogatory except for the purposes of the examinations.

The Bryce Commission had recommended that the Board of Education should coordinate, but not actually administer, a school leaving examination and in 1912 the Board began a round of consultations which led eventually to the setting up of the Secondary School Examinations Council in 1917. The Council was responsible for the coordination of the work of eight separate examining bodies attached to the universities. It consisted of eighteen members of whom half were appointed by the examining bodies, and the remainder by the local education authorities and the teachers. Secondary schools were forbidden by regulation to enter their pupils for any examination below the standard of the School Certificate. In 1936 the Council was reconstituted with thirty-one members of whom one-third represented the examining bodies, one-third the authorities and one-third the teachers.

A more radical reconstitution took place in 1946. The Education Act, 1944, had at last put the public education system under the charge of a Minister of Education whose responsibilities were no longer confined to coordination and supervision but were defined as the 'control and direction of the national policy for providing a varied and comprehensive educational service in every area'.[1] By then the tradition that the government department did not interfere in questions affecting the curriculum had been so well established that the new ministerial powers made little noticeable difference to the freedom of authorities and schools to go very much their own way. In one respect, however, the Ministry did take more control. The Minister of Education, Ellen Wilkinson, announced that, in the sphere of secondary school examinations, 'having regard to the new statutory duties imposed on her under the Education Act, 1944, [she] is no longer justified in limiting her functions to those of a Coordinating Authority. She will accordingly assume in the future full responsibility with the assistance of the reconstituted Secondary School Examinations Council for the direction of policy and general arrangements in regard to school examinations'.[2] The new

[1] Education Act, 1944, Section 1.   [2] Ministry of Education Circular No. 113.

Examinations Council consisted, as before, of thirty-one members. But, instead of a third of the members being representatives of the examining boards, henceforth the examining boards had no representation at all (although their parent universities nominated members). And the Minister of Education had five nominees on the Council, including the chairman.

More recently the administration of secondary school examinations in Scotland has been transferred from the Department to a newly constituted Examinations Board. This has been not so much the result of a deliberate policy of delegation as a simple measure to relieve H.M. Inspectorate of a responsibility which, with the enormous rise in the numbers of candidates for the examination, had become intolerable. The move had in fact been recommended as long ago as 1947. But the Department postponed making it until they had reorganized – or rather thought that they would have reorganized –the examination system. A new ordinary grade was introduced in 1961 and had been the main cause of the very large increase in the amount of work connected with the conduct of the examinations. The Department also thought that they had reached the stage of introducing a new advanced grade, but opposition to this from senior secondary school headmasters proved to be so strong that the Department set up the Examining Board without further delay and passed to them the difficult task of recommending how, if at all, the advanced grade should be introduced. The Scottish Board in its constitution copies the careful balancing of interests which the English Secondary School Examinations Council has had in its various guises.

It might have appeared that England and Scotland were to have more or less the same kind of body responsible for the general coordination of examinations, subject to the direction of the Minister concerned (though not, of course, the same arrangements for the actual conduct of the examinations because in England this is still done by the examining boards, whereas in Scotland the single[1] national Examinations Board conducts the examinations). But just when this situation had been reached the English decided to alter the function of the Secondary School Examinations Council: it has been replaced by the Schools Council for the Curriculum and Examinations, with very much wider terms of reference. Not to be outdone, Scotland has appointed a Consultative Committee on the secondary school curriculum, but this body is separate from the Examinations Board.

CONTROL OF THE CURRICULUM

In the days of the Revised Code the curriculum of the schools was controlled by regulation enforced by a system of regular inspection and of annual examination:

'If the Inspectorate of a bygone generation had a somewhat authoritarian, and at times even an inquisitorial cast, the explanation is to be sought not in the

---

[1] In addition the Scottish Universities Entrance Board conduct the University Preliminary Examinations, but these are used only for university matriculation purposes, may not be taken by pupils still at school, and therefore are not an alternative to the Leaving Certificate.

personal qualities of the talented men recruited to that service but rather in the function assigned to them and in the conditions under which they had to work. Their rigour was of a piece with the autocracy of the headmaster and the coercive force of the external examination. All alike were features, and it may be necessary features, of a national system of education rapidly expanding and having to consolidate its standards as it grew.'[1]

In England, when the payment by results system was abandoned, the Code continued to lay down 'broad and general lines which the school work should follow'. The 1905 *Handbook of Suggestions*, however, went so far as to say that 'the only uniformity of practice that the Board of Education desire to see in the teaching of the Public Elementary school is that each teacher should think for himself'. There was nevertheless still some uncertainty about leaving it entirely to the class teacher to devise his own curriculum, and some doubt about who should in fact carry the responsibility: 'The number and character of the subjects chosen, and the extent to which the subjects chosen may be developed in the teacher's hands, are left sufficiently open to enable individual authorities, managers and teachers to adapt the instruction to local requirements.'[2] But the uncertainty has resolved itself over the years in favour of the teachers. Authorities and managers or governors do not normally exercise any real control over the school curriculum. In strict terms of the Education Act, 1944, the local education authorities have power to control the secular education in any school maintained by them (save a voluntary aided secondary school) except in so far as may be otherwise provided by the rules of management or articles of government. The Act says that such power 'shall include power to determine the times at which the school session shall begin on any day, to determine times at which the school terms shall begin and end, to determine school holidays',[3] etc. The control exercised in practice by the education authority is usually limited to such peripheral matters and to decisions about staffing, buildings and equipment, and to the broad policy of secondary school organization.

The governors of secondary schools commonly have power to control the school curriculum conferred on them by the articles of government of the school. In practice this usually means no more than that the headmaster is under an obligation to report to the governors on the work of the school: instances of any refusal to approve his actions must be very rare. The managers of primary schools normally have no control over the actual work of the school at all.

To come back to the central government, however, the practice has been, since the first edition in 1905, to publish from time to time an official *Handbook of Suggestions* giving fairly general advice to teachers on questions of curriculum and teaching method, as well as rather more detailed monographs dealing with particular subjects. Relieved of their inquisitorial function, H.M. Inspectors have been cast in the role of advisers. Their collective wisdom has gone into the writing of the *Handbooks*. Apart from that they have been seen as individuals

[1] *Report of the Scottish Advisory Council on Secondary Education*, p. 138.
[2] Board of Education, *Handbook of Suggestions*, 1905, p. 2.
[3] Education Act, 1944, Section 23.

whose words of advice have carried as much weight in the schools as the prestige of each inspector and the value of his advice has merited. Each area inspector has, however, always been free to call in specialist advice from colleagues and the regular visits to the schools in his area by the local inspector have been reinforced at intervals of a number of years by the 'full inspection' when a team of H.M.I.s descends on a school, occupies it for a week or more, and publishes a printed report on its work (which is then debated by the governors or managers, who are usually powerless to do anything about most of the recommendations contained in it). But in the past few years it has been possible to discern a change of attitude. There is less inclination than before, within the inspectorate itself, for each individual to go his own way, and far more collective effort by the inspectorate, both nationally and within the area teams. The inspectorate's suggestions still have no external sanctions, but are no longer merely words of advice from one individual. Rather are they backed by the joint opinions of several H.M.I.s who each contribute, not only their personal point of view, but often also their own particular expertise. H.M.I.s have always made a double contribution to the work of the inspectorate: firstly as 'general inspectors' for a limited area, and secondly as expert advisers to their colleagues in some particular field either within a more extended district or nationally. There has been a shift of emphasis from the first function to the second.

Concurrently with this change of emphasis in the work of the inspectorate, the Ministry and its successor, the Department of Education and Science, have shown more interest than ever before in the curriculum of the schools. Sir Edward Boyle, as Minister of Education, announced his intention of setting up a curriculum study group within the Ministry. This came as a shock to the teachers' organizations and they protested at what they regarded as a plot to interfere with their freedom. They had been accustomed to Ministers of Education who were eager to get on their feet, in answer to questions in the Commons from M.P.s who did not know any better, to assert that it was no part of the Minister's job to interfere with the teacher in the classroom and that he either had no power to control the curriculum or at least was determined to exercise a self-denial in this respect which was one of the strengths of English education and of British democracy. Unlike some continental governments the British government did not try to dictate to teachers what they should teach, and were absolutely determined never to be remotely guilty of any suspicion of indoctrinating the children of the land. But, in spite of the teachers' protests, the Minister gave a few assurances and early in 1962 went ahead with the formation of his curriculum study group. 'There is no intention', said the Ministry's annual report for 1962, 'of detracting from the proper responsibilities of the teachers and the local education authorities. On the contrary, the intention is rather to help them discharge their responsibilities more fully.'

The next step was the suggestion that the Secondary School Examinations Council should be replaced by a Schools Council for the Curriculum and Examinations. This proposal was tackled more cautiously. A Working Party[1] was set

[1] Under the Chairmanship of Sir John Lockwood.

up to recommend the constitution and terms of reference of the new council. It reported in the spring of 1964, and its recommendations were submitted to the local education authorities and the teachers' organizations for comment before any further action was taken. The Working Party in fact recommended that the council should be entirely independent of the Ministry, with its own executive separate from the civil service. They reaffirmed that the schools should retain the fullest possible measure of responsibility for their own work. The new council should be a free association of partners with representation from all interested educational organizations. Member interests would retain the right to make decisions affecting themselves but would be able to use the council as a forum for discussion to coordinate their policies with others. 'The Schools Council would not, in other words, be advisory to the Ministry of Education alone; it would be advisory to all its member interests.' Its recommendations would carry only the weight attributable to suggestions arrived at as the result of a planned programme of study or research going beyond what might be achieved on their own by busy teachers. The new Council for Curriculum and Examinations held its first meeting in October 1964.

In Scotland there is still a Code. The Education (Scotland) Act, 1962, defines primary education as 'progressive elementary education in such subjects as may be prescribed', and secondary education as 'progressive courses of instruction of such length and in such subjects as may be approved'.[1] The Code, made under these provisions, prescribes the subjects to be taught in all primary schools and requires that, for each primary and secondary school, the education authority shall prepare a scheme of work, in consultation with the headteacher, showing the scope of work in each subject, and submit it for the approval of the district inspector of schools. The district inspector may not alter the scheme but has power to call upon the authority to produce another. The headteacher is then required by the Code to draw up detailed programmes and timetables based on the approved scheme of work (though he does have power to authorize occasional departures from them). Perhaps the limitations on the teachers' freedom imposed by this system are more apparent than real, since headteachers are normally given the initiative in preparing schemes of work for submission to the district inspector. Nevertheless it must add to the authority with which the Scottish H.M.I. speaks that he is responsible, not only for visiting the schools and reporting on their work, but actually for approving their curricula.

But the interplay of forces is much more complex than the bare terms of the Code would suggest. For one thing, there is the paradoxical situation that English local education authorities, which have far less formal power to determine the school curriculum than their counterparts in Scotland, are nevertheless in the habit of employing local advisers or inspectors, both for specialist subjects and, in many cases, for general school subjects. The main function of these local advisers is to supervise probationary teachers and to organize in-service courses but, inevitably, there is some overlap with H.M. Inspectorate. (Perhaps the main result of this in England is that visits to the schools by two different sets of

[1] Education (Scotland) Act, 1962, Sections 2 and 3.

inspectors serves to weaken the impact of both.)[1] Scottish education authorities do not normally employ local inspectors at all, and even when advisers or supervisors of some specialist subjects are employed, they frequently perform the function more of a visiting teacher than of an inspector. This weakens the position of the authority in drawing up curricular suggestions even though they have the responsibility for doing so. What happens in practice is that, although the headmaster will, of course, be consulted about the particular scheme of work for his own school, the education authorities, or rather the directors of education, act in the role of coordinating authority. They organize working parties of teachers in their area to draw up schemes of work which may be officially promulgated by the authority but they are acceptable to the teachers because they have had a hand in preparing them. This tends towards a degree of uniformity in each area, but is a way of obtaining the collective advice of the teachers which does not often exist in England.[2] The fact that the Scottish Working Party on the Arrangements for Consultation between Education Authorities and Teachers, which reported in 1962, had nothing to say on the question of schemes of work is at least negative evidence that teachers are satisfied with existing arrangements.

In contrast to the recent tendency for the English inspectorate to take a more forceful line in advising the schools, there is to be discerned in Scotland the adoption of a much less authoritarian attitude by H.M.I.s than was usual a few years ago. This has been coupled with 'an innovation which the Department have made in the preparation of general memoranda on the curriculum' – giving the same sort of official advice as is to be found in the English *Handbooks of Suggestions*. The authorship of these documents is usually confined, as it was in England before the establishment of the Schools Council for Curriculum and Examinations, to members of the inspectorate, but practising teachers and training college lecturers were invited to serve with H.M.I.s on the panel charged with the writing of one memorandum (on primary education). The document which they have produced spells out the new freedom accorded to the schools:

'This Memorandum avoids prescription of either subject-matter or methods. Its predecessor (in 1950) was cast in a form which made it a useful hand book but also conveyed probably some impression of stating official requirements in a manner that appeared inflexible. This new Memorandum, however, discusses general principles governing primary education. . . .'[3]

HEADTEACHERS

Within the schools themselves the abandonment of the annual examination under the Code, both in England and Scotland, meant that responsibility for the

[1] Except under the former London County Council, whose local inspectorate had a considerable prestige.

[2] Perhaps Cheshire has gone further in this respect than most authorities, but Cheshire is not typical of English L.E.A.s.

[3] *Memorandum on Primary Education In Scotland*, 1965, p. vii.

maintenance of standards in the schools fell more heavily on the headteachers. They naturally continued to use the methods which the inspectorate had relied on. As far as England is concerned the 1905 *Handbook of Suggestions* admitted that examinations had been 'largely discredited by their mechanical use for the inspection of schools' and wanted to restrict their use as far as possible: 'In no case should they be held more often than four times a year: and in schools whose size and organization allows the Headteacher constantly to supervise the work of his staff, two formal examinations in the year are often sufficient.'[1] Nevertheless it was clearly envisaged that it was the headteacher's duty to 'arrange that the school shall be periodically tested by a formal examination which he should supervise, and in which his staff should take such part as he may determine. He will communicate to them any obvious faults in method which are made evident by the results of the examinations.'[2] The 1927 *Handbook* is interesting in that it plays down the importance of the headteacher's examination: he will still test the school, or certain classes, from time to time and discuss the results with his staff, but at the same time there is the lingering assumption that examinations ought to be 'external' in the suggestions that the Head's examining load might be relieved if class teachers were allowed to examine each other's classes.[3] But, by 1937, examinations had assumed a new importance. An entirely new section on internal examinations appears in the new *Handbook*. It starts by saying that the class teacher will 'naturally' test his own class at fairly frequent intervals, but that there will be times when the need is felt for a more comprehensive review of the work done in a school. The need for such a review, as far as the headteacher is concerned, is, however, carefully related to almost every part of a headteacher's job *except* that of keeping a check on the work of the class teachers:

'If the headteacher does not know with some degree of certainty whether his pupils are making the progress which they are capable of making, whether his classification of them is satisfactory, whether their attainments compare favourably or not with those of previous years, whether his schemes of work are as suitable as they might be, and so on, he and his staff will be working with less efficiency than they might and under a self-imposed handicap which need not exist . . .'

They are not explicitly a check on the efficiency of the staff, but at the same time these general examinations are, throughout this section, referred to as the headteacher's examinations. The word 'headteacher' appears ten times and the phrase 'headteacher and his staff' only once. Moreover in a word of warning to headteachers about the possible pitfalls of examinations, the *Handbook* does let fall a hint that the results will still be used to form a judgment of the work of the class teachers:

'A Headteacher may be fully justified, in certain circumstances, in limiting his examination of a class to what has been done in the "Three Rs", but unless he

---

[1] *Handbook*, 1905, p. 13.   [2] ibid, p. 16.   [3] *Handbook*, 1927, pp. 60–62.

takes other aspects of the work of the class into account in forming his judgment of the value of the teacher's effort, it may follow that little else but the "Three Rs", as he examines them, will receive adequate attention.'[1]

In the next twenty years any uncertainty about the headmaster's role as examiner has been completely resolved. Examinations are now no longer seen as being the headteacher's tool for assessing the work of his school: they are a cooperative effort by the whole of the staff. The rather shorter section on internal examinations in the 1959 *Handbook* consistently uses the phrase 'head or assistant teacher', where it does not refer simply to the class teacher alone. The only occasion when the word 'headteacher' is used on its own is when it is suggested that, when forwarding the school record cards or other reports for the purposes of the eleven plus selection, 'there is always opportunity for the Head to make additional observations'. There is now only passing reference to the head-teacher's tasks of organization, and none to the job of drawing up schemes of work.[2] Instead,

'it is the Head's personality that in the vast majority of schools creates the climate of feeling – whether of service and cooperation or of tension and uncertainty – and that establishes standards of work and conduct. A Head is likely to fulfil all these functions better if he continues himself to be a good teacher and is seen to be so. As a fellow practitioner of quality he is more likely to win the regard of his colleagues and to inspire confidence in the inexperienced ones; as a teacher he meets the children in the normal circumstances of the classroom and therefore knows them better. . . . In thought, idea and practice the good Head leads his whole team. The commonest way of sifting and disseminating ideas is through discussion, and in small schools it is not difficult to find occasions for them. In large schools . . . the occasions for serious discussion should be regular for, where the Head withdraws from being the mainspring of the school or where there is insufficient sharing of thought and experience, the inspiration of a commonly accepted purpose dies.'[3]

For this kind of role the headteacher of an English primary school needs the attributes of 'patience, good sense, humour, humility and sense of purpose'.[4] His opposite number in Scotland was, until recently, thought to need 'energy, efficiency, judgment, tact, and a sense of duty'.[5] Whether or not the different choice of words in the Scottish Education Department's *Memorandum on the Primary School in Scotland*, 1950, is as significant as it appears when they are taken out of their context and put alongside those from the English 1959 *Handbook*, it is quite clear that they were based on a different conception of the proper function of the headteacher. 'The distinction of *function* between a headmaster and other members of the staff is more important than the distinction of *status*',[6] the Scottish Advisory Council had said in 1947. And it is clear that this difference in function involved a measure of control over the class teacher and of leadership

---

[1] *Handbook*, 1937, p. 59.   [2] *Handbook*, 1959, pp. 97–101.
[3] Ibid., p. 92.   [4] Ibid., p. 94.   [5] *Memorandum*, 1950, p. 140.
[6] *Advisory Council Report on Primary Education* (Cmd. 6973), 1946, p. 82.

by precept rather than by example. The 1950 *Memorandum* described the duties of the headmaster as follows:

'He should view the school as a whole, determining the organization, arranging the timetables, deciding the teaching methods (individual, group, class) and prescribing the methods of instruction to be used in a particular subject when – as in subtraction – the same method ought to be used throughout the school.'

The examination was an important part of the Headmaster's stock in trade:

'He must be familiar with the profession of work and attainments of each class, and be on the alert for symptoms of insufficient progress in a class or an individual pupil. . . . If the Headteacher is to "know his school" he will have to visit every classroom regularly in order to confer with the teacher; he should be ready to take a lesson with a class; he should conduct periodic oral tests and, in addition, written tests where these are appropriate: if the size of the school precludes him from personally testing a class in writing, he should himself set the tests, or have submitted for his approval the questions proposed: he should scrutinize the scripts and, after considering the results, take such action as may be called for. Without the knowledge gained in these and other ways he cannot give the necessary guidance, and exercise effective oversight of the work of both pupils and staff.'[1]

But the 1965 *Memorandum on Primary Education in Scotland* rejects the thesis that the difference between a Headmaster and his staff is one of function rather than of status: 'The Headteacher must regard himself, above all, as a teacher and must see his main functions as educational rather than administrative.' He must, of course, be in full control of his school:

'By reason of the overall view which he has of the whole establishment, and through his contact with parents, officials and the secondary schools to which his pupils will go, he is in a position to see, more clearly than his teachers or the parents of his pupils, the part that the primary school has to play in the whole educational process and to ensure the continuity that the pupils need. It is essential, therefore, that his should be the last word on organization and planning, the content of the curriculum, the utilisation of time, teaching methods and the rules of behaviour.'

But he is now seen much less as a director of the school and more as the leader of a team. Although he must still exercise general supervision over the work of each class, and satisfy himself both that adequate ground is covered and that appropriate progress is made, he is now limited to guiding his teachers in their planning only 'where necessary'.[2] Examinations are out of favour: certainly they are no longer the headmaster's normal tool for satisfying himself that the class teachers are doing their job – though, as in the English 1937 *Handbook*, there is a hint that examinations may still be imposed upon the class teacher by the head: 'Much time can be mis-spent in the holding of weekly or monthly tests in the

[1] *Memorandum*, 1950, p. 141.   [2] *Memorandum*, 1965, p. 26.

various school subjects . . . worse still, the existence of tests of this kind in a school may cause some teachers to limit the content of their teaching to those aspects of the curriculum which are known to figure regularly in the examinations.' Nevertheless in the section on internal school examinations there is now no explicit reference to the headteacher at all.[1]

The precise role of the primary school head obviously worries the writers of official reports on Scottish education. The Ministry of Education had felt it sufficient simply to state baldly that 'the over-riding responsibility for planning and supervising the life and work of the school rests with the Head'[2]; they were content to assume that his personality would create the right climate within the school and they thought that a head could best fulfil his functions if he continued to be a good teacher without apparently considering the possibility that he might be a somewhat indifferent teacher, or that, at least, a member of the staff who knew himself to be a better teacher than the head might therefore be tempted to challenge his authority. In Scotland the Advisory Council had pointed out in 1947, that: 'The members of a school staff, speaking generally, are all of a certain order of intelligence and of similar training; some may have academic distinctions superior to those of the headmaster. It is extremely unlikely in a staff of any size that the headmaster will have gifts and capacities superior in every respect to those of every member of his staff'[3], and therefore came to the conclusion that the only justification for the position of the headmaster lay in the special functions of the post. The 1965 *Memorandum* in coming to the opposite conclusion made a less forthright point of the fact that heads are but teachers like the rest: 'The Headteacher's knowledge and experience, vision and vitality, may well be less than his staff can muster as a whole, and he is wise to give scope to the talents of his team so that their combined thinking may have weight in determining the policy of the school.'[4]

It would seem that the concept of leadership, which the English accept as a fact of nature, is rather more open to question in Scotland. Certainly ideas of leadership fit more readily into an aristocratic system of government like that of England than they do into a democratic system in which positions of authority are open to all men of talent (provided that they do in fact show that their talents are superior). Or the explanation may be a much simpler historical one: the function of headship is one which is still a matter for discussion in Scotland because the tradition inherited from the secondary schools of a hundred or more years ago is one of anarchy in school organization. The practice in the nineteenth century has been described in the following terms:

'In general, it had not been customary in Scotland to grant the headmaster (or "rector", as he was traditionally called) any very extensive authority over his colleagues on the staff. Though nominally in charge of the internal affairs of the school, he had only limited powers of discipline, hardly any control of appointments to the staff, and little to do with regulating the work done, since there was

[1] Ibid., pp. 48–52.   [2] *Handbook*, 1959, p. 92.
[3] *Advisory Council Report on Primary Education*, p. 81.
[4] *Memorandum*, 1965, p. 27.

no compulsory course of studies and normally a separate fee was charged for each subject taken, at the option of the parent. This inherent anarchy was increased by the fusion of grammar schools and academies, when in some cases two rectors were retained, as in Perth, and in others the office of rector was abolished altogether, as in Dundee. In other cases there was a tendency for the virtually independent heads of the separate departments to form a council of masters, sometimes presided over by each in turn, to manage the internal affairs of the school in republican fashion. Even to this day, though notions have changed and a fully fledged rector sits in authority over all, the head of each department of study at Dundee High School retains the title of headmaster (e.g. of mathematics, modern languages, etc.). Strangely enough, this competitive system seemed to commend itself to Scottish opinion as good for the schools, and in some cases local sentiment was resolutely against consolidation of the work under one headmaster. As the century advanced, however, it became usual to appoint a rector with a good deal of influence in all matters affecting the school, as in Inverness Royal Academy and in Glasgow in both High School and Academy. In a few cases, on the other hand, particularly where English influence made itself felt, as in the case of Edinburgh Academy, the Headmaster was from the first granted supreme authority over the working of the whole school, with the power to appoint and dismiss his staff almost at pleasure. Thus the variations within the system were great.'[1]

The variations of size and range of organization of secondary schools in both parts of the Kingdom are such that it is more difficult to compare the functions of their headmasters. Suffice it to say that English opponents of comprehensive schools make a great point of the fact that a head's managerial responsibilities are bound to predominate over his teaching role in a very large school. Obviously they are right. Whether or not this is a valid objection to large schools, it is clear that the opponents of comprehensive schools expect most Englishmen to regard it in that light.

[1] H. M. Knox, *250 Years of Scottish Education*, 1963, p. 40.

CHAPTER FIVE

School and Community

GEOGRAPHY

Two out of three Scottish schools with secondary pupils are, in English term-inology, 'all-age' schools. But they are called secondary schools and are a permanent feature of the system. In England any remaining all-age schools are classified meantime as primary schools and are regarded as being obsolete. Since 1926 the process of 'Hadow reorganization' has proceeded at whatever pace economic and other conditions have permitted. The 1944 Act required that primary and secondary education should be given in separate schools, though it was not until 1958 that the Minister of Education felt able to forecast definitely that the all-age school would finally disappear by about 1965.[1] It will go un-mourned. In Scotland on the other hand, although a definite break at about the age of twelve between primary and secondary education was worked out in the early years of this century, the actual separation of primary from secondary schools has never been regarded as essential, and by many is regarded as undesirable. The Education (Scotland) Acts do not require it. It could be claimed that Scottish schools were completely 'reorganized' by 1936, although nearly half the schools at that time were all-age schools, whereas England cannot yet claim to have com-pletely 'reorganised' her schools. Clearly the word is used with a quite different meaning. An apparently similar process of rearrangement of the schools has been going on in both countries over the past forty years or so. It so happens that in 1950 the proportion of maintained and assisted schools which were all-age schools – one in four – was almost exactly the same in Scotland as in England, but this figure only represents the stage which had been reached in Scotland in a continuing process of centralization and rationalization of both primary and secondary education, whereas it represents in England the extent to which the authorities had failed to implement a policy of separating secondary from primary schools which had been accepted twenty-five years before.

One differentiating factor is clearly the geographic one. The view expressed by the Moncrieff Commission in 1881 that a separation of elementary from more advanced work would be 'dispiriting to the master' would seem to presuppose schools which were so small that the staff were called upon to teach children of all ages. Since then the population of Scotland has increased by forty per cent, but most of the increase has been in a very concentrated area and in other areas there has actually been depopulation so that one-third of all Scottish schools still have less than fifty pupils. (The population of England during the same

[1] *Secondary Education for All – A New Drive* (Cmnd. 604), 1958, p. 7.

period has increased by eighty per cent and only one school in seven has less than fifty pupils.) The geographical isolation of some settlements in Scotland is such that an all-age school is the only solution (short of boarding education for all children of secondary age). It is worth underlining the obvious because the sparseness of the population in some ninety per cent of the land mass of Scotland must have had a considerable effect on the attitudes of administrators and teachers even in the urban areas. To record that one-third of Scottish schools are in industrial areas whereas in England and Wales one-third are in areas officially classified as rural is merely to suggest that the balance is different. The contrast is greater than that. It will cause no surprise that the Scottish Education Department classify fifteen of the thirty-five education authority areas as being 'mainly rural', but there is a further category (covering another seven authorities) classified as 'areas mainly of heath and moor'. Scotland has in fact a population roughly the same as that of Lancashire spread over an area about three-fifths that of England. The following table shows how it is spread:

TABLE 9. *Scottish Education Authorities*

CLASSIFICATION OF AUTHORITIES:	LAND AREA %	SCHOOL POPULATION %
Cities and industrial areas	5	60
Mixed industrial/rural	8	20
Mainly rural	40	15
Mainly heath and moor	47	5
All Scotland	100	100

In England teachers get a special 'London allowance' to meet the extra cost of living in the metropolitan area. Scotland has both problems. There was recently a suggestion that a special 'Glasgow allowance' should be paid. There is also a special 'remote school allowance'. This is paid to teachers in a school which is more than fifteen miles by land, eight miles by sheltered water or two miles by exposed water from a 'centre of population'. A 'centre of population' is defined as a community which is large enough to support a three-teacher school! Nor is this the end of the story: there is, in addition to the remote school allowance, an extra 'distant island allowance'.

Centralization in such circumstances is difficult enough. But, where depopulation is a serious economic and social problem, there is also a natural desire to postpone as long as possible the admission of defeat implied by closing or 'decapitating'[1] the local school.

The geographical nature of the country has, of course, an effect on the staffing of Scottish schools. Overall, Scotland claims a slightly better staffing ratio than England and Wales. The number of very small rural schools, however, makes for uneconomic staffing and it is necessary for the urban schools in Scotland to accept larger classes than in England, in spite of the fact that the staffing of the small schools is rather less generous than most English local education author-

[1] i.e. transferring the senior pupils to a central secondary school.

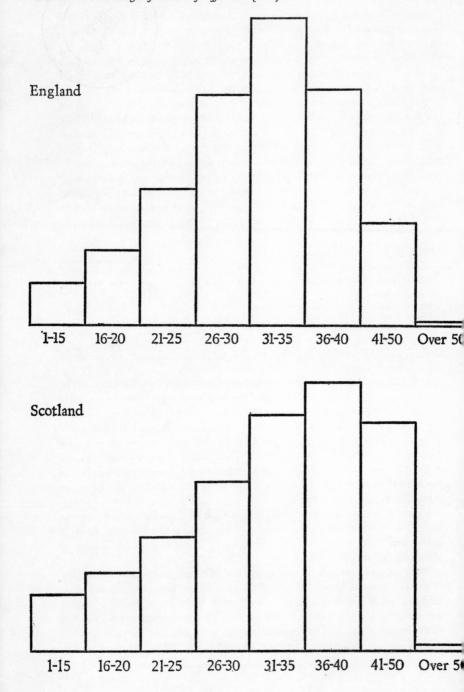

TABLE 10. *Percentage of classes of different sizes* 1962

England

1-15   16-20   21-25   26-30   31-35   36-40   41-50   Over 5(

Scotland

1-15   16-20   21-25   26-30   31-35   36-40   41-50   Over 5(

ities allow to their schools of comparable size, and in spite also of the fact that England squanders rather more of her available teachers by permitting a very much better staffing ratio in the direct grant and independent schools. The School Regulations covering maintained schools in England and Wales prescribe a maximum of forty for primary classes and thirty for secondary classes. The Scottish Code lays down forty-five for primary classes, forty for classes in the first three years of all secondary schools and thirty for the higher classes. A comparison of the number of classes of given sizes in 1962 is given in table 10.

The fact that the population is scattered is not, however, the only reason for the retention of the all-age school in Scotland. The pattern of school organization was, on the whole, set by the parochial school. It was only gradually that the few large towns began to develop a type of organization which differed from that of the rural areas and the smaller towns (though even now not to the exclusion of the all-age school even in the cities). The process of centralization made slow headway up to the second world war, in spite of attempts to hurry it along by the Scottish Education Department, but has shown a sudden spurt since the war.

The designation of the various types of post-primary schools has changed over the years: nevertheless the totals of all-age schools and 'separate' schools respectively in table 12 give a fairly clear picture of the extent of 'reorganisation'.

The trend is a continuing one and has clearly gone hand in hand with a process of centralization since the total number of schools has dropped: the number of secondary schools has fallen between 1950 and 1964 from 909 to 726 and the number of schools with primary pupils has decreased by 157. This picture should be contrasted with that in England where, over the same period, the number of all-age schools has been much more drastically reduced at the same time as the number of secondary schools has increased by 1,100 and of primary schools by nearly 6,000:

TABLE 11. *Types of school: England*

	ALL-AGE	SEPARATE		TOTAL
		Secondary	Primary	
1950	6,357	4,765	16,776	27,898
1963	775	5,890	22,416	29,081

TABLE 12. *Types of School: Scotland*

	ALL-AGE		SEPARATE 'Secondary' only		'Primary' only		TOTAL all schools
1908	Secondary with Primary Dept.	32	Secondary Higher Grade	23	Elementary	1,250	
	Higher Grade with Primary Dept.	162		7			
	Elementary with Adv. Division	1,899		——		——	
		2,093		30		1,250	3,373
1938	Secondary with Primary Dept.	203	Secondary Adv. Division	49	Primary	1,620	
	Elementary with Adv. Division	1,224		50			
		1,427		99		1,620	3,146
1950	5-year Sec. with Primary Dept.	128	5-year Secondary	74	Primary	2,103	
	3-year Sec. with Primary Dept.	639	3-year Secondary	68			
		767		142		2,103	3,012
1964	Secondary with S.C.E. courses	171	Sec. with S.C.E.	210	Primary	2,266	
	Secondary without S.C.E. courses	276	Sec. without S.C.E.	69			
		447		279		2,266	2,992

TYPES OF SCHOOL

At this point it becomes necessary to define the terms used. An English 'all-age' school was an elementary school which provided for children from the age of five, seven or eight, up to the age of fourteen, or, after 1947, to the age of fifteen. The children who were selected for grammar schools, however, were transferred at the age of eleven and it was only the remainder who stayed on. The senior department of such a school would endeavour, so far as its facilities and staffing allowed, to do the same work as a secondary modern school. There were also before 1944 Secondary (grammar) schools with primary or prepara-tory departments, but the term all-age was never applied to them. Nor is it used in Scotland. And in many cases the analogy of the grammar school with a primary department is a more just one than the English all-age school in the strict sense. In fact more than a third of the all-range schools in Scotland are either schools which are an exact parallel with the grammar-school-with-a-primary-department or are comprehensive schools with an age range of five to eighteen. The remainder are elementary schools which developed a 'top' and in due time provided courses now classed as 'secondary', i.e. junior secondary schools with a primary department: it is these schools which are a closer parallel with the English all-age school.

One difficulty of terminology is that, in England, each particular type of school is described by a different name. For example, a grammar school is one which mainly provides academic courses leading to the General Certificate of Education. Any school which is specifically designed to offer both 'grammar' and 'non-grammar' secondary courses will be classified as a comprehensive, or as a bilateral, school according to the precise nature of its internal organization. In Scotland, on the other hand, schools used to be classified simply by the longest and most exacting course they offered. A five-year secondary school was one which provided courses up to the Scottish Certificate of Education on the higher grade. Such a school was commonly known as a senior secondary school, although the term had no official sanction. But a senior secondary school might also be one offering both five- and three-year courses, i.e. it might be the rough equivalent of a comprehensive or bilateral school rather than of a grammar school. It might or might not also have a primary department. A three-year secondary school was one which took pupils from the age of about twelve to fifteen. It might be a school which offered the first three years of a leaving certificate course (completed by pupils who transferred for the remaining two years to a five-year school) as well as courses for children who intended to leave school as soon as they were permitted to do so – i.e. the rough equivalent of a 'junior' comprehensive school in England. Or a three-year school might in fact offer only non-certificate courses – the type commonly known as a junior secondary school, and the rough equivalent of a secondary modern school with no extended courses. Three-year secondary schools might also have a primary department.

Recent developments have added further complications to the question of nomenclature. Many secondary modern schools in England have developed courses for pupils up to the age of sixteen and beyond leading to the G.C.E. and other examinations. Even so they are mostly still known as secondary modern schools. In Scotland it was always understood that five-year secondary schools would keep some of their pupils for a sixth year and that three-year schools might develop fourth-year courses of a specialist nature (although the fact that the Leaving Certificate could not be taken before the age of seventeen prevented them from preparing for that). With the introduction of the ordinary grade in the Scottish Certificate of Education, however, it has now become possible for former three-year schools to present their pupils for the certificate in exactly the same way as English secondary modern schools do for the G.C.E. All the former junior secondary schools in Aberdeen and Dundee have done so. The Scottish Education Department have promptly changed the classification of secondary schools in their official statistics to show 'secondary schools with S.C.E. courses' and 'secondary schools without S.C.E. courses'. Thus it becomes impossible to distinguish between schools which are the equivalent of English grammar schools and those which are the equivalent of a secondary modern school with a G.C.E. course.

To suggest that a Scottish five-year secondary school with both certificate and non-certificate courses is the equivalent of an English comprehensive school is also misleading. In England comprehensive schools have been established as the result of a definite educational or social policy. Comprehensive schools have recently been established in Scotland, too, from the same motives. But in order to describe the type of 'comprehensive school' usual in Scotland before the war, and still the most common even now, it would be better to use the term 'multi-lateral', or, better still, to adopt the Scottish term 'omnibus' school as a quite neutral description of a secondary school which happens to provide various types of secondary course but without thereby necessarily being committed to any particular educational doctrine. The headmaster of one such school describes the situation as follows:

'Secondary education as it is known and practised in the smaller Scottish burghs has evolved from the old burgh school, itself a product of the parish school system in force prior to 1872. Variations have naturally occurred from area to area. A process of centralization rendered inevitable by social and other considerations and accelerated by the 1947 raising of the school leaving age has affected every county in Scotland, with variations from county to county largely according to topographical variations and differences in density of population. School rolls may in some instances have risen threefold or more over the past forty years, but by and large and certainly in essence the Burgh High or Grammar School in Scotland has retained its original function as the one educational centre of the community catering under a single roof and under a single staff for the educational needs of all its children. Only in the cities and larger towns with their concentrations of population has the pattern deviated from that of the old parish school system. In the smaller burghs the more generous provision of the past ten to fifteen years in staffing, equipment and buildings has allowed all the children of the neighbourhood to share in a common and unsegregated experience known in much more limited ways by their predecessors of a century ago.

'The Scottish claim to a more democratic system of education than that which has existed south of the border is true, however, only in part. The burgh school of modern times has indeed educated all the children in its area under one roof, but the advanced divisions of the 1920s left a legacy of segregation that the modern "comprehensive" senior secondary school has found hard to "offset".

'If Inverurie Academy with its present secondary roll of over 1,000 pupils is typical of such schools – and its history from its higher grade days of the pre-1914 era has been so typical – then "omnibus" rather than "comprehensive" courses have been the order of the day. Strenuous but as yet insufficiently far-reaching attempts have been made over the years to break the iron curtain separating junior and senior secondary streams. Up to the 1940s the two streams in Inverurie were housed in separate buildings and taught largely by separate staff, heads of departments being confined in general to senior secondary classes with assistant teachers "graduating" in time from the junior secondary streams to which in their earlier years they had been appointed. An echo of this cleavage is still discernible in the Inverurie community among those of its members now in middle-age – fortunate or unfortunate, according to one's attitude – taught "in the Academy" or "on the other side".'[1]

Even this description does not cover all the types of omnibus school. It is true that the burgh school normally catered under one roof for the educational needs of its immediate area. Typically it would, like Inverurie Academy, have a Secondary department, advanced division courses and a primary department. Many burgh schools, however, also drew senior pupils from a wider area. In some cases it would be only the leaving certificate course which was open to such pupils: in some cases they would also be admitted to three-year advanced division courses but not to two-year courses: in some all post-qualifying pupils were taken but not, of course, the 'non-qualifiers'. Since the adoption of the 'clean cut'[2], the raising of the school leaving age, and post-war reorganization schemes, some omnibus schools are, indeed, 'comprehensive' in so far as they provide secondary education for the whole of their catchment area: all pupils, both from the school's own primary department and from the 'feeder' primary schools, proceed automatically to the secondary department. It is only in the retention of eleven-plus tests and the bilateral nature of their internal organization that such schools fall short of being truly comprehensive. But other omnibus schools, though they may take into their secondary department all pupils from their own primary department, and perhaps from one or two nearby primary schools, are selective in respect of a more extended catchment area. Children in the outlying districts who do not pass the promotion tests either attend a local junior second-ary school or stay on into the secondary department of their all-age school.

---

[1] N. Dixon, 'Comprehensive Education and the small burgh school', *Education in the North*, Spring 1965, p. 19. [2] See page 96.

At the July 1965 meeting of the Aberdeenshire Education Committee the director of education reported on the steps necessary to achieve a comprehensive system in the county. The six full senior secondary schools (including Inverurie Academy) were, he said, comprehensive: the five other schools which presented candidates for the Scottish Certificate of Education were nearly so. These eleven schools together accounted for 5,931 of the 7,533 pupils on the roll of secondary departments. The remaining thirty-three secondary schools, with 1,602 senior pupils, were not comprehensive. Freely translated into English this statement could be said to mean that some seventy-five per cent of the county's secondary pupils were in attendance at one of the six bilateral schools or one of the five secondary schools which had developed a G.C.E. ordinary level course; the remaining quarter were distributed among thirty-three all-age schools with an average roll of fewer than fifty senior pupils each.

It is the very small all-age schools (in the English sense of the word) with tiny secondary departments which have been drastically reduced in number. Perhaps Scottish administrators have been somewhat complacent in not having eliminated them, but without the drive of a national policy (such as may be given by the move towards fully comprehensive schools) it is easy to see how they could give in to the very real practical problems. The fact is that in matters which they do not regard as important they can adopt a *laissez faire* attitude.

SIZES OF SCHOOL

The conclusion which suggests itself is that Scottish schools have been called upon to provide a variety of different kinds of course according to the dictates of local conditions. They may have to cater for primary children as well as secondary, for non-certificate as well as certificate pupils, according to the size of a reasonably convenient catchment area. This is not to say that the question of efficiency has been ignored. To call an all-age school a secondary school is not a way of glossing over the shortcomings of the educational provision that has been made. Whereas an English all-age school usually lacked many of the facilities necessary for its senior pupils, every Scottish secondary school is required to be staffed for secondary work and to be equipped for it as far as the economics of small schools permit. If the senior pupils of English all-age schools sometimes suffered because the provision made for them was inadequate, in Scotland it is the primary pupils, if any, who suffer from attending a school which is likely to be staffed by teachers, or at least under the control of a headmaster, mainly concerned for the secondary pupils. Nor have Scottish administrators been entirely indifferent to the desirability of establishing schools which would have some kind of cohesion and community spirit. They have not, however, been obsessed, as English administrators have, with theoretical arguments about school organization – with, for example, excluding all but the most intelligent from the grammar schools as the best way of obtaining high academic standards, with the development of schools with a particular kind of specialism or bias to make use of some children's technical aptitude or vocational motivation, with keeping schools small enough to form a society in which everyone can know everyone else and the headmaster at least know the name of all his pupils.

The English, with their obsession with organization, and with uniformity in matters of organization, make administrative difficulties for themselves. It took the local education authorities thirty years to come within sight of full Hadow reorganization. Before it had actually been achieved, one authority (the West Riding) persuaded the Ministry to introduce legislation permitting a variation of the statutory age distinction between primary and secondary education so that they might experiment with schools for pupils between the ages of nine and thirteen. Within two or three years the idea had become so popular that it was confidently being predicted that the Central Advisory Council, which, under the chairmanship of Lady Plowden, had been asked to report on primary education, would be recommending a general change of the age for transfer from primary to secondary schools from eleven plus up to twelve or even thirteen plus. Meantime the Minister announced that he did not intend to give his statutory approval to more than a very small number of experimental schools which bridged the dividing line laid down in the 1944 Act.[1] On the other hand he did intend that secondary schools should be radically reorganized: schools would not have to conform to a single pattern, but a limited number of different models was described.

The range in size of Scottish schools compared with schools in England seems to provide ample justification for the suggestion that many schools north of the border 'just growed', whereas in the south they were designed according to a definite policy. The most telling thing about Scottish schools is not in fact that there are so many small ones. This, in a sparsely populated country, is only to be expected. But Scotland has proportionately very many more quite large schools than England has. It would have come as something of a surprise to most Englishmen a few years ago to find a school with more than a thousand pupils in the Outer Hebrides. It was an all-age school which has recently been split into separate primary and secondary schools. The number of all-age schools which still remain does, of course, explain to some extent the number of large schools in Scotland, though the English solution in such cases would invariably have been to separate them. But it is not only the all-age schools which are big by English standards. Among purely primary schools, taking no child over the age of about twelve, there were in 1962 no fewer than forty-nine schools in Scotland with more than eight hundred pupils on roll, compared with only nine in England.

The numbers of schools of different sizes in 1962 is given in table 13. The figures for Scotland are for July and those for England were taken in January so that to some extent the sizes of Scottish primary schools are slightly over-stated and the sizes of the secondary schools slightly under-stated in comparison with the English figures:

[1] Circular 10/65. (In a later speech the ruling was partially retracted.)

TABLE 13. *Size of Schools 1962*

	0–25	26–50	51–100	101–200	201–300	301–400	401–600	601–800	801–1,000	over 1,000
PRIMARY										
England	1,123	2,633	3,114	5,119	4,548	2,471	1,227	77	9	—
Scotland	587	440	282	193	163	150	297	162	40	9
ALL-AGE										
England	17	46	98	179	209	108	64	3	—	—
Scotland	—	11	47	79	66	53	86	49	50	49
SECONDARY										
England	—	6	27	300	777	1,055	1,948	987	260	131
Scotland	1	3	5	7	7	21	46	59	55	58

The difference is less marked than it used to be forty years ago. The number both of very small schools and of very large schools in Scotland has been reduced during that period as the following rough percentages show:

TABLE 14. *Sizes of Scottish schools: Percentages*

	Under 200 pupils	200–800	More than 800 pupils	All schools
1920–21	70	19	11	100
1962	55	37	8	100

The tendency at that time to tolerate very large schools wherever the concentration of population allowed them to grow is shown by the sizes of schools in the four cities forty years ago:

TABLE 15. *Number of schools of given size in Aberdeen, Dundee, Edinburgh and Glasgow*

	Under 200 pupils	201–500	501–700	701–1000	More than 1,000
1920–21	7	17	32	30	62

The number of schools with more than 1,000 pupils included four with more than 2,000: the largest had 2,709. A good example of the way in which schools tended to be either very small or, by English standards, very large is to be found in Inverness where there were eight schools in all: three had approximately 1,000 and the remaining five had fewer than 200 pupils. The three big schools were 'provided' schools, and the five small ones were all transferred (i.e. voluntary) schools.

As regards English schools of forty years ago the Board of Education simply did not record the sizes of schools with more than 500 on roll (elementary) or more than 600 (Secondary). The proportion of small elementary schools was almost as high as in Scotland. Out of 30,000 schools in all, 11,500 had fewer than 100 pupils, and two-thirds had fewer than 200 on roll. The number of big schools was considerably less: a bare 180 elementary schools had more than 500 pupils. Most of the secondary schools in England forty years ago were considerably smaller than would be regarded as the minimum for efficiency now. The majority fell within the 200–400 range, and, out of a total of 1,300 secondary schools on the grant list, only forty-one had more than 600 pupils. The independent schools tended to be even smaller. The Spens Report gives a picture of the growth in the average size of secondary schools up to the second world war:

TABLE 16. *Sizes of English Secondary Schools*

GRANT LIST	1913	1921	1925	1928	1932	1936	1937
No. of schools	1,027	1,249	1,301	1,338	1,378	1,393	1,397
Average size	182	290	283	294	326	346	347
RECOGNIZED AS 'EFFICIENT'							
No. of schools	121	233	312	353	378	394	397
Average size	186	191	184	181	172	185	185

The implication is that in populous England there was a very strong feeling in favour of the small unit, but that in Scotland the schools grew up in direct relation to the size of the local school population without very much importance being attached to theories about the optimum size for a school. More recently, however, more attention has been paid in Scotland to questions of school size. The Scottish Advisory Council, in their report on *Primary Education* in 1947, said that, at the one extreme, no primary school with fewer than ten pupils was a satisfactory educational unit, and, at the other extreme, no primary school should have an enrolment of over 650. They felt that the best size for a primary school was between 400 and 450, although they based this on arguments about primary school organization and posited much smaller classes than the Regulations at present prescribe. They may therefore perhaps be presumed to have accepted schools with 600 or 700 pupils as reasonably satisfactory with existing class sizes. In their report on *Secondary Education* the Advisory Council thought 600 a good size for secondary schools, but they were so much in favour of the omnibus school that they were quite prepared to push the permissible size up to 800 in view of the organizational advantages of the larger school if it was to cater for children of all abilities. The Scottish Education Department, however, pointed out that even this figure was based on recommendations for the re-organization of examinations which they had not accepted, and therefore suggested a figure of 1,000. Table 13 nevertheless shows that even this figure has been exceeded by one school in five.

A figure of 650 for primary schools seems large in comparison with the optimum figures of 240 and 320 advocated by the Ministry of Education for infants and junior schools respectively. But both sets of figures are in fact based on a two-form entry organization. The English figures presuppose a separation of infants and juniors, the Scottish suggestion does not. Moreover Scottish primary schools keep some of their pupils six to twelve months longer before passing them on to the secondary school.

The official term in Ministry statistics, 'school or department', could well be misleading to a Scottish reader. A 'department' in this context is a school under the control of a separate headteacher. In Scotland a department of a school is merely part of a school all under the control of one headmaster. Over and above the English predilection for comparatively small units, the all-age elementary school showed a strong tendency to split up into separately administered sections, each for a limited age range and each with its own headteacher. The 'unreorganized' elementary school might well have had children from the age of five, or perhaps from the age of seven or eight, up to the age of fourteen, all housed in buildings on the same site, but they would have been organized into distinct departments for infants, juniors and seniors, and at the senior stage would often have separate boys and girls departments. Since the war it has been the practice in the towns to build an infants and a junior school, designed as two self-contained buildings, on adjacent sites. In Scotland, on the other hand, even though rebuilding plans since the war have quite often involved an increase in the accommodation of an existing all-age school by building a new primary department on a nearby site and turning the existing building over to the exclusive use of the secondary department (or vice versa), it has been by no means unusual that the headmaster of the all-age school has retained the responsibility for all departments.

PART III

The Formative Years

As I gaed doon by kirk and toun
I heard the larkies singin,
And ilka burnie treetlin doon,
And wid and welkin ringin.

As I gaed doon by kirk and toun,
Quo I, 'A skweel, gweed feth!'
And there I heard nae sang nor soun',
But bairns quaet as death!

CHAPTER SIX

Primary Schools

The infants school was a Scottish invention. The first infants school was established in Britain when Robert Owen opened his infants school at New Lanark in 1816. But it was in England that the infants school rapidly developed as a separate entity. The first Minutes issued by the newly appointed Committee of Council on Education in 1839–40 show that not only infants departments, but separate infants schools, were in contemplation: model plans for new schools appended to the Minutes included both types. The Newcastle Commission's Report in 1861 classified schools as Infants schools, Day schools, Evening schools and Sunday schools. By the time that the Hadow Committee published their report on infant and nursery schools in 1933, they were able to record that two out of every three children between the ages of five and eight were attending separately classified infants schools or departments. They recommended – if recommendation were necessary – that except in rural areas infants should be separately organized under their own headteachers. That is broadly the pattern today.

The development of a definite break between infants and juniors at 'seven plus' was a hesitant one. The effect of the Code was to fix the definition of infants as those below Standard I, i.e. below the age of about six, though in some schools Standard I was taught with the infants. A committee appointed by the London school board in 1871, with T. H. Huxley as chairman, suggested a classification of London elementary schools into infants schools, up to age seven; junior schools, ages seven to ten; and senior schools, from age ten upwards. This scheme was later copied by other school boards, but with occasional variations and modifications. 'On the whole, however, Junior Schools did not at the outset come much into vogue even in the large town. As a rule the arrangement was preferred of providing infants schools, and so-called "senior schools" for pupils between the ages of seven and twelve or upwards.'[1] It should be remembered that in the early part of the present century the attendance at school of children between the ages of three and five was very much higher than it is at present. In 1900, in England and Wales, no less than 43.2 per cent of the total population in the three to five age group was in attendance at grant aided schools. By 1910 this percentage had dropped to 22.7, and thereafter it steadily dropped until in 1950 it was 12.3. It is now 18.5 per cent. As the relative numbers of infants declined

[1] Hadow Report, *The Primary School*, 1931, p. 12.

and the number of older scholars increased with the raising of the school leaving age, the schools experimented with different types of organization: above the infants department there might even be a 'junior', a 'middle' and a 'senior' department, although either one or two departments other than the infants department were more usual. The attitude of the Board of Education also underwent changes: in circular 1350 at the beginning of 1925 they suggested that all children between the ages of five and eleven should be organized in a single department, but when they published *The New Prospect in Education* in 1928 they felt that 'in the light of further experience it is not now possible to press this preference': in fact they saw advantage in a separation which makes it possible for the infants school 'to preserve its special methods and characteristics'. In the 1927 *Handbook of Suggestions* the infants stage is described as extending from the age of five to about eight and 'these three years should be treated as a single stage and even though the organization of the school may require children to pass from one department to another before their eighth year . . . the method of training should be as continuous as possible'. There are signs in the *Handbook* itself of a shift of opinion: the geography curriculum is described as being divided into three stages of which the first is for children up to the age of nine. But then came the Hadow recommendation for a 'well-defined line of demarcation between the younger and older children', and this confirmed what was already established in the majority of schools even if the actual line was drawn differently in different places. The Hadow Committee settled on the age of seven for their demarcation rather tentatively. They seem to have had most sympathy with 'our psychological witnesses who urged that promotion should be determined by the mental rather than the chronological age, though for administrative reasons a compromise might possibly have to be effected'.[1] The 1937 *Handbook of Suggestions* reveals just how little chance there was of mental age being accepted as an administrative guide. The infants school is there described as being for children between the ages of five and seven; 'the present tendency is to make promotion from one department to another once a year only, and for many reasons this is a sound practice'. It is in fact now well established practice. A few schools persisted in keeping the division between infants and juniors at the age of eight, but this was usually because it provided a neat way of fitting the numbers of children into existing buildings in such a way as to achieve the much more important 'Hadow reorganization' of separating the primary and secondary department. The few exceptions are rapidly disappearing and all new infants schools are built to take an age range of five to seven.

In Scotland, even in the cities, the separate infants school is rare. Before 1939 there were fewer than a score of separate infants schools in the whole country. Since the war the city of Aberdeen alone has adopted a policy of building new infants schools which are designed ultimately to be used as nursery and infants schools. (Note that Hadow thought that 'it seems highly desirable that the nursery school should be developed separately.') Since money has not been made available for the extension of nursery school provision, the authority have so far

[1] Ibid., p. 69.

built only such schools as are needed to provide for infants. But this is a policy adopted by only one education authority. The Scottish Education Department's official memoranda and statistics make no mention of separate infants schools. Outside Aberdeen, with very few exceptions, the infants department is just the first two classes of a primary school, which takes children from the age of five up to eleven or twelve. The particular needs of the youngest children are taken care of by the provision in the Code that in any school in which three or more teachers are employed in the infants classes there must be an 'infants mistress'. This is a post of responsibility for which a special qualification in work with infants is required, and, as most headships of primary schools go to men who feel they had better leave control of the infants department very much to their infants mistress, there is a considerable degree of devolution. Nevertheless promotion from the infants department to the junior part of the school falls into line with the promotion policy for the whole school. The infants department is simply the first two years of a seven year course, and even in Aberdeen the break between the infants and junior schools does not operate in the same way as in England.

The statutory definition of the commencement of compulsory schooling differs in detail as between England and Scotland, and this, combined with the fact that the former has a break at seven plus and the latter does not, has certain consequences for the later stages in the primary schools. The Education (Scotland) Act, 1962, requires education authorities to fix two or more dates in the year, and a child who has not reached his fifth birthday on one fixed date is not deemed to be of compulsory school age until the next fixed date. In England a child becomes of compulsory school age on his fifth birthday. Most authorities will, of course, only admit new pupils at the beginning of each of the three terms in the year (although practice differs), and the assumption in the Acts is that children will start school at the beginning of the term in which their fifth birthday falls.

The effect of these different provisions can be illustrated by the examples of children born on 1 June and 1 December. In Scotland, one of two arrangements might apply: Either a December child would start school at Easter at the age of five years and four months, and a June child would start in September at the age of five years and three months, and the school would be organized in two streams, six months apart in age, with promotion for one stream in April and for the other in September each year. At any given point during their primary school career under this arrangement both children would be of approximately the same age and have had the same length of schooling. Or, alternatively, a December born child would be assimilated at some stage into a school organization based on annual promotion in September only. Thereafter he would either be with children younger than himself and have the advantage of six months in age and two terms of schooling over a child born in the previous June; or, if very able, he might be put with children six months older than himself, having had one term less at school than a child born in the following June. Unless this assimilation takes place at the primary stage, of course, the December child has a six month 'transition' period to put in between the primary and secondary departments.

In England the June child, having been admitted to school in April at the age of four years and ten months, would, after seven terms in the infants school, reach the age of seven years and three months and transfer to a junior school a little over two years after starting school. The December child, on the other hand, would start school in September at the age of four years and nine months, but would not have reached his seventh birthday in September until nearly three years later and would thus transfer from the infants school to the junior school with an advantage of six months in age and two terms at school over the June born child. It is the common experience of junior schools in England which stream their pupils by ability (or apparent ability) that children with birthdays in the winter predominate in their 'A' streams, at least up to the age of nine or ten.

PROMOTION UP THE SCHOOL

Instead of having a break at seven plus, which exaggerates individual differences, Scottish primary schools use their system to even out the differences which exist. At different periods in the last fifty years more or less emphasis has been placed on age or on attainments as the criterion for promotion, but never has chronological age been the sole criterion, as it is in England at present. Just as in England, the Scottish primary schools experimented with different subdivisions within the primary school. The age ranges changed slightly from time to time but by and large they settled for an infants division (five to seven), a junior division (approximately seven to nine or ten) and a senior division above that up to the qualifying stage, after which came the advanced division. The Scottish Code of 1915 said that liberty of classification into these divisions was permitted irrespective of age, provided that H.M. Inspector was satisfied generally as to the reasons for the retention of children over seven and over ten in the infants and junior divisions respectively. (There was apparently nothing to prevent more than usually *rapid* promotion.) The 1923 Code spelled out in rather more detail the fact that attainment was the governing factor in promotion:

'The arrangement of work within each division and the classification of the children may vary according to the circumstances of the school, but shall be such as to afford due opportunity for promotion from class to class, and to secure the advancement of the instruction by easy gradations to a standard appropriate to the average age and capacity of each class. As a rule no child should be promoted to a higher division who has not satisfactorily completed the work of the division below.'

The system advocated by the Department at the present is described as promotion by age, but it is subject to considerable modification to take account of attainments too. The current Code requires a strict designation for each class according to yearly stages: PI for the lowest class in the infants department, and so on up to PVII as the highest class in the primary school (and SI up to

SVI in secondary schools). A class in a small rural school which includes several age groups must be designated as, for example, PIII–PV. This clearly gives more encouragement to promote children year by year according to their age than the old classification into divisions. But the 1950 *Memorandum on the Primary School in Scotland* said:

'The results of the oral and written examinations and of the different tests mentioned in the chapter on Assessment are of great value as the basis of promotion, whether within the primary school or from the primary department to the secondary. In the higher primary classes a pupil's promotion is very largely dependent on his attainments in English subjects and arithmetic. If he fails to reach a satisfactory standard in them, he may or may not be required to repeat the stage. *It may well be to his advantage to do so.*'[1]

The 1965 *Memorandum* is less enthusiastic about repetition though it suggests that this is still justifiable if a pupil is so far behind his contemporaries that his needs cannot be met by group or individual teaching within the class, and if there is no special tutorial class available. The guiding rule suggested is that 'the total time gained or lost through such departures from normal progress by any one pupil should rarely exceed twelve months. . . .'[2]
The practice still commonly followed is in fact that of using a limited amount of acceleration or retardation in order to fit human breeding habits into the framework of an academic year: as the 1950 *Memorandum* suggested:

'When admission to the lowest infant class is on two or more fixed dates, the gap between successive age groups is six months or less. Progress can therefore easily be accelerated or retarded by a few months for those who would benefit thereby. Where pupils leave the primary department for the secondary less frequently than they are admitted to the primary department the obvious administrative problems will be solved by judicious adjustment between consecutive stages.'[3]

A very similar picture of promotion within the primary school was given for England in the *Handbook of Suggestions* for 1927:

'It may probably be assumed that most experiments in classification and promotion will, for some time at least, fit themselves into the general framework of an "educational year". This year is usually divided into terms of four or six months, at the end of which the progress made by the class is tested. This examination offers an obvious opportunity for promoting deserving scholars.'[4]

Such 'bye-term promotions' were seen as offering a welcome flexibility compared with the 'rigid system of annual promotion which was the natural accompaniment of the old annual examination.' But flexibility apparently went too far. Only ten years later, in the 1937 *Handbook*, we read that:

[1] *Memorandum*, 1950, p. 128 (my italics).   [2] *Memorandum*, 1965, p. 41.
[3] *Memorandum*, 1950, p. 128   [4] *Handbook*, 1927, p. 33.

'with the disappearance of the annual examination, teachers found it possible to take individual ability more and more into account in the promotion of children from any one class to another. In consequence the custom spread throughout the country of pushing the brighter children ahead as they mastered their lessons so that they might work with the highest classes while they were still eligible by age to enter for the competitive examinations. . . . The argument for promotion by ability has been reinforced by the doctrine of "mental age" which has become familiar during recent years. It would be folly therefore to ignore the ability factor in organisation . . . but physical growth and social development do not necessarily keep step with intellectual progress. Indeed it is now questioned whether the practice of promoting bright young children to classes where on the average the pupils are considerably older has been an unmixed blessing.'[1]

The solution to the problem of promotion by age or by ability was however happily found in the device of 'streaming', though the fitting of children admitted on more than one date in the year into the streams was still seen as a difficulty: 'Where circumstances permit, it is desirable that a junior school should be at least large enough to have an A and a B stream, and a senior school to have an A, a B and a C stream. . . . Where however six-monthly promotions are the rule, then twice the number of classes will be needed if the same advantages in classifications are to accrue.'[2] In the new-found enthusiasm for streaming by ability it apparently did not matter if junior schools were four-form-entry schools and senior schools had six parallel streams. In the event it was the adoption of a rigid seven-plus break at the beginning of the junior stage and an equally rigidly determined age for promotion at eleven-plus out of it which answered the problem for them. In the English junior school with its four year age-range from seven to eleven there is not much scope for accelerating or retarding the progress of a child through the school. At the same time the admission of children from the infants schools at a fixed age, but with varying attainments and even with varying lengths of previous education, predisposes the schools to try to make some arrangements to produce greater homogeneity in each class.

In Scotland there is a period of seven years in the primary schools within which differential rates of promotion can operate and even the system of transfer up to the secondary schools is not so firmly tied to chronological age. The official suggestion that a child should not depart by more than twelve months from the normal group for his age is, moreover, not strictly observed. In 1962, for example, there were 2,536 children (over two per cent of all leavers) who left school, having reached the age of fifteen, who had not completed the second year of the three-year course in a secondary department and who must presumably have been over thirteen before they left the primary school. The number includes 238 children who had not even completed one full year in a secondary department. At the other end of the scale 868 children left school before their seventeenth birthdays, having completed a five-year certificate

---

[1] *Handbook*, 1937, pp. 31, 32.   [2] Ibid., p. 33.

course, including 106 who left before their sixteenth birthdays, and who must have been only ten when they started in a secondary school.

The only thorough examination of the extent of acceleration and retardation in the schools was undertaken by the Scottish Council for Research in Education just before the war. They obtained information about the age-grade distribution of all children in Scottish schools on 1 January 1937. As they

'found that the proportion might be affected by the chance of date of birth, date of admission customary in the area or . . . the dates of promotion, it was decided to include under the heading of "normal" not only those children who were "at age" but also those who were classified in the schedules one year in advance or one year behind. Thus the children in the lowest class of the Primary Division were regarded as "normal" if they were actually seven plus and also if they were six plus and eight plus. "Normal" thus covers generally a period of 2–3 years.'

The figures they obtained were:

	Retarded by		*Normal*	*Advanced by*	
4 *years*	3 *years*	2 *years*		2 *years*	3 *years*
1,714	7,374	37,764	552,571	336	5
	7.82%		92.13%	0.05%	

The Research Council's own comments on these findings were:

'Pupils "at age" that is with 95–105 I.Q., pupils one year accelerated, that is with 105–115 I.Q. and one year retarded in intelligence, that is with 85–95 I.Q. constitute practically seventy per cent of the school population; about 10 per cent are two years retarded intellectually, that is have I.Q.s 75–85; and the percentage more than two years retarded, that is with I.Q.s below 75 per cent, amounts to 3.4 per cent. A comparison can thus be instituted with scholastic retardation:

	Percentage retarded *2 years or more*	% *normal*
Retardation according to school grading	7.82	92.13
Retardation expected on the basis of I.Q.	13.27	60.79

It is evident that the problem that confronts us is not to account for scholastic retardation in Scotland, but to explain why this does not even equal that expected from intellectual backwardness alone. The mentally dull child is evidently being forced to fit the administrative machine to the neglect of the intellectually bright, the real retardation occurring with the children of superior intelligence.'[1]

The assumptions behind this kind of statement were already out of date. Not only had the 1937 *Handbook* south of the border rejected the view that intel-

[1] *Scottish Primary School Organisation*, 1939, p. 14.

lectual ability could be so closely identified with scholastic progress and advocated a policy of streaming by ability, the Scottish Education Department too were coming down in favour of streaming. The idea had begun to be mooted in the early thirties that the break between primary and secondary education should no longer be dependent solely on a test of attainment such as the qualifying examination represented. It was felt that there should at least be some restriction in the limits of the ages within which children should attempt to qualify for promotion. This brought in its train the idea of streaming in the primary department. In his report for 1930–33 the Senior Chief Inspector of Schools suggested that the idea might be tried out, though he did not call it streaming and obviously felt it necessary to explain to his readers what was meant. One suggestion which had been advocated was 'the clean cut', that is, the granting of an 'age-pass' to children who had reached the age of thirteen without being able to pass the qualifying examination. The Senior Chief Inspector comments on an alternative put forward by one of his colleagues:

'The "clean cut" might be applied, but Mr Lamb expresses the opinion, with which I agree, that the better course would seem to be to devise a curriculum which would obviate the need for this method of violence. A reform such as Mr. Lamb recommends is aimed at by what is known as the tri-partite curriculum. Pupils divide themselves into three main categories – the bright, the average and the slow. The existing arrangements do not suit any of these groups. The bright pupil has to endure the repetition of work, to him mere weariness, and is prevented from getting on at his natural pace. The slow pupil on the other hand is expected to maintain a rate of progress quite beyond his powers, while even the average pupil finds it impossible to cover the profession of work within the period of his school life. The tri-partite scheme is to classify the pupils at each stage according to ability and to remodel the curriculum to meet the needs of each of the three main categories.'[1]

The Department took up the idea. In the *Circular Explanatory of the Day School Code* for 1939 they wrote:

'In the classification of the children, intellectual capacity as well as educational attainments should be taken into account. Where classification into two or three streams is feasible, the curricula provided for these streams should be suitably differentiated; in other circumstances recourse may be had to individual or group methods within the class and to special provision for backward children or dull children.'

But Scottish primary schools have neither quite abandoned the notion that there is a fixed profession of work which each child must get through each year, nor adopted the idea of streaming so whole-heartedly as teachers in England. Any attempt to assess accurately the extent to which children are kept back or advanced by periods of a year or less still encounters the same difficulties that the Research Council met of different dates of birth and different promotion

[1] *General Reports for the Years 1930–33* on *Education in Scotland*, 1934, p. 14.

dates. Table 17 (page 72) traces the movement through the schools of children born in a single year. Of the 92,800 children born in 1948 14,604 had started school by 31 March 1953. On 1 January 1954 3,811 of them were already in Primary II and another 73,674 were in Primary I: 17,966 did not start school until some time during the year 1954. The prospect of being held back in the primary school seems, however, to be greater than the chance of passing through quickly because only 2,373 of these children had been promoted to a secondary school or department by 1 January 1960, 61,164 by 1 January 1961 and as many as 25,181 did not appear in the secondary school returns until 1 January 1962.

The adoption of streaming in some Scottish schools is, of course, hampered by the difficulty mentioned in the English 1937 *Handbook*: 'where six-monthly promotions are the rule, then twice the number of classes will be needed'. In their Report for 1957 the Scottish Education Department gave the following description of the extent to which the schools have adopted the suggestions for streaming or grouping by ability which were made in the circular of 1939:

'In some of the larger primary schools throughout the country the classes, especially from PIII upwards, are "streamed" according to ability. This practice is one concerning which opinions are much divided; but whatever its merits or demerits, it raises interesting questions. . . . The assumption evidently is that, if, for example, there are three classes at the PVII stage, the "A" class will make better progress if the pupils are not kept back by the slower pace of the less able. There is a further implication that class PVIIC, usually smaller in numbers, will be able to command more attention from the teacher to their particular difficulties, and, by concentrating on essentials, cover the groundwork of the course. The purpose of streaming then is differential treatment according to ability, and this type of organisation has been one response to a clamant need. In unstreamed classes the analogous and equally necessary procedure is grouping.'[1] This is probably a slightly biassed picture of the situation because the Department are here pleading for more use of group methods. They complain that group teaching is making slow progress in the schools. In infant classes it 'has spread considerably in all areas, and is almost universal in some. Beyond the infant stages, however, grouping is much less common. There are some signs of an extension to the PIII–PV range but the imminence of the promotion tests appears commonly to restrict group teaching in PVI and PVII.' What was here advocated as 'group teaching' was probably something slightly different from what a primary teacher in England would mean by group methods, and was certainly interpreted in some schools to be so. The grouping of children in a classroom can be something quite fluid, which changes according to the nature of the different activities going on at a given time, and it may have nothing whatsoever to do with their respective abilities. But the term is taken in some Scottish primary schools to mean a fairly rigid 'streaming' within the confines of one class. There are some schools in which the children are put into ability groups and the class teacher is not permitted to change the grouping except on the

[1] *Education in Scotland in 1957* (Cmnd. 407), p. 14.

TABLE 17. *Progress through Scottish primary schools of children born in* 1948

	3 years 'retarded'		2 years 'retarded'		1 year 'retarded'		'At age'		1 year 'advanced'		2 years 'advanced'		Special schools and classes	Total in public schools
At age 5		—		—		—	(PI)	73,674	(PII)	3,811	(PIII)	15	249	77,479
At age 6		—		—	(PI)	17,996	(PII)	67,508	(PIII)	3,401	(PIV)	26	563	89,498
At age 7		—	(PI)	458	(PII)	20,141	(PIII)	64,000	(PIV)	3,540	(PV)	6	686	88,998
At age 8	(PI)	41	(PII)	706	(PIII)	21,598	(PIV)	61,639	(PV)	3,444	(PVI)	11	1,220	88,669
At age 9	(PII)	47	(PIII)	1,221	(PIV)	23,924	(PV)	58,884	(PVI)	2,465	(PVII)	10	1,529	88,090
At age 10	(PIII)	84	(PIV)	1,560	(PV)	24,125	(PVI)	57,799	(PVII)	2,459	(SI)	15	1,719	87,802
At age 11	(PIV)	108	(PV)	1,774	(PVI)	23,587	(PVII)	58,359	(SI)	2,373	(SII)	4	1,725	87,958
At age 12	(PV)	91	(PVI)	1,405	(PVII)	20,814	(SI)	61,164	(SII)	2,192	(SIII)	16	1,458	87,163
At age 13	(PVI)	27	(PVII)	211	(SI)	25,181	(SII)	56,382	(SIII)	3,094	(SIV)	2	1,265	86,625
At age 14	(PVII)	—	(SI)	1,514	(SII)	25,428	(SIII)	55,225	(SIV)	1,492	(SV)	4	1,244	84,907

results of tests and after consultation with the headmaster. Whether or not the Department meant quite this is not clear, though they did mention that one of the objections voiced to the idea of group methods relates to 'headmaster's examinations and to promotion tests. Many teachers feel that it is unjust for the weaker pupils to be asked to sit any examination for which they have not covered all the ground, even though, through being taught in their appropriate group, these pupils know more accurately and securely what they have covered.'

The annual examination was, until very recently, still a very important part of Scottish primary education. The 1965 *Memorandum on Primary Education in Scotland* adopts much more of a development approach to the way in which children acquire the skills and the concepts appropriate to the primary stage, it gives advice on a much more flexible kind of grouping within each class than the earlier outline of a type of 'streaming' inside the class organization, it comes out strongly against the excessive use of examinations, and yet it repeats without modification the earlier recommendations for a policy of promotions through the school.

CHAPTER SEVEN

The Eleven Plus

The best starting point for an account of the Scottish 'eleven plus' is, curiously enough, the Merit Certificate, which was introduced by the Scotch Education Department in 1892 to be taken at 'thirteen plus'. It was intended for children leaving the elementary schools at about the end of their compulsory school life, and was in fact an attempt to examine the 'non-certificate' pupils seventy years before England decided to establish the Certificate of Secondary Education. The Merit Certificate was awarded on the results of a school leaving examination consisting of tests in reading, writing, arithmetic and three other subjects of the pupils' choice.

Only six years after it was introduced, the function of the certificate was changed. It ceased to be a leaving certificate: the age qualification for taking it was lowered by a year to about the age of twelve; and possession of the certificate became a necessary passport to the advanced departments of the elementary schools. But, though its function was changed, its form was not. It remained a test of attainment in basic subjects. It was simply that instead of marking the end of 'elementary' education (in the English pre-Hadow sense) it was henceforth to mark the end of 'elementary' (i.e. 'primary') education before the pupil embarked on a more advanced (i.e. what is now termed 'secondary') stage of his education. At first the Merit Certificate was explicitly only an entrance qualification for the advanced departments, but, *a fortiori*, it was a prerequisite for admission to the Secondary schools.

This change in function was carried a stage further when, in 1903, the title of Merit Certificate was dropped, no actual certificate was awarded, and the examination came to be known as the 'qualifying examination'. Up to 1921 this was conducted on behalf of the Department by H.M. Inspectors because a higher rate of grant was payable under the Code for the work of post-primary departments and part of the inspectors' job was to see that children were not promoted to a higher class in the school than their attainments warranted as a means of earning a higher grant for the school. With the introduction of a standard rate of grant for all pupils the Department decided that the way was clear to delegate the conduct of the examination to the education authorities. The circular announcing this decision shows the nature of the examination both as an attainment test marking the successful termination of the primary stage of a child's career and as a selection test for secondary education. The Department expected that 'the standard of the existing Qualifying Examination, the soundness of which has been proved by an experience of nearly twenty years, will be reasonably maintained. That is, the test to be applied should be such as the average pupil of twelve may fairly be called upon to meet.' At the same time the examination would furnish an opportunity 'for those who have taught and those who are to teach particular individuals to combine in an endeavour to estimate the potentialities of the material to be handled.'[1]

During the next twenty years the qualifying examination came to be regarded more and more as a selection test. The new intelligence tests were adopted by many authorities as an addition to the tests of attainment. Most authorities continued to make all pupils who were judged capable of it by their teachers take the examination, either with an additional test for those who sought a place in a senior Secondary course, or with two or more levels of pass – the higher for admission to a leaving certificate course and the other for other types of post-primary education. A few authorities conducted two separate examinations. But, in spite of increasing emphasis on the prognostic use of the tests, and in spite, too, of moves to lower the standard in the interests of pupils who were unable to pass it, the qualifying examination was still regarded as setting some objective measure of the satisfactory completion of the primary stage. The average child of twelve was expected to be able to pass it and to proceed to the next stage of his education. The less-than-average child was also expected to be able to pass it, even if it took him a little longer to reach the required standard – even, in fact, if it took him so long to pass it that he never reached the secondary stage of his education at all. Up to about the mid-thirties, in fact, the attitude to the qualifying examination in Scottish primary schools was similar to that in the English grammar schools towards the School Certificate. For some it was the passport to more advanced education: for others it was a goal in itself, marking the more or less successful completion of the course of education to which their abilities limited them: for a few, the failures, it represented an unattainable goal.

The Scottish Education Department's statistics recorded the numbers of children leaving the primary departments of the schools for whatever reason, and also those leaving the advanced divisions of the elementary schools. From these figures it is possible to deduce roughly what proportions took the qualifying examination and with what success. Throughout the nineteen-thirties, with some variation from year to year, about thirty to thirty-five per cent of children left the primary schools or departments on transfer to a senior Secondary course. Between twenty and twenty-five per cent left the advanced divisions having completed a course of at least two years in the advanced division (and must be presumed to have entered the advanced division from the primary department at the age of twelve.) These two figures together suggest that at least fifty-five to sixty per cent passed the qualifying examination by about the age of twelve. In addition, between twenty-five and thirty per cent left the elementary schools from the advanced division although they had not completed two full years:

[1] Circular 44, 1921.

some of these children could have passed the qualifying examination at about the age of twelve, but, with compulsory schooling ending at the age of fourteen, they would be able to leave school before they had had two full years in the advanced division if their birthdays fell in the middle of the academic year. Some however would fail to complete two years in the advanced division simply because they had been late in passing the qualifying examination. The figures still leave between ten and fifteen per cent of children who left school without having passed the qualifying examination at all. The Scottish Council for Research in Education found that, in 1931, of the fifteen per cent of leavers from the elementary schools who left school without having passed the examination, 13,468 were, at the time of leaving, still being taught with primary children in the nine to twelve age group and a further 135 were being taught in classes intended for the seven to nine age group. In a system geared to promotion by attainments some children were held back with children very much younger than themselves. In some schools, particularly the very small schools, there was probably no other provision that could be made for less able children. The Education Department had, however, tried to encourage the formation of special classes. In 1921 they had made it plain that some children should not be expected to attempt the qualifying examination: 'To require that boys and girls shall spend two or three years of their lives in striving after the unattainable is as futile from the point of view of the state as it is cruel from the point of view of the individual.'[1] Nevertheless there was a feeling that as many as possible should in fact try to reach that standard which was regarded as the proper end to primary schooling. It was also assumed that the proper place for special classes for all less able children—in fact for all 'non-qualifiers' up to the age of fourteen – was in the primary departments.

By the time that the Research Council published the results of their 1931 investigation two developments had taken place: the concept of a mental age which differed from chronological age had added weight to the view that it was futile for some children to try to pass examinations that were designed for the average among their contemporaries: and it was beginning to be felt that even the least able, unless so handicapped as to need to go to a special school, deserved to have the experience of a fresh stage in their education, even if it was something rather different from what had previously been meant by 'secondary' education. The view gained ground that all children should have some opportunity of taking a post-primary course at their own level. The 'clean cut' began to be adopted, by which every child must be transferred to a secondary department by a given age, usually thirteen, whether or not he had succeeded in passing the qualifying examination. This was not universally applied until after the war. In 1949 the Scottish Education Department reported that 'The new schemes of promotion from primary to secondary education, which provide, as a general rule, for promotion between the ages of eleven and twelve and a half have operated to effect a further reduction in the number of pupils over thirteen years of age on the registers of primary schools from 4,275[2] at 31 July 1948 to 3,459 a

[1] Circular 44.   [2] 5.7 per cent of all thirteen-year-olds in public schools.

year later'[1]. The number was further reduced to 2,312 in 1950 and dwindled very rapidly thereafter.

Nevertheless attitudes which have been firmly established for a long time have a habit of reasserting themselves. At least one education authority had included in its promotion scheme in 1959 a provision that no pupil should be retained in the primary department beyond the promotion date following his thirteenth birthday. In 1961 they submitted, and received the Department's approval to, an amendment to the scheme which was intended to effect a slight reduction in the age at which the 'clean cut' would be applied. The rule now is that any pupil retained in the primary department beyond the age of twelve must be promoted to a secondary course before his thirteenth birthday – unless the promotion board decide otherwise. Since this modification was brought into force just over one per cent of children in the authority's area have been held back each year in the primary departments after their contemporaries have been promoted to a secondary course.

ENGLAND

Frequently one finds that the same sort of ideas have had a brief vogue both in England and in Scotland but have persisted longer in one country than in the other. In 1931 the Hadow Committee felt it necessary to knock very firmly on the head what they regarded as a misguided departure from the recommendations in their 1926 report.

'We adhere to the view, which we have stated at length in our Report on the Education of the Adolescent, that primary education should be regarded as ending at the age of eleven. We think that normally all children should go forward at that age to some form of secondary education. We note with regret that some authorities, in their schemes of reorganisation, appear to have deliberately departed from the principle of the break at the age of eleven. For example several urban authorities seem to contemplate the transfer of about seventy to eighty per cent of the pupils at about the age of eleven, the remainder, consisting of the more backward pupils who have failed to reach a certain degree of attainment in a general examination in English and arithmetic, are regarded as not capable of profiting by advanced instruction and their promotion will accordingly be retarded. We consider that proposals of this character are contrary to the whole spirit and intention of the recommendations in our report.'[2]

But this was only a passing phase in England. The eleven plus there developed not from an examination which all were expected to take and most to pass: it grew out of the 'scholarship' examination which was meant only for the select few. From 1907 onwards success in the scholarship examination would earn a free place in a Secondary school for pupils who had previously attended an elementary school. The Secondary schools had to reserve twenty-five per cent of

---

[1] *Education in Scotland in 1949* (Cmd. 7914), 1950, p.16
[2] Hadow Report, *The Primary School*, 1931, p. 59.

their places for free place holders. By 1930 discretion had gradually been extended to the authorities to increase the number of free places up to fifty per cent if they were so minded. In 1932 the system was changed: the free places were abolished and 'special places' awarded instead. This simply meant that a means test was applied. A child who passed the examination was no longer automatically entitled to a free place, but a 'special place' gave him such remission of fees as his parents' income justified. Further discretion was, however, given to local education authorities to increase the proportion of special places and, by 1938, at one Secondary school in four, every place was treated as a special place – though on the other hand nearly half the Secondary schools in the country still offered less than half their places as special places.

The number of children admitted to the Secondary schools, whether fee-paying or not, formed only about seventeen per cent of the relevant age group in all. The number admitted to the Secondary schools from the maintained elementary schools formed less than fourteen per cent of the age group. The number who gained special places was, of course, even less than that. This compares with between thirty and thirty-five per cent admitted to Secondary schools in Scotland (where education authorities had been under a statutory obligation since 1918 to provide a sufficient number of free Secondary schools to meet the needs of their areas).

Even before the days of intelligence tests the 'scholarship examination' was not regarded as a means of making sure that all the children who passed it had acquired a certain minimum standard in elementary school subjects, but rather as a device for picking out the most promising: the 1927 *Handbook* of the Board of Education sets it firmly in its place by describing the process as 'the selection of children for special educational advantages' which should depend on their 'natural capacity' rather than on special preparation for an examination.[1] There was no general line of demarcation between the primary stage and the post-primary such as the qualifying examination provided in Scotland. The elementary school system, with its infants, junior and senior departments was almost self-contained. For the exceptional few entrance examinations to a different type of school, with scholarships for the brightest of them, provided a route into a different system.

With the advent of secondary education for all in England as well as in Scotland the 'selection' tests, as they are called south of the border, and the 'promotion' or 'transfer' tests, as they are usually called in the north, look much more alike. All, or nearly all, the children take them at the appropriate stage; the form of the tests is very similar, and their purpose is approximately the same. In fact most English local education authorities have at some time or other used tests published by a Scottish College of Education. Nevertheless the tests in England still retain something of the aura of the old 'scholarship' and the tests in Scotland are still regarded in something of the same way as the old 'qualifying examination'. This in spite of the fact that Scotland welcomed the techniques of intelligence testing just as eagerly as England. Indeed rather more research into the

[1] *Handbook*, 1927, p. 56.

use of these tests has been undertaken north of the border, though this may simply be due to the fact that many more Scottish teachers take a second degree in education and the number of theses for the B.Ed. exceeds the number of similar publications in England.

ELEVEN PLUS OR MINUS

The rules for determining the stage at which a child should be considered for selection can also be explained by going back to the origins of the tests. In England the local education authorities heeded the rebuke of the Hadow Committee to such effect that most of them now define the eleven plus age group by reference solely to chronological age. Indeed it is usually restricted to children born within a strict twelve-month period. This is more rigid than the Hadow Report had intended. The Report had stated that 'the expression "age of 11 +" is not intended to be used in a precise chronological sense', because it might in practice be stretched far enough to include the child of twelve plus who had been temporarily retarded by illness or the like.[1] However, the present practice is usually to limit the selection tests to children who will have had their eleventh birthday but not their twelfth by a fixed date. Some authorities do allow exceptionally able children to submit themselves for selection – or rather to be put forward by their primary school – before the age of eleven. But this is regarded as a separate scheme. The children concerned are not picked out as having completed the profession of work of the primary school and therefore to be sent to a secondary school because they have worked their way through the curriculum and there is nothing more for them to do in the primary school. They are selected as showing conspicuous promise of ultimately reaching the university, and are passed forward to the grammar school a year early because they are judged capable of tackling the work of the grammar school. The reason for this is that they will thereby be enabled to reach the sixth form a year ahead of their contemporaries and can spend an extra year at that stage (which is considered the most important for the intellectually gifted child). The very name commonly given to the scheme where it is in operation is significant: the children are referred to as 'high fliers'. Yet many local education authorities are obstinately opposed to any such scheme: they believe that all children should be processed through the selection arrangements at the same chronological age. Nor do English authorities normally countenance the retention in the primary school of children over the age of twelve in order that, with an additional year, they may take the selection tests with some hope of qualifying for a grammar school place. The arrangements for late transfer (for 'late developers') invariably mean that a child transfers to a secondary modern school with his contemporaries and, after a year or two, has the chance of taking a special test for late transfer to a grammar school.

In Scotland the term 'eleven plus' in fact usually means 'between the age of about eleven and twelve and a half'. The reason for this wider age range is

[1] Hadow Report, *The Education of the Adolescent*, 1926, p. 71.

simply that the primary school course is regarded as including a more or less fixed amount of work that each child is expected to get through. The able child will cover this work more rapidly than the others: there is clearly a limit to the speed at which he can be promoted through the school and the worst excesses of promotion by ability alone are avoided by ruling that no child may be transferred to a secondary school before his eleventh birthday. On the other hand some children, not necessarily the least able, may take longer to complete the profession of work. Children may therefore be submitted for selection, perhaps with hopes of a place in a senior secondary course, up to the age of about twelve and a half. For those who will never satisfactorily complete the work of the primary school the clean cut operates to ensure that they will pass to a secondary school by the age of thirteen. What it amounts to in effect is that children take the selection tests at the time when they happen to be in the top class of the primary school, and the headmaster is expected to control the pace of his pupils' progress through the school having regard to the speed with which they master the work but bearing also in mind the rules about minimum and maximum ages.[1]

[1] For a further discussion of the eleven plus see pp. 216–220.

CHAPTER EIGHT

Teaching and Learning in Primary Schools

OFFICIAL ADVICE AND CLASSROOM PRACTICE

'Slates and slate pencils should not be used.'

'Artificial, pointless methods of keeping pupils out of mischief, such as "fold your arms", "neck rest", cannot be too strongly condemned.'

'The onset of fatigue can often be averted by . . . interspersing short recreative exercises between lessons. . . . To prevent lassitude that is a result of a stuffy atmosphere, the ventilation and the temperature of the room should be suitably regulated during class work and the air changed completely in the school intervals.'

'Methods of memorization which demand very little attention from the pupils – for instance the chanting of addition or multiplication tables – are practically valueless.'

To the English reader these four quotations probably evoke a picture of the elementary school just breaking away from some of the methods of the nineteenth century, and they are in fact reminiscent of some of the items of advice contained in the Board of Education's first *Handbook of Suggestions for Teachers* published in 1905 (and dropped in later editions of the *Handbook* as being no longer appropriate). But the quotations are taken from a *Memorandum on the Primary School in Scotland* published by the Scottish Education Department in 1950.

This is not meant to suggest that Scottish primary schools are fifty years out of date. Many of the suggestions made in the Scottish *Memorandum* of 1950 are very different from those made in the 1905 *Handbook*. The following pairs of quotations from the two publications may be compared:

1(a) 'Corporal punishment judiciously used may be salutary in its effects, but its use must be very strictly limited: it should not be administered by the teacher when irritated.'

 (b) 'The undue frequency of punishment indicates faults in the teaching as surely as in the children.'

2(a) 'As the school is a larger unit than the family, it resembles more closely the still larger community of which the pupil will in due time be a member. It is thus in a favourable position to instil those qualities which make for good relations between the individual and his fellows.'

(b) 'The school as a community should have some corporate life of its own in order that the scholars themselves may take part in maintaining a standard of conduct.'

3(a) 'It is essential that the pupils should give full attention to the work in hand and do their very best to master it. In general their attention and effort should spring from interest in the work or from their own desire to master a fact, process or "skill". This does not mean that the work need always be in itself attractive; if the pupils see the purpose of what they are doing, and have acquired the proper habits of application, they will be prepared to undertake a reasonable amount of work at tasks which are not in themselves interesting.'

(b) 'We need not fear that by an appeal to the everyday interests of the child we make education too easy, or deprive it of that bracing effect on the will which results from the effort to overcome the difficulties of studies of a more abstract and less interesting kind. Every teacher should understand that good teaching does not merely enlist a languid interest in the child or allow him to be a passive recipient of information given; on the contrary, the purpose of teaching is to stimulate an active interest and attention.'

4(a) The child 'will often become a more accurate speller by transcribing words which he is liable to mis-spell and also new words which are to be added to his spelling vocabulary. The transcription exercise might well be preceded by concentration on each word.'

(b) 'No spelling lessons as such should be given, for it is absurd to learn to spell words outside one's vocabulary.'

5(a) 'Parsing and analysis, if skilfully presented and judiciously employed, play a useful part in the teaching of English. In parsing it will be sufficient to consider the following:

> Noun – number, case, relation
> Pronoun – personal, interrogative, relative case, relation
> Adjective – qualifying
> Verb – subject, transitive or intransitive; tense, present, past, future.
> Adverb – of time, place, manner: modifying
> Preposition – governing
> Conjunction – joining.'

(b) 'The use of grammatical terms distracts the attention of teachers and pupils alike from what at this stage is all-important, viz practice in the *use* of good English, and the comparatively easy and mechanical character of a grammar lesson is a temptation to the weaker teacher.'

6(a) 'At the age at which the pupil first uses an (arithmetical) process, he may not be able to comprehend fully the underlying theory of that process, but it is not necessary that he should.'

(b) 'The necessary training in mechanical skill should be acquired rather by repeated practice in carrying out principles which the scholars thoroughly understand, than by attempting to work examples in rules of which the underlying reasons have not been firmly grasped.'

It is the first quotation in each of these pairs which comes from the Scottish *Memorandum* of 1950. The second in each pair comes from the 1905 *Handbook of Suggestions* and is so much closer to the kind of official advice which is currently given to teachers in English primary schools (for example in the latest – 1959 – edition of the *Handbook*) that the English reader might have some excuse for concluding that Scottish primary schools must be not fifty years out of date but rather more.

This only underlines the need to examine one's own assumptions before criticizing the practice of schools in other countries. In a survey of the primary school curriculum in England between 1900 and 1925 Bramwell remarks that 'many forces combine to determine what work is to go on in the schools of a particular kind at a given time in any country. Always the conservative is a strong force which ensures that much of what one generation does in school, the next will do also.' He goes on to trace the effect of three forces of curricular change – the social ('schools are social institutions, and so, however dimly and tardily, the work they do will reflect changes in the ideals and values of the society which maintains and administers them'), the educational-philosophic, and the subject-specialist ('where the curriculum is subject based, as it was in England throughout the period covered here, specialists of high standing outside schools influence the work of specialist teachers'). His general conclusions are that

'the most pervasive of general trends discernible in elementary school work during the period 1900–1925 is that towards greater freedom for teacher and pupil.... At first Code-bound teachers did not know how to use the freedom imposed on them. But they learnt, and the work of the schools at the end of the period is in sharp contrast with that with which it opened.... The notion that children were to be regimented and treated en masse became gradually outmoded. Individuality was more and more prized, and there was much talk at this time of the child's right to self-realization and to self-expression.... Substitution of more democratic for more authoritarian leadership in the classroom raised the problem of incentives. How would teachers get children to work without the sanctions of tawse and testiness? Clearly, the interests of children had more and more to be consulted, and, at the end of the period covered here, much educational discussion revolved around the so-called doctrine of interest. Syllabuses and curricula changed slowly but quite certainly to take in content which children might learn readily because they were interested in it. The evolution of syllabuses in geography, history, nature study and physical training all showed the same trend towards including what was thought to be consistent with the first loves of childhood.... Activity methods of various kinds, including dramatization, school walks, excursions and an extended range of handicrafts and handwork, began to play an increasingly prominent part in the work of the schools.'[1]

These conclusions would be widely accepted in England. The assumption usually made is that the first twenty-five years of this century merely started a trend which has continued ever since. To concentrate on these developments in English primary school practice without comparing them with the practice of other countries is, however, to undervalue the extent to which the attitudes implicit in them were already enunciated in the very first *Handbook of Suggestions* to be published by the Board of Education. A comparison of the 1905 *Handbook* with that of 1927 does not at first sight entirely support Bramwell's thesis. The 1927 edition is, in many ways, more 'formal' than its first predecessor. But this single quotation from Bramwell's conclusions merely summarizes, and therefore oversimplifies, the description he gave of the schools at work. He shows convincingly how the development of classroom techniques enabled teachers to put into effect some of the ideas underlying the first *Handbook*. Many of the suggestions made in 1905 lacked concrete example, or needed modification: Sometimes experiment overreached itself. But it is not by reading government handouts that teachers develop new methods. The writers of the *Handbooks* are in any case concerned with the middle of the road teacher, not with the innovator – though they are sensitive to changes in educational fashions. The 1927 edition represents a period of reaction, or at least of caution, in England. When the pendulum swung back again in 1937 the teachers were ready for it. The 1959 edition reveals an even greater self-assurance in the classroom, and a readiness to allow the children to make the running which would not be understood by teachers accustomed to a more authoritarian role.

In Scotland it is even more difficult to judge classroom practice by what the Department write. The published reports of H.M. Inspectors suggest that at roughly the same periods the same swings of fashion have occurred. Scottish schools have been subject to the same educational-philosophic influences. In fact, if Scottish teachers read official *Handbooks of Suggestions* at all before the war, it was those published by the Board of Education to which they turned. The Scottish Education Department sometimes err to a fault on the side of caution. They did not themselves embark on the preparation of a full-scale handbook until just before the war. It was not published until over ten years later. The Scottish Advisory Council issued a full report on Primary Education in 1946 (and had the draft of the Department's handbook before them during their deliberations), but, when the Department's *Memorandum on the Primary School in Scotland* finally appeared in 1950, it was a much more conservative document than the Advisory Council's report. In so far as comparison with the equivalent English publications is valid, it is with the 1927 *Handbook* that the 1950 *Memorandum* has the greatest similarity.

But, with whatever reservations one reads these documents, one is forced to conclude that they can only have been written in a climate of educational

[1] R. D. Bramwell, *Elementary School Work 1900–1925* University of Durham, 1961 p. 127.

thought which differs as much as the climates of Aberdeen and Penzance. In 1950 the Scottish Education Department was writing for teachers who were accustomed to being the centre of attention in their own classrooms, who liked to feel that they were fully in control, and who also erred to a fault on the side of caution. That primary education in Scotland has nevertheless not stood still is evidenced by a second *Memorandum*, published in 1965. This has had a mixed reception. Comments from Headteachers have been varied:

'We've heard all this before.'
'My teachers will find it most helpful.'
'If I'm to be in charge of this school, you must chuck that thing out of the window.'

THE NATURE OF CHILDHOOD

A comparison of the series of English *Handbooks* from 1905 to 1959 with the first Scottish *Memorandum* which, after so much deliberation, was published in 1950, will serve to illumine basic differences in the assumptions about primary education on either side of the border and, at the same time, to set the scene for the change which came over official Scottish thinking with the publication of the 1965 *Memorandum*. In their remarks on discipline and social training there are many points of resemblance between the English recommendations of 1905 and the Scottish ones of 1950. Punishment is to be used sparingly; moral training is to be positive; the best teachers maintain order, not by establishing a dictatorship, but by encouraging the development of self-respect and self-discipline. Order, diligence and obedience are the chief virtues; tales of noble lives and noble deeds will set the right model before the children; and the teacher herself should act as a model of good behaviour. Yet, at the same time, there are essential differences. In England punishment was to be used infrequently because it was a regrettable necessity, and – above all – it might upset 'the personal sympathy between teacher and class which is the most effective agent in securing good discipline'.[1] In Scotland punishment should also be used sparingly but it might nevertheless, when used properly, be salutary in its effects, especially corporal punishment, which was sometimes to be preferred to other kinds.[2] In setting an example of good behaviour, it was quite sufficient that the Scottish teacher should maintain standards of justice and fair play: it was not suggested that the children need actually like her. A belief in 'original sin' was moreover firmly held in Scotland. Moral training should certainly be positive: 'more is needed than example, environment and precept. The pupil must be given opportunities of practising right behaviour.' But this was advice which, children being what they are, could only be followed with extreme caution. For example: 'If the teacher is to develop in her pupils habits of truthfulness and honesty, she must show trust in them. . . . She should train her pupils to correct their own work and to add up their own marks. *But* she must take care that there is no

[1] *Handbook*, 1905, p. 11.   [2] *Memorandum*, 1950, p. 114.

inducement to untruthfulness or petty dishonesty through fear or through pre-occupation with rewards.'[1] Again, 'It is no kindness to a pupil to let him have unlimited freedom. To allow him to ignore the equal rights of others, and to think that nothing matters but the satisfaction of his own immediate desires is entirely wrong, and can only lead to frustration and chaos.' Problems of discipline in Scottish schools apparently began from the very first day in the nursery class.

'An important part of the work of the school consists in helping the children to adjust themselves to their environment. . . . By close contact with other children the child begins to realize that the claims he makes on the community involve the admission of its claims upon him. . . . All normal children have days when their behaviour takes undesirable forms; they will appear unusually aggressive, self-centred, nervous, acquisitive, capricious or deceitful.'[2]

The view taken of children south of the border is much more optimistic. The English child in the nursery school will always, according to the 1959 *Handbook*, display the 'gaiety, curiosity, friendliness and spirit of adventure which are as desirable as they are characteristic of this period of life, and they show also increasing self-control as well as more power of self-expression'.[3] The English child understands quite naturally how to fit into the school community and 'the welfare of individual children is never sacrificed to that of the group. . . . It is surprising to the outsider to see how comparatively rare serious difficulties are', and when they do arise they are almost invariably attributable to 'some strain or emotional upset at home. The arrival of a new baby, anxiety somehow caught (though not understood) from parents, or some change in family habits, are amongst the things that may contribute to some set-back in a child's development.'[4] In the English primary schools it is the children themselves who are seen as establishing and maintaining a code of right behaviour: 'The roughness and carelessness of a few individuals are likely to be resented as much by the other children as they are by the teacher.' Indeed 'a child is apt to become more of a "traditionalist" than his teacher'.[5] The influence of the teacher in setting the environment for this display of moral quality is, of course, important, and he must also set the children a good example. But something much more is needed than merely an example of the virtues of kindliness and fair play. The children follow the lead of a good teacher and 'do what he asks of them because it is he who asks it'.[6] This English belief in the value of personal relationships and in the essential goodness of children runs throughout the 1959 *Handbook*, and can be traced through all the editions of the *Handbook* since 1905. But perhaps its most extreme expression was the sentence in 1937 – quoted with approval in 1959 – which asserts the 'gradual recognition on the part of teachers that the superiority of the adult over the child is a matter of length and width of experience and not of moral ability'.[7]

---

[1] Ibid., p. 112 (my italics).   [2] Ibid., p. 147.   [3] *Handbook*, 1959, p. 29.
[4] Ibid, p. 31.   [5] Ibid, p. 82.   [6] Ibid., p. 83.
[7] Ibid., p. 88.

THE SCHOOL REGIME

At the beginning of the present century the pattern of the elementary school day was firmly established. 'Difficult' lessons, like arithmetic, were timed for periods when the children were freshest and most able to concentrate. As the children grew older their span of attention could be relied upon gradually to increase from the mere fifteen minutes of which infants were judged capable, but lessons would still be marked by an increasing stuffiness in atmosphere and lassitude on the part of the pupils until, with a sigh of relief, the windows could be thrown open, the children perform a few physical exercises, and then the class would turn to concentrate on some quite different activity. In England this pattern changed very gradually. The 1927 *Handbook* kept to the basic idea of introducing variety into the school day, though for slightly different reasons: 'It will probably be found advisable to let occasions of collective work, in stories, games or music, succeed periods when children are left to play as their own choice dictates.'[1] But the timing of the school day was to be more flexible: a change of activity should take place when the children had 'obviously had enough'. In 1937, too, for the older children, 'a sedentary period, or part-period, should be followed, whenever possible, by one of greater physical activity', but in the infants schools a different kind of planning was beginning to establish itself. 'A time-table with minute subdivisions or very short periods defeats its own ends. Children should have time in which to finish whatever they are busied with, and, though they tire more quickly of some things than of others, they are capable, if interested, of applying themselves for surprisingly long periods to some occupations.'[2] By 1959 the change is complete. It is said that, in nursery schools, changes are being made in the arrangement of the day to take account of the fact that children 'differ greatly in initiative and in the length of time they can concentrate'; in the infants schools there is now 'enough leisureliness to prevent the children or the teachers feeling hurried'; and in the junior schools 'there is a strong tendency to assign fairly long periods'. The planning of the work in the infant school should in fact no longer be geared to the school day: 'A time-table for each day, or even each week, is not necessary for the experienced teacher. She can see in outline a month's or a term's work ahead, and knows how the children can work within this general plan towards the objectives she has in mind. She can therefore afford to let them follow the enthusiasms which carry them forward efficiently. . . .'[3]

The fact that Scottish schools were still in 1950 being enjoined to keep to the time-honoured practice of alternating short periods of different activities was based on a very different view of child nature. The nursery school day should be a happy alternation of routine and free play because 'play is both the child's way of life and his emotional safety valve'. The teacher should not be deceived by the sudden bursts of energy which young children display: 'Deprivation of rest and sleep devitalizes the young child, increasing his susceptibility to illness and decreasing his capacity for creative activity.'[4] There should therefore be regular

[1] *Handbook*, 1927, p. 49.   [2] *Handbook*, 1937, p. 95.
[3] *Handbook*, 1959, p. 45.   [4] *Memorandum*, 1950, p. 147.

rest periods. (In England, on the other hand, the practice of regular rest periods is being 'widely reconsidered': 'children vary greatly in the amount of sleep they need' and there is no need to keep them all quiet for a given period each day. While some play, the others can sleep: 'children really in need of rest generally continue asleep through noise or disturbance.') Again, in the first stage of the infants school the Scottish child 'should not be required to concentrate on the more exacting activities for longer than twenty minutes. Lassitude or inattention due to fatigue may be prevented by short breaks for music or physical activity. If the children return to school in the afternnons, their occupations then should be recreative or restful.'[1] (Of the English child at the infants stage it is equally true that 'the span of his voluntary attention is still very brief and it is possible to control it only for a short time', but this does not mean that he needs rest: on the contrary 'much of his day must be occupied in doing things which of themselves focus his powers of mind and body'.)

The need for a suitable alternation of activities was thought, in Scotland, to be necessary throughout the primary school stage: 'As children grow older their span of attention increases; accordingly, at appropriate stages, some lessons, arithmetic for instance, may be as long as forty-five minutes.'[2] But history, geography and similar subjects should usually be taught 'in two periods of half an hour each, rather than in a weekly period of one hour'. And 'although a short spell of physical exercise is very refreshing, a physical education lesson of twenty-five or thirty minutes produces temporary fatigue. A formal lesson in this subject should not be looked upon as a recuperative break, and should not be followed immediately by other work of an exacting character.'[3] (English children apparently have more stamina: 'When a longer period [of physical education] can be arranged on some days only in the week, on each of the other days there should be a shorter and vigorous lesson of not less than 20 minutes. Such an arrangement will do much to ensure that the vigour, alertness and vitality of the children, which the training is intended to produce, lasts throughout the day.'[4] That was in the 1937 *Handbook*. In 1959 we are told that: 'In some schools physical education is thought of solely as an antidote to sedentary work – an opportunity to let off steam. Sometimes that is the only function it can fulfil, because the regime of the school day makes release an urgent need; but children need more than activity, they want to develop mastery, to do different things in different ways, to work out ideas.'[5])

TEACHING METHODS

The English *Handbooks* are full of the 'tireless energy' of primary children, of their intellectual curiosity and their physical vigour, of their inventiveness and power to create. 'The junior school asks much from its teachers. They must possess above all other qualities, enough resilience to deal with the energy and far-reaching demands of the children, and enough resources to meet their ex-

[1] Ibid., p. 10.   [2] Ibid., p. 11.   [3] Ibid., p. 11.
[4] *Handbook*, 1937, p. 165.   [5] *Handbook*, 1959, p. 133.

tremely wide range of intellectual and imaginative power. It is scarcely possible for any teacher.'[1] The teacher can let the children down in many ways: 'Common causes of boredom are that the children either have not enough to do or are given work which seems to them to lead nowhere', and 'sometimes the teacher fails to cultivate in the children the technical skill which they now need and demand.'[2]

If it is the children who set the pace to this extent, teaching method is obviously of secondary importance. The 1959 *Handbook* does see fit to reassure us that 'the traditional arts of the teacher remain as important as ever – the art of vivid narration and of clear description and explanation', but that is only because the whole trend of the arguments in the *Handbook* leads so much to the opposite conclusion that it was obviously felt necessary to correct the balance. Nevertheless the teacher has ceased to expound and to instruct. He has become an organizer of learning. To supply the children with what they demand calls for a grand design rather than detailed lesson-planning.

'Children explore what lies before them, but they do not choose what lies before them: that choice is the teacher's, and he has to choose those things and opportunities which he thinks of greatest value and most likely to lead to fruitful enquiry. Although he cannot foresee just what the children will get from any pursuit on which they set out, his experience should give him an idea of the kind of thing that is likely to happen.'[3]

In Scottish schools, teaching method has been all important. In 1939 the Scottish Education Department published a pamphlet describing the country's educational system for the benefit of the man in the street.

'Much of the teaching at the primary stages', says this pamphlet, 'must be of a formal nature, i.e. it must tidy up and pigeon-hole the child's knowledge. . . . Much of the knowledge acquired in the primary division must be so firmly fixed in the mind of the child that throughout life he will be able to draw on it without effort or conscious thought. Such complete familiarity with any subject can never be achieved except by practice and more practice, drill and more drill. Giving this practice and drill is a great part of the primary teacher's task and it is not an easy part. Repetition readily induces tedium; to disguise repetition and so maintain freshness – there is the problem. It is a problem not only of actual presentation of subjects but also of class organisation and management.'[4]

The *Memorandum on the Primary School in Scotland*, 1950, made several suggestions for maintaining the children's interest in their work, all of which were very similar to the kind of thing that the Board of Education had been saying in 1927:

'(a) the pupil should himself see some purpose in what he is called upon to do.

'(b) by relating topics to the objects of a pupil's interest, the teacher may be able

---

[1] Ibid., p. 27.   [2] Ibid., p. 66.
[3] Ibid., p. 62.   [4] Educational Pamphlet No. 4., 1939.

to bring within the circle of his interests a subject which at first had no appeal for him.

'(c) by communicating her own enthusiasm the teacher can prepare the way for the growth of the children's interest.

'(d) the desire to succeed is by itself sufficient to spur children to effort, and the teacher should do all she can to foster this desire by the use of devices which help the child to realize his own progress.

'(e) new facts should, if possible, be presented both orally and visually.

'(f) during oral class lessons the pupil is not likely to remain attentive unless he can share in some form of activity. Considerable use should therefore be made of question and answer. But the questions should not be asked in such a way – round the class – that the pupil can anticipate when he will be called upon to answer.

'(g) where the interest motive is not dominant – and it cannot always be so – it may be reinforced by an appeal to the pupil's sense of duty or to his determination not to be beaten.'[1]

The phrase 'determination not to be beaten' is perhaps ambiguous. The idea of appealing to the pupil's sense of duty is the only one which does not echo similar suggestions made in the English *Handbook* for 1927. The Board of Education then wrote: 'It may be argued that children should face drudgery from a sense of duty. This is a hard saying and subjects their incipient sense of duty to an intolerable strain.'[2]

The Scottish 1950 *Memorandum* is also very reminiscent of the English 1927 *Handbook* in its treatment of class organization. 'Individual methods have the great merit of enabling both the content and pace of the course to be adapted to each pupil', but 'if used exclusively they have certain disadvantages . . . there is little opportunity for either cooperative effort or emulation . . . they demand considerable skill and versatility on the part of the teacher.' Group methods 'cater for the differing abilities normally found in a class and at the same time secure some of the stimulus of emulation and of cooperative effort . . . but the placing of the pupil in his appropriate group calls for great care and judgement from the teacher . . . and to teach a class by groups does not lighten the teacher's task', 'Class instruction will always have some place.'[3]

But though teaching methods and class organization were superficially similar up to thirty years ago, the different views of child nature have led to a divergence. The English *Handbooks* have dropped any detailed statement of teaching method or of the advantages and disadvantages of different kinds of class organization. The authors of the 1937 *Handbook* grudgingly admitted that 'where numbers of people have to live and work together there must be organization. We should ask ourselves', they went on to say, 'what things are best done by the school taken as a whole, by groups of classes working together, by classes of the

[1] *Memorandum*, 1950, p. 19.   [2] *Handbook*, 1927, p. 17.
[3] *Memorandum*, 1950, p. 14.

traditional type, by sections within such classes, and by children working in voluntary association or individually'. But they did not suggest what answers we should give ourselves to this question, although they did record with approval that 'there are few schools nowadays where children do not at some time or other work in sections within their classes . . . and individual work is a common feature of school work in an increasing number of schools'.[1] By 1959 there was no longer even any need to ask ourselves about class organization: 'The teacher comes to know when to teach groups and when to teach the class or an individual, and in time he knows at what pace and in what ways the different groups of children learn best.' It is still recognized that 'to acquire this art is no mean achievement, though to many who have an understanding of children and a fertile inventiveness it appears to come easily'. The main advice now given to English teachers is that they should 'be themselves' and not be too self-conscious about their methods. 'The ways of teachers differ; but should they attempt to elevate particular methods or procedures to the level of fundamental principles, and cease to be critically aware of what they are doing and of the value of what the children are learning, unfortunate results are likely to follow.'[2]

The only possible conclusion to draw from a comparison of the general advice given by the two government departments on broad questions of school and class organization and general teaching method is that, in England, education is regarded as a perfectly natural activity on the part of both the teachers and the pupil, but in Scotland it is a rather artificial exercise which calls for strongly developed techniques on the part of the teacher and involves something of a strain for the children. This appears to depend on two quite different conceptions of human nature, but there are also, of course, some differences in what is taught.

THE TEACHING OF ENGLISH IN ENGLAND

There is general agreement on both sides of the border that the first essential step in the learning of language is fluency and proficiency in the spoken word. It is the process of developing an acceptable written style from the spoken language which has always caused difficulty and which reveals both changes of fashion over the years and a difference in attitude between England and Scotland. In 1905 training in spoken English was a fairly new development in the schools and the English *Handbook* of that year proclaimed in extreme terms the view that written English followed naturally from spoken English. Apparently no problem need exist at all if only teachers would not make so much of a burden of trying to teach children to write:

'It is of the utmost importance to remember that there is *no* difference between the proper style of written and that of oral composition. . . . In both the same simplicity, which is not to be confused with poverty of vocabulary, the same directness of narrative and clearness of construction are to be required. Good written English is only more careful spoken English.' It followed from this that

[1] *Handbook*, 1937, p. 29.   [2] *Handbook*, 1959, p. 54.

'the formal rules of grammar need not find a place in the time-table as a separate subject if correct speaking, reading and writing are thoroughly taught', and 'no spelling lessons as such should be given'.[1]

Inevitably there was a reaction from this extreme view. In 1927 we were told by the Board of Education that 'when written composition comes to be undertaken its main purpose should be that of disciplining fluency into form'. Written composition was still to be preceded by considerable oral practice but it now cast its shadow before: in oral composition the child should be 'trained to weave his narrative into a more definitely connected whole by the use of subordinate clauses'. Moreover 'a certain amount of spelling drill is probably necessary in the Junior stage', and 'the intelligent study of language will necessarily involve teaching some grammar'.[2]

By 1937 the pendulum was beginning to swing back again. On the one hand, 'teachers would do well to ponder the differences between written and spoken language' and the statement that spelling drill was probably necessary was retained in the new *Handbook*. On the other hand, 'there is no need whatever for a separate grammar lesson in the Junior School, and very little need for written grammar exercises'.[3] It may not be irrelevant that during the period when formal grammar was more in fashion with the writers of the *Handbooks* the number of pupils in grammar schools recognized by the Board of Education as efficient increased by fifty per cent. 'It is natural for teachers', said the 1937 *Handbook*,

'to be concerned that every pupil who is fit for a Special Place shall have his chance to gain it, though as our knowledge of the means of diagnosing children's abilities increases, and it becomes possible to discern with greater certainty the true marks of fitness for specialised education at the higher stages, it may be expected that the task of preparing children for Special Places in Secondary schools will be accomplished without involving the temptation to interfere with the normal course of Junior school work.'[4]

The swing back again to a less formal approach to the teaching of English, such as had obtained at the beginning of the century, and had only been abandoned temporarily during the twenties and thirties, may have been partly attributable to the fact that the pace of the increase in the number of grammar school places had slowed down, and also that the introduction of intelligence tests promised to make attainment tests in English a less important factor in the special place examination. This is, however, by no means the only explanation of the changes in fashion during the inter-war period. In the early days the schools had not yet learned how to find suitable material for the children to write about in order to give them the frequent practice in writing that was advocated. Descriptions of a picture or an object in the classroom or, for older children, the reproduction in their own words of a story they had read or heard the previous day from the teacher – this was as far as the 1905 *Handbook* was able to go in suggesting suit-

---

[1] *Handbook*, 1905, p. 35. [2] *Handbook*, 1937, pp. 96–104.
[3] Ibid., pp. 350–85. [4] Ibid., p. 119.

able topics for composition. 'When written composition first appeared in the Elementary School programme', said later editions of the *Handbook*, 'it generally took the form of a short passage which they had listened to or studied till they had practically got it by heart. In the reaction which followed, "original work" was demanded from the children at all stages'. But the unsuitability of the topics and the immaturity of the pupils had led to unsatisfactory results. It was for this reason that the 1927 *Handbook* suggested both that written composition should be postponed to the later stages of the primary school and that, when it was undertaken, considerable attention should be paid to form. The 1937 *Handbook* marks the beginning of the swing away from grammar and too much attention to form, but the burden of its advice is still that composition should not be begun too soon, or practised too often. As regards subject matter, 'it would be unreasonable to say that children should not begin to express themselves in writing until they feel the need to do so; many would not feel any such need until too late. But the suggestion does contain this truth, that children should feel that what they write has some purpose.'[1]

The 1959 *Handbook* represents a complete reversion to the 1905 school of thought. Admittedly it does not quite subscribe to the statement that there is no difference between good spoken English and good written English. But a good written style is expected to grow naturally out of good oral expression. Indeed, the most praiseworthy elements of written English are no longer directness of narrative and clearness of construction (still less something called 'form') but 'fluency and individuality'. Emphasis on formal accuracy is deprecated as likely to suppress these hallmarks of good writing. 'At the junior stage, as in the infant school, the essentials in composition are to have a reason for writing and something to write about, to have frequent opportunities to write, to have time to finish, to be neither over-anxious about accuracy nor lacking in respect for the reader.' Whereas in 1927 children were expected to speak in subordinate clauses instead of joining every sentence with 'and', the 1959 view is that 'the simple sentence may represent for children a retrogression from the sequence in thought and appreciation of relationships implied in their use of the conjunction "and" '. With older and more able children some attention may be given to form and style, but this should be done by setting good models before them rather than by exercises which 'may blunt children's sensitivity to language'. Grammar is simply not mentioned. Spelling lessons are unnecessary for most children – 'they pick it up'. Written composition should no longer be postponed: children should do a lot of writing from the infants school upwards. Previously the amount of writing they should do was to be strictly limited so that what they did write would be written with care. The composition was to be an exercise in form and grammar and, as such, was to be something rather special. Now there no longer seems to be any problem in finding things for the children to write: the development of fluency is such a natural thing that plenty of practice is almost enough by itself; and since the other virtue to be desired is that of individuality, then, in writing as in painting, the earlier children start

[1] *Handbook*, 1937, p. 381.

to practise, the more will their work display freshness and originality uninhibited by adult conventions. By the end of the junior stage, 'a very wide diversity in type and quality of written work is to be expected, including work prescribed and spontaneously undertaken on every aspect of the curriculum. It should serve the purpose for which it is intended, should reflect with increasing competence children's widening knowledge and should bear also the stamp of their personality.'[1]

THE TEACHING OF ENGLISH IN SCOTLAND

The shifts of fashion in Scotland followed much the same pattern as in England until about thirty years ago. At the beginning of the present century grammar was 'out' almost as much north of the border as it was to the south. In 1908 H.M. Inspector Mr Lamb is to be found protesting that the trend had gone too far. 'No doubt too much time was formerly given to the intricacies of formal grammar. At present it is far too common to find the opposite fault. Pupils get little or no instruction in the structure of sentences, and the general scaffolding required for expression of thought.'[2] In 1927 grammar was 'in' in England and in the same year H.M. Chief Inspector Mr J. M. Wattie is to be found rejoicing that in Scotland, too, 'after a period of neglect, grammar is now fully restored to favour, though shorn of a good deal of its former elaboration'.[3] In favour it has remained ever since. Scotland has not swung back again as England has. Part of the reason is perhaps to be found in the 1950 *Memorandum on the Primary School in Scotland*: when setting out the amount of parsing thought suitable for primary schools (as quoted at the beginning of this chapter) the *Memorandum* remarks that 'the following scheme should meet the needs of the pupil in the primary school and provide an adequate basis even for the subsequent study of foreign languages'. But it is not only that the primary school curriculum is influenced by the requirements of the secondary schools. The academic tradition involves more than the teaching of foreign languages. H.M. Inspector Mr Crawford looked, in his report for 1923, to a model much more in sympathy with Scottish attitudes than the English *Handbooks* when he wrote:

'The teachers of France exercise the most scrupulous and, one might say, reverential care over the study of their mother tongue. One could wish for more of this minute and illuminating analytical work in Scottish schools. The analysis of words, phrases, clauses, sentences, should be constantly practised, so that words may be understood in their precise connotation, so that vocabulary may be enlarged, the diction varied, and the principles of sentence formation thoroughly grasped.'[4]

It is in line with this attitude that the 1950 *Memorandum* recommended a method of teaching English which was formal and carefully graded.

[1] *Handbook*, 1959, pp. 148–65. [2] *General Reports*, Western Division, 1908, p. 38.
[3] *General Reports*, 1926, p. 36. [4] *General Reports*, 1923, p. 81.

'At the appropriate stages the teacher must see to it that they learn, first, how to compose and write a sentence correctly; next, how to construct a paragraph; and, later, how to build up a longer form of composition on a single theme. Paragraphing in the technical sense of logical disposition should not be expected before class VII. Exercises to aid in this progression should be carefully graded, and should give abundant practice in forming sentences of varied structure. The pupil should have a text book to supplement, as need arises, the exercises set by the teacher.'

In contrast with the English recommendation that children should have abundant practice in all sorts of writing, Scottish schools were told not to give the children essays to write more frequently than once every three weeks: 'In the intervening weeks the teacher should set exercises expressly designed to improve the pupil's power of arrangement and to develop his vocabulary.' It is clear, too, that Scottish teachers were still faced with the difficulty which had earlier bothered their colleagues in England – what to find for the children to write about. The advice offered was mainly negative: the subject set for an essay

'should have some relation to his intellectual and emotional experience in order that his ideas may flow easily and that he may be free to concentrate more on how to say a thing than what to say. Teachers should accordingly avoid abstract subjects (Friendship, Thrift), fantastic subjects (Imagine Yourself an Umbrella); vague subjects (Football, Railways).'[1]

THE TEACHING OF NUMBER

Just as there has been agreement on both sides of the Border that proficiency in spoken English is an essential prerequisite to learning to write, but very different views nevertheless on how children should learn to write, so, too, there has been complete agreement that the teaching of arithmetic should be 'realistic', but very different ideas about how children should learn to calculate. That arithmetic teaching ought to be 'realistic' can mean several things. First, it may mean that the subject matter of the arithmetic lesson should be strictly within the pupil's experience. In this sense the English and Scottish *Suggestions* have been in agreement, but they have differed on what might be regarded as falling within the experience of the primary school child. The Scottish *Memorandum* of 1950 was followed by a very full survey of the teaching of arithmetic in the Department's report for 1955, which was published separately as a pamphlet for the guidance of teachers. In this pamphlet it was said that,

'Ideally, the matter dealt with in arithmetic courses should bear a close relation to the processes and to the various units and quantities most likely to be used in practical affairs. In the primary school, where only the foundations are being laid, the limited experience of the pupils must always be borne in mind. Although

[1] *Memorandum*, 1950, p. 64.

the yard, the pint and other measures are in common everyday use, many pupils have only the vaguest notion of what these measures are.'[1]

The English *Handbook* four years later also thought that young children should have plentiful opportunity in school of actually handling these simple measures, but the assessment of what experience the children could be expected to bring to their lessons was rather more generous: 'The vocabularies of even young children contain words such as wavelength, supersonic speed, acceleration, gradient, interplanetary and atomic energy.'[2]

In another sense, 'realistic' arithmetic might mean a course of instruction which is rigidly confined to the arithmetic which the pupils are likely to use in their daily lives. In this sense the Scottish Education Department were quite explicit about what they meant by realism: 'Without a knowledge of arithmetic, the child will be gravely handicapped in his daily life. It is a main task of the primary school to instruct him and give him practice in the processes involved in solving, quickly and accurately, the problems which will confront him in his everyday dealings with money, time, weights and measures.'[3] In England, 'with the advent of calculating machines there is no longer the need for man to undertake long computations; but the design, programming and maintenance of these machines require more advanced mathematical knowledge than mere computation. It may be argued that the mathematics of the engineer and of the atomic physicist is remote from the work done in the primary school. Nevertheless, it is in the primary school that children's attitudes towards mathematics are created.'[4]

'Realism' in arithmetic may also mean that the process of generalization and abstraction from 'practical' or concrete situations should, as far as possible, be made obvious to the children. In this sense, it is more difficult to compare the attitudes of the authors of the English and Scottish *Suggestions* because the Scottish publication was by no means as explicit as the English. Teachers of infants in both countries have for many years been in the habit of prefacing number work with informal activities designed to give the children the opportunity of associating numbers with actual groups of objects, and it has also been common practice to use diagrams or apparatus to illustrate new mathematical processes as they are introduced. But the Scottish suggestion that the period of informal activity before formal arithmetic was introduced 'will depend on the previous experience of the child and may extend to six months'[5] implied a rather more perfunctory prologue than the English statement that

'when learning a new mathematical process children should at least know for what purpose they will use it, and be convinced that it gives the "right answer" to the problem. This implies that they can find the "right answer" by a more rudimentary method or by using concrete material.'[6]

It is common ground that the introduction of written calculations should not

---

[1] 'Arithmetic in the Primary School', an extract from *Education in Scotland in 1955*, (Cmd. 9722), p. 7.   [2] *Handbook*, 1959, p. 181.
[3] 'Arithmetic in the Primary School', loc. cit., p. 3.   [4] *Handbook*, 1959, p. 182.
[5] *Memorandum*, 1950, p. 7.   [6] *Handbook*, 1959, p. 183.

be made too early, but the Scottish teacher found herself under more pressure to ignore this advice.

'An apparent dilemma faces the infant teacher who, though herself convinced of the value of a period of informal training, fears that her professional skill will be called in question if after several months in school her pupils have nothing on paper. This misgiving troubles many teachers of newly enrolled pupils, and causes particular anxiety to those who are in charge of each new "baby" class for only six months.'[1]

There was a good deal of evidence, said the Department's report for 1955, that despite the recommendations made in the 1950 *Memorandum* formal work throughout the country was still begun too soon. The English *Handbook* had some stronger words to say on the need to postpone written work: 'Premature written work often has the effect of producing work which is done completely by rote – "this is the way to do this sum" – and children suffer throughout their lives from lack of understanding.'[1]

It is in this reason for the postponement of written work in English schools that we find the essential differences in attitude to the teaching of arithmetic. The Scottish *Memorandum* of 1950 paid scant attention to the philosophical basis of the subject because it was thought to be axiomatic that arithmetic was a 'fundamental tool' of education. The metaphor is apt. As a tool, the ability to calculate quickly and accurately should be kept sharp and bright. For this purpose frequent polishing by means of practice was all that was necessary. 'Accuracy is the prime essential, and the degree expected should be high': 'oral drill is essential if the fundamental facts are to be thoroughly known and readily applied': 'all written work should be neat and orderly. Correct placing of figures is essential': 'the method adopted for any process, particularly subtraction and multiplication, must be uniform throughout the school': 'constant revision is imperative'. If adequate drill was given, it was not necessary that the children should understand what they were doing, and the teaching of mechanical processes might even be hampered by attempting to explain the underlying reasons for it.[2]

The English 1959 *Handbook* adopted a much more critical approach. 'If the learning of mathematics is conceived of as nothing more than the daily grinding out of pages of mechanical sums, then the answer probably is that there is little justification for spending a great deal of time on it.' The reasons given for including the subject in the primary school curriculum were threefold. First, the historical ('mathematical thought is part, and a great part, of the heritage of the race. Children should not remain unaware of this activity of the human mind'); secondly, the utilitarian ('every adult needs a certain amount of mathematics in order to live in this complex society and feel some sense of mastery over his environment'); and thirdly, the aesthetic ('the elegance, the order, the pattern and the generality which are inherent even in the most elementary work can be

---

[1] *Arithmetic in the Primary Schools*, loc. cit., p. 3.
ʻ*Memorandum*, 1950, pp. 71–6.

appreciated by all children in some measure'). At first sight this seems a far cry from the insistence in the earlier *Handbooks* on the need for 'realism' in the teaching of arithmetic. It does not, however, lead to very different conclusions about what should be taught, nor how it should be taught. This is partly because of the overriding need to confine the subject matter to things which are within the child's experience, but much more to the fact that insistence on the absolute importance of understanding was not a new development.[1] Ever since 1905 it had been regarded as essential that English children should grasp what they were doing in the arithmetic lesson. Even the 1959 statement that 'it is not generally realised how, in mathematics, a class can develop its own mathematical knowledge' is given the lie by the 1927 edition: 'Practical work, if properly directed, may not only introduce rules, but lead the children to formulate rules for themselves', and by the 1905 suggestion that 'the scholars, under the guidance of the teacher, should construct the process or rule'. The 1959 belief that 'mere accuracy of computation is not enough' goes no further than the 1905: 'it is important that arithmetic should be treated not merely as the art of performing certain numerical operations: it should be taught with the view of making the scholars think clearly and systematically'.

In mathematics it is easier than in other subjects to compare the amount of work which the children are expected to accomplish during their primary school careers, and it is quite clear that the curriculum recommended for English schools has been wider than that for Scottish schools. The English infants school is assumed to introduce its pupils to measurements of length, weight and capacity, to money up to £1, to some multiplication and division – all these are implicit in what is said about the teaching of number to infants, even though the 1959 *Handbook* said that it would not be desirable to lay down how much work should be covered in the infants school. The Scottish *Memorandum* laid down a strict profession of work in which all these topics were to be postponed to the junior stage. For the older children, the English *Handbook* was even more cautious about making detailed recommendations because it envisaged considerable differences in attainment by the age of eleven. Most children, by the time they left the primary school would not be ready 'to have the principles of mechanics, or formal geometry, or the motions of the heavenly bodies explained to them mathematically', but some of the ablest could profitably be introduced to such ideas. Though Scottish primary schools retain their pupils rather longer than in England, the recommended curriculum was much narrower: it was confined to the four rules of arithmetic, the application of these rules to money, weights and measures, fractions with small denominators, simple proportion, problems and bills. The very able might cover a few topics which were not suitable for the majority, but in general 'it is not advisable to anticipate the programme for later stages' and it is better that 'a specially high degree of accuracy should be exacted. Some of the examples set should demand considerable thought or more sustained effort than is normally expected.'[2]

[1] *Handbook*, 1959, pp. 180–3.   [2] *Memorandum*, 1950, p. 132.

THE SCOTTISH MEMORANDUM OF 1965

It might be thought that the routine of drill and more drill, practice and more practice, in Scottish schools goes a long way to explain the lassitude, the lack of creative energy (and also the rebelliousness which creates problems of discipline) which in the 1950s were accepted as typical of primary children in Scotland. But cause and effect are difficult to disentangle, there is just as much evidence that the narrowness of the curriculum, and the rigidity of the methods of instruction, were a direct consequence of the assumptions made about the nature of child-hood. The essential difference in the classroom was that, in Scottish schools, the main emphasis was on the teacher. It was her responsibility to see that the children responded in the desired way, or, if she used activity methods, to con-trive situations in which they would learn exactly what she wanted them to learn. In England, the classroom was the scene for 'interplay between the minds of the teacher and of the children, and between the minds of the children them-selves'.

There is an interesting progression in the following quotations from succes-sive editions of the English *Handbooks*:

1905: 'The teacher, therefore, must know the children and must sympathise with them, for it is of the essence of teaching that the mind of the teacher should touch the mind of the pupil. He will seek at each stage to adjust his mind to theirs, to draw upon their experience as a supplement to his own and so take them as it were into partnership for the organisation of knowledge.'

1927: 'All through their period of schooling the children should be led to regard the school as their ally in their efforts after self-discovery.'

1937: 'In the national system of education there must be scope for the free growth of intelligence and adaptability, and the school must see that such scope exists.'

1959: 'The teacher should have a clear idea of what she expects them to learn, though she may not foresee all that any particular child will get out of the opportunities or materials she provides for him, for children's inventiveness and what arrests their attention can be a constant source of surprise to even the most experienced teachers.'
[And also in 1959:] 'As the children's capacity for critical observation of their elders grows, it is especially important that the school should satisfy their needs on all sides. An able child's estimate of the school situation can be devastating.'

The initiative seems to have passed from the teacher to the child some time in the nineteen-twenties, and now teachers find it increasingly difficult to keep up with their pupils' demands. The Scottish Education Department in 1950 took a much more balanced view: 'Throughout the chapters on the curriculum, no matter what the subject, there runs the recurrent note that appeal must be made to the child's experience and that he should be, if not in the radical sense the architect of his own education, at least a willing collaborator.'

Then, suddenly, in 1965, children as seen through the eyes of the Scottish Education Department became quite different creatures. In the Preface to the 1965 *Memorandum on Primary Education in Scotland* an attempt is made to suggest that the difference between the practice of the primary schools now and the primary schools of twenty years ago is the result of a steady development, of changes in the environment and of a 'growing acceptance by teachers of the principles underlying an education based on the needs and interests of the child and the nature of the world in which he is growing up'. A half-hearted attempt is even made to suggest that the earlier *Memorandum* of 1950 had 'to a certain extent' suggested new ways of doing things and had envisaged some of the changes which increasingly have influenced the work of teachers in recent years.[1] In fact the new document represents nothing short of a revolution. No longer are there references to lassitude in the classroom:

'The five-year old is constantly active, and does not sit still for long. . . . His curiosity about the world around him, his desire to learn, and the delight and satisfaction which he derives from each fresh discovery, make him willing to co-operate in his own education and ready to respond to the stimulus which can be provided in the classroom by a rich environment and an understanding teacher.'[2]

No longer is it a question of the teacher 'bringing within the circle of his interests a subject which at first had no appeal for him': instead 'he enters enthusiastically into pursuits which interest him and his enthusiasm can be killed by an adult who tries too insistently or overtly to direct his activities'. No longer is the child's attitude to the teacher merely one of respect, and discipline a matter of justice: even the impulses which lead to bad behaviour can be turned to good account:

'In an atmosphere of security and affection, and in the hands of a teacher who understands the developing pattern of his emotions, his increasing desire for independence, which occasionally reveals itself in hostility and rebelliousness against authority, can be diverted into rewarding channels, and used to motivate him in the pursuit of his own education'.

Corporal punishment is no longer 'salutary'; its use should be unnecessary.

There are still, of course, differences between the new *Memorandum* and the English *Handbook* of 1959, but they are now differences mainly of emphasis. The English primary school teacher, for example, 'sees' in outline a month's or a term's work ahead, and 'knows' how the children can work within her general plan. The Scottish teacher is advised, in consultation with her headteacher, to draw up a plan for perhaps a month ahead, but within its framework she

'must plan a programme for each week or each day, covering all the activities which she wishes to include, and allowing for group or individual work, and

[1] *Memorandum*, 1965, p. vii.   [2] Ibid., pp. 5, 6.

occasions when the whole class will be taken together. For this purpose it is best to portion out the school day in large blocks of time within which the teacher can achieve as much flexibility of organisation as she desires.'[1]

There is no longer any discussion of the relative advantages and disadvantages of individual, group and class teaching: as in the English *Handbook*, it is assumed that all kinds of organization are necessary at some time and it is assumed that the arrangements will be very fluid. But,whereas the English teacher 'comes to know' what kinds of class organization are best, Scottish primary teachers are given some useful advice on how to train their pupils from the first infants class onwards to accept varied patterns of teaching.[2] The English teacher cannot foresee what any individual child will get from any pursuit on which he sets out: the Scottish teacher now also relies on the individual assignment but she must be clear about its purpose in order to ensure that it really gives practice in those elements of the subject which she wishes to emphasize. The ablest of English children, by the end of their junior school career, 'need books and materials worthy of their abilities, for no teacher has enough time, even if he has the knowledge, to satisfy these children's intellectual and creative needs'[3]: similarly one of the most important things for the Scottish teacher to realize 'is that learning rather than teaching is the most essential element in the education of the able pupil. Her function, therefore, is not to teach him all that he wants to know – she may not have the knowledge to do so – but to create situations in which he will learn for himself.' The authors of the Scottish *Memorandum* are, however, not completely happy to accept this situation: they go on to suggest that the ablest children at the top of the primary school might be given special tutorial instruction by teachers with special skills, or even that all such children might be gathered from a number of neighbouring schools to a special centre which might cater for perhaps the most gifted two per cent who, even though a policy of acceleration through the primary school is still to be coupled with earlier transfer to a secondary school, might otherwise spend some time with too little to occupy them.[4]

It is in the teaching of mathematics that the 1965 *Memorandum* shows the greatest change from that of 1950. Arithmetic is no longer simply a tool of education. Speed and accuracy in computation are now of secondary importance. The purpose of mathematics teaching is now to help the child to understand those aspects of his environment which are best expressed in terms of number, which show qualities of regularity, order, pattern, structure or form. The teaching of mathematics is in fact described in the chapter headed 'Environmental Studies'. The method of approach to mathematics is of the utmost importance, discussion among groups of children and with the teacher will help to classify vaguely conceived ideas, the concepts which are at the very core of mathematics must be formed. Essential skills must still be practised and basic facts mastered, but excessive drill in mechanical calculating and in learning standard methods

---

[1] Ibid., p. 39.
[2] Ibid., pp. 64–8.
[3] *Handbook*, 1959, p. 74.
[4] *Memorandum*, 1965, pp. 57–9.

of solving problems should not be allowed to 'dull the children's interest or cramp their initiative'. Needless to say the recommended syllabus is completely new.[1]

In the chapter on the teaching of English (or, rather, the 'Language Arts') the assertion is made that 'speaking and writing are essentially different', but the purpose of the statement is to encourage a new freedom in the development of spoken English: to make the point that children should be allowed to talk without insisting that they always speak in complete sentences, and to avoid any suggestion that spoken English is only a preparation for written English. At the same time,

'written English, like spoken English, is a means of communication as well as of self-expression. Like speech, it may be personal and individualistic, but it is subject to more conventions and involves more skills which must be learned. In teaching written English, therefore, the aims are two-fold:

(a) to encourage fluent expression in as spontaneous and varied a form as possible;

(b) to train the pupil gradually to a mastery of the accepted conventions.'

In pursuit of these aims children are to be encouraged to write much sooner and much more frequently than had previously been considered desirable: the limitation now is not that writing must only be undertaken after careful forethought, appropriate consideration of the requirements of grammar and style, and with meticulous care: the only limitation is that the teacher should be careful not to force the pace of natural development and, after all, 'not all children have something to write about every day'. Nevertheless, though 'some children absorb the patterns of normal written English unconsciously through imitation of what they hear and read, and reproduce them in their writing from quite an early age, the majority of pupils do not seem to make marked improvement in their ability to construct sentences unless some supplementary training is given'. Exercises should therefore be given by a systematic treatment of basic sentence patterns, and progressive understanding of the structure of sentences should be nurtured by a classification of words according to their function. These exercises in grammar, syntax and style should, nevertheless, proceed side by side with ample opportunity for practice, should be carefully related to the points which the children's own writing has shown to need attention, and the depth to which study of this kind should be taken depends not only on the ability but also on the interest of the pupils. The final word on the matter is that 'for the ablest pupils grammar may become an interesting and rewarding study in its own right'.[2]

[1] Ibid., pp. 145–58.   [2] Ibid., pp. 97–125.

PART IV

The Academic Tradition

Syne look at gabbin Jamie Broon!
A teem, lang-leggit, glaiket loon,
Wha'd nivver worn a college goon,
Na, but for me!
And noo they ca' him Doctor Broon,
An Ll.D.!

CHAPTER NINE

The School and Leaving Certificates

SCOTLAND BEFORE 1951

The histories of the development of Secondary school certificate examinations in England and Scotland show many more points of similarity than does the 'eleven plus'. In spite of important differences of form, the main purpose to be achieved was the same in both countries. The first task was the establishment of some kind of uniform standards in the Secondary schools. And the need for this was equally pressing on both sides of the border, for, although Scottish Secondary schools were more numerous than in England, the fact that there had been no matriculation test for entrance to the universities meant that standards in the schools were at least as variable. Even though, in Scotland, it was the state which took responsibility for the examination of Secondary school pupils rather than the universities (who have retained it in England), it was inevitable that, at first, a school leaving certificate, in Scotland no less than in England, should be linked to the university preliminary examinations and should draw on the experience of the universities in having set examinations at this level. As the Secondary school provision in both countries improved during the first half of the present century the certificate examinations have tended to move away from university requirements both in terms of the standards demanded and in terms of the subjects examined.

The attempt has been, as progress has been made in the development of suitable Secondary schools, to define an adequate level of achievement which could mark the successful completion of a secondary course. The certificate which was to testify to this level had still, of course, to provide some testimony of the pupils' ability, if they so desired, to pursue some further course of study. The prestige of the universities meant that they still had the most considerable influence on the determination of such standards and on the pattern of school examinations. But at least they no longer had a monopoly. Technical colleges, teacher training colleges and the professions have all defined their own admission requirements.

When the Scottish Leaving Certificate was introduced the universities had no matriculation test, but they did have a preliminary examination and students who could pass it were able to complete the degree course in three years instead of four. At first the Leaving Certificate was a 'subject' examination. Papers were set in six subjects: English (including history and geography), mathematics, Latin, Greek, French and German. Passes were awarded at three levels: lower, higher and honours. Candidates might take the examination in any subject at any level. The standard of the higher grade was intended to correspond to that of the examination preparatory to the three years' course at the Scottish universities, and from 1894 the universities accepted passes on the higher grade in individual subjects in the Leaving Certificate as equivalent to passes in their own preliminary examination. The next step was to make the examination a more adequate test of the total secondary course instead of allowing pupils to take any subject they chose at any age and in any order. By degrees between 1901 and 1908 the Department turned the examination into one for a 'group' certificate which could only be taken at the end of a four-year course, and would only be awarded to pupils who obtained four passes on the higher grade or three passes on the higher grade and two on the lower grade. Higher English was compulsory: so was mathematics on either the higher or the lower grade: for their remaining subjects candidates might take either science and one or more languages, or languages only, but if more than one language was taken one of them had to be Latin. The honours grade was dropped in 1907 as being unnecessarily exacting. In 1911 the process of reducing the requirements for a certificate continued with a reduction of the group requirement to three highers and one lower. On the other hand the certificate was now only awarded on the completion of an approved secondary course of five years instead of four. In 1918 the four Scottish universities set up a joint entrance board to conduct a common universities preliminary examination, as well as to decide whether 'the length and general character of the course or courses of secondary education, the satisfactory completion of which was attested by the Group Certificate of the Scotch Education Department', might qualify for university entrance. The requirement for admission to a degree course in arts at this date was also three higher grade passes and one lower, although a candidate with higher English and higher mathematics together with lower Latin and Greek might in fact qualify for admission with only two highers and two lowers. It was not until 1924, when the group requirement for the Leaving Certificate was further reduced to two highers and two lowers, that the minimum number of passes required for university entrance always exceeded the minimum number required for the award of the Leaving Certificate. In 1924, also, the group of practical subjects – art, music, applied science and domestic science, was added to the range of subjects in the Certificate. The universities had always insisted on a stricter selection of subjects. Indeed as early as 1899 the Department had introduced science as a leaving certificate subject, but the universities were not prepared to recognize a pass in science for their purposes. Finally, in 1939, history was separated from English, and geography ceased to be linked as a 'half' subject with the sciences, so that both became full examination subjects in their own right. The group requirement for the certificate was increased from two highers and two lowers to two highers and three lowers, but the universities put up the minimum numbers of passes which they required to four highers or three highers and two lowers.

The award of the Leaving Certificate at the end of a four-, and later a five-year coarse, with a choice of the level at which individual subjects might be taken, antedated the introduction of the Intermediate Certificate. This certificate was at first designed merely to give an opportunity to take the examinations on the lower grade to pupils who had followed a course of the type offered by the higher grade schools after 1903, but who were going to leave school at about the age of fifteen. From 1907 to 1924 Leaving Certificate candidates were also required to pass the Intermediate Certificate at the end of three years in the Secondary schools before proceeding into the fourth and fifth years of the senior secondary course. For a period of seventeen years, therefore, the Scottish Leaving Certificate was a two-stage examination, as the English School and Higher Certificates were. But there were important differences, and the examinations were taken at the ages of fifteen and seventeen instead of at sixteen and eighteen. In 1924, however, the Intermediate Certificate was abolished and the Leaving Certificate again became what its name implies, a certificate which was only awarded to pupils on the point of leaving school on the results of an examination taken at the end of the secondary course.

ENGLAND BEFORE 1951

The English School Certificate, finally established at a much later date than the Leaving Certificate, can be said to have approached the same problem from the opposite direction. In Scotland the Certificate had been seen as a test of the individual (though of course the work of the schools would have to be of a standard to enable the individual pupil to submit to that test). But in England the School Certificate was designed explicitly to test the work of the schools (though of course the individual pupil would never see it as anything other than a trial of his own abilities). At any rate, the School Certificate was intended to 'provide a suitable test of the ordinary work of a Secondary school at the fifth form stage, suitable in the sense that whole Forms, and not only picked pupils, would probably be presented for it with the expectation that a large proportion would pass (what proportion was never stated), and that without special preparation or undue disturbance of the normal work of the Form'.[1] The idea was that the examination should be conducted on the basis of easy papers and a high standard of marking. The same examination would serve both as a test of the work of the whole form and, with a higher level of pass, as a university matriculation examination for the better pupils. Even so the School Certificate was later criticized for subjecting children to too great a pressure. The blame was, however, attached not so much to the examination itself as to the fact that

'a matriculation certificate, which should mean nothing more than a certificate entitling the holder to admission to a university, has come to mean a superior kind of school certificate with its own special value in the eyes of employers and the general public, and to be the aim of thousands of Secondary school pupils who neither intend nor desire to enter the doors of a university.'[2]

[1] Report of Panel of Investigators appointed by Secondary Schools Examinations Council, quoted in *Report of the Consultative Committee on Secondary Education* (Spens), 1939, p. 255.
[2] Spens Report, 1939, p. 258.

The School Certificate, like the Scottish Leaving Certificate, was a group certificate which was only awarded on the basis of a minimum of five passes with certain prescribed subjects. There were three main groups of subjects: (i) English subjects, (ii) foreign languages, and (iii) science and mathematics. Candidates, like their Scottish contemporaries, were expected to satisfy the examiners in each of the three groups. The Board of Education did recognize the existence of a fourth group of subjects (including music, drawing, manual work and housecraft) but argued that these subjects were not capable of being tested by a written examination. In response to protests from the teachers' organizations the Board agreed to ask the examining boards to experiment, and from 1918 onwards a pass in one subject taken from Group IV was allowed to count towards the certificate granted by the Northern Universities Joint Matriculation Board. With some reluctance the other Boards followed suit in due course. The matriculation requirements of the English universities before the war conformed to roughly the same pattern as the entrance qualifications laid down by the Scottish Universities Entrance Board: both in turn are similar to the kind of rules prescribed for the award of a 'group certificate' both by the English examining boards and the Scottish Education Department.

Thus far the main difference was that the English system provided for syllabuses in each subject which demanded approximately the same attention: distinctions were made in the standard of performance in an examination set both to the potential university scholar and the bare pass mark candidate. The Scottish system allowed the pupil himself to decide the level at which he would take the examination, whether at the lower grade or, with a wider syllabus, at the higher grade.

The Scottish universities, however, had viewed with some reluctance the introduction of a school examination which demanded a higher standard than that reached by many of their own students on admission: at the time they did not want to give up their junior classes: the Department's attempt to offer an even higher standard in school examinations with the 'honours' grade was abandoned. No one now regrets the passing of the university junior classes, but the attitude to the higher grade in the Scottish Certificate of Education is emphatically that it represents an adequate demand on entrants to the universities, and that it would be wrong to try to raise this standard, especially if to do so would open the door to specialization in the secondary schools. The faculty requirements of the Scottish universities are expressed within the framework of the general entrance requirements (with a minor exception in the case of mathematics), and there seems no desire to see the schools taking on work which has been the province of the universities.

In England, on the other hand, the matriculation standard was regarded as the minimum standard for admission, and it was the faculty requirements which served to encourage the development of more advanced work in the schools. Matriculation was based on the School Certificate, but the faculties became more interested in performance in the Higher School Certificate. The entrance requirements of most English universities have been revised since the war and are now expressed primarily in terms of the faculty (and therefore specialist) demands, leaving the candidate's general education to be looked after by subsidiary subjects which simply supplement his main subjects. Whereas in Scotland the 'highers' perform the same function as before, in England the main emphasis in university selection is now on the advanced level of the G.C.E. The period between the wars led up to this, as the universities were able to turn their attention from a theoretical minimum standard to the standards they could actually demand of applicants – from the School Certificate to the Higher School Certificate. These two examinations were officially known as the First and the Second School Examinations. The Higher School Certificate was also a group certificate in the sense that it was only awarded on the basis of a minimum number of passes. The several examining boards differed in their prescription, but a candidate usually had to pass in three 'main' or 'principal' subjects, or else in two main and two subsidiary subjects. The subjects professed did not, however, have to be chosen from different disciplines. On the contrary, the main subjects, at least, would normally be taken from related fields, for example, mathematics, physics and chemistry; or two foreign languages; or English and history. The subsidiary subjects might either be supporting subjects from the same general field of study or, alternatively, might be used to give some balance to the sixth form curriculum. For example, a school might require all its scientists to take mathematics as a subsidiary subject or, alternatively, might insist that they all took subsidiary English, or perhaps that they studied some German. As in the School Certificate, passes in the main subjects in the Higher School Certificate were awarded with credit or distinction, though the subsidiary subjects were usually taken on a simple pass or fail basis.

ENGLAND: THE G.C.E.

Such was the situation up to the introduction of the General Certificate of Education in 1951. Various schemes of reform had previously been put forward but none had been put into effect. In particular the Norwood Report had wanted to abolish the School Certificate altogether and replace it by internal examinations. The Higher School Certificate would be replaced by a system of subject examinations at a standard intermediate between the existing main and subsidiary levels: it would be taken at the age of eighteen plus and would not be designed to provide evidence of a general or all-round education (that would be supplied by the pupil's school record) but would simply 'provide such evidence [of an ability] to pursue a particular line of study as individual faculties of universities and particular Professional Bodies may see fit to require'.[1] The G.C.E. was, in the event, a compromise. It was intended to provide a much more flexible system of examinations, and could be taken in any number of subjects at any level. The group requirement was abolished. An ordinary level was retained at a standard roughly corresponding to the credit standard of the old School Certificate (i.e. a stricter standard of marking would be used but the syllabuses

[1] Norwood Report, *Curriculum and Examinations in Secondary Schools*, 1943, p. 42.

K

would not necessarily be changed). The advanced level would approximate to the standard of the former 'main' subject level in the Higher School Certificate. It was hoped that the schools would adopt a much freer organization of their work. Indeed the stated intention was that they should no longer use the ordinary level (as the School Certificate had been used) as a barrier between the lower school (in which pupils took at least six or seven subjects from all branches of study up to the age of sixteen) and the sixth form (in which they specialized in two or three). The hope was that any pupil who intended to take a subject at the advanced level would either bypass the O level examination in that subject altogether or, if he took it at all, would do so incidentally and without diverting from his advanced studies to prepare specially for it. The idea was that the G.C.E. should be in spirit, if not in strict form, a school leaving examination. Pupils would not be (as Scottish pupils had been) required to postpone sitting any examination until they were on the point of leaving school, because it was thought to be impossible for them to carry on all their subjects to the end of their school careers without distracting too much of their attention from the specialist subjects which would properly be their main concern in the sixth form. But they would only take an external examination in any subject at the highest level to which they proposed to pursue their study of it, and at the point when they were about to abandon that particular subject. The intention was that, in course of time, the O level examination should be deferred to a later stage in the school course and its standards raised.

Many grammar schools have not used the new examination in this way. The tradition of taking the School Certificate in all subjects before proceeding into the sixth form was too strong: the ordinary level has been used in exactly the same way as the old School Certificate. Another miscalculation was that back in 1951 no one realized the extent to which schools would contrive to present many more pupils than hitherto for the certificate examination. The raising of the standard of the ordinary level was expected to reduce the number of candidates. The reverse has happened, and the ordinary level has been given a new importance by the large and increasing number of children who are put in for it. This use of the ordinary level by children who carry their school studies no further has made it impossible to develop the O level, as it was intended to be developed, mainly as an examination at subsidiary level for pupils taking advanced level subjects in the sixth form. The new ordinary level in 1951 took the place both of the former School Certificate and of the subsidiary level in the Higher School Certificate. This in itself was probably a mistake. It is impossible to devise an examination which is equally suitable for some who have studied a subject only up to the age of sixteen, for some who have carried it on (with reduced attention) for a year or two longer, and for others who have perhaps only taken it up for the first time at sixteen and spent two years on it as a subsidiary subject in the sixth form. Some of the examining boards soon saw the necessity for different examination syllabuses for different purposes and introduced an 'alternative ordinary' level as the equivalent of the former subsidiary subject in the Higher School Certificate. The Cambridge Board for example currently offer examinations in forty-eight different subjects. In more than one-third of these it is possible to take the 'alternative ordinary' level.[1] The distribution of subjects according to the levels at which they may be taken under the Cambridge Board is shown in Table 18.

TABLE 18. *Cambridge Local Examinations Syndicate: Levels of G.C.E. subjects*

Ordinary level only	15
Both Ordinary and Advanced level	10
Advanced level only	6
Alternative Ordinary level only	4
Alternative Ordinary and Advanced level	2
All three levels	11

But some of the other examining boards make no distinction between the types of O level examinations.

One of the main controversies affecting the English grammar schools at present is that concerning the examination of subsidiary subjects in the sixth form. The attention being given to this problem suggests that it is not fair to criticize the sixth forms for excessive specialization or the universities for pressing them into it. Schools and universities alike were content formerly to rely for evidence of an all-round education mainly on an examination which was over and forgotten by the time the pupil was sixteen. They are now concerned about the attestation of satisfactory performance in subsidiary or complementary studies up to the age of eighteen. Dissatisfaction with the O level as evidence of all-round study by the prospective university student, and the complication introduced for the pupil who will leave school at sixteen by the fact that he will now have a choice of taking the G.C.E. or the C.S.E., have led some to suggest that the O level should be dropped altogether. If anything should ever come of this suggestion it would seem that something like the old subsidiary subject of the Higher School Certificate must be reintroduced.

SCOTLAND: THE S.C.E.

In 1951 the Scottish Leaving Certificate also ceased to be a group certificate. Pupils might take any number or combination of subjects and might take them on either the higher or the lower grade. Candidates were still required to have followed a five-year secondary course, and the Department's regulations prescribed the broad nature of these courses, but they could at the end of the course be presented for examination in any number of subjects. The regulations governing secondary courses were relaxed at the same time, so that henceforth a school could submit proposals to the Department for the omission of either mathematics or a foreign language. There was also a concession for 'pupils who are unable to complete the approved five years' course': a pupil in the fourth year who decided to leave school at the end of the year might be presented for

---

[1] Or, as this particular Examining Board describe it, 'Ordinary level for sixth form candidates.'

the certificate on the lower grade in any subjects which the school authorities considered him fit to attempt. The standard of the lower and higher grades remained unchanged.

This was only an interim measure however. In 1961 there was a more radical alteration marked by the change of name from Leaving Certificate to 'Scottish Certificate of Education'. A new ordinary grade, designed to be of approximately the same standard as the ordinary level in the G.C.E., was introduced in lieu of the lower grade which was abandoned. It is intended to be taken in the fourth year of the secondary course, that is, at about the age of sixteen. The higher grade remains unaltered and is still a fifth year examination.

The new ordinary grade is of a lower standard than the old lowers, because it is to be taken a year earlier (though the date of the examination was changed so that less than a full year would be lost). But it is not intended that pupils should take the ordinary grade before proceeding to the higher grade. There is the possibility that they may take the ordinary grade 'in their stride', but if they do so it is much more likely than in England that they will genuinely take it as an incidental to their studies for the higher grade. For one thing the Scottish schools have not been accustomed, as have the English schools, to a two-stage examination. For another, there is only one year between the ordinary and the higher grade against the two years between the G.C.E. ordinary and advanced levels, and pupils who are to have any prospect of success on the higher grade will necessarily have embarked already on the wider syllabus at the time of the ordinary grade examination.

Even though the introduction of the ordinary grade means that a pupil who is following the full five-year course can drop some of his subsidiary subjects at the end of the fourth year, there has been no consequent increase in the standard of the higher grade. It was not the intention that in the fifth year pupils should concentrate on a narrower range of subjects. On the contrary the opportunity to drop, say, two subjects at the ordinary grade may well enable a pupil to achieve passes in four or five highers, whereas previously the need to keep on his lower grade subjects as well would have limited him to only three or four highers. The suggestion was made, too, that some pupils might take up a fresh subject in the fifth year with the intention of taking it on the ordinary grade in the sixth year after two years' study. Scotland is thus also faced with the difficulty that the ordinary grade may be used for two quite different purposes and be required to test both the very able child who takes up a subsidiary subject towards the end of his secondary school career and also the average child who has carried the subject as far as he is likely to be able to do by the end of his fourth year. Already in 1964 the Department reported some headmasters as doubting the suitability of the O grade examinations for sixth year pupils taking a short course in some new subject since they were of the opinion that the pupils would be better served if their approach to such subjects were a more mature one than would be expected in an ordinary grade syllabus.[1]

The use to which the ordinary grades in the two examinations are being put

[1] Report for 1964, p. 47.

is much the same on both sides of the border but the reasons for introducing them were directly opposed. The G.C.E. was devised with only the grammar schools in mind. The main motive behind it was to emphasize the unity of the grammar school course by removing the artificial break at sixteen and treating the course as one which developed naturally from the age of eleven straight through to eighteen. Difficulties in the use of the O level have been mainly created by the unexpectedly large numbers of children taking the examination who have no intention of completing a six or seven year grammar school course. The standard of the examination was raised in order to exclude these unwanted candidates. But, in fact, only some sixty per cent of candidates for the O level are currently pupils of maintained, direct grant and independent grammar schools. The balance is made up of secondary modern school pupils (ten per cent), students in maintained establishments of further education (seventeen per cent), plus comprehensive, multilateral and other types of secondary school. In addition, but not included in official statistics, are private candidates, pupils of unrecognized independent schools, candidates from outside England and Wales, etc.

The Scottish ordinary grade on the other hand was introduced, in spite of misgivings from the senior secondary schools that it would lower standards and upset the traditional curriculum for the most able pupils. It was adopted specifically in order to attract the more run-of-the-mill secondary school pupils to take it. And, far from trying to exclude other candidates, it was only with the introduction of the S.C.E. that the Department's examinations were made open to candidates other than those presented by a secondary school. The Leaving Certificate could only be taken by pupils from an approved secondary school: the S.C.E. is open to students in further education establishments and to external candidates. The motive behind the change was quite simply that

'rather less than a third of the pupils who embark on [a Leaving Certificate] course actually gain a certificate, even including those whose certificate records a single lower grade pass. The majority of the others leave school without completing the fourth year of their course; many do not complete even the third. . . . Pupils who, on reaching the statutory school leaving age, are very doubtful about their success in the Scottish Leaving Certificate as at present organised, may well hesitate to spend two further years at school in the hope of gaining a certificate. We believe that the prospect of gaining a certificate of accepted national standing in *one* additional year will induce many of these pupils to remain at school and complete a four year course.'[1]

AN ADVANCED GRADE IN SCOTLAND?

The introduction of the S.C.E. ordinary grade was a compromise. It is, so far, the only outcome of a recommendation made in 1947 that the Leaving Certificate should be completely recast on the English pattern. The Scottish Advisory

[1] *Report of the Working Party on the Curriculum of the Senior Secondary School*, 1959, p. 7. (See also the 1947 Report on Secondary Education which is discussed on page 174.)

Council based their report on the development of post-war secondary education entirely on the institution of a school certificate to be taken at sixteen and a higher school certificate to be taken at eighteen. For ten years nothing was done. Then it was decided to introduce the ordinary grade, but without changing the highers. Some members of the working party set up to consider the effects of the new O grade had thought that the higher grade should be postponed to the sixth year and that there should be a new advanced grade as well as the higher grade. But the majority had preferred

'that the examination on the Higher Grade should continue to be, as at present, essentially a fifth year examination, and that an Advanced Grade should be allowed to develop naturally from the system of Ordinary and Higher Grade examinations, if the need for such a grade becomes strong enough. They felt that the advantages which might accrue from the introduction of an Advanced grade are, as yet, not clearly enough established. We suggest therefore that another committee might be set up.'

The second committee appointed to consider the question reported in 1960. They considered, first, the possibility of abolishing the higher grade, but because

'it is precisely the exacting standard of the higher grade pass that has given the Leaving Certificate its prestige and value' and because 'the practical recognition given to it by the universities enables the pupil seeking admission to a university to complete the formal entrance requirements at the end of his fifth year', they unanimously recommended that it be retained. They also took into account that the abolition of the higher grade would lead to a 'severe shrinkage in examination presentation among that group of pupils whose level of intellectual attainment has hitherto been regularly attested by a limited number of Higher grade passes.'[1]

One consequence which, they thought, would follow directly from such a diminution in the number of pupils staying on to seventeen or eighteen would be the difficulty of organizing efficient senior secondary schools.

'In Scotland, before the growth of large urban and industrial areas, the typical community was the small provincial town, in which the educational provision beyond the primary stage was the small local academy or secondary department. Although radical changes have come about both in the size and in the character of many Scottish towns that educational provision has continued to be made in the same typical way. If the Higher grade were discontinued the "top" of the small senior secondary school would be so diminished in numbers that it would no longer be economic.'[2]

The Committee went on to suggest that a new advanced grade, to be taken at the end of the sixth year, should nevertheless be introduced as an addition to the ordinary and higher grades. There is one slightly anomalous precedent for this

[1] *Report of the Working Party on the Post-Fourth Year Examination Structure in Scotland*, (Cmnd. 1068), 1960, p. 8.   [2] Ibid., p. 8.

in the Scottish examination system. It is in the field of mathematics. Although there is no external examination for which pupils who have already passed the higher grade can study to a more advanced level while still at school (apart, of course, from the bursary competitions) there have for many years been additional papers in mathematics which lead to an endorsement on the Leaving Certificate. In spite of this precedent Scottish opinion is very divided about the introduction of an advanced grade. Following the 1960 recommendation the Scottish Education Department started to prepare syllabuses and specimen examination papers, and consulted the teachers about them. Much of the criticism they received was not related to the details of the proposed syllabuses, but cut at the very basis of the A grade. Its introduction was therefore postponed: the Department have passed to the new Examining Board the task of recommending whether an advanced grade shall in fact be adopted, and of preparing syllabuses.

In practice about one Scottish senior secondary school in four is believed to have had some experience of entering some of its pupils for the A level examinations of the English G.C.E. examining boards. Half of these – one school in eight – only present the odd pupil occasionally: usually because a pupil with English connections asks for the opportunity to sit English examinations. The other schools prepare candidates for the A level in a few selected subjects, largely by way of experiment. The new advanced grade of the S.C.E. is therefore being planned with some care, and, if it is eventually introduced, is bound to be very different from the English advanced level, mainly because of the retention of the higher grade and the entrance requirements of the Scottish universities, but partly because the English A levels have been looked at closely and in a spirit of criticism.

There is, of course, in both countries, continuous appraisal of examination syllabuses, the introduction of new material and the deletion of old. In Scotland such revision of syllabuses has perhaps been more radical, especially in science subjects, than it has in England because administrative control has been in the hands of the Department. H.M. Inspectors have been in a powerful position to persuade the Department to adopt new syllabuses, and at the same time to encourage the schools to use them (and of course, to give them advice on teaching to them). But in terms of the general standard and function of the examinations there have been important changes at the ordinary stage in both countries, whereas the higher grade and the advanced level,[1] in spite of various proposals for change or for the introduction of new grades, have remained essentially unchanged.

[1] For proposals which might have affected the English A level see pp. 154, 226 and 263.

CHAPTER TEN

The Pre-war English Grammar School

1904–1939

An English Secondary school was defined in the 1904–05 regulations as providing education 'up to and beyond the age of sixteen'. The Board of Education were at first concerned mainly to establish four-year courses in the Secondary schools. It was not until 1917 that regulations were introduced covering the provision of courses of advanced study (i.e. sixth form work) although some schools had already started advanced courses before that date. Between 1904 and 1937 the number of Secondary schools on the grant list increased from 575 to 1,397 and the number of pupils attending them from 94,698 to 484,676. The growth in the numbers in the sixth forms was even more satisfactory:

TABLE 19. *Sixth forms: England*

	(a) No. of pupils in grant aided Secondary schools	(b) No. of sixth form pupils included in (a)	(b) as a percentage of (a)
1904–05	94,698	?	—
1911–12	166,831	9,500 (est.)	5.7
1925–26	367,564	20,500 (est.)	5.6
1934–35	467,217	31,170	7.3
1935–36	478,085	36,849	7.7
1936–37	481,767	39,597	8.2
1937–38	484,676	40,589	8.3

As might be expected the number of candidates for the School Certificate increased proportionately with the growth in size of the schools. But it is unexpected to find that the number who took the Higher School Certificate in England, in spite of the continuing growth in the sixth forms, reached its peak by 1930 and thereafter dropped slightly. In fact the number taking the Higher School Certificate in 1937 was no greater than it was in 1931, even though the number in the sixth forms had increased by forty per cent.

TABLE 20 *Certificate Candidates: England*

	No. of candidates for School Certificate	No. of candidates for Higher School Certificate
1925–26	43,122	6,380
1928–29	48,155	7,654
1931–32	57,681	10,725
1934–35	58,348	9,811
1935–36	64,829	9,498
1936–37	64,005	10,057

An apparent contradiction which is even more unexpected is that during the 1930s the number of 'early leavers' from the English Secondary schools increased appreciably:

TABLE 21. *School Leavers from English Secondary Schools*

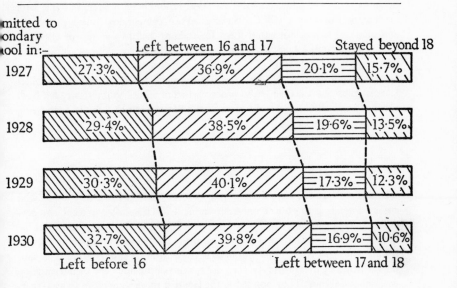

The growth in the numbers of pupils was not primarily due to the admission of more children. Admissions increased slightly in the late twenties and early thirties, but not sufficiently to account for the growth in the size of the schools. Pupils were, however, admitted at an earlier age and if fewer were willing to stay until they were eighteen more stayed on until they were sixteen or nearly so. In London, for example, in 1910–11 only twenty-six per cent of entrants to the Secondary schools had been under the age of twelve: by 1925–26 the proportion had increased to fifty-three per cent and by 1939 virtually all were under the age of twelve on admission. What was true of London was true of the rest of England, as the break at eleven plus became established practice. Children started their Secondary course younger, and it proved easier to persuade them to stay for a minimum course. The primary schools had proved more efficient at preparing them for Seconday school entrance and the Secondary schools, in turn, proved more efficient at preparing them for the first external examination.

This helps to explain how more children could leave school before the age of sixteen even while at the same time the number who took School Certificates increased. It also helps to explain the growth in the size of the sixth forms. Many local education authorities made parents sign an undertaking that they would keep their children at school until they were sixteen before offering them a Secondary school place. Some authorities nevertheless allowed a child to leave before sixteen if he had passed the School Certificate. Others stuck to the letter of the law and made them stay on even if they had passed the examination. To that extent the sixth forms were filled with children waiting until their sixteenth birthday, or perhaps until the end of the year in which they became sixteen, with no intention of remaining for the two years necessary to take the Higher School Certificate. Some children stayed at school even longer, but still with no intention of taking H.S.C., because certain professions (notably teaching and nursing) would not admit them for training before the age of eighteen. The percentage of leavers from the Secondary schools over the age of fourteen who went on to some form of higher education declined between 1925 and 1937 from 23.7 per cent to 19.3 per cent. By the same token the number of older leavers (those over sixteen) who proceeded from school to university fell both relatively and absolutely. It dropped from 3,865 in 1932 to 3,035 in 1937 (from 8.1 per cent down to 5.4 per cent).

THE SPENS REPORT

The Spens Report in 1939 was enthusiastic over the 'fact that many pupils who are not intending to go to a university remain at school after sixteen', and described it as 'a natural growth from the life of the schools themselves, from the keenness of the teachers and pupils, from the longer views of parents. It is a spontaneous growth, and its vigour is derived from its spontaneity.' The support which they drew from the statistics for this optimistic view of the situation was rather dubious. They pointed to the fact that there were more sixteen-year-olds in the schools than there had been in 1925 although admitting casually that 'the proportion of pupils remaining to form this group is not so high as in that year and there has been some falling away recently in actual numbers'. In fact the proportion of fifteen-year-olds in the schools who stayed on beyond the age of sixteen had declined steadily from 50.4 per cent in 1931 to 40.1 per cent in 1937. The Spens Report also mentioned that early leaving was greater among fee-paying pupils than among those paying no fees, but did not, apparently see the significance of this fact for a situation in which grammar school places might be made more readily available to the children of poor parents.[1]

But the Spens Committee were out of sympathy with the grammar school in its traditional role. They were convinced that it had

'already been proved in most European countries that there is a considerable danger both to the individual and to society in looking upon secondary educa-tion as only, or chiefly, preparatory to higher institutional education; such a situation must inevitably lead to an over-production of "intellectuals", and the unrest consequent on their inability to find a niche in an economic world for which they regard themselves as fitted and prepared.'[2]

The Committee were quite sure that an academic course was not only useless for all save a select few in the modern world but also out of tune with the true needs of the adolescent. 'The rapid growth in the number of pupils in Grammar schools during and since the war has resulted in the inclusion in the schools of a number of pupils who are not quick at seizing the relatedness of things or ideas, and who find French and mathematics difficult, and so find the School Certificate Examination beyond their reach.' They estimated that in some schools the pro-portion of such misfits would be between twenty-five per cent and thirty-five per cent.[3]

The fact that the schools had been as successful as they had in preparing their pupils for the School Certificate could perhaps be partly attributed to the gradual relaxation in the demands of the examining boards. In England children were under pressure, nevertheless, to aim at more than a bare certificate because of the importance attached to the possession of a matriculation certificate. The Spens Report recommended both that matriculation requirements should be separated from the School Certificate and that the requirements for the School Certificate should be relaxed even further.

WHICH TRADITION?

The Spens Report recommended what they conceived to be a new attitude to the curriculum and methods of teaching in the grammar schools. Their accusation was that the Board's *Secondary School Regulations* of 1904 had taken 'the existing Public Schools and Grammar Schools as their general cadre or archetype for secondary schools of all kinds', and that 'that conservative and imitative tendency which is so salient a characteristic in the evolution of English political and social institutions, is particularly noticeable in this instance'. But it has been argued that this is an unfair criticism of Morant's 1904 regulations. The new Secondary schools after 1902 inherited two traditions: that of the old endowed grammar schools and also that of the higher grade and other schools which had earned grants from the Science and Art Departments. The existing regulations had in fact distinguished between 'division B' schools with a predominantly literary curriculum, which were only required to devote one third of their time

[1] Spens Report, 1938, p. 96.   [2] Ibid., p. 144.   [3] Ibid., p. 168.

to science, mathematics and manual subjects, and 'division A' schools which were allowed to give most of their time to scientific and practical subjects. The Bryce Commission in 1895 had thought that the development of scientific and technical education might swamp the tradition of literary education in the grammar schools.

'There is little danger at the present day that we shall fail to recognise the necessity for improving and extending scientific and technical instruction. It is less certain that we may not run some risk of a lopsided development in education, in which the teaching of science, theoretical or applied, may so predominate as to entail comparative neglect of studies which are of less obvious and immediate utility, though not of less moment for the formation of mind and character. In efficient grammar schools, as existing examples prove, it is possible to harmonise modern requirements with the best elements of that older system which has produced good results in the past, and which in our own day still represent so much that is fundamental and indispensable in a properly liberal education.'[1]

Morant's regulations can therefore be seen as an attempt to redress the balance or to effect that harmony which the Bryce Commission commended: they made both linguistic studies and scientific subjects an essential ingredient in the curriculum of all Secondary schools. Perhaps they went too far. When, from 1912 onwards, the Board tried to relax their requirements in order to permit some Secondary schools to adopt a bias towards industry, commerce or agriculture, the response was small. Some schools took immediate advantage of the opportunity: in 1913, out of a total of nine hundred Secondary schools, thirty-four offered a course with a rural bias, twenty-five a commercial course, fourteen a course in domestic subjects and eight a course directed towards employment in the engineering industries. But the movement did not grow. The courses offered were usually alternatives to a certificate course, and little effort was made to tie in the course with a vocational objective with the normal course leading to a School Certificate.

The Spens Report said no more than the Board of Education had been saying since 1912. The Board had argued that the Secondary schools must provide for two classes of pupil; those who would stay at school until the age of eighteen and those who intended to leave at sixteen. 'The needs of both classes of pupil will best be met if alternative courses of instruction are established at the end of the first or second years; the one leading up to the examination necessary for entry to the university, the other more limited in scope, and often modified in its later stages by a vocational bias.'[2] But Spens wanted to push the pendulum much further. The committee seem in some of their statements to have disapproved altogether of the academic approach of the grammar school. They thought that the Board of Education's *Handbook of Suggestions*, 1937, 'with its enlightened analysis of the aims and problems of the Modern School, is a

[1] Bryce Report, *Secondary Education, 1895*, p. 48.
[2] Board of Education Circular 826, 1912.

challenge to the grammar schools to take stock of their position which cannot be ignored'.[1] They felt that the presence in the schools of some who would go on to take an honours degree should not be allowed to affect the lower school course. Secondary education should cater 'for the special needs of adolescence: that is to say, it should be related to the natural activities of body and mind during that period, and both illumine and guide the pupils' experience. . . . It should *not* consist to any considerable extent of courses which are only of value if carried further'. The curriculum should be organized quite clearly into two parts – up to, and beyond, the age of sixteen – on the assumption that the majority would leave at sixteen. The sixth form was to be divorced almost completely from the main school.

THE SIXTH FORM

The sixth forms were more sensitive to the climate of opinion than the main sections of the grammar schools. The pre-war sixth form was a very small affair. Detailed numbers are difficult to discover but there is a fair amount of circumstantial evidence. For example, the number of pupils from each school going on to a university is not related exactly to the size of the sixth, but it gives some guide:

TABLE 22. *Grant aided schools sending pupils to a university: England:* 1926–27

Number of pupils entering a university from each school	Number of schools
Nil	384
One or two	462
Three or four	248
Five to ten	186
Eleven to fifteen	24
Sixteen or more	15

Back in 1919 the Board of Education had advocated some kind of mutual understanding between neighbouring grammar schools so that the sixth form work might be concentrated in the interests of economy and efficiency. Effective organization, they said, was impossible 'if each school is treated as an isolated unit free to take its own line independently of all other considerations except its own efficiency and prestige, competing and not cooperating with other schools'. The appeal had little effect except in so far as neighbouring boys' and girls' grammar schools sometimes cooperated in the combination of science teaching. The Spens Report repeated, twenty years later, that in a large number of schools it would not be possible to provide teaching up to university standard in more than one subject save by imposing an altogether improper strain upon individual teachers, or at a financial cost, by way of providing additional teachers, which would be prohibitive. At the same time it was essential for every grammar school to have some sort of sixth form 'both for their effect upon the corporate

[1] Spens Report, 1938, p. 144.

life and internal affairs of a school, and for their effect upon the length of school life and the after careers of individual pupils'. The solution recommended therefore was some specialization of function by different sixth forms in an area, since 'there are relatively few schools in which it would not be possible to secure at least one teacher who could prepare pupils for the university in his own subject'. The example was quoted of one school with some 300–400 pupils in which

'a laudable effort was made to organise the work of the Sixth Forms so as to allow all pupils to follow that course of study for which they appeared to be individually best fitted, up to the Higher Certificate standard. The experiment was continued over a period of seven years. At the end of this period there were three parallel Sixth Forms, of which two were taking full courses for the Higher School Certificate; the third consisted of pupils taking varied one year courses. The numbers were six and eight in the two H.S.C. classes and nine in the class taking one year courses.'[1]

It is possible that the new state grammar schools would not have persisted with this grossly uneconomic and often rather inefficient 'top' to the school but for the example of the Public Schools. In the English Public School, with admission at thirteen rather than eleven and with most pupils staying until seventeen, eighteen or even nineteen, the sixth form is a much more significant part of the whole. The new grammar schools needed a sixth form if any opportunity of proceeding to Oxford and Cambridge were to be given to the outstanding pupil who came up through the state system. But, just as the Public Schools swelled their numbers with pupils who were destined for the army or a business career, so the grammar schools also developed, at their own economic level, 'general' sixth form courses for pupils who would stay at school until seventeen or eighteen but had no intention of taking a university degree, 'Today', wrote the Board of Education in a pamphlet published in 1938, 'the university offers only one among a large number of careers intended to be followed by pupils in Sixth Forms; and these pupils include a substantial number whose abilities in kind and amount do not suit them for a University career.'[2] The pamphlet – on *The Organisation and Curriculum of Sixth Forms in Secondary Schools* – included separate chapters on courses in engineering, commercial work, art and craft, domestic subjects and handicrafts. Some of these present a very different picture of the sixth form from the usual idea of it as a power house for the intellectual. Having, for example, outlined their suggestions for a commercial course, the Board remarked, obviously in the expectation that this would commend it to grammar school headteachers, 'the charge of being academic could never be brought against such a course'.[3]

THE NORWOOD REPORT

Only five years later the Norwood Report represented a complete reaction. It was at pains to reassert the academic function of the grammar school, and had its

[1] Spens Report, 1938, pp. 333–7.
[2] Board of Education Pamphlet No. 114, 1938, p. 6.   [3] Ibid., p. 17.

own explanation of why this had been forced to take second place: 'The truth seems to stand out quite clearly: the Secondary schools, which alone have provided full-time education up to and beyond the age of sixteen years, have often been asked to do too much.'[1] The typical grammar school pupil was, to the Norwood Committee, one

'who is interested in learning for its own sake, who can grasp an argument or follow a piece of connected reasoning, who is interested in causes, whether on the level of human volition or in the material world, who cares to know how things came to be as well as how they are, who is sensitive to language as the expression of thought, to a proof as a precise demonstration, to a series of experiments justifying a principle. He is interested in the relatedness of related things, in development, in structure, in a coherent body of knowledge. He can take a long view and hold his mind in suspense; this may be revealed in his work or in his attitude to his career . . .'[2]

The committee regarded it as being of the first importance that the standards of work in the grammar schools should be maintained at a high level. They therefore recommended very careful selection of the pupils who were to attend these schools. They regarded the full grammar school course as continuing to the age of eighteen and hoped that a much larger proportion of pupils would stay the whole course. In spite of the fact that they hoped that the School Certificate would eventually be abolished they did not so far break with the existing organization of the grammar schools as to suggest that the dividing line between the main school and the sixth form at about the age of sixteen should be removed or glossed over in any way. Their attitude to the sixth form was, nevertheless, quite different from that of the Spens Committee and the Board of Education in their 1938 pamphlet. Even though they recognized that large numbers of sixth form pupils would continue to enter commerce and industry, they considered that vocational training should find no place in the sixth form. The most they would admit was that some courses in the sixth form might be recognized as valuable preparation for such professions as nursing and medicine; these courses would be 'as such vocations themselves require, not unduly narrow or specialised'.

A valuable touchstone to the attitudes of the schools towards vocational training is always to be found in the provision they feel it proper to make for employment in commerce: this has always presented them with a problem because they feel unable to justify training in the skills of shorthand and typewriting as having much educational value, yet these are skills which are in considerable demand. The Board of Education had decreed in 1913 that the office skills might be taught in grammar schools to pupils over the age of fifteen. The Spens Committee came to the same conclusion, adding that five lessons a week would be a reasonable allocation of time. The Board's 1938 pamphlet admitted with a rather greater show of reluctance that commercial courses in the sixth form might include shortland and typewriting for those who thought they

[1] Norwood Report, 1943, p. 13.   [2] Ibid., p. 2.

needed it. The Norwood Committee, however, were quite clear that pupils entering office work after a school career ending at about the age of sixteen should in no case make a start on shorthand and typing until after their main school course had been completed. For pupils staying in the sixth until the age of seventeen or eighteen they thought that the office skills were best acquired in an intensive course at a commercial college after leaving school. But they did not quite rule out the possibility of shorthand and typing being taught in a grammar school which happened to be in an area where no other provision was made for them.

The main Norwood recommendation that there should be a 'tri-partite' organization of secondary schools was quite explicitly motivated by a desire to relieve the grammar schools of the work which they had taken on because of the lack of development of other types of secondary school. It has often been said that the report distinguishes three different types of children during adolescence, which happen to coincide with the three different types of school then existing. It was not, however, so much a question of their arguing from the existing organization of secondary education to false psychological conclusions, as that they cast around for schools which would relieve the grammar schools of unwanted pupils, saw in the existing technical schools and the nascent modern schools the opportunities for further development, and described in glowing terms the attributes of the pupils for whom such schools could cater admirably, in order that the grammar schools might be relieved of them. The Norwood plea for 'parity of esteem' was not simply a sentimental appeal to the public to regard the human worth of all children regardless of their intellectual ability, but an appeal to parents to look upon other types of school as a real alternative to the grammar schools in the hope that fewer would send their children to a grammar school for the wrong reasons, thereby filling up the schools with unsuitable material. Parity of esteem was not suggested for the benefit of the other types of school at all, but in an attempt to keep the academic standards of the grammar schools pure and unsullied either by concessions to the less able or by the taint of vocational training.

CHAPTER ELEVEN

Tripartitism

TECHNICAL SCHOOLS

In 1943 neither the junior technical school nor the secondary modern school was yet a serious competitor to the grammar school. The Norwood Report stated no more than the truth when it said that the grammar schools alone had provided education up to the age of sixteen. Full-time day trade schools date from the beginning of the century and were concentrated mainly in London and in the north of England. The Board's regulations had made it possible in 1905 for technical colleges to receive grants for day technical classes attended by boys at or near the end of their elementary school course. The intention was to fill in the gap between the end of compulsory school attendance and the beginning of apprenticeships. In 1913 day technical schools were recognized under a separate set of regulations. These were, however, limited in scope. 'These schools were definitely not intended to provide courses furnishing a preparation for the professions and Universities, or for higher full-time technical work or commercial life' – that was the job of the Secondary schools which had been empowered the previous year to offer courses with a technical or commercial bias – 'They were designed to prepare their pupils either for artisan or other industrial occupation.'[1] The minimum age for admission was fixed at thirteen. The schools were not allowed to teach any language other than English or Welsh.

By 1926 the Hadow Committee could distinguish two types of school, the 'trade school' which prepared its pupils for specific employments and the 'junior technical school' with a rather broader aim of offering preparation for a group of industries (e.g. engineering or building). Both types together, however, only made up an insignificant part of the total provision of post-primary education. Their pupils represented only 0.3 per cent of all children between the ages of eleven and sixteen. The Hadow Report limited itself to the recommendation that, as the schools appeared to be doing a useful job, they should be encouraged to develop wherever the demand for their pupils from local industry seemed to justify their work. The report recommended no change in their organization: it noted that the ban on teaching languages had been lifted, but saw no purpose in the schools taking advantage of this; the age of admission should certainly not be reduced below thirteen. The technical schools were compared unfavourably with the central schools, which not only postponed any distinctive vocational bias to the last two years of their courses but were also in a position to offer alternative courses to any pupil who found that his desire to enter industry

[1] Spens Report, 1938, p. 83.

had weakened in the meantime. The Hadow Report repeated the suggestion that any local education authority which wanted to reduce the age of admission to technical courses to eleven, or to provide courses of a wider scope than those of the junior technical schools could legitimately do so by conducting a school with a technical bias under the Secondary school regulations.

But, in spite of the fact that they found no real place in the Hadow scheme of things, the junior technical schools actually made remarkable progress during the next ten years. The number of such schools grew from eighty-six in 1922 to 224 in 1939: the number of their pupils from 10,413 boys to 20,229 and from 1,793 girls to 7,672. Although they had been seen as standing outside the main stream of post-primary developments, they came to occupy an importance in educational thinking during the 1930s out of proportion to their numerical strength. They were originally intended only to train artisans, but many of their pupils in due course filled positions in higher technology. H.M. Inspectors in a report on London schools in 1928 wrote that

'In whatever capacity the boys enter employment they make rapid progress, as a rule, and often rise to positions of high responsibility. Some have risen to posts as managers, chief engineers, heads of department, designers, research workers; others have set up in practice for themselves as consulting engineers, architects. These are, of course, exceptional boys, but investigation leaves little doubt that boys from the schools make good progress in industry, and that they supply far more than their proportionate share to the ranks of foremen or shop managers.'[1]

The Spens Report recommended that they be given added importance in so far as selected schools which were providing technical courses of a general type should be designated technical high schools, and should admit their pupils at the age of eleven and offer a five-year course (but they were not expected to keep their pupils beyond the age of sixteen plus). Even so the technical schools were, by the time of the Norwood Report, still only a numerically very small part of the country's post-primary education.

MODERN SCHOOLS

The Hadow Report set out to show how the new secondary modern schools might develop exciting ideas from the traditions they would take over from the senior departments of the elementary schools. At the same time it was necessary to insist that they would not offer an education quite so inferior in type to that available in the Secondary schools as their lowly origins might suggest. The need to keep the door open for pupils who might wish to transfer to a grammar school was paramount. In many areas the provision of grammar schools fell so far short of the demand that inevitably the new secondary modern schools would be called upon to supply the needs of many who, had the provision been more abundant, would have been found in the grammar schools. The hope was ex-

---

[1] *Education*, 28 December 1928 – see O. Banks, *Parity and Prestige in English Secondary Education*, Routledge & Kegan Paul, 1955, p. 114.

pressed that there would be more frequent opportunity for transfer of pupils between the various types of secondary school at the age of twelve or thirteen. In fact the report went so far as to recommend that 'in the earlier years the curriculum in the secondary modern schools should have much in common with that provided in the schools at present commonly known as "secondary"; it should include a foreign language, subject to permission being given to omit it in special circumstances; and it should be given a practical bias only in the last two years'. The report was very much concerned to emphasize that the modern schools should not develop such strictly vocational courses as were at that time being provided in some trade schools. It insisted that 'a humane or liberal education is not one given through books alone, but one which brings children into contact with the larger interests of mankind; and the aim of the school . . . should be to provide such an education by means of a curriculum containing large opportunities for practical work and related to living interests'. It is worth quoting Hadow at some length on this issue:

'We are concerned with the growth – which has begun already, and which we desire greatly to accelerate – of selective and non-selective central schools and of senior departments in elementary schools. This growth, in our view, will run side by side, but in no sense counter to the growth of secondary schools: and, while it will differ in kind, it will not be inferior in its promise or quality. The central school and senior departments, like the secondary schools, will give a humane and general education. It will be shorter in its duration; it will terminate at the end of three or four years; but it will be directed so long as it lasts to the general fostering of mental power. Two methods, which will differentiate them to some extent from secondary schools, will generally be followed in central schools and senior departments. One will be the method of practical instruction and manual work, on which we set high hopes, believing that there are many children who think as it were with their hands and will profit greatly by a method of instruction which follows the natural bent of their capacity. Another will be the method of giving a trend and a bias, which for want of a better word, we may call by the name of 'realistic', to the general course of studies. English and a modern language, history and geography, mathematics and natural science, will all be studied in central and senior schools no less than in secondary schools. But the study of these subjects, we hope, will be related more closely to the living nature of industrial, commercial or rural life; and it will be designed to stimulate interest in boys and girls who are beginning to think of the coming years and a career in life, and are likely to feel the liveliest quickening of mind when they see the bearing of their studies on that career.'[1]

It is clear that the Hadow Committee were very conscious of their own recommendation that the school leaving age should be raised when they were making their suggestions about the curriculum of the secondary modern school. They recommended that courses with a practical (i.e. vocational) bias should only be introduced in the third or fourth year of the course. But adequate provision

[1] Hadow Report, *The Education of the Adolescent*, 1926, p. xx.

should also be made, even in the final year of the course, for the needs of pupils who would gain greater advantage from following a more general course of study. The committee envisaged that some children would not have made up their minds about employment before they left school.

The Hadow proposals for reorganization made fairly rapid progress: in 1931 about one-third of pupils over the age of eleven were in reorganized senior departments, and by 1938 the proportions had increased to nearly two-thirds. But this had had a negligible effect on the growth of extended courses in the new modern schools and the existing selective central schools had not been much more successful. The number of pupils between the ages of fourteen and fifteen staying on for one year in elementary schools of all types had in fact remained almost stationary between 1922 and 1938, though the number over the age of fifteen who, having stayed for one year, remained even longer, had increased by about six or seven thousand. The Norwood Committee, in urging the development of other types of Secondary school to divert unwanted pupils from the grammar schools were considering a situation in which some fourteen per cent of the total age group in the country might be expected to stay at school until the age of sixteen, of whom over ten per cent were in the grammar schools, about two and a half per cent in central and modern schools, and only just over one per cent in the technical schools. Beyond the age of sixteen the percentage of pupils in any schools other than the grammar schools amounted in total to less than one in a hundred.

TRIPARTITISM

The idea of tripartite organization of secondary education caught the popular imagination in England as much as had the notion of a 'rising tide in the veins of youth' at the age of eleven. So much so that it is commonly assumed that it developed naturally and logically through the three main reports on secondary education: Hadow, Spens and Norwood. 'This principle', wrote the Ministry in 1947, 'was clearly recognized in Chapter III of the Hadow Report and it was convincingly restated in the first chapter of Part I of the Norwood Report.'[1] This is a distortion of the facts. For one thing none of the three reports was concerned with the whole field of secondary education. For another, though they may each have contributed arguments which led to the formulation of the policy, they did so for very different reasons.

The place of the secondary technical school is crucial to the whole notion of a tripartite system. The Hadow Report said very little about the junior technical schools and was not interested in altering their limited role. It is a measure of the reversal of attitude from the Spens Report to the Norwood that the former recommended that technical schools should admit pupils at the age of eleven because otherwise the grammar schools stole the best material, and that the later report came to the same conclusion, but for the opposite reason that, if technical schools did not admit at eleven, the grammar schools got material they did not

[1] *The New Secondary Education* (Pamphlet No. 9), 1947, p. 22.

want. However, the doctrine of parity of esteem meant that the development of secondary technical schools was taken a stage further. The Norwood Committee were not satisfied that the technical school course should stop short at sixteen. It was above all in the grammar school sixth forms that the dilution of the academic by the merely vocational was taking place. Secondary technical schools were therefore to offer facilities for advanced work between the ages of sixteen and eighteen. It was most important, they thought, that the road to the technical faculties of the universities should be open to all who might profit from university studies. It was precisely on this upgrading of the technical school that the whole Norwood structure depended. It could not really be pretended, in spite of the eloquence of the Hadow Report, that the modern school would achieve effective parity with the grammar schools. The introduction of advanced courses in these schools to any significant extent was still far in the future: it was only expected that they would take children up to the end of their compulsory school life. To have attempted to distinguish between the different types of school solely on the basis of the intelligence range of their pupils or on the length of course provided would not have relieved the grammar schools of the large numbers of pupils who at that time were quite prepared to stay at school to sixteen or seventeen, though not usually to eighteen, who were deemed to be incapable of the highest academic achievement, or simply not interested in the traditional academic type of curriculum. But once you could introduce the idea of parallel types of school, with the choice between them dependent on aptitude and interests rather than on ability, you could present the alternative types as each being attractive in its own way.

The Hadow Report did use the word tripartite. But it was used to describe an existing situation (and one which should be abandoned), not to advocate a new idea. It was used to criticize the fact that the senior departments of the central schools were still administered under the elementary school Code, Secondary schools had their own regulations, and the regulations governing the junior technical schools were ones which derived originally from the field of further education. The recommendation was that this 'tripartite' system in administrative matters should be replaced by a single code for all secondary schools. The Hadow Report envisaged the possibility of at least eight different kinds of secondary school: the secondary, or grammar school; the secondary school with a vocational bias; the junior technical school; the trade school; the selective central school, the secondary modern school which would cater only for the children left after a double 'creaming off' to grammar and central schools; the secondary modern school which would serve an area where only one layer of cream was removed; and the senior classes in elementary schools where re-organization proved impossible. The Spens Report dropped the category of secondary-school-with-a-bias because they thought that all secondary schools should offer courses with a vocational bias: it wanted select junior technical schools to be promoted to the category of technical high schools: it left the trade schools still to play a minor part in the scheme of things: it was not concerned with any other type of school, but there is one remark in the report which clearly envisages that there would be both selective and non-selective modern schools. The tripartite principle might be regarded as just a simplification of the various suggestions in the Hadow and Spens Reports, but it involved important changes in the conceptions of all three types of school.

The Hadow Committee, with their suggestions for selective and non-selective modern schools and for senior classes, were more concerned with the grading of schools according to the length of course offered and the abilities of their pupils than they were with the separation of secondary schools by function. They assumed that the existing Secondary (grammar) schools would continue to provide a predominantly literary and scientific curriculum, but seem to have hoped that they would develop other courses too. They assumed that the selective central schools would be kept in being, indeed they seem to have intended that any area large enough to support both types should have both selective and non-selective modern schools. They went on to counter the possible objection that children who did not qualify for admission either to a secondary school or to a central school should not receive a 'secondary' education at all. They asserted that

'the desirability of schools which will offer advanced instruction to children who do not pass to selective post-primary schools is not, we think, open to question. Even when places in the latter, and in the Secondary school of the existing type, are more numerous than they are today, it seems probable that there will still be a considerable number of children who, for one reason or another, are somewhat slower and more backward than their fellows. For such children it would be discouraging and depressing to enter a school where they always found difficulty in keeping pace with the work of other pupils, and for them it is therefore advisable to contemplate the provision of a school where the pace will be somewhat slower, and where practical work will play an even larger part in the curriculum than it does in the Central Schools of today.'[1]

The pattern in the Committee's mind seems to have been not dissimilar to the post-primary provision made in Scotland with its Secondary and its advanced division courses (but with provision within the secondary sphere for 'non-qualifiers'). Yet, if so, the unit was to be the school and not the course within the school: the pattern was that of urban Scotland and not of the rural omnibus school. As the Ministry of Education were later to claim, 'Past experience shows that schools with a limited and well-defined aim are the most likely to succeed in reaching and maintaining the highest standards within the particular field they serve'.[2] The possibility of multilateral schools is not mentioned in the Hadow Report.

[1] Hadow Report, *The Education of the Adolescent*, 1926, p. 89.
[2] Pamphlet No. 9, p. 22.

CHAPTER TWELVE

The Post-war English Grammar School

THE ECONOMIC CLIMATE

When the 1944 Act was being debated the doctrine of tripartitism coloured all discussion of secondary education. The Ministry of Education's pamphlet, *The Nation's Schools*, published in 1945, nevertheless marks several changes of emphasis from pre-war days. So far as the grammar schools are concerned it repeats the Spens view that they should play a less important part than they had done before the war – because the increase in numbers had led to the admission of children who could not benefit from a predominantly literary and scientific curriculum, and because the popularity of the grammar schools was diverting the brains of the country into white collar jobs instead of into industry and commerce. (It also adds a new reason for hoping that the grammar schools would prove less attractive in future compared with other types: the grammar school led to white collar jobs which were relatively safe in times of unemployment, but the welfare state would remove the fears of unemployment which had hitherto kept people out of less secure kinds of work.) But it carried overtones of the Norwood Report in seeing the grammar schools as the place for intellectually demanding courses leading mainly to the universities and other courses of further education of university standard: indeed it goes further than the Norwood Report in regarding the grammar school course as one 'providing a coherent and unified programme of studies for pupils from the age of 11 to 18, and at the same time a course as reasonably complete as is possible for those who will continue to leave at 16'.[1] The sixth form is no longer to be a separate stage tacked on to the main school, and its requirements seem likely to influence the work of the lower school even at the expense of a slightly unsatisfactory curriculum for those who leave without taking a sixth form course.

The Norwood Report had succeeded in its main object of freeing the grammar schools from the task of providing suitable courses for every child who might want, for any reason, to continue his or her secondary education beyond the age of fifteen. The economic climate has also been very much in the schools' favour. The Spens Committee had been told that 'the capacity of the professions in the widest sense to absorb the product of secondary schools is less than it was, and may be further reduced'.[2] The Central Advisory Council's report on *Early Leaving* in 1954 still thought it necessary to warn that 'it is unrealistic to encourage some boys and girls to imagine that they are entitled to follow certain

---

[1] Pamphlet No. 1, 1945, p. 16.   [2] Spens Report, 1938, p. 144.

sorts of superior careers',[1] by offering them a type of education which goes beyond their economic expectations, but at least the report had 'no hesitation, so far as employment openings are concerned, in expanding the science sixth forms as much as possible'. It could also point to the fact that most of the professions had recast their entrance qualifications in terms of the General Certificate of Education in such a way as to make it possible to qualify either by the possession of ordinary level passes or by a combination of ordinary and advanced level passes, and it seemed clear to them that an education up to at least sixth form standard was highly desirable as a background for entrants to the professions. As regards commercial work, too, the attitude had changed. A considerable proportion of grammar school leavers still found their way into office work – particularly those who left at about the age of sixteen, but it was now felt to be a matter for regret that 'a good deal of the work is inevitably of a character which would not fully extend boys and girls of the best grammar school calibre'. By the time of publication of the Crowther Report five years later the emphasis had swung completely – beyond a concern whether the products of the sixth forms would find suitable employment to a fear lest they should not all be able to secure admission to the universities or other institutions of higher education.

But, much as the economic situation has changed since the thirties, and much as scientific and technological developments have increased the demand for well-educated men and women, one of the most important factors in the growth of the grammar schools in the past two decades has been the need for more teachers. It has been the needs of the teaching profession itself which have largely contributed to the success story of the grammar schools. Perhaps it is not in the actual number of recruits required for the profession that the chief importance of this factor lies. It may well be that many parents have been prepared to let their children stay on at school because of the comforting knowledge that, though they might aim at some other career and fail, yet they could always fall back on teaching in the last resort. The willingness of the teaching profession to take in graduates in almost any subject means that there is always a second line of defence, and promotes a sense of security which may have its importance in the growth of higher education. The report on *Early Leaving* spoke comfortingly of the continuing shortage of teachers, and the Crowther Report urged the needs of the teaching profession as one of the main reasons for developing what it described as 'Sixth forms with a difference'. The ninth report of the National Advisory Council on the Training and Supply of Teachers (1965) recognized how far this development had gone by posing the question whether the educational system could justify the absorption of such a large proportion of its own products as would be necessary to staff the schools by accepted standards in the 1970s and 1980s.

[1] *Early Leaving*, 1954, p. 2.

SIXTH FORMS WITH A DIFFERENCE

Crowther's sixth forms with a difference are the old 'general sixth' in a new guise and form part of a quite different pattern of sixth forms. When, in 1938, the Board of Education's pamphlet on the sixth form had encouraged the schools to offer more general courses, the number of sixth form pupils proceeding straight from school to the universities had accounted for just under ten per cent of all leavers from the sixth forms. By the date of the Crowther Report the universities were taking just over one half of the boys and between one third and a quarter of the girls from the sixth forms.

Since the war the sizes of sixth forms have been steadily increasing, even though they still do not, on average, compare with the sixth forms of the independent schools. The Crowther Report gives the following figures derived from detailed inquiries from a sample of schools of all kinds.

TABLE 23. *Sizes of sixth forms 1952 and 1959*

			Sixth Forms		No. of schools with	
	No. of Schools	Year	Range in Size of Sixth	Average No. of pupils	less than 20 pupils	20–39 pupils
Maintained schools:						
Boys'	36	1952	8-137	52	6	4
		1959	13–178	79	1	3
Girls'	38	1952	5–99	39	8	13
		1959	12–134	56	2	7
Mixed	26	1952	2–76	33	7	10
		1959	22–130	61	0	7
All maintained schools	100	1952	2–137	41	21	27
		1959	12–178	65	3	17
Independent schools:						
Boys'	23	1959	56–303	165	—	—
Girls'	18	1959	8–79	43	4	3

'General' sixth form courses before the war were usually only one-year courses and were not intended to lead to the Higher School Certificate. The 1954 report on *Early Leaving* gives the first accurate figures available of the extent to which grammar school pupils were attracted to the general courses – which for this purpose were defined as sixth form courses not leading to presentation for the advanced levels. A survey was undertaken of just over 4,000 boys and just over 4,000 girls who were attending, or had attended, a grammar school. Rather more than half the sample were still at school at the time of the survey, and of these 4.1 per cent of the boys in attendance at boys' schools were following a general sixth form course compared with 31.8 per cent of the girls who were pupils at a girls' school. (The percentage of all pupils, boys and girls, in mixed schools who were in a general sixth was 13.8.) Head teachers were asked, in respect of all children in the survey (whether they had left school or were still in attendance), to state which of the courses offered by the school would have been the most suitable if they had stayed at school to take the course for which their ability best fitted them. The distribution of replies was as follows:

TABLE 24. *General sixth form courses*

RECOMMENDED COURSE	Boys	Girls
	%	%
Sixth form course leading to two 'A' levels	37.1	28.3
General sixth form course	6.7	22.5
Ordinary level only	56.2	49.2
All pupils in the sample	100	100

Two-thirds of the boys' schools covered by the sample had no general sixth form course at all. Those that had, had only small groups of boys following it, and only one course in a boys' school had any distinctive vocational aim. In the girls' schools the general courses were designed specifically for girls who intended to take up such careers as teaching and nursing for which, although ordinary level passes would suffice, one or two A level subjects would be an advantage, and which, in any case, prescribed a minimum age of eighteen for admission to further training so that there was every incentive to stay on in the sixth form even if prospects of success in two A level subjects were not very bright.

Among its recommendations for persuading more pupils to stay longer at grammar schools the report on *Early Leaving* suggested that there should be less of a break between the main school and the sixth form, and that more pupils should be given a foretaste of sixth form work before the age of sixteen (as the reorganization of the examinations allowed and the report of the Secondary School Examinations Council had advocated when the G.C.E. was introduced in 1951). The report also thought that there was scope for an increase in the number of general courses for girls and hoped that the schools would be prepared to experiment with such courses for boys. By 1959, however, there were signs that things were about to change. A subcommittee of the Secondary School Examinations Council examined a proposal that a new 'General level' of the G.C.E. should be introduced at a standard intermediate between the existing O and A levels, and suitable for those staying in the sixth form but with no intention of going on to a university. They rejected the idea mainly on the grounds that the new level of certificate might attract many who could, and should, aim higher and take the advanced level.

So we come to the Crowther Report's sixth forms with a difference. The report distinguished three types of course in the sixth form which might be taken mainly by girls intending to enter teachers' training colleges. There was the 'earlier pattern' of general course which might include one or two additional subjects to be taken on the O level plus a selection of subjects to be studied, not for examination, but because they appealed to the individual pupil or might be thought to be useful to her in her chosen career. There was the full academic course leading to two A levels. And there was an intermediate type of course. This would essentially be of two years' duration, unlike the older type of general course which was usually only for one year. It would also be of a different composition in that it would give especial prominence to one or two subjects which would attract more time and more attention because of the relatively extensive syllabus and difficult examinations involved. It would aim at the advanced level, even though some of the pupils might not in fact pass the examination.

'A course of this type seems to us appropriate for the great run of ordinary candidates for training college places including most of the academically weaker ones who, in the past, have followed the earlier pattern. The only rider necessary to safeguard their interests is that, while it may be appropriate for them to take an advanced level course in one or two subjects, we do not think they should be automatically excluded from a training college if they fail to secure a pass.'[1]

In short the sixth form with a difference became not so much a development of the earlier type of general course as a full academic course which differs from the standard sixth form course only in that some of the pressure is off: there is no need to be sure of a pass at A level (and certainly no need to get a pass with credit or distinction) in order to secure admission to a course of professional training, and the choice of subjects to be taken is not rigidly controlled by faculty requirements and the like.[2]

The Robbins Report on Higher Education in 1963 gives ample confirmation of this trend in the sixth forms. It records that 'in recent years' the proportion of sixth form boys who are preparing for, or have already passed, in at least two advanced level subjects has been constant at about ninety eight per cent or more. The proportion of girls aiming at, or having achieved, two A levels rose from eighty-seven per cent in 1957–58 to ninety per cent in 1960–61.

It seems clear that the role of the grammar school in providing literary and scientific courses up to the age of eighteen is for the present much more secure than it has ever been before. The great fear of comprehensive secondary education has always been that it would lead to a dilution of this role. Such fears have by no means been entirely allayed, but they should have been calmed a little, although the comprehensive debate may have led the grammar schools to exaggerate their academic purity.

[1] Crowther Report, 1959, p. 306.   [2] See also Chapter 22; Specialization.

CHAPTER THIRTEEN

Tripartitism since the War

PARITY OF ESTEEM

The Ministry's first pamphlet, *The Nation's Schools*, also marked a change of emphasis in its attitudes to the secondary modern schools. These schools are now seen as typically non-selective. Forgotten are the more refined gradings of schools of the pre-war reports. The advantages or disadvantages of the selective central school are not discussed, but the assumption obviously is that the modern schools will take all the children who do not gain admission to a grammar or technical school. This, too, is linked with assumptions about the future needs of industry and society which the event has proved to be false. It is said that, as the mechanization of industry increases, there will be an increasing need for highly skilled operatives (supplied by the grammar and technical schools) but there will be a growing field of routine and repetitive process work so that the modern schools will have to act on the assumption that the majority of their pupils will get no satisfaction at all from their work in later life.

Post-war developments in the secondary modern schools show how wrong were some of the assumptions made in 1945. To some extent they have taken upon themselves the pre-war functions of both the grammar and the technical schools. They should be encouraged, said the Ministry of Education in 1958, to develop courses leading to technical apprenticeships, to careers in commerce, to nursing, etc.

The introduction of the G.C.E. in 1951 with a pass standard for the ordinary level at about the standard of a credit pass in the School Certificate, coupled with the prescription of a minimum age of sixteen for presentation, had been expected to put the external examination designed for grammar school pupils well beyond the range of children in secondary modern schools. The hope was that the G.C.E. would gradually become a genuine school leaving certificate and that, as the grammar schools abandoned the practice of using it as an entrance test for their sixth forms, the minimum age for presentation, and therefore the standard of the O level pass, could be raised. The fact that the grammar schools continued to use the examination in very much the same way as they had used the old School Certificate left the way open for the modern schools to surprise the administrators by achieving considerable success at the ordinary level, and even in a few cases at the advanced level.

The result is a blow to the pure doctrine of tripartitism. It is not merely that the dividing line between schools shifted. The dividing line is now seen to be rather less definite. It is no longer sufficient that there should be opportunity for transfer from one school to another for children who are obviously a misfit in one type of school. There still needs to be that opportunity but

'transfers can never be anything but exceptions to the normal rule and there must be – and be seen to be – opportunities in all the secondary schools, and not just in the grammar and technical schools, for boys and girls to go forward to the limits of their capacity. The essential conditions of success are that all secondary schools should be enabled to be good in their own ways, and that there must be full recognition that, where separate grammar and modern schools exist, there will be an overlap in the capacity of the pupils and that therefore the courses offered must overlap also.'[1]

This was no more than a recognition by a Minister of Education who was still defending the tripartite doctrine of the proven fact that some pupils of secondary modern schools could be presented at the ordinary level of the G.C.E. and could acquit themselves as well as some grammar school pupils. But the breach was made. The next step was for the Ministry, albeit very reluctantly, to accept the notion of a national examination below the level of the G.C.E. – and then to equate a good performance in the new examination to a pass on the G.C.E. ordinary level.

THE CERTIFICATE OF SECONDARY EDUCATION

Even before the secondary modern schools existed at all in England, a majority of the witnesses who submitted evidence to the Hadow Committee were opposed to the establishment of any special external examination, mainly on the ground that the institution of a public test of the schools' work would adversely affect the free development of their curricula. On balance, however, the committee themselves came down in favour of the eventual introduction of an examination to be taken at about the age of fifteen. One of the reasons they gave for this was that, in default of a recognized examination of their own, the schools would attempt to push too many of their pupils through the School Certificate, and for the majority of them this would be a quite unsuitable test. But the Report, though favouring a new examination, recommended that its introduction should be postponed for a period of at least three years to give the new schools time to settle down. In the event the postponement was long enough to run into a period during the 'thirties and early 'forties when external examinations, even for grammar school pupils, were in disrepute. The debate over the advantages and disadvantages of external examinations in which the arguments aired by the Hadow Committee set the main lines, continued until the mid 1950s. Meanwhile, however, such bodies as the Royal Society of Arts, the College of Preceptors and the Union of Lancashire and Cheshire Institutes, whose examinations were being taken by the pupils of many central schools and some senior elementary schools back in 1926, continued to attract the support of many schools in spite of the fact that the Hadow Report had described them as

[1] *Secondary Education for All – A New Drive* 1958 (Cmnd. 604), p. 6.

unsuitable. In this, too, Hadow merely foreshadowed the grand debate of the fifties.

The continued activity of the unofficial examining bodies, coupled with the initiative of one or two local education authorities in establishing regional examinations in cooperation with the teachers in their schools (e.g. the scheme for South West Hertfordshire) forced the Ministry to show some interest in the prospect of examinations below the level of the G.C.E. In 1955 they opened a public discussion by the issue of circular 289 inviting people to submit their views on the question to the Minister. The circular however, set out the Ministry's own very definite opinion that the standard of the G.C.E. ordinary and advanced levels should be maintained, that they did not favour the establishment of any new general examination, but that further experiments by local groups of schools in conducting their own examinations were to be welcomed. The Ministry appeared to have the whip hand in that they made it clear that they proposed no alteration in the grant regulations which prohibited the schools from entering any pupil under the age of sixteen for any external examination other than the G.C.E.

Two years later, having considered the response to circular 289, the Ministry issued circular 326 in which their own earlier views were substantially upheld, but the door was left open for further discussion, and in particular the Secondary School Examinations Council and the Central Advisory Council were invited to give closer attention to the problem.

The Beloe Committee (a sub-committee of the S.S.E.C.) reported against a background of a rapidly accelerating increase in the number of secondary modern schools presenting their pupils for some kind of external examination. The number presenting for the G.C.E. was by this time considerable. It was matched by the number preparing pupils for other examinations, many of them taken in the pupils' fourth year, i.e. at about the age of fifteen. That this was in apparent contravention of the Ministry's regulations was explained by the fact that the children were not entered for the examinations officially by the schools, but were presented by their parents (with or without the direct connivance or encouragement of the schools, but presumably much more frequently with it than without). Thus the spirit, if not the letter, of the regulations was being broken. No national figures were available of the extent to which the schools were preparing their pupils for the examinations but, out of a sample of 272 schools replying to a questionnaire, which included 164 secondary modern schools, 81 grammar, 12 secondary technical and 15 comprehensive schools, the following numbers had entered candidates (or permitted their pupils to enter):

TABLE 25. *Schools preparing for external examinations: England*

	1946	1950	1954	1958	
G.C.E.	78	80	95	123	} out of a total of 272
Other than G.C.E.	18	22	53	133	

In their fourth report the Secondary School Examinations Council supported the recommendations made by their sub-committee and gave additional information about the increase in the habit of secondary modern schools of submitting their pupils for external examinations. The following figures relate only to examinations taken by pupils in their fifth year of secondary education:

TABLE 26. *Pupils taking external examinations: England*

	1958	1959	1960
G.C.E.	8,700	12,800	17,400
College of Preceptors Senior Certificate	50	100	200
London Chamber of Commerce	11,000	11,000	11,000
R.S.A. School Certificate	3,900	6,800	8,600
East Midlands Educational Union	—	—	400
Union of Educational Institutes	700	1,600	3,400
Union of Lancashire and Cheshire Institutes	1,900	3,300	4,600
Total (nearest thousand)	26,000	36,000	46,000

In addition many schools were said to be presenting pupils for external examination at the end of their fourth year, so that they were able to leave school at, or shortly after, the end of their compulsory schooling, in possession of a certificate.

The schools had not planned for this: they had not devised courses from the age of eleven with the expectation that some pupils would prepare for external examinations. It would seem that the majority of children made the decision to stay on as late as the beginning of their third, or even of their fourth, year in the secondary school. The Crowther Report expressed the view that extended courses must have an entirely beneficial effect on the whole school, but it is clear from what was said on this score that the usual way of introducing an extended course had been to graft it on to the existing three-to-four-year course:

'There is a new seriousness about work because there is a recognisable purpose to it; recognisable, that is, to pupils and parents as well as to teachers. The outward and visible signs of this new attitude is the introduction of homework, often enough at the request of parents. At first homework and hard work may be confined to the last year or two, but it does not take long to realise that a G.C.E. course, for instance, cannot be improvised on top of three years of very much less arduous work than the abler grammar school boy or girl has had to put in.'[1]

This has, of course, been realized by teachers as well as by pupils and their parents, and, particularly where an extended course has been directed towards the G.C.E. so that existing examination syllabuses have had to be adopted, headteachers have been faced with the problem of deciding how early they can select their G.C.E. classes.

The conclusion reached was that the question of a new examination had been

[1] *15 to 18*, p. 91.

taken out of official hands. The schools were in fact using these examinations, and no attempt to stop them would be effective. Some of the examinations were deemed to be unsuitable, and it was felt that the practice of presenting pupils for external examination at the end of their fourth year was of doubtful value. The only course of action therefore was to provide an official examination, suitable for pupils in their fifth year, and more under the control of the teaching profession, in the hope that schools would thereby be persuaded to turn from some of the less-well-conducted examinations and that the pupils would be attracted to stay at school for an additional year. The Secondary School Examinations Council said:

'The great majority, if not practically all, of the pupils remaining for a fifth year in the schools in question are being entered for external examinations. In this connection we would also draw attention to the information given in our Committee's Report which showed that a number of schools not yet using external examinations in 1958 had plans for doing so shortly, and indicated that the addition of these would bring the proportion of schools entering pupils for external examinations to over 80 per cent of the schools in their sample enquiry. If these findings are even approximately valid, we would submit that the time is already past when it serves a useful purpose to debate *whether* these pupils in their fifth year should be externally examined. The question is *how* they should be examined.'[1]

The Council confirmed, too, their Committee's view that the G.C.E. was only suitable for about twenty per cent of the age group. They conceded that some who were well below the top twenty per cent at eleven plus would achieve good results in the G.C.E. at sixteen: but by the same token some who were in the top twenty per cent at eleven would only obtain poor results in the G.C.E. They submitted as a working approximation that about twenty per cent of pupils aged sixteen might be expected to achieve a useful number of O level passes at the age of sixteen, on the assumption that four or more passes was a fair criterion of success. They quoted in support of this view some figures from six comprehensive schools: in the best of them fifty per cent of the pupils had been presented for the O level; forty-five per cent had achieved one or more passes, but only twenty-two per cent had passed in four or more subjects.

The Ministry capitulated. They have even made a virtue of necessity, and are taking a lively interest in the new examination. The new Certificate of Secondary Education will be taken in the fifth year, and is designed so that the next twenty per cent of children below the G.C.E. group may be expected to achieve four or more passes and up to a further twenty per cent attempt the examination in individual subjects. Passes in the C.S.E. are to be graded as they are in the G.C.E., and the intention is that a very good pass in the C.S.E. shall be approximately equivalent to a pass in the same subject in G.C.E.

The introduction of the C.S.E. causes some problems. One is the extent to which the pupils of grammar schools should be permitted to take it. Some fears

The Certificate of Secondary Education, Fourth Report of S.S.E.C., 1961, p. 5.

have been expressed that a softer option may tempt some of them away from the G.C.E. The implication of this, even more clearly than of the success of some secondary modern school pupils in the G.C.E., is that, whether or not the modern schools have achieved parity of esteem, it is now recognized that the range of ability catered for by the two types of school overlaps considerably. And, already there is talk of abandoning the G.C.E. and replacing it with the C.S.E. once the new examination has proved itself.

THE NEWSOM REPORT

The other problem is that the introduction of an examination which brings a majority of secondary school pupils within the examinable range may enhance the feeling of inferiority among those who can never aspire to take an external examination with any hope of success. The optimism of the Newsom Report may counterbalance criticism of the C.S.E. on this score.

'We have been impressed by what the schools have achieved since the concept of secondary education for all was initiated. We have been particularly struck by the steady growth in the standards of literacy, and there is no sign that the rate of improvement is slackening. But there is some evidence that young people of the same ability who attend recognised private schools and remain there in small classes until well beyond the statutory leaving age can achieve standards very different from those normally found. Moreover in many other countries the pupils remain at school till a later age than in the United Kingdom. From this we deduce that it is not possible to generalise about the capacity of the average and below average until we have had an opportunity of keeping them at school for a longer period and in smaller classes.'[1]

But the most remarkable change of heart is to be found in the Foreword to the Report. 'The essential point', writes the Minister of Education, 'is that all children should have an equal opportunity of acquiring intelligence.' This has all the appearance of having been planted deliberately. In a country where Ministers of Education do not make *ex cathedra* statements about psychological theory it is nevertheless possible for the ministerial blessing of an advisory council report to imply the decent burial of old dogmas about intelligence.

The Newsom Report asks that the schools should use with children of average and less than average ability some of the practices which they have long used with abler pupils. They should

'allow the pupils themselves some choice in the subjects they study and in the kind of programme they follow. This is not uncommon now for the abler boys and girls, but in many schools it would be a revolutionary step so far as "our" pupils are concerned.'

And:

[1] Newsom Report, *Half Our Future*, 1963, p. xiv.

'The abler pupils in secondary schools are regularly required to do a substantial amount of homework, which considerably lengthens their working day. But large numbers of pupils, and the majority of "our" pupils, commonly do none. We are strongly of the opinion that all boys and girls would profit from undertaking some work for themselves outside what is done in lessons.'[1]

But, if the modern schools are being recommended to duplicate some of the work of the grammar schools and to emulate some of their methods, the Newsom recommendation that they should provide courses in the later years of the secondary stage with some vocational bias suggests that they may also be usurping the role of the secondary technical school. Up to a point this is so, even though the Newsom recommendations refer to a range of ability below that for which the technical schools, even before Spens and Norwood, were intended. But the insistence in Newsom that pre-vocational courses should emphatically be 'vehicles of general education' implies that they are to do the same kind of thing as is done in the technical schools as they have become and not as they were in the 1930s.

SECONDARY TECHNICAL SCHOOLS

Attention was directed in Chapter 10 to changes in the character of the pre-war grammar school which explain such apparent inconsistencies as the growth in the size of sixth forms without an equivalent increase in the numbers taking the Higher School Certificate. Attention has been drawn in the last few pages to changes in the character of the secondary modern schools by describing their growing use of external examinations. The story of secondary technical schools since the war must take account of both changes in the size and structure of the schools and their use of examinations.

Examinations

So long as they were closely associated with a technical college or with local industry the junior technical schools had no need of external examinations: they were able to recommend their pupils personally to the staff of a technical college who knew the value of their recommendations. On this point, as on so many others, the Spens and Norwood Reports took diametrically opposite stands. The Spens Committee were impressed by the fact that the schools had hitherto been wholly free from any system of external examination and by the emphatic statements of witnesses that this freedom had been an important and vital factor in the successful development of the schools. They thought, however, that in order to give reality to their recommendations for the complete equality of status between technical high schools and grammar schools, some kind of leaving certificate having general currency was required. As a compromise they suggested that the technical schools should have an internal system of examinations subject to external assessment by assessors approved or appointed by the

[1] Ibid., p. 33.

Board of Education. The Norwood Committee thought that the School Certificate had been so long associated in the public mind with the grammar schools that to retain it for that type of school only would prejudice the parity of esteem which they desired the technical and modern schools to enjoy. The alternatives were either that all forms of secondary school should normally look towards the school certificate examination – 'a hypothesis which is so out of relation to the needs of the Technical School, where an internal examination, we understand, is working well, and so inimical to the character and future development of the Modern School as to be unthinkable'[1] – or alternatively that external examinations should be abolished in all secondary schools. They took the view that the grammar schools should enjoy parity of esteem with the technical schools in being trusted to conduct their own internal examinations, though a period of experiment would be necessary before the School Certificate could be finally abandoned.

In fact things have worked out in the opposite direction to that in which the Norwood Report hoped that they would go. Examinations have become a more important feature of the educational scene, and the reorganization of the technical schools has brought them more into line with the grammar schools. In particular the growth in the numbers of non-grammar school pupils presented for the G.C.E. led to the formation of a 'ninth' examining board, the Associated Examining Board, as the only G.C.E. examining body not connected with the universities, for the specific purpose of providing a G.C.E. examination which would be exactly comparable in standard with the G.C.E. of the other eight boards, but with syllabuses more suited to the needs of secondary modern and technical schools.

The extent to which in recent years the pupils of secondary technical schools have become accustomed to taking the G.C.E. examination, and also the extent to which they find their way into apprenticeships in industry may be judged from the figures of leavers from the schools in 1962 given in Table 27.

TABLE 27. *Leavers from Secondary technical schools* 1962

	BOYS	%	GIRLS	%
Did not take G.C.E.	3,170	28	2,740	38
Attempted O level	6,500	57	4,030	55
Attempted A level	1,660	15	490	7
All leavers	11,330	100	7,260	100
Entered full-time Further Education[2]	1,800	16	1,050	14
Took apprenticeships	4,280	38	560	8
Entered other employment	5,250	46	5,650	78
All leavers	11,330	100	7,260	100

[1] Norwood Report, 1943, p. 46.
[2] Including those who took temporary employment before entering a course.

A recent apologist for the secondary technical school explains that

'the sixth form of the secondary technical school differs from that of the grammar school in that it acts more as a retrieving mechanism of ability and caters for pupils who wish to take O level subjects and to take other subjects for professional purposes including also the taking of foreign languages in intensive courses. In addition, subjects are taken at A level. But the sixth forms of secondary technical schools, accepting in so many cases pupils transferred at fifteen or sixteen from secondary modern and other schools, is not as homogeneous a unit as is the sixth form of a grammar school providing as it does almost exclusively, intensive courses of A level standard mainly for university purposes.'[1]

In fact the difference is probably not quite so marked as he suggested in those technical schools which have well established sixth forms, though the variations between technical schools are considerable. The Crowther Report stated that in 1958 just half of the technical schools in England had a sixth form. The average size was twenty-one (compared with sixty-five for grammar schools) and only ten per cent of the schools with sixth forms had more than fifty in the sixth (whereas in the grammar schools eighty per cent of the schools in the Crowther Report's sample had sixth forms of more than forty pupils). The 1958 figures showed that sixty-three per cent of the technical schools' sixth formers were taking courses leading to presentation in two or more A level subjects.

Raising the Sights

The statistics relating to secondary technical schools and their pupils which call for some explanation are set out in the following table:

TABLE 28. *Pupils in secondary technical schools*

Year	No. of technical schools	Total No. of pupils in technical schools	14-year-old pupils in technical schools as a percentage of all 14-year-olds
1922	86	12,206	0.6
1938	224	27,901	1.7
1946	317	66,454	?
1950	301	72,449	4.7
1962	220	97,411	2.8

In the last twelve years the number of secondary technical schools has dropped by eighty, the number of their pupils has increased by 25,000, yet the proportion of children attending them has fallen sharply. The explanation is quite simple. The increase in the total number of pupils is to be attributed to the extension of the age range of the schools: the whole of the increase between 1950

[1] R. Edwards, *The Secondary Technical School*, 1960, p. 22.

and 1962 was in pupils under the age of thirteen or over the age of fifteen. In every other respect the technical schools have been losing ground. By far the most important factor has been the lowering of the normal age of admission from thirteen plus to eleven plus, to bring the schools into line with other secondary schools. Of the total increase of 25,000 in the number of pupils in the schools, eleven and twelve year olds account for 18,000. At the same time, the schools have ceased to be junior appendages of technical colleges and have become ordinary secondary schools comparable with other secondary schools, and with far less of a distinctive flavour about them. Some of the new technical schools with post-war buildings are very difficult to distinguish in their planning and equipment from grammar schools and their staffs tend to have less industrial experience than did the staffs of the old junior technical schools. Moreover in all technical schools there has been a marked tendency to increase the variety of course offered. Of the two hundred junior technical schools just before the war about half were preparing their pupils for one or more groups of industries and the other half were more specialized, training their pupils for a particular industry and variously known as trade schools, junior commercial schools or junior housewifery schools. The available courses included courses in engineering, building, nautical work, book production, boot and shoe manufacture, cabinet making, catering, hairdressing, the meat trades, photo-engraving and photography, silversmithing and jewellery, tailoring and dressmaking, millinery, corset making, embroidery, upholstery, domestic service and laundrywork. Direct training for particular industries has now been abandoned, and many of the more specialized courses have been dropped. The crafts now offered in secondary technical schools include woodwork and metalwork, building, plumbing, brickwork, plastering, painting and decorating, pottery, weaving, spinning, fabric printing and bookcraft. These are still much more specific than the technical courses offered in Scottish secondary schools but, compared with the pre-war English technical school, the courses are undoubtedly broader. Probably the best single indication of the change of attitude is that, whereas the original junior technical school was typically single sex, and mixed schools were almost unknown, the two hundred odd schools at present include no less than eighty-eight mixed schools.

The age range has also been extended upwards. The original junior technical school was confined by regulation to courses finishing at about the age of sixteen. From the Norwood Report onwards the intention has been that selected technical schools, if not all, should develop sixth forms comparable with those of the grammar schools, and in the last twelve years the technical schools have, during a period of rapid expansion of courses for older children in all types of secondary schools, increased their share of the number of pupils over the age of sixteen still in full time attendance at school from 5.6 per cent to 6.6. per cent.

The secondary technical school is no longer a place for vocational training. In this respect the 1945 pamphlet *The Nation's Schools* had foreseen quite clearly that it would be different from the junior technical school of pre-war days:

'Its aim is not to produce little engineers or builders nicely adjusted to strict industrial requirements, but rather, through the interest created by a curriculum with a broad relation to future careers, to send out pupils equipped with a good general education that will stand them in good stead in whatever occupation they may enter, and will certainly enable them to embrace skilled employment with interest and competence.'[1]

Where secondary technical schools still exist they do just that – and a little more. 'Skilled employment' now comes some way down the hierarchy of industrial life, and the secondary technical schools see their task as including the education of the future technician and technologist. It is in this raising of their sights to provide a road to the technological faculties of the universities that, as any Scot could have foreseen, they have removed the justification for their own existence.

THREE PARTS OR TWO?

The tripartite system, even before the Labour government was returned to power in 1964, was beginning to disintegrate (if it can be said ever to have existed). Nevertheless there were many who at least clung to its familiar nomenclature. In the Ministry of Education statistics for 1962, for example, the explanation was given that 'secondary education is provided broadly speaking in three types of school – the secondary modern, the secondary grammar and the secondary technical'. This in spite of the fact that the statistics themselves showed that the approximate distribution of children of secondary school age in maintained schools was as follows:

TABLE 29. *Percentage of pupils in the several types of secondary school: England 1962*

Secondary modern schools	59
Secondary grammar schools	25
Secondary technical schools	4
Other types of secondary school	12
All secondary pupils	100

It is difficult to trace the development of secondary schools of different types in England and Wales since the war because of changes in classification in the Ministry's statistics, as the following comparison between the pattern of provision in 1950 and in 1962 will suggest:

[1] p. 16.

TABLE 30. *Types of secondary school: England*

TYPE AS GIVEN IN MINISTRY STATISTICS:	1950		1962	
	No. of schools	No. of pupils (nearest hundred)	No. of schools	No. of pupils (nearest hundred)
Secondary modern	3,227	1,095,200	3,889	1,676,000
Secondary grammar	1,192	503,000	1,287	708,300
Secondary technical	301	72,500	220	97,400
Grammar-technical	8	3,600	included with grammar schools	
Bilateral: Modern-grammar	19	7,600		
Modern-technical	4	2,300	63	45,300
Multilateral	4	3,500		
Comprehensive	10	8,000	152	157,500
—	—	'Other types'	269	151,300
All types of secondary schools	4,765	1,695,683	5,880	2,835,712

The Ministry may not have abandoned the tripartite way of thinking. But, by giving up the separate classification of technical streams in bilateral and multilateral schools they indicated some awareness of the trend in English education to become bipartite rather than tripartite. This trend has been emphasized with the introduction of the C.S.E. Even bipartitism as practised (or at any rate preached) in the past few years is much more flexible than the pure doctrine of tripartitism ever was, and the number of multilateral and comprehensive schools has grown rapidly.

CHAPTER FOURTEEN

Secondary Education in Scotland

1903–1939

Chapter 10 traced the growth of numbers in English Secondary schools after 1904. Scottish Secondary schools also were originally encouraged to establish a four year course and this was lengthened in 1911 when the course leading to the Leaving Certificate was extended to five years. There is no point in trying to make exact comparisons between the two types of Secondary school because the Scottish schools did not have an 'advanced' course beyond the Leaving Certificate. Nevertheless the same general tendency both to increase the Secondary provision made and to extend the usual length of Secondary school life is suggested by the figures in Table 31:

TABLE 31. *Fifth and sixth forms: Scotland*

	(a) No. of pupils in Secondary schools	(b) No. of pupils in Fifth and Sixth year	(b) as a percentage of (a)
1911–12	36,452 (Higher grade and Secondary)	1,772 (post- intermediate)	4.9
1925–26	74,448	6,576	8.8
1934–35	92,654	7,715	8.3
1935–36	92,075	7,912	8.7
1936–37	90,875	8,333	9.2
1937–38	90,984	8,459	9.3

The actual number of Secondary schools did not increase in Scotland: it remained more or less constant at around the two hundred and fifty mark, but the number of pupils, and in particular the number of older pupils, went on growing.

As in England, the number of pupils in the top forms of the schools – in the fifth and sixth years – grew faster than the number of pupils aged sixteen, seventeen, and eighteen. The ability of the primary schools to put their pupils through the qualifying examination and get them into the secondary departments earlier was probably an even greater factor than in England in enabling children to reach the Leaving Certificate stage younger than before. But the number of Leaving Certificates actually awarded did go on rising more or less in hand with the numbers in the upper classes of the schools and did not, as with the Higher School Certificate, reach a limit.

The higher grade of the Leaving Certificate cannot, however, be compared with the English Higher School Certificate. Nor were there any interesting developments in Scottish sixth forms which can be set beside those in England because Scottish schools do not have sixth forms. The post-leaving certificate year, the 'sixth year' in Scottish schools, was only taken before the war by those who had already got their 'group'; they would be working for the university bursary (open scholarship) examinations. Sixth year courses for other pupils were non-existent.

FIVE-YEAR COURSES

Just as English Secondary schools had inherited the traditions of both the division A and the division B schools of the pre-1904 regulations, so the Scottish Secondary system assimilated after 1903 some of the short-lived higher grade schools. This was of less significance because the higher grade schools had been so short-lived and because they had been seen to be outside the main stream of Scottish education. Courses for the Leaving Certificate were naturally governed mainly by the entrance requirements of the universities. Moreover in Scotland technical and commercial courses of certificate standard were necessarily integrated with the main school course and not grafted on after it. Pupils were eventually enabled to take a course with a technical or a practical bias leading to presentation in the Leaving Certificate, but some of the subjects they took would be common to the pre-university course. Technical courses in fact made little headway, but the commercial courses were more successful than in England.

The Scottish Education Department were constantly trying to persuade the schools to broaden their curricula, but one does not get the feeling of intense self-questioning which appears in the Spens Report. This is understandable. The English grammar schools were selective enough for them to feel that their pupils were an élite, enjoying educational advantages denied to others. So they felt aggrieved if many rejected the opportunities given them, either by leaving school early or by failing their School Certificate. At the same time, the door into the English grammar schools, though still narrow, had been perceptibly widened: the municipal grammar schools only dated from 1902; their growth had been rapid – perhaps too rapid. But in Scotland it was not merely that the schools were carrying on an academic tradition which was less open to question. They had, since 1918, when most of them had been made free, been carrying on a policy of generous access which had always been accompanied by a high wastage rate. Although far from indifferent to the fact that a majority of their pupils rejected learning, the schools were not unaccustomed to it. Children had to stay the full course to seventeen if they were to obtain the Leaving Certificate: they were more committed than their English contemporaries since they might thereby forfeit the chance of an apprenticeship or a trainee post in commerce for which sixteen was the upper age limit. So some of those who left school early could hardly be blamed. Yet something was being done to extend the schools' scope. Secondary education was not a mushroom growth: it had its roots in tradition but it could also adapt.

But there is more to it than that. There was no fear in Scotland that the academic type of secondary course would lead to over-production of intellectuals. with the implication that it would be healthier for the majority to receive some more down-to-earth training. On the contrary, few Scots appear to have believed that mental power might be fostered in some children through work with their hands rather than with their brains, or to have thought that a 'realistic' bias or trend should be given to the whole course of study for some children. All this was as foreign to Scottish ways of thinking before the war as was the feeling that different kinds of children needed to be taught in different kinds of schools. Mental growth was fostered by the traditional academic subjects. For an all-round education it might be desirable to undertake practical and aesthetic, as well as academic, studies. But it was just as natural for the able boy in a senior secondary school who wanted to take a technical course to continue with his study of French up to the higher grade as it was for the future language specialist to continue with mathematics.

THREE-YEAR COURSES

The same attitude is to be found in the design of the three year advanced division courses. It is worth quoting in full the introduction to the 1923 Code:

'The first and principal aim must be the continuance and development of general education on the moral and physical, no less than on the intellectual side. It is, therefore essential that every course should provide for training in Morals and Citizenship, for Music and for Physical Exercises. [This is identical with the statement in the Secondary School Code] Intellectual training can best be secured through a proper discipline in a selected number of the branches specified below. The main instruments here will be the English subjects together with Mathematics and Science and, as a rule, Drawing. These should be studied throughout, the amount of detail varying with the length of the course. General provision of this kind having been made for all, Education Authorities may reasonably proceed to take account of local conditions and of the needs and aptitudes of individual scholars to such extent as the circumstances of each school may require and its resources permit. The point at which any specialisation that may be attempted is begun, will depend partly on the length of the course and partly on the nature of the special subject to be studied. Normally the longer the course and the more definitely vocational the subject, the later will be the period to which specialisation is deferred.'

The curriculum prescribed in the Code for the three-year advanced divisions was as follows:

1. English, history and geography
2. Mathematics and science
3. Drawing

4. One or more of the following:
> (a) Practical subjects, e.g.
>> technical drawing, benchwork, mechanics
>> navigation, seamanship
>> gardening, agriculture, dairying
>> needlework, design, dressmaking
>> cookery, laundrywork, housewifery
>
> (b) Commercial subjects
>
> (c) A foreign language
>
> (d) Any other approved subject.

The Department were anxious that the advanced division courses should not be regarded simply as truncated versions of the full leaving certificate courses. But the regulations for the award of the Day School Certificate (Higher) followed very much the same pattern as those for the Leaving Certificate and the choices of subject made by the majority of pupils (or on their behalf by their parents and teachers) meant that the courses taken by most pupils in the three-year advanced division were not very different from the first two or three years of a five-year course. The Day School Certificate (Higher) was a group certificate which was awarded on the basis of performance in all the subjects taken. In 1932 the regulations were modified. The Department wrote:

'At present candidates are normally presented in five subjects, including either a foreign language or mathematics, or both. Experience has shown that for many pupils these requirements lead to over-pressure or to the neglect of subjects like music and physical exercises which are not tested by examination. The Department have accordingly decided that in future candidates need not be presented for examination in more than four subjects, though other subjects may continue to find a place in the curriculum.'

It continued to be compulsory for every candidate for the certificate to be presented in English, history and geography. But mathematics was no longer a compulsory subject, though every candidate had to take arithmetic; any candidate taking a foreign language had also to take algebra and geometry; so did any boy taking a technical course; and any pupil taking a commercial course had to take algebra. Science became completely optional and art or crafts became additional optional subjects. Perhaps a change of emphasis is indicated by the fact that the other options – technical subjects, housecraft, navigation, commercial subjects, a foreign language – were now described as 'the characteristic subjects of their course'.

It was in the same year, 1932, that the regulations for the Leaving Certificate were changed so that the second subject on the higher grade (after English) could be taken from the group of practical subjects. Thus the trend in the three-year course was the same as in the five-year course. The changes in the popularity of different subjects in the Leaving Certificate and the Day School Certificate (Higher) can be compared in Table 32.

TABLE 32. *Percentages of pupils offering certain subjects*

A. DAY SCHOOL CERTIFICATE (HIGHER)

	French	Latin	Art	Technical subjects	Commercial subjects	Domestic subjects	Science
1925–26	89	19	97	9	8	4	—
1935–36	67	18	67	15	16	11	—

B. SCOTTISH LEAVING CERTIFICATE
(BOTH LOWER AND HIGHER GRADE)

1927–28	97	65	19	—	0.3	0.8	48
1937–38	100	57	14	0.3	6	4	57

With the introduction of the new Code in 1939, and the expectation that the upper age of compulsory schooling would be raised to fifteen, the curriculum for the new three-year secondary course was virtually the same as that which had been prescribed for the Day School Certificate (Higher) in 1932. The Department explained the reasons behind the curriculum rather more fully than they had done before. They repeated that the course should not be regarded merely as an abbreviation of the leaving certificate course but 'as complete in itself and having a definite character of its own, determined by the length of the course and the local conditions'. It should offer a general education with English as the main instrument of culture. Aesthetic sensibility should be cultivated through music and art.

'While facilities may be offered for the study of languages other than English, it is not anticipated that this will be a general requirement. Some of the abler pupils, however, may find a knowledge of Latin or a modern foreign language an advantage, and it is necessary to leave the door open for those who may desire transference to the five year course.'[1]

Alongside an insistence on the importance of general education ran an equal insistence on the need for a realistic assessment of the children's abilities and of their vocational needs. Although they were careful not to lay down any fixed pattern, it seems clear that the Department thought that pupils who intended to leave school at fifteen should have made up their minds about the course they wanted to follow not later than the age of thirteen, and should be made to think about their futures even before that.

'The pupil's choice will be largely determined by his natural aptitudes and by the kind of employment which is common in the neighbourhood, or which he may desire to follow. With a view to determining at an early stage the most suitable type of course for individual children, efforts should be made from the time of entry on the secondary course to discover or develop the pupils' vocational desires. In these efforts the collaboration of the parents and of the teachers in the primary classes which the child has attended should be sought.'[2]

[1] *Memorandum Explanatory of the Day School Code* ,1939, p. 10.   [2] Ibid, p. 13.

The success of the three-year advanced division courses varied from area to area, but it seems clear that success went with the practical recognition given to the Day School Certificate in further education, or by employers, rather than with any belief that it gave a more appropriate type of education to some secondary pupils. The Department had been careful to ensure that the standard of the Certificate was no lower than that of the Intermediate Certificate with which employers were familiar, and the addition of vocationally useful subjects helped some to find employment. As H.M. Chief Inspector Mr Fraser wrote in 1934: 'a pupil who has obtained the Day School Certificate (Higher) with really good marks in commercial subjects need not fear comparison with others of like age who hold the commercial certificates of external examining bodies'.[1] In Arbroath, for example, the advanced division course with a commercial bias attracted a large number of pupils. Dundee, on the other hand was 'averse from the introduction of commercial or technical subjects in the academies except with a view to presentation for the Leaving Certificate, mainly because the number of suitable vacancies, at least in clerical posts, is relatively much smaller than in other towns of comparable size'.[2]

TWO-YEAR COURSES

The pattern of the two-year advanced division courses as outlined in the Code differed very little from that of the three-year courses. But a comparison between the subjects recorded on the Day School (Lower) Certificates which were awarded and those in the Higher Certificate suggests that the schools did have a rather different attitude towards pupils who were not going to stay at school much longer than they were compelled to. In 1925–26, for example, as many as forty-three per cent of the boys gaining the Lower Certificate had taken bench-work; thirty-nine per cent of the girls had taken needlework and dressmaking, and thirty-five per cent cookery and laundrywork. Even so, as many as nineteen per cent had taken French, and this proportion probably remained steady up to about 1930, after which it probably declined.

The system of Day School Certificates represented a well-designed attempt by the Scottish Education Department to foster the bipartite organization of courses which they had been advocating since 1903. In some schools it suceeded. In many, however, the three-year advanced division courses, stemming as they did from the former intermediate courses, were too often only a watered down version of the five-year leaving certificate courses. The two-year courses, in turn, were frequently only a watered-down version of the three-year courses. The Department wanted secondary education to be diversified: the Educational Institute of Scotland had, in the 'twenties, expressed the view that 'All post-qualifying education must be the same for all pupils'. Perhaps the compromise which was reached was that there were two types of course – one in preparation for the Leaving Certificate (which the pupils were expected to master), and another which was not very different (except that the pupils were not expected

---

[1] General Reports for the years 1930–33.   [2] Ibid.

to master it). At any rate this is the judgement which, in retrospect, many Scots themselves make of their pre-war secondary education.

SCOTTISH SECONDARY EDUCATION AFTER THE WAR

In 1947 the Advisory Council on Education in Scotland published a report on *Secondary Education* which called for a complete reorganization of the system by replacing the three- and five-year courses with four- and six-year courses. The omnibus school was advocated no longer simply as a matter of local expediency but because of 'the great gain on social as well as educational grounds if the country could get rid of segregation at twelve and, within a system of omnibus schools, preserve the unity of general secondary education up to the age of sixteen'. It is the choice of the age sixteen which is significant here. Not only did the report take into account the prospect of the age of compulsory schooling being raised to sixteen, it also recommended that Scotland should adopt an examination system very similar to that in England. There was to be a school certificate taken at sixteen and a higher school certificate taken at eighteen. The identification of a watershed at the age of sixteen was hailed with almost as much enthusiasm as that with which the Hadow Committee had discovered the eleven plus:

'Throughout the English speaking world there is now agreement that sixteen is the age at which general education should end, and within a reasonable period the full-time education of all Scottish children will be extended to that age. Sixteen is a kind of educational divide: till then, with due allowances for individual differences, the schooling remains one broad stream; thereafter its parcelled state reflects the developed differences in aptitude, interest and vocational needs of late adolescence. If there is to be a general assessment of the work of the school, here surely is the natural point at which to make it.'

There was a practical consideration, too, behind the recommendation:

'In England young people are certificated and ready for employment (in apprenticeships, and a great range of clerical, commercial and semi-professional work) at about sixteen: in Scotland at present they have the unsatisfactory choice between a truncated course and no certificate or an additional year which too often gives no adequate return. . . . Moreover it should be noted that the great majority of the professional associations themselves are content with the School Certificate in England, whereas in Scotland they are forced to demand the Senior Leaving Certificate, because there is nothing else.'

The Council thought that their recommendation would be 'as advantageous to the few as it would to the many, since it would give them at the post-certificate stage the stretching room and time to look about them which cannot be had in the brief year between the Senior Leaving Certificate and the university'.[1]

It is clear that their main preoccupation was, like that of the Spens Committee, not with the intellectually most able of secondary pupils but with the ordinary

[1] *Secondary Report*, p. 54.

run of children. Many of their statements are very reminiscent of the Spens Report ten years earlier. The curriculum of the secondary schools was criticized as being overcrowded; the schools should concern themselves with the bodily growth and well-being of their pupils; every child should be able to experience the quickening and development of mind which come from purposeful activity directed to concrete ends; the arts should give opportunity for aesthetic experience and appreciation; above all every aspect of secondary education should be tested by the question 'How does it stand related to the reality of adolescent life?' Like the Spens Report the Scottish Advisory Council's Report makes much of the three distinct phases of the learning process – the phase of romance, that of precision and the final phase of application, which had been postulated by Whitehead, Nunn and others. It even out-Spens Spens in its enthusiasm for project methods:

'Typical of informed but cautious opinion in this country is the oft-quoted verdict of the Spens Report, which, after admitting the seductiveness of the doctrine and the great value of the project in the teaching of young children goes on:

But our general doctrine forbids us to go much further than this: for its essence is that the school "subjects" stand for traditions of practical, aesthetic and intellectual activity, each having its own distinctive individuality, and we hold that the profit a pupil derives from them does not come from casual or episodical contacts, but by his being, so to speak, put to school to them, and so getting to make their outstanding characters part of the equipment and habit of his mind. If this is to happen, the subjects must be pursued as such – though we have urged that they should be pursued actively and not merely be assimilated by memory and understanding.

'The criticism has substance, and the high claim for systematic training is indeed vindicated in the finest products of the system, the relatively few in whom native aptitude and long study unite to produce the good fruits of a rounded education, be it mathematical or scientific, linguistic or historical. But as one passes in thought from the few to the many, to the thousands of ordinary children who in the class rooms of our land have been "put to school" to the subjects, a very different picture takes shape – of uninterested, restless boys and girls, drifting or muddling through the years of secondary schooling and, in many cases, carrying away at the last little more than gobbets of ill-digested knowledge and a distaste for what has yielded to little.'[1]

The aims of the Advisory Council were justified in so far as their strictures on the pre-war Scottish secondary schools were correct.

'For Scotland, secondary education still remains pre-eminently a schooling in academic subjects. Our educational past, the great influence of the universities, and the extent to which in a country of limited resources higher education has always been an education away from more active pursuits into the learned pro-

[1] Ibid., p. 25.

fessions – all these have combined to attach immense prestige to the traditional bookish curriculum and to the school which provides it. This alone would have imposed a heavy handicap on the short course schools in the years between the wars but the difficulty of establishing them in general regard has been aggravated by many other factors. . . . A big proportion of the headmasters and teachers appointed to the short course schools have themselves been in the older tradition, academically trained and partial to the familiar ways. Hence, in a situation where the only hope of success was with the pioneer, too many have kept close to the known paths, and, confronted with children who came to them unwillingly, found little to hold their interest and left at the earliest possible moment, they have tended to think that their professional lot was not an enviable one.'[1]

The report recommended that there should be no external examination for children who left school at fifteen. The outbreak of war had prevented the Junior Leaving Certificate from being introduced nationally, and the Council thought that in their short courses the schools should be free from the limitations imposed by examinations. They said that there was ample evidence that the fruitful development of the senior elementary schools in England owed much to the fact that they stood clear of external examinations; they recalled that very few children had been able to reach even the modest standards required for the Day School Certificate (Higher); and they felt that a certificate on a national standard was unnecessary for children who would usually go into local employment.

The report was followed up eight years later by a very full *Memorandum on Junior Secondary Education* published by the Scottish Education Department in 1955. This *Memorandum*, too, expressed the opinion that 'the effects of an external examination would be especially dangerous while junior secondary education is still striving to find how best to achieve its purpose'. In its general plea for a realistic approach, attention to individual differences, the fostering of a community spirit in the schools, etc. etc., the *Memorandum* spelled out in detail many of the principles suggested by the Advisory Council. But on the fundamental question of the integration of subjects through projects, etc. it was more cautious:

'Those who are most dissatisfied with the present results of junior secondary education have sometimes suggested that the traditional curriculum should be abandoned entirely and a fundamentally different system devised, in which few, if any, of the orthodox subjects would appear in anything like their present guise. Drastic action of this kind is neither necessary nor wise. An educational course based, for instance, on the study, not of the usual school subjects, but of topics or centres of interest, chosen for their relevance to everyday life, probably requires more favourable teaching conditions than could possibly be looked for in the majority of schools today. There is no reason why, so far as the curriculum is concerned, the aims of junior secondary education should not be achieved through a course of study organised broadly on present lines. The framework of subjects should probably be less rigid than it commonly is, and the detailed

[1] Ibid., p. 32.

content of the individual subjects should be carefully reviewed, but there are still cogent reasons for retaining the subjects themselves.'[1]

In their annual report for 1961 the Department devoted some space to a survey of junior secondary education. It was couched in the usual measured – not to say grudging – style with which the Department habitually write their general surveys of what the schools are doing:

'Some definite if limited progress has been made in pursuance of the aim of providing an education suited to the needs of pupils in junior secondary courses. Much thought has been given to the problem, and there has been a good deal of experiment in the presentation of subjects and in developing activities. These advances are greatly to be welcomed; yet a feeling of disappointment must remain that after five years progress is so slow and so uneven.'

The Department repeated their views on the value of the traditional curriculum:

'The curriculum provided in non-certificate courses includes almost invariably English, history, geography, mathematics, science, art, music, physical education, religious instruction, and one of the five groups of practical subjects – homecraft, technical subjects, commercial subjects, rural subjects, nautical subjects. In some areas girls taking commercial subjects may add French; and a foreign language – usually French but occasionally German – is sometimes studied by the abler boys' classes. The number of subjects may seem excessive for pupils who are not of the highest calibre, for it differs from the senior secondary curriculum only in its much smaller linguistic element. There are, however, strong grounds for the inclusion of each of those subjects at some stage in the course, but care has to be taken to adapt their treatment to the abilities of the pupils. In general the present balance of subjects appears to suit most pupils.'[2]

But, however disappointed the Department may be at the general pace of change in the junior secondary schools, there can be no denying that some individual schools have, in the last ten years, adopted much more flexible curricula than have ever been known in Scotland before: they have been prepared to organize projects, or introduce short courses of a pre-vocational nature, and rest content that the pupils should gain some experience of value from them, without being too much concerned that some of the ingredients of the traditional curriculum may thereby be lost. Perhaps it has helped them to do this that, in the hundred years since Scotland first tried to provide post-primary courses for children other than those aiming at the Leaving Certificate, it is only during the last twenty-five that such courses have not also led to an external examination.

THE FOURTH YEAR

Though the Advisory Council in their 1947 report advised against examinations for pupils who left school at fifteen, and though they were against external

---

[1] *Junior Secondary Education*, 1955, p. 13.
[2] *Education in Scotland in 1961*, Cmnd. 1673, p. 42.

examinations for any secondary school pupils, they nevertheless recommended the institution of a school certificate to be taken at the age of sixteen on the basis of internal examinations externally assessed by the Scottish Education Department. Moreover they expected that this would not only prove a much more suitable examination for pupils following a leaving certificate course than the existing Senior Leaving Certificate, but that some of the short course schools would develop fourth year 'tops' and that 'pending the raising of the leaving age to 16, the institution of a school certificate would do much to promote continued attendance through the fourth year, thus closing the gap between school and apprenticeship'.[1] Fourteen years later the ordinary grade of the Scottish Certificate of Education was introduced.

It was realized that some short-course schools would be attracted by the certificate too, but it was explicitly stated by a working party set up by the Secretary of State to consider the effects of the introduction of the ordinary grade that 'Junior secondary schools certainly ought to develop courses which will encourage pupils to stay on at school, but the objective set should be one within the reach of the pupils concerned, and for the great majority it should not be the acquisition of the Certificate'.[2] The new ordinary grade, moreover, was quite different from the school certificate envisaged by the Advisory Council. It was not based on an internal examination: it continued to be conducted by the Scottish Education Department – the establishment of a new examining board, which would permit the participation of practising teachers in the administration of the examinations, did not precede its introduction but came three years later. But the response of the junior secondary schools to the ordinary grade was immediate. The proportion of children allocated to certificate courses went up to forty per cent. One hundred and seventy schools which previously had no certificate course have started to prepare some of their pupils for the new examination:

TABLE 33. *Scottish Secondary Schools*

1959: Schools with a 5-year course	213	with no 5-year course	563
1961: Schools with 4- or 5-year courses	306	without 4- or 5-year courses	465
1964: Schools with S.C.E. courses	381	without S.C.E. courses	345

In 1963, only the second year of the ordinary grade, 2,367 candidates were presented from four-year secondary schools compared with 22,432 from the fourth year of the five-year schools, and the number two years later had increased to 3,418 (compared with 22,200 from senior secondary schools). The following figures of school leavers in 1959, 1961 and 1963 show the big jump in those who had completed a four-year secondary course in 1963:

[1] *Secondary Report*, p. 54.
[2] *Report of the Working Party on the Curriculum of the Senior Secondary School*, 1959, p. 37.

TABLE 34. *School leavers*

Numbers of children leaving school:

	Without completing	After completing					
	SI	SI	SII	SIII	SIV	SV	SVI
1959:							
from 5-year courses	24	671	4,104	7,242	2,950	3,710	4,043
from other courses	229	2,112	20,132	24,717	624	—	—
1961:							
from 4- and 5-year courses	11	505	3,515	7,492	3,580	4,780	5,137
from other courses	215	1,463	18,593	23,603	769	—	—
1963:							
from Certificate courses	48	506	3,907	6,679	6,121	5,129	6,242
from other courses	162	1,599	21,415	29,746	671	—	—

S.C.E. candidates from the four-year courses in Scotland appear already to have come nearer to the level of candidates from the senior secondary courses than do secondary modern candidates to the achievements of grammar school pupils entering for the G.C.E. in England. One of the facts which led the Beloe Committee to acquiesce in the introduction in England of an examination below the level of the G.C.E. was the comparatively poor showing of secondary modern pupils who had taken the G.C.E. From their sample survey they found that G.C.E. ordinary level passes awarded to candidates in secondary modern schools in 1957–58 averaged out at 2.3 passes per candidate, whereas grammar school pupils had succeeded in obtaining an average of 4.2 passes per candidate. The gap appears to have widened: in 1962 pupils from secondary modern schools attempting O level subjects obtained an average of 2.1 passes per candidate compared with the grammar school average of 5.0 passes. In Scotland in 1963, however, S.C.E. candidates from four-year courses obtained an average of 3.7 passes per candidate compared with an average of 4.3 for candidates from the fourth year of senior secondary courses. Too much should not be read into these figures, and they should certainly not be taken as a basis for comparison between the standards of English and Scottish schools or examinations; there are too many different factors involved. The average number of passes per candidate depends on the number of candidates, and schools may adopt either a cautious or an open-handed policy in deciding which pupils to present for the examination: the number of ordinary grade or ordinary level passes obtained by children who intend to stay longer at school will depend on the schools' policy in expecting their pupils to by-pass the examination in subjects in which they are aiming at a higher or advanced level: it is not even certain that an examination 'subject' means the same thing in different examinations. Nevertheless the figures do suggest that the short course schools in Scotland have, by the success of the pupils they have presented, entirely justified the speed with which they have responded to the introduction of the ordinary grade.

But the expansion of ordinary grade courses is in marked contrast with the failure to develop any other kind of extended course. It had always been understood that the three-year secondary schools might develop a fourth year, but until the advent of the ordinary grade they had not done so. Since the ordinary grade was so new it was decided to wait and see how it worked in practice before experimenting, as English schools were doing, with examinations below the level of the S.C.E. At present the extended course of the type which the English secondary modern schools developed spontaneously in the late fifties is virtually non-existent in Scotland. There were in 1962 only twenty-eight schools in the whole country with a fourth-year course not leading to the ordinary grade – nineteen of them were in the County of Fife.

THE FIFTH AND SIXTH YEARS

As regards secondary school work beyond the fourth year the important change in the scheme of examinations was the abolition of the group requirement in 1950. Thereafter the Scottish Leaving Certificate could, like the G.C.E. after its introduction in 1951, be taken in any number and any combination of subjects. Even before that date there had been considerable flexibility in the choice of examination subjects provided only that the candidate offered at least two subjects on the higher grade and three on the lower grade. But in their report for 1949 the Department bemoaned the fact that so few pupils made full use of the freedom they had been given. 6.3. per cent of the candidates in that year were presented in a group including mathematics or science but no language, 4 per cent in a group including a foreign language but neither mathematics nor science, and only 0.2 per cent in a group which included neither a language nor mathematics or science. 'It will be seen that there was still little tendency to depart from the traditional type of secondary course.'[1] The dropping of the group requirement obviously meant that more candidates would be successful in obtaining a certificate, and in 1950 a number of pupils seem to have stayed on at school in order to get the certificate which up to then had been beyond them. This is the only possible explanation of the sharp rise in the number of certificates awarded in that year and the fall in numbers thereafter:

TABLE 35. *Leaving certificates 1946–53*

| | No. of pupils in | | No. of candidates presented in S.L.C. | No. of certificates awarded |
	SV	SVI		
1946	7,134	2,095	8,245	4,522
1949	6,824	2,386	?	4,110
1950	7,359	2,486	10,133	8,201
1951	7,058	2,641	10,286	6,702
1952	6,957	2,681	10,210	6,212
1953	7,174	2,681	10,504	6,314

[1] *Education in Scotland in 1949* (Cmd. 7914), 1950, p. 26.

The Department did in fact explain the drop in numbers from 1950 to 1951 by saying that a number of pupils had taken the examination in order to add extra passes to their certificate, and in the following two years they stated that the number who had done this was 3,400. This habit of taking extra subjects in the sixth year of the course has persisted, as may be deduced from the figures for the year 1961 (Table 36), the last in which the Scottish Leaving Certificate was awarded before the introduction of the Scottish Certificate of Education.

TABLE 36. *Higher grades* 1961

	No. of Higher grade subjects taken					
	0	1	2	3	4	5 or more
Candidates in S V	1,568	2,315	2,255	1,768	1,143	690
Candidates in S VI	624	1,875	2,934	2,383	684	121
	No. of Higher grade passes obtained					
	0	1	2	3	4	5 or more
Certificates awarded to pupils leaving school in 1961	1,350	2,000	2,156	1,897	1,501	1,722

Changes in the popularity of particular subjects since both the abolition of the group requirement and the introduction of the ordinary grade may be judged from the following table. It would appear that the changes are mainly a continuation of the trends that were already implicit in developments in the school curricula before the alteration of the examination system.

TABLE 37. *Higher Grade presentations by subject*

	Leaving Certificate	Senior Leaving Certificate	S.C.E.	Percentage increase 1963 over 1948
	1938	*1948*	*1963*	
English	5,737	6,629	14,514	119
Latin	1,313	1,342	2,629	96
Greek	194	156	259	66
French	3,016	2,986	7,013	135
Mathematics	3,396	3,699	7,087	92
Science	2,127	2,954	9,389	224
Art	519	664	1,255	89
Music	91	145	298	105
Technical subjects	14	269	1,156	330
Commercial subjects	204	289	493	70
Domestic subjects	160	226	924	310

The effect of the abolition of the group requirement on the work of the schools in their sixth year has, however, caused some misgivings. Previously all pupils in the sixth year had obtained their 'group', were all at much the same level and had much the same interests and ambitions for their higher education.

Since 1950 that has been changed. The fact that at the same time the extension of financial assistance from the Scottish Education Department has meant that the winning of a university bursary in order to pay one's way at the university is no longer necessary has, for some pupils, robbed the sixth year of its immediate point. This is not regarded as important. On the contrary, the purpose of the sixth year is that the ablest pupils should, in the words of the 1947 report on *Secondary Education,* have 'stretching room and time to look about them'. But the true spirit of the sixth year is diluted by the presence, alongside those who are taking a 'proper sixth year', of others who are seeking to add to their certificate, not subjects which they are studying purely for interest, but subjects which they must have in order to meet university entrance requirements, etc. Hence the debate over the introduction of a new advanced grade in addition to the existing ordinary and higher grades. There is the feeling that there is no tangible goal for pupils in a 'proper' sixth year, and it is argued that an advanced grade might provide this. On the other hand there is a very definite fear that it would interfere with the freedom of the schools to plan the extra year in the best interests of their ablest pupils, and that, although the advanced grade would necessarily be something very different from the G.C.E. advanced level because of the retention of the higher grade, it would nevertheless bring in specialization because it would come to be assumed that pupils went on to the advanced grade in the subjects in which they had shown most promise at the higher grade.

In contrast with the English sixth form, however, the Scottish sixth year has had one clear purpose up to now. It is intended for the best of academically in-clined pupils. The 'proper' sixth year has only been taken by pupils intending to proceed to a university and, typically, by those who hoped to take an honours degree. It is only they who have had any reason for staying at school until the age of eighteen. Many who sought only an ordinary degree and most who pro-ceeded to other institutions of higher education, including girls who went to teachers' training colleges, have been able to do so at the age of seventeen (or rather at the end of their fifth year at school provided that they obtained the necessary passes in the Leaving Certificate). The Scottish senior secondary schools have not been presented with the problem (if problem it is) of catering for those who had obtained a School Certificate and were simply staying at school until they were allowed to leave, or until they reached the minimum age of eighteen at which they could enter a teachers' training college.

CHAPTER FIFTEEN

From School to Further Education

HIGHER EDUCATION

The Scottish Advisory Council have described Scottish secondary education as being 'at once peculiarly academic in type and utilitarian in intention'. This is so accurate a judgment that one hesitates to elaborate on it. So far as certificate pupils are concerned the point is obvious enough – acquisition of a certificate may be a sufficient vocational aim in itself: once the pupil has his certificate is time enough to start thinking about the next stage. It is nevertheless worth looking briefly at the different patterns of higher education on either side of the border for the light they throw on the different intentions of the grammar and senior secondary schools, and on the different percentages of pupils admitted to certificate courses.

In both countries it is the growth of opportunities in advanced further education and in the universities which has helped the certificate course to expand so rapidly. But, only a few years ago, the provision of advanced courses was much more generous in Scotland than in England, the provision of 'non-advanced' courses of further education much more generous in England than in Scotland. The scale of provision is now more nearly equal simply because the two countries have concentrated on the fields in which they were weak.

The fact that a university education has been more readily available to the pupils of Scottish schools after they leave is well known. But it is wrong to equate this with a predominance of the humanities over science and technology. On the contrary, Scottish universities have made more generous provision for engineering and applied science, for medicine and dentistry, for agriculture and forestry. They still do so. Table 38 shows this diagramatically for the years 1954 and 1962. During recent years the rapid expansion of the universities throughout Britain has been accompanied by considerable variations in the proportions admitted to different faculties. In the diagram the vertical line represents the norm for British universities as a whole in 1954 and 1962 if distribution between faculties had been the same on both sides of the border. Representation of the places provided in Scottish universities to the right of this vertical line means that they provide more than their 'share' of places in the faculty concerned.

As regards higher education other than in the universities, the Scottish Code of 1901 had attempted to regularize the provision of further education, but it is to an exception to the Code that Scotland owes the rise of her most important

TABLE 38. *Places in Scottish universities by faculty in relation to all British universities*

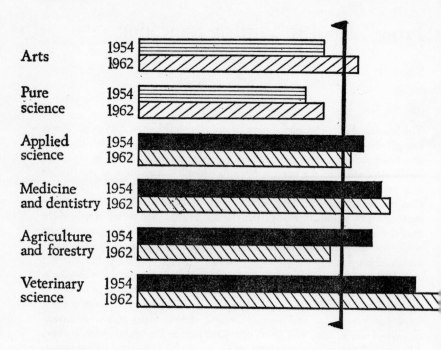

and characteristic institutions – the group of colleges known as central institutions. The Department explained their reasons for this exception:

'My Lords are of opinion that any scheme of technical education would be incomplete which did not provide instruction of the very highest kind in Applied Science and Art to selected students who will devote their whole time to study. They think, therefore, that a further differentiation of institutions is necessary, and that instead of all alike being subjected to the same set of regulations, as has been done hitherto, a few which have had an outstanding record of success in the past, which are well staffed and well equipped for a considerable variety of work, and which are situated at the natural centres of population for large areas may be allowed to proceed upon lines of their own, in the hope that they may develop into institutions worthy to rank, not in number of students, but in quality and advancement of work, with the best of their kind in any other country.'

By 1938 the central institutions had 2,500 full-time students following advanced courses compared with only 4,000 in the whole of England and Wales (advanced courses being used in the sense employed in the Robbins Report of courses beyond the advanced level of the G.C.E. or of the Ordinary National Certificate). But the existence of the central institutions had the effect, or else the pattern of industry in Scotland was responsible for the fact, that technical education of a less advanced standard did not prosper. Since the last war, therefore, the Scottish Education Department have been at pains to encourage the education authorities to establish technical colleges to serve more local needs, and to persuade industry to make use of them. In 1953 they complained that 'some Education Authorities have not shown all the enthusiasm they might', and that some of the provision made for technical education 'has received scant support from local industries'.

South of the border the emphasis has been different. Although there has been an all-round development of further education, the greatest effort has been put into the more advanced courses. The selection of Imperial College, London, and other university centres, for special development in 1953, a more generous exchequer grant for advanced courses in technical colleges, the designation of the colleges of advanced technology in 1956, the establishment of the National Council for Technological Awards in 1955, were all part of the government's policy for the encouragement of technological education at a level equivalent to that of the universities which has been capped by the Robbins Report. As a result the number of students in full-time advanced courses increased from a mere 4,000 in 1938–39 to over 35,000 in 1961–62: the more modest increase in Scotland during that period (from 2,500 to 4,500) only means that England has been able almost to catch up. Most of the changes have taken place within the last ten or fifteen years and Table 39 shows the alterations in the pattern of full-time higher education in less than a decade.

TABLE 39. *Full-time students in Higher Education*

	Teacher training (including U.D.E.s)	Universities	Advanced Further Education	Non-advanced Further Education
ENGLAND AND WALES				
1954–55	27,900	76,600	9,700	36,000
As percentage of all full-time	20	48	7	25
1961–62	37,700	93,700	35,200	61,500
As percentage of all full-time	16.5	41	15.5	27
SCOTLAND				
1954–55	3,500	14,100	2,700	4,600
As percentage of all full-time	14	57	10.5	18.5
1961–62	5,500	19,400	4,500	6,600
As percentage of all full-time	15.3	53.9	12.5	18.3

ENTRANCE REQUIREMENTS FOR HIGHER EDUCATION

The predominance of the universities and central institutions in Scotland before the war, and the comparatively meagre provision of training courses at craftsman level must account not only for the importance of the Leaving Certificate, but also for the Department's comparative lack of success in introducing technical subjects in certificate courses: the engineering faculties of the universities might demand mathematics and science, but were not interested in metalwork, technical drawing and mechanics.

In England the rise in numbers taking G.C.E. courses has gone hand in hand with the expansion of advanced further education and also with a recasting of the entrance requirements. Now the normal requirement for admission to a college of advanced technology is a pass in two subjects at advanced level. Even for an Ordinary National Certificate course the normal requirement is now expressed in terms of the G.C.E. ordinary level.

But there appears to be another difference between England and Scotland. In both countries admission to higher education depends on the Certificate of Education, but in competitive England the student knows that he must get at least the prescribed passes and preferably one or two more. In Scotland it seems possible to succeed with a near failure.

The Robbins Report gives evidence of the extent to which 'qualified' school leavers go on to advanced higher education. The difference between the G.C.E. and the Scottish Leaving Certificate makes it impossible to compare children leaving the schools with equivalent qualifications: yet it appears that if one takes the quite different standards for minimum university entrance requirements in the two countries one is in fact dealing with approximately the same percentage of children. In England a minimum of two passes at the advanced level of the G.C.E. is demanded by most universities: in Scotland in 1961 the minimum was three passes on the Higher grade and two on the lower grade. The Robbins Report also gives details of pupils who fell just short of the minimum university requirements – with only one A level in England and with two highers and three lowers in Scotland. The percentages of school leavers in 1961 at these levels of qualification were:

TABLE 40. *School Leavers with certain minimum examination successes:* 1961

ENGLAND AND WALES				SCOTLAND			
	Boys	Girls	B & G		Boys	Girls	B & G
2 or more A levels	8.7	5.1	6.9	3 H plus 2 L	7.4	6.1	6.8
1 A level but not 2	2.0	2.2	2.1	2 H plus 3 L but not 3 H	1.7	2.2	1.9

The extent to which pupils in both these groups proceeded to courses of higher education is shown in Table 41.

TABLE 41. *Initial entrants to full-time higher education in* 1961 *as a percentage of qualified school leavers*

	ENGLAND AND WALES			SCOTLAND		
	Leavers with two or more Advanced levels			Leavers with three Highers and two Lowers (or more)		
	Boys	Girls	B & G	Boys	Girls	B & G
Percentage entering:						
Universities	63	47	60	70	47	60
Training Colleges	6	27	14	2	27	13
Advanced Further Education	13	4	9	9	14	11
	82	78	83	81	88	84
Percentage entering:						
Part-time advanced courses:						
day	6	1	4	9	1	5
evening	4	—	2	4	—	2
Percentage receiving no higher education other than by private study	8	21	11	6	11	9
	100	100	100	100	100	100

Initial entrants to higher education with lower qualifications than above:

	ENGLAND AND WALES			SCOTLAND		
	Leavers with only one A level			Leavers with two Highers and three Lowers		
	Boys	Girls	B & G	Boys	Girls	B & G
Percentage entering full-time:						
University	2	—	1	45	6	23
Training Colleges	17	39	28	7	73	45
Advanced Further Education	23	6	15	12	11	11
	42	45	44	64	90	89
Percentage entering part-time advanced courses:						
day	27	2	15	10	—	5
evening	14	1	7	10	—	4
Percentage receiving no higher education other than by private study	17	52	34	16	10	12
	100	100	100	100	100	100

It will be seen that not only is there a very close correspondence between the percentages of children who achieve the minimum university entrance requirements (as separately defined in each country) but also a very close similarity, except in the case of girls taking further education courses, in the percentages, of those obtaining these qualifications who do in fact proceed to the universities and other higher institutions of higher education respectively. But remarkable differences occur in the next band – of those who nearly, but not quite, achieve the standards laid down by the universities. In particular there is what the Robbins Report calls the 'somewhat surprising fact' that forty-five per cent of Scottish boys who fall just short of minimum university entrance requirements nevertheless contrive to enter a university.

THE NEWSOM AND BRUNTON REPORTS

Below the level of the G.C.E. and S.C.E. the schools have recently been called upon to introduce a more overtly pre-vocational element into the last year or two of the secondary school. The paradox here is that if the emphasis in the Newsom Report for England on increased standards of attainment can be dubbed 'academic', then English schools are being encouraged to become more academic in intention if not in the means employed. Whereas in Scotland the Brunton Report has recommended the schools to be less academic and more practical in the content of their courses. At the same time the Scottish approach is distinctly more utilitarian than the English.

These two reports were both published in 1963. The remit of the former was to 'consider the education between the ages of thirteen and sixteen of pupils of average or less than average ability who are, or will be, following full-time courses either at schools or in colleges of further education. The term education shall be understood to include extra-curricular activities'. The Scottish working party under the chairmanship of the Senior Chief Inspector of Schools, Mr J. S. Brunton, was required to 'consider means of improving the arrangements for coordinating the later stages of secondary courses and the earlier stages of vocational further education, with particular reference to the educational needs, both vocational and general, of those young people who either do not follow or do not complete courses leading to the Scottish Certificate of Education'. The Newsom Committee had three H.M.I.s as assessors and one member of the Ministry staff, and felt itself empowered to reiterate the recommendation that the school leaving age should be raised; the Brunton Committee had nine H.M.I.s and two representatives of the Department as members and only felt able to recommend what should happen if the government should feel able to take action to raise the school age. But, for the first time two committees, one in Scotland and the other in England, were considering simultaneously the education of almost exactly the same group of school children: Newsom was concerned with the sixty per cent of children aged thirteen to sixteen who would not be taking either G.C.E. or C.S.E. and Brunton was concerned with the sixty-five per cent over the age of about thirteen for whom the S.C.E. was judged to be unsuitable. Their recommendations are very similar: the Newsom Report suggested that 'all schools should provide a choice of programme, including a range of courses broadly related to occupational interests, for pupils in the fourth and fifth years of a five-year course';[1] its Scottish counterpart thought that 'the case is un-answerable for the use in schools of the vocational impulse as the core round which the curriculum should be organised'.[2]

But, though they found general agreement among their witnesses that it would be desirable to introduce vocational elements into secondary education, the Scottish working party were told, by some, that any such vocational elements should be of the most general nature and should not relate exclusively, or even very closely, to any particular occupation or industry. Others believed that vocational courses should prepare pupils for entry into specific trades. In be-tween these two were those who believed that secondary school courses should provide a broad general preparation for a group of occupations associated with a particular industry or service. The working party themselves believed that the very general approach advocated by the first group of witnesses emphasized one aspect of the environmental considerations which should influence secondary education from the very start and should play a growing part in the instruction throughout the schools. The middle course – preparation for a broad general class of occupation – had its place in the third year of the course, and the narrower and more specific kind of vocational training was appropriate at the stage when the young person's vocational ambitions had become clearly crystal-lized, i.e after the age of fifteen, and should be limited either to an extended course in a secondary school or in the first year at a college of further education. They thus envisaged a secondary course for children of average or less than average ability which would progressively focus more closely on the pupils' career intentions, and would go hand in hand with a system of vocational guidance which 'at a much earlier stage than is normal at present, probably at the beginning of the second year', would encourage children to consider the major question that would arise when they came to decide what sort of job they would like to take up. The purpose of vocational guidance would be not only to provide an adequate background knowledge from which the pupils might make sensible decisions when the time came to choose an occupation but also to assist the school in guiding them into appropriate courses in the later years of their secondary school life. In spite of their insistence that the central core of vocational courses should be one that allowed a broad approach, and of their statement that, the individual's needs being much wider than those of his voca-tion, preparation for working life must not be made at the expense of the development of the personal, social and civic aspects of life, it is nevertheless clear that for the working party the pre-vocational side of secondary education was all important. The fact that they had almost nothing to say about prepara-tion for the enjoyment of leisure may be attributed to the limitations in their terms of reference: two brief paragraphs were devoted to the informal aspects of education in secondary schools.

In the section on less able children, however, the working party, having said that they had no reason to believe that the vocational interest was any less

---

[1] Newsom Report, 1963 p. xvi.   [2] Brunton Report, 1963, p. 24.

marked for them than for more intelligent children – though it would have to develop in a different way and at a rather different level – went on to remark that hobbies periods would be an additional way of enlisting their interest. Perhaps it is unfair to draw from this the implication that the only children whose interest should be aroused by an appeal to their leisure interest would be those who, because of their limited ability, would be unlikely to find full satisfaction in their jobs. The fact remains that the report is almost exclusively concerned with ways in which the schools can foster the kind of qualities in their future employees which industry and commerce require. The one paragraph in the report headed 'General courses in schools' reads as follows:

'The value of courses which include recognisable vocational elements has been emphasised in the above paragraphs. The interests and needs of some able boys and girls who will seek employment in commerce and in the public services may, however, best be met through courses which are of a more general nature. The schools should, so far as their resources permit, give these pupils the opportunity of studying more intensively the subjects which, on general or vocational grounds, are of particular interest to them. It is of great importance that they should be encouraged to attain their full potential, and the necessary modifications should be made to their courses to enable them to do so.'[1]

This sounds like another way of saying, as the Spens Report had said, that a liberal education is only a vocational education for the liberal professions.

This attitude contrasts with some of the reasons given by the Newsom Report for the basically similar recommendations made therein. The Newsom Report, too, was anxious to encourage 'well-designed courses in schools, which, without in any way being narrow trade-training, guided pupils' interests and helped them to see the way ahead into further education and future training for a career', and recommended that such courses should be fairly broadly based up to the age of about fifteen, reserving more specialized courses to the fifth year of a five-year secondary course. The Newsom Report also saw some difficulty in designing pre-vocational courses for children of limited ability. Nevertheless the reason for making use of the vocational impulse is stated, far more explicitly in the Newsom than in the Brunton Report, to be that it will provide a more stimulating approach to school work and offer an incentive to extend the pupils' general education. The main reason for suggesting that the schools should provide a variety of vocationally biased courses is quite simply that this makes it possible to offer the pupils a choice. Their more able contemporaries in the grammar schools are able to choose what subjects they will take, and to give 'average' children also some choice in the kind of programme they follow will give them the illusion of participating in the planning of their own education. Because this is the reason for the suggestion it is not necessary that every school course should revolve around vocational interests:

'For some pupils, rewarding courses may be built around interests which are not necessarily tied to any occupational theme – hobby interests in photography

[1] Ibid., p. 29.

or gardening or dressmaking or model building or sailing, for example, or in all the wider aspects of home-making and marriage.'[1]

There are references to the importance of vocational guidance in the Newsom Report: they are less explicit than those in the Brunton Report and, in particular there is no specific recommendation about the stage in a pupil's school career at which the process should begin: the sections on the Youth Employment Service and the role of careers teachers are included in a chapter which appears to be solely about the last year of the secondary course.

It must be admitted that the English recommendations contained in the Newsom Report are more imaginatively expressed and more comprehensive, yet they lack some of the conviction of the down-to-earth Scottish recommendations. The idea is to give the pupils a choice of programme, but little is said about the kind of advice they should receive before they make their choices: the idea is to capitalize on the pupils' intense interest in the careers they are likely to follow when they leave school, yet,

'the range of choices in any one school does not need to be very wide. The schools cannot possibly offer courses related to all the jobs which their pupils will eventually enter, nor do they need to do so. Choice itself is important as a symbol that pupils are taking a hand in their own education, and the morale of many boys and girls will be strengthened by the sense that what they are doing has some relevance to earning a living.'[2]

The Brunton Report is realistic enough to see that boys and girls may have doubts about the value of the whole exercise, if, in the event, it is shown not to have been particularly relevant to what they in fact find themselves doing.

The Newsom Report seems not to foresee the danger that adolescents who have recently left school may regard the vocationally biassed courses of their school days as a confidence trick to keep them interested. The Report in fact says surprisingly little about the requirements of technical colleges and employers: it seems to assume that a good general education is all that will be asked. Its basic thesis is that

'In spite of popular belief to the contrary, technological advance . . . is not leading to widespread unemployment among skilled workers or to the destruction of the level of the skill. . . . If anything, the progress of automation and the application of other technological developments are likely to be delayed by lack of trained personnel.'[3]

And its purpose is to encourage the schools so to appeal to the interest of their pupils that the already rising standards of attainment in the schools will rise still further.

The Brunton Report on the other hand records that formal further education was in the past largely confined to National Certificate courses and goes on to

[1] Newsom Report, 1963, p. 37. [2] Ibid. p. 35.
[3] Newsom Report, 1913, p. 5.

describe the various levels of City and Guilds courses which can be made available:

'In general, courses for operatives make very limited demands on academic ability and attainment. . . .

'Basic craft courses are offered to the average craft apprentice who, if he proceeds no further with his studies, is likely to remain in the craft grade all his working life. . . .

'The ablest apprentices among the boys with whom we are concerned *might* take a technician's course which, though still biassed towards a practical skill, calls for some academic ability. . . .'[1]

Beside this Scottish attempt to evaluate the careers open to boys at different levels should be set the advice contained in an English pamphlet on vocational guidance in schools:

'Educational choices may have a profound vocational significance, particularly in the later stages of the secondary school. With the increasing use of optional courses there is some possibility that vocational decisions may be made almost inadvertently at the ages of 13, 14 or 16, or in changing from school to school, or from school to further education. We need to guard against the tendency of some boys and girls to assess themselves too narrowly, and against the tendency of some parents to think of only a few occupations as suitable for their sons and daughters. Such restricted attitudes may be encouraged by school systems which require early decisions about alternative courses. The options offered within school courses should be so arranged that they do not shut the door on a whole range of careers.'[2]

[1] Brunton Report, 1963, p. 15 (my italics).
[2] *Careers Guidance in Schools*, 1965, p. 7.

CHAPTER SIXTEEN

Comprehensive Schools

ENGLAND UP TO 1965

Public discussion of the organization of secondary schools between 1926 (when the Hadow Report was published) and 1938 made it essential that the Spens Committee, when they came to write their report, should consider the principle of multilateralism. They defined a multilateral school as one which, by means of separate streams, would provide for all types of secondary education except that provided in junior technical schools (since they depended for their special function on their association with technical colleges and on the joint use of equipment, etc. with the colleges: 'Special courses in multilateral schools would not be a satisfactory substitute for junior technical schools. This view would probably be accepted by the majority even of those who would wish to substitute multilateral schools for Grammar and Modern Schools.'[1]) The Spens Report came out against establishing multilateral schools as a matter of policy, although some measure of experiment might be undertaken, especially in new areas. The objections to it already included the fact that reorganization on Hadow lines had gone so far that it would be wrong to consider setting up a quite different type of school unless it was clear that a substantial balance of advantage would justify the expenditure involved. In order to secure a satisfactory number of pupils in each stream the size of multilateral schools 'would have to be very considerable, say 800 or possibly larger'. Moreover:

'There is general agreement that much of what is valuable in the grammar school tradition depends on the existence of the Sixth Form. But a Sixth Form can only play its traditional part in the life of a school if it contains a reasonably high proportion of the pupils in the school. This could scarcely be the case if only half the pupils, or probably less, were on the grammar school "side" and were with comparatively few exceptions the only recruits for a Sixth Form.'

This is a particularly interesting statement in view of the fact that the report recommended that the provision of grammar school places should be restricted to about fifteen per cent of children leaving the primary schools plus a margin of about three per cent for children entering from independent schools. Even allowing for an enormous expansion of technical high schools, the committee can have thought of the grammar streams of a multilateral school as approaching half the total number of pupils in the school, only if they were thinking in terms of selective secondary modern streams, or, more probably, if they had in

[1] Spens Report, 1938, p. xxi.

mind something like the typical small-burgh omnibus school in Scotland drawing its selected pupils from a wide catchment area, but its non-selected children
only from the immediate neighbourhood. In rural areas they did in fact see
advantages in what they described as 'small grammar schools which incorporate
modern schools', but thought that such a school would be more efficient in
operation if the modern school side were of a selective nature.[1]

The Norwood Report attempted to side-step the issue altogether by suggesting that the term 'multilateral' had been used in so many different senses as to
lead to complete confusion.

'We consider it essential to the variety which secondary education should display
that there should be alternative courses suited to the degrees of general intelligence and special abilities of its pupils; . . . thus the secondary Modern school
should distinguish kinds of curricular or special methods of treating subjects to
suit the varied interests and capacities of its pupils; the secondary Grammar
school should admit of alternative courses in which differing weight is placed
upon Languages or Natural Science or Mathematics or whatever combination of
subjects is desirable. Thus each school offers alternative courses which conform
to its general type, and each may be described as a school with two, three or
more courses. Such variety within the type we regard as highly desirable if the
needs of its pupils are to be satisfied; but it is evident that variety cannot be preserved if the number of pupils falls below a minimum figure [not stated].'[2]

The Norwood Committee nevertheless went on to consider the question of
combining 'two-type' or 'three-type' schools under one roof and one direction.
They thought, like the Spens Committee, that technical schools should be
excluded from any multilateral system, not because of their links with the technical colleges, but for much the same reason, that they owed much of their
success to their close association with local industry. They were, however, prepared to admit the possibility of experiment with schools combining the
grammar and the modern type within the limits of size imposed by the need for
each side to have a minimum number of pupils for the sake of variety of courses,
and a maximum imposed by the tradition of English education which had
always valued human contacts and been unfavourable to schools so large that
the head could not know every pupil. Again the actual numbers represented by
these limits were not stated.

The tripartite idea completely dominated the government's thinking while
the 1944 Act was being piloted through parliament, though it has been claimed
that a protest from the National Executive of the Labour Party was mainly
responsible for the fact that the Act 'did not have the term "three types of
secondary school" . . . which left the way open for the comprehensive or
common secondary school'.[3] Such an explicit reference to tripartitism was pre-

[1] Ibid., pp. ix–xx and 297.
[2] Norwood Report, 1943, p. 18.
[3] Report of the Labour Party Conference, 1950, pp. 92–95: see O. Banks, *Parity and Prestige in English Secondary Education*, 1955, p. 133.

sumably abandoned in favour of the implicit reference in the third word in the famous trio 'age, ability and aptitude'.

Nevertheless, Pamphlet No. 1, published under a Labour Minister of Education, took a strictly tripartite view. It expressed the belief merely that some experiments in the provision of multilateral schools might be profitable. It did not satisfy the party advocates of the common school and the Minister was under pressure to withdraw it. This she did not do, though she undertook to print no more copies, and to produce a fresh pamphlet on secondary school organization. Pamphlet No. 9, *The New Secondary Education*, when it appeared, was no more favourable towards the establishment of multilateral schools than its predecessor had been, and it made explicit the arguments for a minimum size of school which was exactly double what the Spens Report had felt to be too big for any school. The various changes in emphasis affecting all three parts of the tripartite system came into play. The belief that secondary technical schools should now be separated from their parent technical colleges in order to be able to cater suitably for the needs of the adolescent meant, of course, that a technical stream could now be included in a multilateral school. The dropping of the selective modern school meant that all children not allocated to a grammar stream would go to swell the numbers. A new insistence on the value of the sixth form made it essential that every school should have an adequate sixth form. The resultant contention was that no multilateral school should have less than 1500–1700 pupils, because otherwise it would not have a sixth form of viable size.

The assumptions made about secondary schools at this time meant that a very large intake of pupils was necessary because so few would stay on at school after the age of fifteen. For example a school which admitted 360 eleven-year-olds could not expect that more than about thirty of them would remain in the sixth form. Table 42 suggests approximately how its internal organization might work out.

TABLE 42. *Notional organization of an English comprehensive school*

	1	2	3	4	5	6	7	8	9	10	11	12	
11–12	30	30	30	30	30	30	30	30	30	30	30	30	360 in 12 classes
12–13	30	30	30	30	30	30	30	30	30	30	30	30	360 in 12 classes
13–14	30	30	30	30	30	30	30	30	30	30	30	30	360 in 12 classes
14–15	30	30	30	30	30	30	30	30	30	30	30	30	360 in 12 classes
Fifth	30	30	30										90 in 3 classes

SCHOOL CERTIFICATE

Sixth { 30 first year
{ 30 second and third years

Total: 1,590 pupils in 51 classes
plus sixth form

HIGHER SCHOOL CERTIFICATE

For comparison the organization of a Scottish secondary school with the same intake of 360 might be as in Table 43.

TABLE 43. *Notional organization of a Scottish omnibus school*

	1	2	3	4	5	6	7	8	9	
SI	40	40	40	40	40	40	40	40	40	360 in 9 classes
SII	40	40	40	40	40	40	40	40	40	360 in 9 classes
SIII	40	40	40	40	40	40	40	40	40	360 in 9 classes
SIV	30	30	30	30						120 in 4 classes
SV	30	30	30	30						120 in 4 classes
LEAVING CERTIFICATE										
SVI	45									Total: 1,405 pupils in 35 classes plus the sixth year

In both cases the supposed organization is purely theoretical. Both assume a larger proportion of children staying on to the end of the course than did in most schools just after the war: in particular the high degree of wastage from certificate courses in Scotland is ignored. The point of the comparison is not to show that a Scottish school admitting exactly the same number of pupils each year as an English school (even if it took all the children from the catchment area) would be nearly two hundred smaller in numbers and have sixteen fewer classes below the sixth year. The point is that, whereas a twelve-form entry school was about the lowest limit of size for an English comprehensive school which aimed to prepare pupils for the Higher School Certificate, an omnibus school in Scotland of very much smaller size could be expected to provide a perfectly satisfactory variety of courses up to the Leaving Certificate because the main organizational problem which faced Scottish schools was much the same as that faced by English schools in their fifth form: Scottish schools did not have to concern themselves with a minimum size for the sixth. In practice there seems to have been little interest in Scotland in making this kind of calculation. It did, however, give a basis for planning new schools in England.

The history of the common secondary school in England since the war has depended very much on the political fluctuations of power in certain local education authorities. The greater or lesser reluctance of the Ministry of Education to authorize what are still often described as 'experiments' with common secondary schools has been of secondary importance. Nationally the Labour party's policies during the years of opposition between 1951 and 1964 hardened, but this is no more than happened locally in the plans of those L.E.A.s which were Labour-controlled for most of the period. Derbyshire, for example, had an overwhelming Labour majority on the county council from 1946 onwards. The county's development plan prepared under the 1944 Act soon after the party took control, however, allowed complete freedom to each of the five divisional executives and the excepted district of Chesterfield to choose whichever kind of secondary organization seemed to them to be most suitable for their (very different) areas. The west side of the county, which is mainly rural, was to be served exclusively by separate grammar and modern schools. Mid-Derbyshire showed considerable interest in secondary technical schools and converted a boys' and a girls' selective central school into a mixed secondary technical school as well as building a new one. Only on the coal-fields of north-east and south Derbyshire were there to be three or four com-prehensive schools. But in 1961 the county education committee decided that the whole county, whatever particular areas might think of the matter, should go fully comprehensive, leaving only the excepted district to follow its own policy.

At the same time the term 'multilateral' has largely been superseded by the word 'comprehensive'. They were never synonymous, though it is not easy to define the precise difference in meaning. A multilateral school is supposed to be one in which the three 'sides', though within one school and with freedom of transfer from one to another, are separately organized. A comprehensive school will usually divide its children according to their ability, either into streams or into sets, but may be regarded as having more of a common core of studies lead-ing to a diversity of courses in the later years, yet without such a marked dis-tinction between the 'sides'. The terms themselves are to be distinguished mainly by their emphasis and the change from one to the other implies a change in emphasis in thinking about the common secondary school.

A few local education authorities embarked immediately after the war on the establishment of a fully comprehensive system based on the ideas then current. London and Coventry in particular set about building schools with over a thousand pupils. Coventry was content with about 1,250 though it was the intention that the schools might be made bigger later. London thought in terms of schools with up to 2,000 pupils. (Both authorities, incidentally, fell foul of the principle that, although comprehensive schools might be allowed as an experiment, existing schools must not be affected. In London the Ministry refused to sanction the closure of Eltham Hill secondary school so that its pupils might be incorporated in the new Kidbrooke comprehensive school. In Coven-try the continued existence of direct grant schools in the town meant that they took the first 'creaming' of able children from the whole town and left the com-prehensive schools with the remainder). But the West Riding was never con-vinced that a comprehensive school needed to be quite so big. Middlesex, too, proposed to establish comprehensive schools with only eight or nine hundred pupils. The Ministry of Education were distinctly worried by this proposal and limited the authority to two, later three, schools as yet another 'experiment'. The defeat of the Labour group in the county council elections in 1949 led to an amendment of the original plan in favour of the separate grammar school. But the idea gained ground that a comprehensive school could be much smaller than the Ministry had recommended and growing interest began to be shown in smaller schools which had been established in rural areas mainly because a common school provided the most economical answer to the problem of giving secondary education to all in sparsely populated parts of the country. The com-prehensive schools in Anglesey excited especial interest.

The Croydon authority considered, but did not adopt, the suggestion that a single sixth form 'college' might serve the whole borough, and therefore make it unnecessary to plan the other schools in such a way as to ensure that each had a sixth form of adequate size.

Then S. C. Mason, Director of Education for Leicestershire, realized that the lengthening of secondary school life opened the way for a compromise between the comprehensive principle and the English predilection both for small schools and for the stratification of schools into limited age ranges. This would make it possible to abandon the classification of secondary schools by function, create a new break at thirteen, and cut the size of the common secondary school by considerably more than half. Three or four junior high schools in an area would cater for all children between the ages of eleven and thirteen or fourteen as well as those who chose to remain there until fifteen rather than transfer to a senior high school, and would thus be presented with opportunities for 'leadership' in the junior high school which would otherwise be denied them. These schools need not be very big because the senior high school would rely for its sixth formers on several contributory schools. The senior high schools would still provide opportunity for that interplay between the sixth form and the main school which the Croydon plan lacked. Selection at eleven could be abolished because parental choice would be a much more realistic one at fourteen than at eleven. The new schools would fit conveniently into existing buildings. On grounds of cost and convenience, and in face of mounting public objection to selection at eleven plus, the Leicestershire plan, or variants of it, caught on all over the country.

Some of the variants abandoned the logic of the Leicestershire scheme. The original idea was that if the choice of school were postponed to fourteen, parents could be given complete discretion to decide whether their child was to stay at school for only one more year or longer. This might well mean that children of limited ability might choose to go on to a senior high school, but, in spite of misgivings, the logic of this was accepted. In other areas the implication has usually been that the senior high school should only be expected to provide advanced courses and that, somehow or other, unsuitable children should be dissuaded from transferring. In practice the opposite danger appears to have been more significant: some parents of able children have proved more reluctant than was hoped to transfer their children to the senior schools. Class differences could be discerned in the proportions of children transferring. The prospect of compulsory schooling being extended to sixteen introduced a new factor, and in a number of areas (including Leicestershire itself) it has been decided that all children should transfer from the junior to the senior high school at the age of thirteen or fourteen. The original Leicestershire plan is now the least favoured of the various two-tier systems outlined in circular 10/65. Nevertheless it served its purpose in introducing new ideas for the organization of secondary schools in England.

THE ORGANIZATION OF CERTIFICATE COURSES

In order to understand some of the complexities of comprehensive organization in the two countries in recent years it is necessary to look a little more closely at the effect of differences in their examination structure. In England, the normal G.C.E. course takes five years up to O level and a further two years to A level, which brings the pupil already up to the age of eighteen. But yet another year in the sixth form is essential for those who wish to attempt the open scholarship examinations for Oxford and Cambridge, is normal for all who wish to go to Oxford or Cambridge whether or not they hope to win a scholarship, and is advantageous to those who will proceed to some other university. A year gained on the route to the O level is therefore invaluable in the sixth form. Even though some local education authorities have a special arrangement for the admission of 'high fliers' to the grammar schools a year early, therefore, most grammar schools of sufficient size to do so also organize an 'express stream' leading to the ordinary level stage in four years instead of five. This is much more common in boys' schools than in girls' schools. The Crowther Committee devoted some attention to it in their report. They found themselves unable to distinguish the extent to which early admission and express streaming were being employed but suggested that it was a measure of the combined effect of both devices that, in 1958, 23.3 per cent of all boys aged fifteen in the grammar schools (maintained and independent) took their O levels before they reached the age of sixteen. The figure in girls' schools was thirteen per cent.[1]

There are in fact two conflicting principles which the Heads of grammar schools have had to keep in mind. An 'express stream' involves, of course, streaming by ability. This will mean keeping together in one class all the ablest pupils regardless of whether they see themselves as future scientists or as arts specialists. At the same time there is pressure to allow the child of scientific bent to start studying the separate branches of science, and the linguist to embark on another foreign language, in good time to acquit themselves well on the ordinary level as a preparation for their sixth form work. Suffice it to say that streaming by ability serves as some sort of counterbalance to pre-specialization. But, for the purpose of comparison with Scotland the important point is that, although the course up to the ordinary level may be four years or five, and although some may stay for an extra year after the advanced level, the period of two years between O and A levels has usually been regarded as fixed.

In Scotland there is no point in enabling the very able pupil to rush even further ahead of his contemporaries at the secondary stage. He probably had the opportunity of putting his foot on the accelerator in his primary school. If he enters the secondary school at the age of eleven, he can have passed sufficient highers to obtain university entrance qualifications by the age of seventeen. He therefore has enough time to spend one more year at school in which to consolidate and develop his studies and prepare for the university bursary com-

[1] Crowther Report, 1959, p. 208.

petitions. The sixth year is an extra year added to the normal secondary course, but for the able pupil it simply offers an alternative to entering the university at the tender age of seventeen.

The introduction of the ordinary grade has, however, brought in its train a complication. The idea of the old highers and lowers was that there should be some differentiation in the syllabus for pupils aiming at each grade from perhaps the third year. Theoretically at least any pupil could be aiming either at the lower or at the higher grade in any subject, and therefore 'setting' might be employed in every subject offered in the school. The schools did not in practice go as far as the examination system encouraged them to do. The working party which considered the effect on the schools of the introduction of the new O grade described the position as follows:

'Hitherto it has too often been accepted that all Certificate course pupils should initially follow in each subject a syllabus essentially designed to lead to presentation on the Higher grade. The intention has undoubtedly been to give as many pupils as possible the chance of obtaining Higher grade passes; in consequence, the decision to transfer pupils to a Lower grade section in any subject is normally postponed as long as possible. Not infrequently the decision is taken as late as the end of the fourth year and in a number of cases even half way through the fifth year; that is, although the pupils may take the Lower grade examination, they have been following a Higher grade syllabus. . . . This practice of treating all Certificate course pupils more or less alike has, however, proved unsatisfactory.'

They recommended that

'for each pupil a decision as to which subjects he will study with a view to presentation on the Ordinary grade in the fourth year, and which subjects, if any, he will study with a view to presentation on the Higher grade in the fifth year, cannot be postponed beyond the end of the second year without prejudicing the chances of success of the majority of the pupils concerned.'[1]

Most Scottish schools have accepted this recommendation. It means that, in every subject which it is possible to take on either the ordinary or the higher grade, there can be at least two 'sets' from the third year onwards, so that in some of the larger schools the form as such completely disappears. But, for the purposes of comparison with the English the point is that the period between the ordinary and the higher grade can be either one year or two. The pupil who is selected at the beginning of his third year to take a subject on the higher grade will be able to take it on that grade at the end of his fifth year – three years later. But the pupil who does not embark on the higher grade syllabus in a particular subject, but perhaps takes the ordinary grade examination in his fourth year, will still not be denied the chance of taking it up to the higher grade – provided that he is prepared to spend a further two years on it after the O grade, i.e. four years later.

[1] *Working Party on the Curriculum of the Senior Secondary School*, 1959, p. 13.

A COMPREHENSIVE POLICY

In circular 10/65, issued by the Department of Education and Science, the government called upon English local education authorities to submit plans for the organization of their secondary schools on comprehensive lines. The circular listed six main forms of comprehensive school:

(i) the orthodox comprehensive school with an age range of eleven to eighteen. (The circular explicitly states that it is perfectly satisfactory for an all-through comprehensive school to be only half the size which had been thought necessary in 1945.)

(ii) three variants of a two-tier system: in the first *all* pupils transfer at eleven to a junior comprehensive school, and, at thirteen or fourteen, *all* go on to a senior comprehensive school: in the second, *all* pupils go to a junior comprehensive school at eleven, and *all* transfer to a senior school at thirteen or fourteen, but there is a choice of senior school – each senior school will cater either for pupils intending to stay at school until eighteen or for pupils intending to leave school at sixteen (in other words the senior schools will not be comprehensive). In the third variant *all* pupils go to a junior comprehensive school at eleven but at the age of thirteen or fourteen *some* transfer to a senior school offering courses up to the age of eighteen, the *remainder* stay on to sixteen in the junior comprehensive school.

(iii) comprehensive schools with an age range of eleven to sixteen providing for all children up to the age at which they will be permitted to leave school, and 'sixth form colleges' providing courses for pupils over the age of sixteen.

(iv) a new system of primary schools for children up to the age of eight or nine, 'middle schools' for pupils aged eight or nine to twelve or thirteen, and comprehensive schools providing secondary education for all pupils between the age of twelve or thirteen and eighteen in a single school.

The orthodox comprehensive school with an age range of eleven or twelve up to seventeen or eighteen is, of course, equally practicable on both sides of the border. Scotland has some advantage in that the schools of this type do not have to be as large as was once thought necessary in England, and perhaps not even as large as the six- or seven-form entry schools which are now advocated as the minimum size.

The comprehensive school for pupils from eleven or twelve to sixteen combined with a sixth form college is not really practicable in Scotland. There is no natural break at sixteen such as has always existed in English grammar schools in spite of some attempts to bridge it. On the contrary, pupils who intend to take examinations in the higher grade in their fifth year must be actively preparing for them in their fourth year, and a change of school a mere nine months before the examinations would be intolerable. A sixth form college could only operate at the expense of all pupils taking the ordinary grade examinations at the end of their fourth year, and those who wanted to go on to take the highers spending an extra year over it and taking the higher grade examinations at the end of a sixth year.

The experimental system of truncated primary schools, middle schools and comprehensive secondary schools from the age of twelve or thirteen was first mooted in England, where it needed legislative dispensation because the middle schools do not conform to the 1944 Act. It has not been tried in Scotland, where it could more easily have been introduced.

It is the several variants of the 'two tier' system which reflect most clearly the differences in length of secondary schooling and in examinations. England here has the distinct advantage that the minimum length of secondary course is longer. Once the school leaving age is raised to sixteen, children can spend two years in one 'tier' and three, or nearly three, in the other. 'Two years is not ideal as a period in one school at any stage', says circular 10/65, 'but a choice has to be made, and the balance of argument seems to favour transfer to a senior school at thirteen.' The reasons given for this evidence a desire to preserve as far as possible existing arrangements which English grammar schools make for 'pre-specialization' by their pupils: 'Although for subjects such as history and geography the age chosen for transfer might not be very important, for others, such as science and modern languages, delay of transfer until fourteen would probably be harmful. A two-year course geared to an external examination would be likely to be planned on the basis of giving a large amount of time to comparatively few subjects; this is the very reverse of liberal education.' The main concern here, however, seems to be to encourage transfer at thirteen rather than fourteen, not so much in order to facilitate early 'pre-specialization' as to mitigate the effects of schools clinging to the existing basic choices of subject for presentation in the G.C.E. but trying to compress into two years the teaching of some subjects which now cover three. Any two-tier system, of course, makes it difficult for the schools to organize an 'express stream' – which is why provision for promoting 'high fliers' from the primary schools at the age of ten was an important feature of the original Leicestershire plan. In any comprehensive scheme some form of selection has a habit of creeping in through the back door.

Circular 10/65 makes it quite clear that any variant of the two-tier system which permits of any kind of parallelism is not truly comprehensive: it is merely a postponement of segregation from eleven to thirteen, though this postponement certainly provides opportunity for less formal methods of selection than were usual for the 'eleven plus', and enables parents to participate more fully in the decision about their children's education. In particular the circular insists that the variant in which *some* children transfer at thirteen to a senior school while the remainder stay behind at the junior comprehensive school is only acceptable if the junior schools provide courses leading to the Certificate of Secondary Education. Whether they should also provide courses leading to the ordinary level of the G.C.E.

'is a more open question. Where staffing permits, there is much to be said for including G.C.E. courses in the junior schools. This gives an added stimulus to the work and to the teaching; it gives intellectually able pupils who do not transfer an opportunity nevertheless of gaining the qualifications which they would have won if they had transferred; it makes it easier for them, through gaining G.C.E. Ordinary levels, to transfer in due course to the sixth form in a senior school or to a college of further education: and it reduces the danger of creating social differences between junior and senior schools with the junior schools regarded as "poor relations".'

In Scotland, if any two-tier system is to be adopted, there is really no choice of the stage at which transfer should take place, and the variant in which the junior school provides courses up to the age of sixteen for those who do not transfer to a senior school at fourteen is really the only practicable one. At present over one-third of Scottish pupils taking non-certificate courses leave school before they have completed three years of secondary education. Unless the raising of the minimum school leaving age to sixteen is also to be accompanied by some modification in the arrangements for transfer from primary to secondary education, or by some increase in the number of children staying on at school at least long enough to complete their final academic session, there will, for a substantial number of children, still be less than four years of secondary education. Even if everyone completed the minimum of four years, as short a period as two years in any one school, undesirable as it is as one stage of a child's school career, is obviously something which authorities will try to avoid at two consecutive stages.

As for certificate pupils the fact that it is generally regarded as desirable that they should make their choice of examination subjects, and the grade on which they will take them, at the end of the second year points to that stage as the best for transfer from a junior to a senior comprehensive school. But the very fact that it is thought desirable to identify the prospective higher grade candidates at the age of about fourteen, and provide for them a curriculum which diverges from that followed by pupils who will be content with the ordinary grade, has led in Scotland to a number of arrangements in which there is some parallelism. The examination structure makes for a rather more inflexible parallelism than obtains in English two-tier systems. In England, at age thirteen, it is only a question of whether a pupil aims at O level or not. His decision whether to go on and take A levels can be postponed until after his O level results are known. A child who was likely to stay at school until eighteen would certainly be well advised under a two-tier system to transfer at thirteen to the school providing A level as well as O level courses, but, as circular 10/65 points out, O level G.C.E. courses in junior comprehensive schools would allow the able pupil who did not transfer at thirteen to transfer across to the sixth form of the senior school without loss of time. In Scotland the pupil who transfers to a school offering courses up to the higher grade will be able to take the highers after three years; the pupil who does not transfer may have the opportunity to take the ordinary grade after two years, but if he then decides to go on to take his highers it will cost him another two years. Yet it is precisely this kind of parallelism, based as it is on the supposition that it is possible to discriminate at fourteen between higher grade and ordinary grade candidates, which is fundamental to most of the two-tier comprehensive systems which have been introduced in Scotland in recent years. It is a curious twist of educational history that the country which prides itself on the traditions of its omnibus schools (which could so easily become comprehensive schools of the orthodox type) should, in trying to devise other forms of organization consistent with the comprehensive principle, adopt a form which depends on a refined system of selection and one which must serve to discourage the 'borderline' pupil, the late developer and the child who receives little encouragement from his parents to contemplate higher education. Tripartitism in England had the excuse that it distinguished between three kinds of children, among whom the academic could be clearly identified. In Scotland there are no misgivings about discriminating quite simply between the most able and the not-quite-so-able.

The so-called comprehensive schools in Glasgow are based on this kind of parallelism. There are in the city several six-year schools, providing tuition up to the higher grade and beyond. Associated with each are 'four-year' comprehensive schools. Very promising pupils are transferred from the four-year to the six-year schools at the end of their second year. The remainder stay at the four-year schools, all of which provide courses up to the ordinary grade of the S.C.E. But there has been a tendency for the four-year schools to transfer very few at the second-year stage and to hold the majority of their certificate pupils until they have completed the ordinary grade course. There has been some disappointment that pupils who, after passing the O grade, might have gone on to a six-year school for the higher grade have not in fact done so. As a result two of the four-year schools have recently been promoted to become six-year schools, i.e orthodox comprehensive schools.

The Labour government's policy for comprehensive education in Scotland is outlined in circular 600. This goes into less detail than the English equivalent, circular 10/65, and makes rather more of the practical difficulties. It states categorically that the most effective and most desirable form of organization is the orthodox 'all-through' secondary school, makes a tentative plea for experiment with the middle school for pupils aged nine or ten to fourteen, and goes on:

'In some areas geographical factors will make the "all-through" comprehensive school impracticable, because it would impose on very many pupils an intolerable burden of daily travel, or even the need to live away from home. In other areas, where there are very real difficulties of adapting existing accommodation without a much larger rebuilding programme than will be practicable for a long time to come, authorities may, as an alternative to long delay in achieving comprehensive reorganisation, have to develop, along with full six-year comprehensive schools in appropriate centres, a series of schools providing four years of secondary education and offering certificate as well as non-certificate courses. Pupils intending to continue their secondary education beyond the fourth year would transfer to central schools in which courses would run from at least the third to the sixth year. Transfer to a central school would be made at a time which suited local circumstances and the parents' wishes but would not take place earlier than the end of the second year.'

This offers scope for education authorities to drag their feet. Alterations in the system of allocating pupils to the schools would be little more than a postponement of selection from eleven or twelve to thirteen or fourteen. The circular adds that 'in some areas where the population is most scattered and where communications are most difficult' the principle of comprehensive education may be ignored altogether.

In their annual report for 1965 the Scottish Education Department describe the types of secondary school which exist at present. The categories they list are as follows:

	Number of schools
A. SELECTIVE SCHOOLS	
1. Offering non-certificate course only	306
2. Offering certificate courses only	70

B. COMPREHENSIVE SCHOOLS

Offering non-certificate courses and complete ordinary and higher grade certificate courses   **134**

[i.e. true all-through comprehensive schools, schools which are comprehensive in respect of part of their catchment area and selective in respect of other parts of their area, and bilateral schools – see Chapter 5]

C. PART SELECTIVE/PART COMPREHENSIVE

1. Offering non-certificate courses and years I and II of both ordinary and higher grade certificate courses   **33**

[i.e. selective beyond the age of thirteen as between certificate and non-certificate]

2. Offering non-certificate courses, years I and II of higher grade, and years I to IV of ordinary grade certificate courses   **66**

[i.e. selective beyond thirteen as between ordinary and higher grade]

3. Offering non-certificate courses, and years I to IV of ordinary grade certificate courses (no higher grade)   **59**

[i.e. the equivalent of a secondary modern school with a G.C.E. course]

PART V

The Democratic Tradition

Alas for Scottish education!
They say it's heidin for Salvation
Wi' universal acclamation
Fae a' the airts!
But, man, fut is't that mak's a nation?
The lad o' pairts!

CHAPTER SEVENTEEN

The Education of an Elite

SCOTLAND

In the days of the Revised Code the Managers of Kirkwall Burgh School had an acrimonious correspondence with the Secretary to the Committee of Council for Education because he had refused to authorize payment of grant to the school. Payments under the Code were intended for schools attended by the children of the classes who supported themselves by manual labour, and the view was taken in London that it was 'simply idle' to claim grant for a school which offered instruction in mathematics, advanced Latin, Greek and French for university entrance. The dispute was settled when one of H.M. Inspectors was persuaded to visit Orkney and conduct a survey of all the parents of pupils of the school. He reported that a large proportion of them were indeed manual workers and the grant was reluctantly paid.

In 1864 it was reckoned that sixteen per cent of the students at Scottish universities were the sons of skilled labourers and artisans. This compares with the twenty-five per cent of undergraduates in 1955 and 1961 in all British universities whose fathers were manual workers – an overall percentage which ranges from nine per cent at Cambridge to twenty-four per cent at Scottish universities, and forty per cent at the University of Wales.

The democratic tradition of Scottish education has been the object of considerable admiration by English observers, even when they have not appreciated the precise flavour of it. One reason for their admiration has been that there is much of the charitable in the English attitude towards state education. At first it was a grudging charity, which was, moreover, confused by the assumption that children of the lower classes would commonly prove to be less capable of the highest academic achievements than their more fortunately placed fellows – and that any exceptions to the rule might well be misfits in society. It is nowadays a much more generous charitable view which sees the intellectual potential of children from environments unfavourable to academic success and wishes to help them to realize their potential in spite of those disadvantages.

But such an attitude is no part of the Scottish democratic tradition. It is true that the poor student was helped by the very cheapness of university education, and that there were sources of financial help from charitable foundations. It was estimated in 1830 that the annual cost to a student of attending a Scottish university might vary from as little as £15 up to perhaps £25. The bare minimum cost at Oxford and Cambridge at the time was estimated at £100–£120, although the average expenditure might, it was thought, be anything between £150 and £300. The cost of studying at a Scottish university was in fact less than that of attending many of the secondary schools in Scotland, and it was often for that reason that the lad o' pairts would proceed straight from his parish school to the university. Moreover, although the value of most bursaries was less than ten pounds, it was reckoned that one student in every ten or twelve at Edinburgh and Glasgow, one in four at St Andrews, and one in three at Aberdeen, was in receipt of a bursary.[1] Nevertheless it was not a *nouveau riche* industrialist or the proprietor of an expensive private school who said: 'If people choose to pay for their education, no teacher can refuse.' It was a witness before the Scottish Universities Commission of 1826–30 who was giving his reasons why it would be undesirable to impose a matriculation test for admission to the universities.

The Scottish democratic tradition has been an object of admiration, and it has also been a source of considerable surprise to the English. They have admired the extent to which the children of poor families have been able to take advantage of higher education, but they have been surprised that the Scottish middle classes have, in the main, been quite content to send their children to the schools provided for the generality of the population. 'Where in England could we produce such an example of interest and confidence in a public school among the middle classes or our rural population?' asked one of the Assistant Commissioners appointed by the Taunton Commission to visit and report on Scottish schools in 1866.[2]

The golden age of the democratic tradition in Scotland was the eighteenth century and it is worth quoting at some length an account of the parochial schools of that time:

'The parish school was an equalising agency in so far as it was a common school designed for the education of children of all classes, and actually attended by them at least in the country districts. The schooling provided was neither compulsory nor free, yet education was generally accepted as a parental obligation and the inability to pay the school fees or to provide clothing and shoes for children of school age was often regarded, like the inability to pay the rent of a church sitting, as a public confession of either failure or laxity. A general education was valued as something more than a preparation for employment. It was an end in itself, and associated with the Sabbath exercises, the ministerial catechisings and family training and discipline. It helped to define the worth and duty of the individual in terms that were relatively independent of class and circumstance. The average parish school gave the oncoming generation an early experience of a simplified world in which there were few artificial distinctions; it inculcated some universal standards of self-respect and an appreciation of intellectual and moral effort. The result was to create a community of values that made for an easily recognizable national character and outlook.

'As a selective agency, the parish school was expected to prepare an élite

---

[1] See G. Balfour, *The Educational Systems of Great Britain and Ireland*, 1903, p. 277.
[2] *Report of the Schools Inquiry Commission*, 1868, vi, p. 60.

for the universities and the professions. It therefore professed to provide the necessary instruction in the Latin tongue, still the technical qualification for admission to the higher learning. With the economic expansion of the 18th century the horizon of business opportunity had widened and the schools responded to the new needs by the introduction of such utilitarian subjects as book-keeping, surveying and navigation. But in this preparation for either profession or business, the economic situation to the end of the 18th century still put a premium on general intellectual and moral training rather than on specialized instruction. The selective process was in terms of personal ability and character as tested by an equalitarian competition rather than in terms of technical knowledge or social expectation, and in the larger world professional repute and business success were still largely due to the same factors. In medicine and commerce alike the "general practitioner" had to supplement a limited fund of specialized experience with common sense or inspired guess-work and in such a situation general intelligence, integrity and diligence counted heavily and could be appreciated by an interested public. The effect was to recruit the professional and business groups in Scotland from a wider range of the population than elsewhere. Family connection and social status were always assets of value, especially in a conservative profession such as law or a conservative business like banking, but the movement into the clerical and medical professions was indeed so apparent as to justify a pervasive liberal expectation that every career could and should be entered by those exhibiting the requisite character and talent. For these, the parochial schools led to the university and the university to an open profession. Along this line of advancement competition would winnow out the unfit, nor was it advisable that the survivors should have things made easy for them, but it was widely admitted that there should be a range of educational opportunity and a right of passage for the "lad o' pairts" who had no initial advantage beyond his own ability, industry and energy.[1]

With the industrial revolution and the growth of the large cities (in which in any case the democratic tradition had not been so well founded as in the rural areas) it is true that an increasing section of the community did not see a liberal education as important either in itself or as a preparation for the liberal professions. It is also true that the current of reform in the English Public Schools was matched not only by the establishment of a few proprietary boarding schools in Scotland but also by the opening of day secondary schools which were patronized by the more affluent sections of the urban population. Edinburgh Academy, for example, founded in 1824, charged a fee of three guineas a quarter (compared with the ancient High School, maintained by the Town Council, whose fee was only half a guinea a quarter). But to this day Scottish education and Scottish society retain something of the flavour of the eighteenth century as described by Professor Saunders.

There are nevertheless a few independent schools in Scotland which stand completely outside the state system. The more important of them are English

[1] L. J. Saunders, *Scottish Democracy 1815–1840*, 1950, p. 241.

in every sense of the term except the geographic. Modelled on the English Public Schools, they prepare their pupils for the English G.C.E. and for admission to English universities.

Apart from these few schools the Scottish state system includes, as it were, the private sector within itself. There are a few 'direct grant'[1] schools. But even in the matter of fee-paying there is no division between maintained, direct grant, and independent schools. In England, maintained schools are forbidden to charge tuition fees. The Education (Scotland) Act, 1962, however, repeats earlier legislation from 1891 onwards to the effect that, provided they have first secured adequate provision of free education to meet the needs of their areas, education authorities may retain a proportion of their schools as fee-paying schools. A number of authorities still do so, although many Labour-controlled councils have abolished fees in their schools over the past twenty years. Nevertheless Scottish education has traditionally been democratic enough to ensure not only that the clever child of poor parents shall not thereby forfeit his chance of the best that education can provide, but also that parents who wish to pay for their children's education shall have the opportunity to do so. There has, however, been much less tendency to distinguish certain schools by their social cachet rather than their academic prestige. The distinction is largely irrelevant in Scotland. Aberdeen Grammar School (non-fee-paying and maintained by the Labour-controlled city education committee) is, for example, on at least equal terms with Robert Gordon's College (fee-paying, a former Hospital, which now receives direct grant and is a Headmaster's Conference school) and it may even claim a slightly higher rating by virtue of having been founded in the fifteenth, as against the early eighteenth, century – 'scratch a Scot and you rouse a traditionalist'.

ENGLAND

But it is not the democratic tradition of Scottish education which should cause surprise. Rather the length of time which it took the English to realize that education is more a matter of the individual's ability than of his social status. Elementary education was first seen as a charity for the poorer classes, but secondary education was to be based on a much more refined class system: the Taunton Commission recommended in 1868 that there should be three grades of secondary school – the first for the children of parents of ample means or of good education but 'confined' means; the second for boys whose parents' means were 'straitened', or who wished to enter professions which required that they should enter specialized training at about the age of sixteen; the third for the sons of 'the smaller tenant farmers, the superior artisans'. The three grades of school would correspond 'roughly, but by no means exactly with the gradations of society'.[2] If the precise wording of the Taunton Commission's recommenda-

---

[1] i.e. they receive grants direct from the Scottish Education Department. The financial arrangements are however different from those in England – see the glossary.

[2] Taunton Report, p. 16.

tions now seems rather quaint and class distinctions among the pupils in state-maintained schools have largely disappeared, it must nevertheless be admitted that this is comparatively recent, that it has been gained at the expense of an even wider gulf than before between the public and the private sector in education, and that the state system is still administered by those who have not been brought up in it themselves.

Yet one must be careful not to give the impression that the class structure of English education is rigid and exclusive. It, too, has been an agent of social mobility.

A century ago the English Public Schools were largely the preserve of the upper classes, and had become so inefficient that they were in danger of losing the support of the rising middle classes.

'With the growth of the power and wealth of England and the need for every kind of leadership at home and overseas that the new century demanded, a great increase of secondary education was essential. And it was to some extent supplied, but in an unexpected way that had important social consequences. It might have been supposed that the age of Reform and the approach of democracy would lead to the improvement and multiplication of Endowed Grammar Schools by State action; in that case a common education would have been shared by the clever children of very various classes, as had been done in the Grammar Schools of Tudor and Stuart times with excellent results. But in the Victorian era the Grammar Schools remained less important, in spite of some striking exceptions, as at Manchester. At the same time the Dissenting Academies, so useful in the previous century, petered out. The new fashion was all for the "Public Schools" modelled on the old ideals of Eton, Winchester and Harrow, of which Rugby became the great exemplar. . . . The "middling orders of society" found in the reformed Public School the door of entrance for their sons into the "governing class". The old landed gentry, the professional men and the new industrialists were educated together, forming an enlarged and modernized aristocracy . . . and by the same process were further divided from the rest of the nation brought up under a different educational system.'[1]

The middle classes continued to associate themselves with the more privileged classes even after the particular reasons for it in the nineteenth century had passed: 'the fusion of the older gentry with the parvenus was completed before the Boer War. Empire building ceased soon after it. . . . Yet the hold of the public school on the middle class mind has not weakened.'[2] Up to 1945 there was, however, a fairly smooth gradation from the more prestigious Public Schools and better founded independent schools down through the endowed grammar schools (which had accepted both state recognition and financial assitance from the local education authorities) to the new municipal grammar schools, provided and maintained by the L.E.A.s but still, to a greater or lesser extent, fee-paying. Many of the endowed, but municipally assisted, grammar schools sought,

[1] G. M. Trevelyan, *English Social History*, 1942, p. 519.
[2] R. Lewis and A. Maude, *The English Middle Classes*, 1949, p. 190.

immediately after the passing of the 1944 Act, a middle road between complete absorption into the public system and the complete independence which most of them would have preferred (but feared that they could not afford to assert). They applied for direct grant from the Ministry of Education. But Ellen Wilkinson, the Minister, was determined that the exceptional class of direct grant schools should not be enlarged.[1] Some schools gave in and became voluntary schools maintained by the local education authorities. Others took a chance and went independent. The reaction of the middle classes was clear. They

'evidently interpreted those provisions of the 1944 Act which affected the independent grammar schools to mean that these institutions would be converted into something like replicas of State secondary schools. Those who could afford it promptly turned to such private schools as remained – even if, in the past, these had given a poorer education. A correspondent to *The Times Educational Supplement* reflected that "Many supporters of his [Mr R. A. Butler's] Education Act must have chuckled cynically to think that his all-embracing logic had pushed the grammar schools down from competition with the public schools, and so damaged their prestige that the most miserable boarding school that escaped bankruptcy in 1939 now has a long waiting list at enhanced fees.'[2]

In both England and Scotland the aristocracy educates its children in schools which are beyond the reach of the ordinary people. The difference lies in the alignment of the middle classes. This does not mean, of course, that there is merely a different dividing line between the education reserved to the children of the privileged or the monied and that which is provided for the rest of the population. The education provided in the English Public School was the education of the gentleman. It has been copied by the grammar schools, though not with complete success. The reason that so many positions of influence in the community still go to the products of the Public Schools and the two ancient universities is not only that their academic standing is greater than that of other educational establishments but that they are thought to give their students something in addition to intellectual training which fits them to be leaders of men. Stanley Baldwin was probably not concerned to enquire whether the Harrovians he brought into his government had distinguished themselves academically at school. Britain has had no fewer than eighteen Old-Etonian Prime Ministers: of these two – Robert Walpole and Harold Macmillan – were scholars at Eton.[3]

Social class in England has never been entirely fixed. The governing classes have always been ready to recruit new talent. But it has been for the individual to gain access to the 'establishment' – whether by marrying into the aristocracy, by sending his children to a Public School, or by winning a scholarship from a state grammar school to the University of Oxford. The institutions themselves have usually been not only willing but even eager to take in new blood. The

[1] The number of Direct Grant Schools fell from 232 in 1943 to 164 in 1952.
[2] Lewis and Maude, op. cit., p. 187.
[3] See A. Sampson, *Anatomy of Britain Today*, 1965.

Public Schools only survived because they took in the children of the rising middle classes. In 1919 they offered to take pupils from the elementary schools, but the Board of Education did not take up the offer. The Fleming Report in 1944 made recommendations for a considerable proportion of the places at Public Schools to be taken up by 'boys and girls capable of profiting thereby, irrespective of the income of their parents', but even English authorities boggled at the difficulties of selecting the *crême de la crême* to enjoy these special advantages.

The different roles of the independent schools may be regarded as but a symptom of the fact that the two countries set about much the same task in rather different ways. On both sides of the border the schools are concerned, as one of their aims, to produce an élite. But the English do this by charging particular institutions with the responsibility of preparing the élite for their part in society. The Scots do it by sieving the whole of the oncoming generation in order to discover those who are fitted to form an elite.

CHAPTER EIGHTEEN

Selection and Survival: Secondary Schools

Because of the importance of favoured institutions in England, competition to get into them is an important part of the system. Sometimes the competition is on the basis of merit alone, sometimes on a mixture of merit and financial or social privilege, sometimes purely on privilege. But it is the competition and the prestige of particular schools or colleges which are important. Standards are maintained, and not infrequently forced up, simply by the excess of demand over supply. This has a spiral effect: a particular schools gains in reputation: competition for a place there becomes stronger: the school can become more selective; with more able pupils its reputation goes on increasing.

In Scotland much less reliance is placed on particular institutions. The attempt is made to set objective standards to mark the end of a course of study or a stage in a child's educational career. To reach that standard is the main thing. Some institutions will be better than others at preparing their protégés for it, but in the last resort, what matters is not the environment in which one took a particular course of study but one's successful completion of it. The Scottish system places as much emphasis on the selection of students as does the English. In fact the classification of children as being capable of tackling this course or that tends to be more detailed. But at the same time care is taken that demand exceeds supply, by generally admitting more students than are expected to complete the course successfully. The main reason for this is concern for the individual – that he may be given the benefit of the doubt and allowed to prove his own worth. But it does help to maintain standards in examinations if it is an accepted part of the system that there is bound to be a fair crop of failures or 'drop outs'.

This is rather too sweeping a generalization. Its truth can best be judged by considering firstly selection at eleven plus and examination practice in the secondary schools, and secondly selection for higher education and examination practice in the universities.

ALLOCATION TO CERTIFICATE COURSES

Intelligence testing had as big a vogue in Scotland as in England. The names of Thomson and McClelland rank among those who did most to spread the use of these and other objective tests in selection for secondary education. McClelland found, just before the war, that the number of pupils deemed fit for a senior secondary course on the basis of test results who actually completed such a course successfully amounted to 10.6 per cent of the appropriate age group. He calculated that, by making financial assistance available to those whose parents could not otherwise afford to allow them to stay at school until the age of seventeen, the percentage could be raised to 15.4. He considered that an ultimate ideal of 30.1 per cent was not entirely unrealistic, but this implied both a far-reaching improvement in social and environmental conditions and also considerable modifications of the senior secondary course which, without necessarily relaxing standards, would bring about an increase in the variety and attractiveness of the courses offered. As an immediate practical recommendation he thought that the top twenty-five per cent should normally be admitted to senior secondary courses.[1] At the time Scottish education authorities were admitting, on average, something over thirty per cent. They were not only more generous than McClelland recommended, but were tolerating a very considerable measure of 'wastage'.

The Advisory Council on Education in Scotland in their report on *Primary Education*, 1946, made no reference to the percentage of children to be admitted to senior secondary courses, but they did enunciate the principle that 'in cases of doubt the pupil should generally be given the option of taking the longer or more onerous course, at least for a probationary period'.[2]

In 1961 a Special Committee of the Advisory Council considered the whole question of transfer procedure. They found, no less than McClelland had, that there was considerable wastage: 'On an average some thirty-six per cent of an age group are admitted to senior secondary courses, and only some twelve per cent of that age group are ultimately presented for Leaving Certificate examinations.' Nevertheless they pointed to the many changes both in the organization of schools and of examinations and in the techniques of selection since McClelland's survey and their final recommendation was that about thirty-five per cent of an age group should be admitted to certificate courses, although they thought that only about twenty per cent should be aiming at the higher grade and another fifteen per cent would be expected to have a reasonable chance of success only on the ordinary grade.[3] This recommendation has been accepted by the Secretary of State.[4] It represents a remarkable comparison with England, since the Scottish Certificate of Education on the ordinary grade is intended to be of approximately the same standard as the ordinary level of the G.C.E. In Scotland, at the time of the Special Committee's report, there could be no experience of the actual performance of pupils on the ordinary grade because it had only newly been introduced, but the feeling was that about thirty-five per cent of children should be allowed to take it and the expectation should be that a child who was just within the top thirty per cent of the age group should have a reasonable prospect of obtaining at least three passes. In England the Beloe Committee assumed, and most people, including the Ministry of Education, have since also assumed, that only twenty per cent of children could reasonably be expected to attempt the ordinary level in four or more subjects. In the event

---

[1] W. McClelland, *Selection for Secondary Education*, 1942.   [2] Cmd. 6973, p. 123.
[3] *Transfer from Primary to Secondary Education* (Cmnd. 1538), 1961, pp. 13 and 28.
[4] Circular 501, 1962.

the introduction of the ordinary grade in the S.C.E. has resulted in an increase in allocation to certificate courses and the Scottish Education Department seem quite happy about this. 'As was to be expected', they wrote in the 1964 annual report, 'there has been a considerable increase in the percentage of pupils attracted to Certificate courses in S I. In 1953 it was just over thirty per cent of the age group: in the period 1958 to 1961 the figure had grown to just over thirty-five per cent: in 1963 and 1964 it was over forty per cent. This is probably as high as is desirable.'

This overall percentage covers variations from about twenty-five in some areas to as high as fifty in others. The English grammar school, according to the area and the policy of the local education authority, may admit anything between fourteen and forty per cent of the age group, with an average over the country as a whole of about twenty per cent.

ELEVEN PLUS ANXIETY

A larger percentage of children than in England is admitted to senior secondary courses north of the border. But this does not mean that Scotland is relieved of 'eleven plus anxiety'. Before the last war, at least in the rural areas, the arrangements for promotion from the primary to the secondary departments worked extremely smoothly. References in the Scottish Education Department's reports in the nineteen-thirties to the way in which allocation to secondary courses was often settled by discussion between the headmaster and the parents are enough to make any hard-pressed director of education at the present time green with envy. Even in the cities the situation was not too competitive. The demand for Secondary places from the children of poor parents was not so great that the education authorities found much difficulty in meeting the statutory requirement that they should provide sufficient free places to meet the needs of their area, and the fee-paying places, which they were allowed to provide in addition, were able to meet most of the demands from middle-class parents whose children under a more competitive system might have lacked the ability to win a place for themselves. Since the war things have become tougher. One Scottish observer has an explanation for it: 'At the present time, and possibly through English influence, class distinction is far from being absent in the cities.'[1] This is a long way from being the only explanation. It is doubtful whether class distinctions were ever absent in the Scottish cities. The reduction in the number of fee-paying places coupled with a rising demand for senior secondary education from all classes of the community has led to a more competitive spirit. But the academic tradition demands that the route to the universities shall be kept open for as many children as possible for as long as possible. Dr Douglas M. McIntosh, Director of Education for Fife, reported in the *Scottish Educational Journal* in February 1963 on an investigation he had carried out in the county to compare parental plans for their children's education with what actually happened to the children after the selection procedure had been applied. Thirty-nine per cent of

[1] M. Mackintosh, *Education in Scotland*, 1962, p. 8.

the parents in the investigation had wished their children to follow a senior secondary course. One-third of the children of these parents were in fact excluded from the senior secondary courses by the selection tests. Dr McIntosh commented:

'The tendency in Scotland has been to dictate to parents what is educationally good for their children. As long as parents could enrol their children in fee-paying schools where the charges were modest, this attitude did not arouse too much hostility. With this avenue barred, antagonism to the system of transfer from primary to secondary education develops, particularly where pupils are segregated into junior secondary schools in which *no language is taught*.'[1]

In the Scottish cities moreover the senior secondary schools, both free and fee-paying, both local authority and state-aided or independent, tend to form into a strict hierarchy, based almost exclusively on academic prestige. The competition to win a place in the desired schools is every bit as fierce as in English towns. In fact it may well be more fierce because there just are no second-rate, but fee-paying, independent schools to which the middle-class parent can send his 'eleven plus failure' as an alternative to the 'recognised' schools. To a much larger extent than in England the whole community is competing together for places in the same schools, whereas in England the children of different classes of society are often aiming at places in quite different schools.

Scottish children have an additional cause for anxiety in that selection is more refined than in England. It has been mentioned that the working party on transfer from primary to secondary education in 1961 quoted separately the percentages of children they thought should be deemed capable of aiming at the ordinary and at the higher grade of the Scottish Certificate of Education. They in fact recommended that the transfer tests results should distinguish between these two groups of children. The English eleven plus is a simple 'pass or fail' examination as a result of which the child either wins a place at a grammar school or does not. The Scottish working party's recommendation for two grades of 'pass' on the other hand was actually an attempt to persuade education authorities to simplify their procedures. Many have done so. But it was possible until recently in one area or another of Scotland for children to be allocated, as a result of the transfer procedure, to one of the five following categories (though there was perhaps no single authority which used all five categories):

1. Allocation to a senior ('five-year') secondary school to take, up to the higher grade, a 'two language' course
2. Allocation to a senior secondary school but to a 'one language course'
3. Allocation to a 'four-year' secondary school for a course up to O level
4. Allocation to a junior secondary school for the ordinary three-year non-certificate course
5. Allocation to a 'modified course' which might be provided in the junior secondary school or, in a few areas, in a 'top' to a primary school.

[1] My italics.

Allocation to a modified course is a relic of the old qualifying examination. Before the war the secondary schools had barely begun to provide for the bottom ten to fifteen per cent of the age group at all. When they did, they admitted them as 'age pass' children or as 'non-qualifiers'. Nowadays all children above the age of thirteen, other than those in special schools, attend the secondary schools. But, according to the area, anything between about ten and as high as thirty per cent of the total age group will be classified as needing 'modified courses': the term implies that these present-day 'non-qualifiers', though they may now proceed to a secondary school, need a type of education which is not properly secondary: the 'normal' curriculum has to be modified for their benefit.

The Scottish Education Department now say that

'the commonly accepted pattern, whereby the Transfer Boards allocated pupils to at least four different types of course – two language, one language, junior secondary and modified – has almost completely disappeared: and in most cases the allocation is now simply to Certificate courses or non-Certificate courses. (An exception is where the presence of schools providing only four-year courses alongside those providing five-year and six-year courses necessitates a sub-division of the allocation to Certificate courses.)'

The Department goes on to exhort that 'the assignment made by the Transfer Boards should be regarded by the Boards and by the schools as no more than tentative, and it should be open to the secondary headmasters, with the minimum of formal procedure, to transfer pupils from one course to another or to make alterations within a pupil's course'[1]. This exhortation sounds slightly odd to English ears: south of the border the allocation of pupils is usually to a school; some formality will be necessary for a change of school, but it is almost unthinkable that a headmaster should need to refer to anyone (other than the parent) to decide which course within his school a pupil should follow.

Finally, of course, there is more chance of eleven plus anxiety communicating itself to the children in Scotland because of the feeling, which still persists in spite of the great similarity between selection techniques in both countries, that it is an examination in which success will come to the child who has put the most effort into his primary school work. English parents and teachers drive their children to greater efforts by spurring them on to the eleven plus, too, but there comes a point at which they accept that it is a purely predictive device which assesses capability rather than achievement, and they accept that further urging is useless. That point is perhaps reached earlier in England than in Scotland.

WASTAGE

English readers will probably be most interested to learn whether the bigger intake into certificate courses results in a bigger proportion of children obtaining

[1] *Education in Scotland in 1964*, Cmnd. 2600, p. 34.

a certificate. But it is not as simple as that. A typical English comment is to be found in the report of an investigation carried out under the auspices of the Population Investigation Committee of all children born in one week in March, 1946 (and therefore aged fifteen in 1961) which showed that the 'wastage' in Scottish schools is significantly higher than in England and Wales:

'The reputation of Scottish education is high and it is unexpected to find that early leaving is more the pattern there than in the south. It is not just that more of the less able leave: the greatest difference between Scotland and the rest of Britain is found amongst youngsters who are above average in measured ability:

Level of test score at Eight Years

	51 or less	52–60	61 or more
	% leaving school at 15	% leaving school at 15	% leaving school at 15
England and Wales	74.4	43.8	15.6
Scotland	89.6	58.3	17.4[1]

Something is being done to check early leaving. The ordinary grade was introduced to check this wastage and in their 1964 report the Scottish Education Department are to be found rejoicing at

'the very marked increase in the percentage of pupils assigned to Certificate courses who have remained at school beyond the age of fifteen. The number of Certificate pupils in S IV as a percentage of Certificate pupils in S I three years earlier was, in 1961, 61.2 per cent, in 1962, 66.6 per cent, in 1963, 71.3 per cent, and in 1964, 78.2 per cent. This remarkable increase – 17 per cent in three years – must mainly be accounted for by the introduction in 1962 of the ordinary grade.'[2]

Nevertheless the best of these figures is still very little better than the Central Advisory Council found in England in 1954, when they undertook an investigation into early leaving because it had been causing great concern south of the border, and it falls very far short of the ninety-one per cent of English grammar school pupils who, in 1962, completed at least five years before leaving school.

Beyond the ordinary grade the end result is much the same in Scotland as it is in England – that is to say that, in spite of the much more generous allocation of pupils to certificate courses, the percentage of the total age group who obtain a certificate at the age of seventeen which will qualify them for university entrance is almost exactly the same as the percentage in England who, from a smaller intake into the grammar schools, obtain such a certificate at the age of eighteen.

But it is no part of the democratic tradition that all children admitted to a certificate course should necessarily complete it successfully. Although there is selection, it errs markedly on the side of generosity, because the real test comes during the course itself and in the examinations at the end. The accent is on the

[1] J. W. B. Douglas, *The Home and the School*, 1964, p. 126.
[2] *Education in Scotland in 1964*, p. 32.

individual. As he has the opportunity, so he has the responsibility of contributing his own efforts. The original conception of the English School Certificate was that it should be a test of the whole form. The Scottish Leaving Certificate was always a matter for the individual candidate and the schools took very seriously the decision whether each pupil should be presented for examination.

EXAMINATIONS: THE PASS RATE

It is not easy to make a straightforward comparison between examining practice in the two countries because several factors need to be taken into account – particularly during the period when both the school and leaving certificates were awarded on a 'group' basis. Up to 1950 rather more than seventy per cent of candidates for the English School Certificate obtained a certificate compared with just over fifty per cent of candidates who achieved a Scottish Leaving Certificate. But the percentage of passes awarded in each individual subject was probably much the same – certainly it was just over seventy per cent in Scotland: the percentage of candidates awarded a pass in individual subjects in the English School Certificate seems to have been at least seventy: but only about fifty per cent passed with 'credit'. The rather different group requirements – and, in particular, the fact that passes on the higher grade were needed in Scotland – obviously account for differences in the award of group certificates, though it would also seem that English candidates took more subjects and therefore allowed themselves a greater margin for failure.

The introduction of the G.C.E. in 1951 and the S.C.E. ten years later means that group requirements are no longer a factor. It also means that the percentage of successful examinees in England is now lower than in Scotland. An ordinary level pass in G.C.E. is supposed to be of the same standard as a credit pass in the old School Certificate, and the examining boards have in practice ensured that it should be so by only awarding passes to some fifty per cent of candidates in each subject. England has abandoned the principle of an easy pass standard, if not the principle of discriminatory levels of marks.

Nevertheless, even though fewer English than Scottish pupils embark on a G.C.E. course at eleven and the failure rate is higher, just as many achieve a certificate as in Scotland and a higher proportion acquire more passes. Over eighty-four per cent leave school with a certificate showing passes in four or more subjects compared with only seventy-eight per cent in Scotland. Over fifty-two per cent pass six or more subjects compared with forty-four per cent in Scotland. It would seem that English candidates still leave themselves a large margin for failure. (In 1962 3,300 pupils who attempted six or more subjects failed the lot.) This may simply mean that English teachers realize that the G.C.E. is operated as a 'percentage fail' examination, so that the more candidates they enter the more will pass. Nevertheless, teachers in English grammar schools seem conspicuously successful, in comparison with Scottish teachers, in keeping their pupils at school until the examinations and seem conspicuously optimistic in presenting their pupils for examination.

INTERNAL ASSESSMENT AND EXTERNAL EXAMINATION

In England it was only during the second world war that significant use began to be made of teachers' estimates as part of the normal examining machinery. They are now used in the G.C.E. in order to reach a decision about borderline candidates. But, as the Secondary School Examinations Council say:

'Many other European countries are surprised to find that the public examinations in England and Wales make so little use of teachers' assessments. Here, it seems to be assumed that where a teacher's opinion of a candidate is in conflict with the result of the examination, it must be the teacher who is wrong. And there is, by and large, no machinery for taking teachers' assessments into account except through the machinery of appeals.'[1]

When the Ministry of Education yielded to pressure from the schools to scrap the rule that no child might take the G.C.E. below the age of sixteen they added a face-saving clause that under-sixteens might be entered for the examination provided that the school was satisfied that they had a good chance of passing. The published statistics do not allow a full check on the efficiency of this rule, but twenty per cent of pupils leaving school under the age of sixteen after having taken G.C.E. in 1962 failed in every subject attempted compared with ten per cent of such leavers over that age. This does not give much confidence in the teachers' obedience to the only rule which attempts to restrict the entry to the examination.

In Scotland, before the war, teachers presenting pupils for the Leaving Certificate had the difficult job of deciding which candidates to put in for the higher grade and which for the lower: they had to submit an estimate of their pupils' capabilities: they had to be prepared to discuss the examination results with H.M. Inspectors. During the last war the Department delegated the conduct of the Senior Leaving Examination entirely to subject panels of teachers in each area, with an H.M.I. in the chair, and to panels of assessors composed of headteachers, directors of education and an H.M.I.

The introduction of the ordinary grade in the S.C.E. has lessened the teachers' responsibilities partly because it is now possible for a pupil to make sure of an O grade pass on his way to the highers, and partly because the Department have introduced the device of awarding a 'compensatory' ordinary grade pass for a near miss in the higher grade examination, but mainly because the number of candidates has increased so much that it is impossible to consult the teachers, and the examinations are held later in the year. The teachers' participation in the examining process has been reduced in Scotland, too, to the submission of estimates which may be taken into account if an appeal is lodged against failure. But the past history of the examination leads to more appeals being lodged (at, of course, the discretion of the school).

It also means that Scottish children do not reach the examination room at all unless their teachers consider that they deserve to.

[1] Examinations Bulletin No. 1, 1963, p. 25.

CHAPTER NINETEEN

Selection and Survival: Higher Education

ADMISSION TO COLLEGES OF EDUCATION

Whatever anxieties Scottish children may have at eleven plus, at least they are spared some of the worst features of competition at seventeen or eighteen. At this stage Scotland has the regional, non-residential college or university with a more generous supply of places to start with, and, because there is no need to provide living quarters, more flexibility in providing extra places to meet rising demand. In England, the nation-wide provision of boarding schools and, more particularly, of predominantly residential institutions of higher education, means that students from the whole country are in competition with each other for places in establishments which are strictly graded in the prestige they enjoy. Oxford and Cambridge started, of course, by drawing their students from every area between Land's End and Berwick on Tweed (if not John O'Groats) simply because they were the only universities in the country. They have continued to be national universities.

A more instructive example of the differences in practice between England and Scotland in the selection of students for higher education is to be found in the field of teacher training. It is the proud boast of the Scottish colleges of education that they have never turned away a qualified applicant. In the nineteen-thirties, when there threatened to be some over-supply of teachers, there was admittedly a decision to limit the numbers of students accepted by the training centres. In the event the students themselves saw the difficulties of obtaining employment after training and did not present themselves in sufficient numbers to make any limitation of intake necessary. That apart, the Scottish training colleges have never, in all their history, refused to admit an applicant who was academically qualified for admission. To be sure the academic requirements for admission have been adjusted from time to time. It was the steadily improving staffing situation in the schools between the wars which made it possible to insist on graduation for all male teachers and to raise the standard for admission for women too, as well as lengthening the non-graduate course from two years to three. The minimum requirements for entry to a Scottish college of education are at the present time slightly higher than for English training colleges. Non-graduate women must possess two higher grade passes (of which one must be English) together with four Ordinary grade passes, and they must hold a pass at one grade or the other in arithmetic or mathematics. This requirement has been translated into equivalent terms in the English G.C.E. as a total of seven passes including one at advanced level, English language, English literature and mathematics. On these terms at least one-third and perhaps more than half of the women students actually admitted to English training colleges in 1962 would not have been qualified for admission to the non-graduate course at a Scottish college.[1] On the other hand the Scottish colleges have, apart from a medical examination, no other criteria for admission: there is no need to have more than the minimum qualifications to get in: there are no interviews. Indeed to conduct interviews of prospective students would be an intolerable task for the college staffs. It is impossible to decide as the result of a short interview whether or not an applicant can be turned into an acceptable teacher, and rejection at this stage would simply mean that the applicant was refused the opportunity to train as a teacher at all. The staffs of the English colleges are in a far different position. They only demand, as a minimum, five ordinary level passes in the G.C.E., and there are no requirements as to the subjects which shall be included. Every college, however, has the experience of receiving many more applications than it can possibly accept. The more popular colleges therefore adopt the practice of demanding more than the minimum academic qualification, and all colleges interview. There can be no guarantee that the minimum qualification required by the Ministry's regulations will secure a training college place, and the competition for places in the last few years has resulted in a considerable rise in the average attainment of the students actually admitted. Nor can there be any guarantee that the most impressive academic record will secure a place for the applicant who cannot survive an interview. From the point of view of the college interviewers they need have no qualms about rejecting the applicants they do not favour. They are not called upon to decide whether or not a young man or woman can be turned into an acceptable teacher: they only have to decide which of those who appear before them they happen to prefer. Those they reject will have other chances at other colleges. Those who, in the event, fail to gain admission to any training college can be regarded as having failed to impress any one of the hundred and fifty or more colleges in the whole country. The responsibility for rejecting a potential teacher is not laid at the door of any one college interviewing panel but at the door of the Clearing House which is supposed to ensure that every available place is taken up by a qualified applicant.[2] Certain English training colleges enjoy a much higher reputation than some others. They get the most applicants and can make a stricter choice. Just as

[1] The academic qualifications of 9,613 women admitted to general courses at Training Colleges in September 1962 were analysed by the A.T.C.D.E. Apart from 6 per cent who had qualifications other than the G.C.E., 29 per cent had no 'A' level pass (the number of 'O' level passes held by those who also had an 'A' level pass was not stated but a few may have had less than seven subjects in all); 59 per cent did not have a pass in Mathematics (although it should be noted that in Scotland a pass in Arithmetic alone suffices, but the English boards do not have examinations in Arithmetic); 2 per cent did not have a pass in English Language

This does not of course mean that such a large proportion of these women would have failed to qualify for a place at a Scottish College of Education had they been working towards the requirements laid down by Scottish regulations. It simply shows how different are the criteria for selection.

[2] In 1963–64 there were 21,198 applications for admission to Training Colleges in England and Wales registered with the Clearing House. Of these, 2,146 were not accepted by any college. The reasons given for rejection included: Unqualified, 735; Quite unsuitable, 49; Borderline, 1,272.

Q

Oxford and Cambridge draw off the cream from the other universities, some training colleges start with a higher reputation than others and are able to improve on it even further because they have the pick of the students. The other result of this situation is that schools already disposed to emphasize the development of 'personality', qualities of leadership, social ease of manner and an acceptable accent, are led to attach even more importance to this aspect of education because of the need their pupils have to acquit themselves well in interviews.

ADMISSION STANDARDS AND THE G.C.E.

The English system, with its selection for particular institutions, may attach an importance to qualities of personality and environment which is entirely beneficial. It may cast an aura around certain establishments which scares some potential applicants away. The system may, because of the intensity of the competition which it provokes, be an extremely effective means of forcing up academic standards. The objection is that it may do this in a quite uncontrolled way. The influence of particularly favoured establishments is almost certainly excessive. The entrance requirements for Oxford and Cambridge affect the work of most grammar schools and the sixth form studies of large numbers of pupils who are certain to go to other universities, as well as of those who are certain not to go to any. The system is completely uncoordinated. Individual faculties as much as individual universities have had their effect on the pattern of sixth form studies. It is also arguable that, in undertaking the difficult task of selecting the lucky few from far too many applicants, the faculties of the provincial universities have used the wrong criteria. At least Oxford and Cambridge used their own selection schemes and their own scholarship examinations – much as they have been criticized. But there has been a tendency elsewhere to attach too much importance to small differences in the marks obtained by candidates in their advanced level passes.

It has always been a feature of the English system that weight has been given not merely to the standard of a student's attainments but to the quality of his performance. In the School Certificate there were not just passes and fails; there were credits and distinctions. In the G.C.E. it was originally intended to abolish grades of pass. But the policy of the examining boards differed. Some refused to divulge marks: some made them available to the schools but asked that they be treated as confidential: some published them. Public opinion seemed to be in favour of the disclosure of marks.

As regards the advanced level in the G.C.E. the Secondary School Examinations Council in their third report seriously considered, and saw considerable force in the arguments for, the introduction of a new level of school examination – the 'U' or university level – at a standard above that of the advanced level. 'Papers at the new level would be specially designed to test promise rather than achievement.'[1] On balance they rejected the idea, but, nevertheless, made two proposals which have been carried out. Firstly that, without any alteration in the

[1] *The General Certificate of Education and Sixth Form Studies*, H.M.S.O., 1960, p. 5.

standard of the advanced level pass, there should be no less than five grades of pass mark: these would be published as A, B, C, D and E. The refinement of five grades was thought necessary to help the universities in their selection of applicants, and it was implicit in the Council's report that only those with a pass at grade C or above would be likely to secure a place at a university. Secondly the Council recommended that there should be additional 'S' or special level papers, set on the same syllabuses as the advanced level but with questions of a more searching nature or requiring somewhat wider reading. This really amounted to the retention of the former 'scholarship level' papers which had been used to give extra refinement in the selection of pupils to be awarded state scholarships on the results of the G.C.E. examination, but it was felt that with the abandonment of the state scholarships the universities would still need the additional papers to help them to discriminate between applicants in spite of the A, B, C, etc. grades of pass.

In much the same way the standards for admission to teacher training colleges have been raised. Although the minimum entrance requirements are still expressed in terms of the ordinary level, by 1962 sixty-five per cent of entrants to the colleges had in fact got at least one pass at advanced level including forty per cent with two or more A level subjects. Only a little over five per cent had the bare minimum of five ordinary level passes. Some of the more popular colleges are not only demanding A level passes for admission but are expecting students to hold an A level pass in the subject they propose to take in a 'main course' at the college: 'faculty requirements' are entering into this field too. One interesting point about the demand for A level before admission to a training college is that it may be said to be approximately of the same standard as the final examination in training colleges in the nineteen-twenties. (The final examination was supposed to be of about the same standard as the London intermediate degree examination, which in turn was about the same as the main subject in higher school certificate, on which in turn the advanced level G.C.E. was based. But perhaps this is an area in which the logic of A=B=C=D does not apply.)

ADMISSION STANDARDS AND THE S.C.E.

Standards for admission to institutions of higher education in Scotland have been raised too. They have not been forced upwards so far or so fast as in England. But when they have been introduced they have been adopted advisedly. In teacher training for example the last radical tightening up of the requirements was in 1931 when there threatened to be an over-supply of teachers and the opportunity was taken to control the flow of students by raising the standards. Since then the basic admission qualification has remained substantially the same except when the replacement of the lower by the ordinary grade in S.C.E. called for an adjustment. There have been minor modifications from time to time – either as a matter of policy or from expediency – but this has been done nationally, not at the whim of each college. At certain periods a pass in arithmetic or mathematics has been required: at others it has not. For some years the rule was that a girl must have been presented in arithmetic in the Leaving Certificate but need not have passed. By and large the desired standard has been insisted upon whenever it was practicable to do so, but has been relaxed to some extent in times of shortage. Currently, however, in spite of a shortage of teachers, the entrance requirements have been slightly tightened up. The fact that the proportion of students who seek admission to the colleges with more than the minimum requirements has been rising is a tribute to rising standards in the schools without the kind of external pressures which operate in England. (It also reveals the extent to which girls who are quite capable of taking a university degree prefer, even in academic Scotland, to take the shorter non-graduate course.)

For the universities, too, policy on admission standards has been decided nationally. The four Scottish universities have had a common matriculation standard administered by the Scottish Universities Entrance Board. This Board has been responsible for granting the Certificate of Attestation of Fitness. The Certificate attests that an applicant is gratified for admission to a university though it is then up to him to apply to the university of his choice. But the universities have, until recent years, usually been able to accept all qualified applicants. Faulty requirements represent no more than a bias within the 'group' needed for an Attestation. Scotland has been in the happy position that candidates knew exactly where they stood, and were not faced with the multiplicity of requirements and the multiplication of examinations which have made application to the universities so complicated for English students. The control of the Universities Entrance Board over admission requirements has, however, been broken by the grant of university status to Strathclyde. It is not in membership of the Board. With more new universities to come and some doubts being expressed by the older foundations, the future of the board is under discussion.

The requirements for the attestation of fitness were raised between the wars. Recently, for the first time, discrimination in the level of pass mark in the examinations has been introduced. The Scottish Certificate of Education and the University Preliminary Examination are now awarded with passes at credit and very good standard on the higher grade. The attestation of fitness is granted on the basis of four highers, or of three highers if one of them is obtained with a very good pass or two of them are passed at credit standard (provided of course that the 'group' requirements are also met). It is said, however, that this has been done, not in order to discriminate between too many applicants chasing too few university places, but because the universities had evidence that students who had passed their highers comfortably did in fact prove to be more capable when they reached the university.

ORDINARY AND HONOURS DEGREES

The fact is that the Scottish universities, with four years at their disposal to bring a student up to the level of an honours degree, have less need to insist on high achievements in the subjects in which a student proposes to specialize at the university (if indeed he proposes to specialize at all). The universities are not under the same need to control the quality of the candidates they admit, because they are not called upon to select the potential honours student before he arrives. The headmaster of a comprehensive school has no need to use the eleven plus results to select his G.C.E. candidates: he can sort them out after he has had the chance of teaching them for two or three years. The Scottish universities, if not comprehensive, are at least 'bilateral'. Approximately two-thirds of their students enter in the hope of taking an honours degree, and approximately one-third succeed in doing so.

But to say that two-thirds of Scottish students start at the university in the hope of obtaining an honours degree is not the same thing as saying that they start on an honours course. It is in England that well over two-thirds of undergraduates enter direct into an honours course and stand the risk of being thrown out if they do not reach the required standard. In Scotland all arts and pure science students take courses in their first two years which are common to the honours and the ordinary degree and it is by their performance in the subjects in which they would like to take honours during those first two years that they earn the right to proceed to honours. The Robbins Report[1] makes this plain in a table showing the three broad types of course taken by students in their first year in 1961–62 (honours, pass, or studies common to both honours and pass degree courses) and the types of course they were expected to finish by taking in their final year.

TABLE 44. *Percentage of students taking honours and pass degree courses and common studies.*

| | Type of course in first year | | Type of course in final year | | |
	ALL STUDENTS		Honours	Pass	Common studies
ENGLAND AND WALES	Honours	72	68	4	—
	Pass	4	—	4	—
	Common Studies	24	13	8	3
SCOTLAND	Honours	19*	19	—	—
	Pass	—	—	—	—
	Common Studies	81	34	44	3

* This figure represents students of technology at the Universities of Glasgow and Strathclyde. At the other Scottish universities (and in other faculties at Glasgow and Strathclyde) there is no allocation to honours in the first year.

Relegation from the honours to a pass degree course is just as important a route to a pass degree in England as direct entry: which is another way of saying that it is regarded as very much a second best by half the students who take it, and represents a partial failure. When students start in common studies for pass and honours, the eventual division of them between honours and pass

[1] App. IIB, Table 5, p. 211.

courses is more nearly equal than where all students start on an honours course and those who fail to reach the required standard are transferred to a pass course: which is another way of saying that the Scottish universities know, when admitting students, that a large proportion of them will be perfectly content with a pass degree, whatever their secret aspirations may be – and that is another way of saying that there need be fewer inhibitions about refusing some students admission to the honours course. A higher degree of selection may be operated with less sense of failure being felt.

DEGREE EXAMINATIONS

Even so there are more outright failures at Scottish universities. Some four-teen per cent of students who entered the Scottish universities in 1955 left with-out success before the spring of 1958, compared with twelve per cent at London, ten per cent at the other English universities and only four per cent at Oxford and Cambridge. The Robbins Report[1] gives the following figures with the intention of showing that 'first generation' undergraduates are not less successful than their fellows whose fathers were non-manual workers (a point which seems proven except in the case of Scotland):

TABLE 45. *Percentage of undergraduate entrants in 1955 (excluding medical students) who left without success by the Spring of 1958.*

	Father's occupation	Men		Women	
		%	Total entrants	%	Total entrants
Oxford and Cambridge					
	Non-manual	4	2,780	6	450
	Manual	3	386	6	32
London					
	Non-manual	13	1,260	13	830
	Manual	12	486	10	166
Civic					
	Non-manual	12	3,335	8	1,730
	Manual	10	1,844	11	564
Scotland					
	Non-manual	13	950	8	645
	Manual	18	400	14	132

But, although there is a marked difference between the failure rates of Oxford and Cambridge and the other universities, and some difference between Scottish universities and English universities as a group, the difference between any one Scottish university and any one university in England is not great. The Robbins Report also lists[2] the failure rates of twenty-four individual universities: the list shows that each university is fairly consistent in the percentage of students it fails from year to year. They are listed in random order and are anonymous. If in fact the failure rate in each individual Scottish university were enormously different from the rest of British universities it would be possible to identify the

[1] App. IIA, Table 13, p. 135.   [2] App. IIA, Table 5, p. 129.

Scottish universities in spite of the fact that the list is anonymous. In fact it seems impossible.

On the other hand the outright failure rate is not the only factor of importance to undergraduates. Altogether some five per cent of students in arts and science complete their courses but take more than the normal period to do so. In technology and agriculture the proportion who need an extension of the course is eight per cent and in medicine it is thirty per cent. Unfortunately there are no separate figures for England and Scotland.

Further, it is possible to fail an examination at the first sitting, but recoup the failure at a resit without loss of time. The Hale Committee on University Teaching Methods records that 'All the Scottish universities and some others rely on a resit at the end of September to enable a sizeable proportion of their students (upwards of forty per cent in Scotland) to qualify for further study after failing or partly failing in examinations held in June'.[1] Their enquiry showed that a rather higher percentage of students claimed to have spent their long vacation in study if they had re-sits in September than did those who had no examinations to prepare for!

It must be remembered that Scottish students in any case have more examinations than other undergraduates. The ordinary M.A. is awarded on the basis of seven distinct courses each of which is assessed by a final examination. Some figures recorded by the Scottish Council for Research in Education in 1936 reveal a remarkable tolerance by the university of students who needed more than one attempt at an examination before they could achieve a pass. They traced the careers of all students entering one of the Scottish universities in 1928. Students who qualified for admission on the basis of passes in the Leaving Certificate were shown to have been more successful than those who did so by virtue of passes in the University Preliminary Examination. Even so, it was found that, of the 340 with a Leaving Certificate who had been following a course in arts or pure science thirty per cent had not yet graduated four years after their admission to the university. (Of the 123 students with other entrance qualifications as many as forty-nine per cent had not graduated four years later.) The same sort of figures were produced for medical students. The university record of the leaving certificate group was expressed in terms of the number of degree examinations they had taken but failed:

TABLE 46. *Scottish university students: exam failures.*

NO. OF FAILURES	0	1	2	3	4	5	6	7	8	9	10	11	12	13	14	15	16	...20
Arts and Pure Science	155	54	40	19	22	9	7	10	7	4	2	3	2	1	1	3	1	—
Medical	24	6	4	6	4	3	3	—	1	1	2	2	—	—	1	—	—	1

The rules have been tightened up at some Scottish universities since 1936. Normally a student will be excluded if he has not obtained at least two passes by

[1] *University Teaching Methods*, 1964, p. 21.

the end of his first year and at least four by the end of his second year. It is therefore no longer possible to accumulate as many as a dozen or more failures during a degree course. Nevertheless failure in some part of the course is still a very common experience.

Some figures have been collected of the university careers of ordinary graduates training for teaching in Aberdeen. They show that there has been some increase in the number who obtained more than the minimum number of seven passes for the ordinary M.A. but that it took them rather more 'second shots' to get them. How far these figures are typical of all Aberdeen graduates it is impossible to say:

TABLE 47. *University passes in ordinary M.A. degree passes and re-sits.*

Graduating in	1929–31	1936–38	1941–43	1947–48	1959–61
Percentages with:					
Minimum 7 passes	19.3	20.1	12.8	24.0	6.5
8 or 9 passes	48.0	54.9	50.4	38.5	65.3
10 or more passes	32.7	25.0	36.8	37.5	28.2
	100	100	100	100	100

Number of sittings of degree examinations required to obtain the above passes:

			1941–43	1947–48	1959–61
Percentages with:					
Minimum number of sittings			53.0	33.7	30.2
1 or 2 re-sits			34.8	40.3	35.3
3 or more re-sits			12.2	26.0	34.5
			100	100	100

Two-thirds of ordinary graduates entering teaching in north-east Scotland recently have had the experience of failing one or more degree examinations. With honours graduates the situation is different. In finally adopting the English pattern of honours degrees alongside the traditional ordinary degree the Scottish universities also adopted, for this purpose only, a different system of examinations. The honours examination is usually a once-for-all assessment in which one's 'class' is irrevocably determined. It is only the courses leading to the ordinary degree (including those common both to ordinary and to honours students) which are assessed by examinations in which re-sits are possible. Nevertheless, in 1959–61, among honours graduates entering the teaching profession in Aberdeen the average number of re-sits in those subjects in which re-sits were permitted was 0.5. This does not mean that half of the honours graduates had had one re-sit during their course: it does mean that to the extent that fewer than half had that experience an equivalent number must have had more than one re-sit.[1]

[1] See J. Scotland, 'The Quality of Student Teachers' in *Scottish Educational Journal* Vol. 47, pp. 115–17 and 133–34: 1 Jan. and 7 Feb. 1964.

INTERNAL ASSESSMENT AND EXTERNAL EXAMINATION

At university level the difference in examination practice lies not so much between English and Scottish universities as between Oxford, Cambridge (and London) and the rest of British universities. At Oxford and Cambridge the colleges do the teaching and the university does the examining. But in the newer English universities, as in Scotland, lecturers are called upon to combine the function of teacher and examiner of their own students. The Hale Report on *University Teaching Methods* shows that, in a sample survey, only fifty-one per cent of university teachers at Oxford and Cambridge expected to participate either officially or unofficially in the setting and marking of examinations in 1962. At British universities other than Oxford, Cambridge and London the proportion was as high as ninety-four or ninety-five per cent. This is not to ignore that the amount of examining is greater in Scotland than in England: but the actual conduct of the examinations is much the same in the universities of both countries.

CHAPTER TWENTY

Boarding Education

COLLEGES OF EDUCATION

The poor student of Scottish tradition was prepared to tolerate the Spartan existence in his garret with his bag of oatmeal in the pursuit of knowledge. The English Public School boy also had to endure a Spartan existence, but not as a means to an end: it was an end in itself, because it was thought good for his soul. If this is a gross exaggeration of the living conditions of the modern Public School boy, no less than of the present-day Scottish undergraduate, it is never-the less true that the former goes to an expensive school largely in order to learn how to live, whereas the Scot still goes to a university in order to learn how to earn a living. And there is an element of the monastic still in the regime of many English universities, colleges and schools.

At least seventy-five per cent of the teachers[1] who staff the state schools of England moreover experience something very similar to the monastic atmo-sphere of the Public Schools and older universities during their three years at a training college. The colleges have changed considerably in the last twenty years, but they inherit the tradition established by Kay Shuttleworth. His proposal for a State Normal College having been rejected by the government in 1846 – 'sacrificed on the altar of sectarianism' – he founded the Battersea College as a private venture. It served as a model not only for the church colleges but also for the local education authority colleges which were to follow. 'At Battersea, life in college was regarded as a definite educational instrument. For many years corporate life of this kind was looked upon as of the highest value in the training of the teacher.'[2] In this attitude Kay Shuttleworth was not alone among the pioneers of teacher training. Joseph Lancaster consistently referred to the students of his Borough Road college as his 'family'. The first Principal of the St Mark's College, Chelsea, the Rev. Derwent Coleridge, wrote that 'The College must be an adapted copy, mutatis mutandis, of the elder educational institutions of the country . . . with their noble courts, solemn chapels and serious cloisters. . . . It must create the same esprit de corps among its alumni'.[3] Until very recently all English training colleges were still 'families'. In 1938, of eighty-three recognized colleges, only five had more than two hundred students.

---

[1] A. Sampson, *Anatomy of Britain Today*, 1965, p. 200:
   84 per cent of women on three year general courses; 73 per cent of men on such courses; 75 per cent of women on specialist courses; this compares with 22 per cent of students resident in hostels attached to Scottish colleges of education.

[2] R. W. Rich, *The Training of Teachers during the Nineteenth Century*, 1933, p. 76.

[3] D. Coleridge, *The Teachers of the People*, 1862, pp. 33–34.

Many of the new colleges which were established after the last war were of a similar order of size, and it was only in 1957 that the Ministry of Education ventured to suggest that a college with between 450 and 500 students was perhaps about the optimum size. The expansion of the teacher training system was carried out largely by the enlargement of existing colleges. The Robbins Report went slightly further in thinking that something nearer 750 was the right size for a college. At present half the English colleges have under 400 students, but there are now six colleges with more than 800.

It is only very recently that new training colleges in England have been established as a matter of policy in large towns (preferably university towns) so that the students, while still enjoying the essential experience of community living, might also share something of the cultural life of the neighbourhood. It is only as a matter of expediency that a few day training colleges have been opened in order to attract into the teaching profession those who could not train away from home.

In Scotland before the war there were no training colleges at all, but only 'training centres' in which some teachers received most of their training and all received some of their training. The centres have now become colleges. With the exception of two Roman Catholic colleges and the specialist college for the training of women teachers of physical education, all are non-residential and have more than 800 students: the largest has nearly 3,000. Three new colleges are being established, for 600 and 900 students.

UNIVERSITIES

So far as the English universities are concerned policy has swung back and forth: first Oxford and Cambridge (where the rule of celibacy for fellows of colleges was only abandoned in 1871); then the group of civic universities in Manchester, Birmingham, Sheffield, Leeds, etc.; more recently the wholly residential Keele[1] and new universities at Colchester, Norwich, York and similar towns; then another swing with the Robbins recommendation that 'of the new universities to be founded and the existing colleges selected for the eventual granting of university status we hope that the larger number will be in great centres of population or in their vicinity'.[2] But even the civic universities soon became national rather than regional institutions. They attach considerable importance to the provision of halls of residence and the Anderson Committee in 1958 recommended the payment of university awards at the higher 'resident' rate even to students in residence at a university within daily travelling distance of their homes. The proportion of English undergraduates living at home has fallen by over half since before the war.

The Scottish universities have always been regional and non-residential, which made them much more accessible and, of course, cheaper, quite apart from the fact that their tuition fees have always been considerably lower than

[1] Keele has now decided to 'experiment' by admitting non-resident students.
[2] Robbins Report, 1963, p. 163.

those in England. Until the recommendations of the Anderson Committee brought about greater uniformity with England,[1] the Scottish bursary regulations allowed education authorities to give an award for attendance at any university, but to limit the amount of the grant to the sum which would have been paid had the student attended the university nearest to his home. Authorities normally followed this practice in any case in which the recipient of the grant could have taken his chosen course at his nearest university. The alteration in the regulations has not so far brought about any change in the tradition of going to the university for the region. In 1961–62 eighty-four per cent of undergraduates at universities in England and Wales said that they had submitted applications to universities other than their own. In Scotland only twenty-nine per cent (most of whom were probably English) had even applied to another university. The percentages of university students by type of residence in 1961 was:

TABLE 48. *University students: residence*

	COLLEGES OR HALLS OF RESIDENCE	LODGINGS	AT HOME
English universities	31	54	15
Scottish universities[2]	13	40	47

SCHOOLS

In a country with such sparsely populated areas as Scotland has it might have been expected that there would be many more boarding schools than in England, but this is not so. That boarding is out of favour throughout the educational system is suggested by the fact that fewer than 10 per cent of handicapped children attend boarding schools in Scotland compared with 32.5 per cent in England.

The same attitudes are to be found outside the sphere of education altogether. The basis of the old poor law in Scotland was that relief was administered on a parish basis with the deliberate intention of keeping those in receipt of assistance in touch with their relatives and friends, whereas the English poor law showed much more of a tendency to institutionalize those who needed relief. In fact, in Scotland, there were no poors' houses at all outside the very largest towns.

There was a move to provide residential accommodation in Scotland for secondary school pupils in the nineteen-twenties. It was financed partly by the

[1] Anderson Report, *Report of the Committee on Grants to Students* (Cmnd. 1051), 1958.
[2] The percentages for each university are:

	COLLEGES OR HALLS OF RESIDENCE	LODGINGS	AT HOME
Aberdeen	6	52	42
Edinburgh	13	51	36
Glasgow	7	24	70
Strathclyde	3	36	61
St Andrews	37	47	16

education authorities and partly by the Carnegie Trust. But the solution normally adopted was to build a hostel in the same town as a day secondary school, not necessarily adjacent to the school, and, in some cases, the headmaster of the school had no jurisdiction over the hostel. A score of these hostels was built between the wars: the number of secondary schools with residential accommodation still remains at twenty.[1] In other areas, in default of boarding schools or hostels, pupils – even eleven- and twelve-year-olds – have to take lodgings in the town. When there were complaints about the school bus taking pupils from Lairg to school in Golspie recently the Director of Education for Sutherland retorted that there was no need for dissatisfied parents to send their children on the bus since the education authority were quite prepared to pay lodging allowances for them to stay in Golspie during the week. When pupils have to live in lodgings it is usual for the education authority to make it quite clear that finding and paying for, the lodgings is the parents' responsibility. The authority may offer advice and grant financial assistance, but they will not exercise any oversight.

It is not that Scotland never had any boarding schools. At an earlier date a number of boarding schools were actually converted into day schools. Starting with the George Heriot Hospital, founded in 1624, several so-called hospitals (cf. Christ's Hospital) were established as charitable institutions providing both boarding accommodation and tuition. The Argyll Commission in their third report in 1868, mentioned eleven of them. The commission had not investigated these schools themselves but they suggested that some enquiry should be made, with the implication that they thought that the endowments might be more profitably employed in maintaining efficient day schools, particularly in the large towns where working-class parents experienced greater difficulty in securing a good education for their children at a reasonable cost than those living in the rural areas. This suggestion was followed up by the Merchant Company which controlled four of the hospitals. An enquiry was carried out on their behalf by S. S. Laurie who eventually reported:

'I have been led to conclusions even much larger and more antagonistic to the present constitution of things than I have felt myself at liberty here to record.' His general conclusions have been summarized as follows: 'Neither intellectually nor morally did he consider the system a wholesome one, and he summed up its wants under the heads of moral and intellectual ventilation, self-dependence and family life. . . . Accordingly he advocated the breaking up of what he called the monastic character of these institutions, either by converting them into boarding establishments pure and simple and sending the foundationers to outside schools for their education or alternatively converting them into fee-paying day schools (as suggested by the Argyll Commission) and boarding out the foundationers with relatives or friends'.[2]

---

[1] A new programme has recently been announced for building hostels in the Highlands to meet the raising of the school age and further centralization of secondary education.

[2] H. M. Knox, *250 Years of Scottish Education*, 1953, p. 75.

Laurie later became Secretary of the education committee of the Church of Scotland. Legislation following on his recommendations to the Merchant Company permitted the enlargement of the scope of the hospital trusts. Most of them have now become the rough equivalent of English direct grant day schools; they may still have a boarding hostel but the boarders form a minority of their pupils. At least two of them became day schools in the 1870s but have acquired a hostel within the last thirty years. The trust funds have been diverted to other educational purposes, including further education.

PART VI

Specialization

And gin ye're ettlin for a bigger skweel,
And want at interviews to mak' yer mark,
Profess to cairry a'thing in yer creel
Fae mathematics doon te needlewark.

CHAPTER TWENTY-ONE

Universities

SCOTTISH DEGREE COURSES

A discussion of specialization presupposes some definition of what is meant by 'general education'. However, it will be sufficient to side-step that particular problem by treating the matter historically, and taking as the basis of 'general education' the classical conception of a liberal education as embodied in the study of the seven liberal arts. Both England and Scotland are sufficiently within the western European tradition for it to be possible to trace the gradual modifications which have been made in the curricula of their universities and schools to the original *trivium* (grammar, rhetoric and dialectic) and *quadrivium* (arithmetic, geometry, astronomy and music). In England, at any rate since the Renaissance, this process has been one of narrowing down the range of study. Particularly at Oxford the greater emphasis given to Greek as well as to Latin resulted in a concentration on the subjects of the *trivium*, while the sciences of the *quadrivium* were merely incorporated in the miscellaneous learning associated with rhetoric. Cambridge took a rather different line: at the beginning of the nineteenth century the only tripos examination was that in mathematics. But Oxford's influence was the more important in Scotland. Much of the heart-searching of the Scottish universities during the nineteenth century was related to the low standards of Greek scholarship compared with those at Oxford, and to the absence of any sound grounding in the language on the part of students entering the universities. John Burnet, Professor of Greek at St Andrews, attributed the comparative backwardness of the Scottish universities in the teaching of Greek to the fact that the medieval curriculum of grammar, logic, ethics and physics had in Scotland survived both the Renaissance and the Reformation. There had, he wrote, been various attempts to give to classical philology the predominance it enjoyed elsewhere but they had always been 'defeated by our old enemies the philosophy regents'.

In the Scottish universities at the beginning of the nineteenth century a prescribed curriculum led, after a four year course, to the degree of M.A. Though the subjects differed slightly from one university to another, the course in general consisted of Latin, Greek, logic and moral philosophy, mathematics and natural philosophy (i.e. physics). Courses in rhetoric, astronomy and music were still offered but they had no value as graduating subjects. In fact few students followed the prescribed course and few troubled to graduate: they did however take such courses in arts as were considered necessary to give them an adequate general background for the professions they intended to enter. The

R

commission of 1826–30 endeavoured to place graduation on a more systematic basis. They proposed to revive the B.A. degree which had fallen into disuse and devised a four-year course which should include double courses (i.e. two years' study) in Latin, Greek and mathematics and single courses in logic and metaphysics, moral philosophy and natural philosophy. Students who had obtained the B.A. might then proceed to an M.A. after a further year of more specialized work in literature, philosophy or science, though continued attendance was also prescribed at classes in political economy, natural history and chemistry. Alternatively the B.A. would be followed by a second degree in law or theology. This scheme was not put into effect. Its successor in 1858, which was, followed similar lines. The attempt to revive the B.A. degree was dropped but instead the M.A. might be awarded as an ordinary degree after a three- or four-year course (depending on entrance standards) for which the prescribed curriculum followed the earlier recommendation except that rhetoric – renamed as English literature – was added. The honours M.A. was to be awarded after a further year's study; the LL.B. and the B.D., too, could only be taken by graduates in arts.

But the 1858 scheme was not given much time to prove itself. In 1876 yet another Commission was appointed. In their Report

'not merely was the old general degree to be virtually abolished but a clean sweep was to be made of the native experiment with Honours courses which introduced the special only as a follow-up of the general, and, in lieu of these two existing types of course, there was to be introduced a new kind of qualification, hitherto unfamiliar in Scotland, of a severely specialist type. In short the aim of the Commissioners was the final realisation of the anglicising ideals which had for so long been pressed on a suspicious nation by an influential minority.'[1]

This is something of an overstatement. The commission in fact recommended a three-year degree course in one or other of the following fields:

Literature and philology (with courses in classics, English and one other language);

Philosophy (including logic and metaphysics, ethics, psychology and physiology);

Law and history (comprising civil law, constitutional or international law, political economy and a branch of ancient or modern history);

Mathematical science (pure and applied mathematics, natural philosophy and astronomy);

Natural science (natural philosophy and chemistry with a selection from mathematics, physiology, botany, zoology and geology).

There would be no separate course or examination for honours: an honours degree would simply be awarded for outstanding performance in the normal examinations. It would no longer be necessary to graduate in arts before taking

[1] G. E. Davie, *The Democratic Intellect*, 1961, p. 78.

a degree in law, medicine or science. But it is not fair to conclude that the commission were unsympathetic towards the ideal of a general education: indeed the curriculum within each department of study was not particularly narrow. Their purpose, however, was quite clearly to make the university the home of specialist studies and to confer on the schools the task of looking after the general education of their pupils, even if this meant a considerable revision of the part played by the schools in the educational system as a whole. It was a far more important part of the 1876 commission's report than of its predecessors' that there should be an adequate matriculation test for admission to the universities, and their view was that such a test should include examination in Latin, Greek, mathematics and English, plus, as soon as it became realistic to demand it, physical and natural science. What would be lost would be the compulsory study of logic and philosophy.

But the 1876 recommendations proved too drastic and premature. They were shelved until finally the compromise of 1889 was adopted whereby an honours M.A. course even more specialized than the courses suggested in 1876 was instituted but the old general degree was retained as the ordinary M.A. degree.

These are quite distinct alternatives even though students for both ordinary and honours degrees commonly attend the same classes in their first year or two. The curriculum for the ordinary degree has been considerably modified over the past fifty years, but students are still required to take at least seven one-year 'courses'. They are required to study five or six subjects: that is they will either take three subjects for only one year – at the 'ordinary' level – plus two subjects for two years each, up to the 'advanced' or 'second ordinary' level; or they may in some cases substitute for one of their two-year courses, two one-year courses in two 'cognate' subjects. In other words they take either five subjects of which two are taken to the advanced level or they take six subjects of which one is taken to advanced level and other two must be in related fields. In all four ancient universities – the University of Strathclyde does not conform – either logic and metaphysics or moral philosophy was, until recently, a compulsory subject. But in the last few years there have been several changes in the requirements: the precise regulations governing choice of subjects differ from one university to another but in general the effect has been that it is now possible to obtain an ordinary M.A. by taking either a classical or modern language, or mathematics or a science subject, instead of having to take, as was previously the case, both a language and maths or science. It is still usually difficult or impossible to take such subjects as English, history or geography without taking a language other than English or maths or science. It is interesting that the Edinburgh or Glasgow undergraduate who wants to concentrate on the arts side can avoid taking a course in mathematics by taking music as an alternative, and at Edinburgh the mathematician can similarly avoid taking a language by choosing music. Music is offered as a graduating course at all four universities and astronomy at three of them.

The University of Edinburgh explained to the Robbins Committee that they regarded their present ordinary degree course as 'a compromise between coherence, closer integration and greater depth on the one hand and breadth on the other: it is not therefore an honours degree with the top cut off, but a relatively broad-based general degree'. Even so, they felt it necessary to defend themselves from the charge that 'specialist was being substituted for liberal education. In justification it may be said that the polymath and the educated man are becoming increasingly difficult to equate'.[1]

In contrast with the maximum of two years' study of any subject which is an essential feature of the ordinary M.A., the honours course at all the Scottish universities requires four years' study of one's special subject. Two 'outside' subjects also have to be taken but there never was a requirement that these should be in completely unrelated fields: students are advised to take courses which have some relevance to their honours subject. The conception of the honours course is therefore the opposite of that for the ordinary degree. In practice, nevertheless, honours students during their first two years attend the 'ordinary' and 'advanced' course in their honours subject along with students who are aiming at the ordinary degree. (There are exceptions in some faculties). For their 'outside' subjects, honours students also take classes alongside ordinary degree students. It is therefore possible to plan one's course for the first two years in the hope of being permitted to take honours and, if one fails in this, to devote one's third year to logic and moral philosophy and such other subjects as are necessary to complete the requirements for the award of an ordinary degree. For science degrees the decision whether or not to proceed to honours may even be postponed to the end of the third year.

Eight examples are given in Table 49 of courses which were actually taken by recent graduates of the university of Aberdeen. They have admittedly been chosen to show what a wide breadth of subjects is possible. The five examples of an ordinary degree are all of students who chose to take one more than the minimum seven courses. There are two examples of a five-year course leading to both an ordinary and an honours degree, and one of a normal four-year honours course. The subjects taken in the Scottish Leaving Certificate are given as well as courses at the university.

It would have been quite impossible from the subjects in the leaving certificate taken by each of these students to guess what subjects they would go on to take at the university.

A LIBERAL EDUCATION

The division between general, pass, degrees and specialist, honours, degrees applies to England as well as to Scotland, but the general degrees are organized very differently and only twenty-five per cent (instead of over sixty per cent) of students take them. The Hale Report on *University Teaching Methods* summarizes the position as follows:

'While courses in one main subject have hitherto accounted for the majority of honours degrees, courses in three or more subjects have almost always led to

[1] Robbins Report, 1963, App. II B, p. 206.

TABLE 49. *Examples of Degree Courses*

ORDINARY M.A.

Example	A	B	C	D	E
Leaving Certificate passes at age 17	English (H) Maths (H) Science (H) Geog. (L) French (L)	English (H) Maths (H) French (H) Latin (H) Greek (H)	English (H) Maths (H) Geog. (L)	English (H) Maths (H) Science (H) French (H) Latin (H) History (L)	English (H) Maths (H) Latin (L)
and at age 18		Geog. (L)	Latin (H) French (H) Science (H)		French (H) Science (H)
University: 1st year	Botany Zoology	Maths Latin Psychology	Geog. French Chemistry	Maths Physics Chemistry Zoology	Maths Physics Logic
2nd year	English Geog. Moral Phil.	Logic Psychology (Adv.)	Geog. (Adv.) English	Maths (Adv.) Latin	Maths (Adv.) Psychology Latin
3rd year	English (Adv.) Spanish British Hist.	Scots Law English Zoology	Logic British Hist. Psychology	Psychology Logic	English Scottish Hist.

	ORDINARY AND HONOURS		HONOURS ONLY
Example	F	G	H
Leaving Certificate at age 17	English (H) Maths (H) Science (H) French (H)	English (H) Maths (H) French (H)	English (H) Maths (H) Latin (H) French (H)
at age 18	Biology (H) Latin (L)	German (H) Geog. (H)	German (H) Geog. (H)
University 1st year	Logic Political Theory Maths	English German Maths Philosophy	German Geog. French Geog. (Adv.)
2nd year	French Music	Maths (Adv.) Geog.	Botany Economic Hist. Scottish Hist.
3rd year	Botany Physics Chemistry	Geog. Geology	Geog. Geology
4th year	Chemistry	Geog.	Geog.
5th year	Chemistry	Geog.	

ordinary or pass degrees, and though there are certain notable exceptions at Oxford and Cambridge (e.g. Philosophy, Politics and Economics at the former; Natural Sciences Part I at the latter), and though some other English universities award honours degrees for general courses in arts or science, the number of students receiving honours degrees after general courses is at present inconsiderable. The position is probably changing, partly owing to the advent of new universities which are introducing honours courses in a wider range of subjects than has hitherto been usual, and partly owing to the introduction of joint honours courses in a number of other universities.[1] But these changes have not yet gone far enough to have much effect on the general statistical picture, and at the moment it remains true that honours and specialisation tend to go together.'[2]

Yet it is by no means certain that the difference between the English specialist honours course and the Scottish broad ordinary degree course implies any difference in the ultimate and professed aim of a university education. The difference in the means employed is considerable: the object is much the same. The Robbins Report, which favoured the introduction of more multi-subject courses, said that the 'essential aim of a first degree course should be to teach the student how to think'[3]: the Hale Committee, who saw considerable drawbacks in the general type of course, echoed this:

'The aim and nature of the undergraduate course seem to us to be quite distinct. This should be not only or even primarily to equip the student with knowledge, but also, and more importantly, to teach him to think for himself and work on his own. We shall assess the methods and practice of university teaching accordingly.'[4]

They proceeded to do so in a manner critical of Scottish practice. Both reports expressed concern at the extent to which first degree courses were becoming overloaded as the result of the increases in knowledge, and felt that without severe pruning of the curriculum there was a danger that the amount of fact to be assimilated would militate against the prime purpose of teaching the students to think for themselves. It would in fact be fair to adapt the statement by Edinburgh University and say that the dilemma in which the English universities find themselves is that the specialist and the educated man are becoming increasingly difficult to equate.

There is, however, another aspect to the traditional conception of the liberal education. Not only was a liberal education to be an education in breadth, it was regarded as the appropriate training for the free man – for the amateur in politics or in business, as against the technician or the wage-slave. In so far as the English have retained the attitudes of the amateur and the gentleman towards certain callings they have been guilty of a confusion of thought towards liberal education which the logical Scots have avoided. In Scotland a general education

[1] Including the Scottish universities.
[2] Hale Report, *University Teaching Methods*, 1964, p. 13.
[3] Robbins Report, 1963, p. 90.   [4] Hale Report, p. 9.

is seen quite clearly as the essential preparation for vocational training which, even if it be postponed until after graduation, is as necessary for all the professions as general education, even if it be abandoned at an earlier stage, is for more humble callings. The Scottish universities have been the stronghold of general studies: they have also been the places where vocational training is given to the lawyer, the minister, the accountant, the doctor, the veterinary surgeon, the engineer, the farmer, the forester and the scientist. (The teachers have been left out of the university scheme of things, but professional training has been regarded as no less necessary for them). The fact that at Oxford and Cambridge – after some slight hesitation – new specialisms were admitted, not as subjects for further study after a basic course in classics or in mathematics, but as alternatives, meant that the older 'liberal studies' were kept as the appropriate course for some, while others took courses more obviously related to their future employment. So it was that the Spens Report could epitomize a liberal education as being simply vocational education for the liberal professions. But the confusion of thought made it easy to assume that some specialists were better educated than others. Complaints were heard that scientists were illiterate, but until the Crowther Report coined the word 'innumerate' there were fewer complaints that specialists on the arts side were not fully educated.

CHAPTER TWENTY-TWO

Specialization in Schools

WHAT IS SPECIALIZATION?

When describing first degree courses at universities the term 'specialization' can be used in a fairly unambiguous sense. The undergraduate who specializes is concerned exclusively with one particular field of study: his course may not be confined to one subject; it is in any case difficult to delimit what is meant by a 'subject'; but everything he studies will be related in some way to his central specialism. The distinction between the Scottish honours course with its two 'outside subjects', some English honours courses which include ancillary subjects, and others which explicitly contain only one subject, is more apparent than real. But if one turns from the universities to the schools which serve them the picture is not quite so clear. There is almost certainly no English sixth form in which the pupils specialize exclusively in their interrelated advanced level subjects. Commonly between one-quarter and one-third of their time is devoted to other subjects. This 'minority time' (as the Crowther Report calls it) is usually taken up with a large number of subjects none of which gets an allocation of more than two or three periods in the week. But even if minority time is set aside only for physical education and games, a certain amount of essay writing on general topics, a period or two on current affairs and religious instruction, plus, perhaps, one lesson a week on musical appreciation, nevertheless it must be accepted that the school curriculum includes something other than pure and exclusive specialization. There is also the difficulty that some combinations of subjects can clearly be regarded as specialization: the boy who is taking pure and applied mathematics and physics at advanced level must be dubbed a specialist: but some combinations of subjects on the arts side are not quite so obviously within the normal definition of specialization: advanced level courses in English, French, and history for example. Specialization must therefore be taken to mean a course in which the pupil concentrates the major part of his time and his more serious attention on a group of science subjects; or science and mathematics; on linguistic studies with perhaps some history to supplement them; or on a rather less obviously interlocking group of arts subjects. Regardless of the amount of time devoted to them he will look upon his subsidiary subjects as being less important: they may or may not be modified in some way to take account of his specialist interests; he may or may not be studying them for examination purposes. The examples quoted above of the subjects taken by Scottish students include one (example B) who took five higher grade subjects in one year: English, French, Latin, Greek and mathematics. This is for Scotland an extreme example of 'specialization'. It is not comparable with any course that a pupil in an English sixth form might take because to take these five subjects concurrently to the advanced level would be far too heavy a commitment. It is true that this particular student would follow exactly the same syllabus in mathematics as any who took an equally biased course on the science side. It is true that he would regard his mathematics just as seriously as his language subjects because he was preparing for an examination at the same standard in all five subjects. It is true that he would have to regard his mathematics seriously not simply in order to gain a higher grade pass but in order to qualify for admission to a Scottish university. Nevertheless what really distinguishes the Scottish system from the English is that this would be true of all schools and of all pupils. The English sixth former who combined A level maths with A level languages would have made a deliberate choice to step outside the usual pattern of specialization. The Ministry of Education's statistics for 1961–62 define a specialist by reference to three groups of subjects:

Science group: Biology, botany, chemistry, geology, mathematical subjects, physics, zoology.

Arts group: Economics, English literature, geography, history subjects (including British constitution), languages (modern and classical).

Other subjects: All other subjects, including art, general studies, practical subjects, music, religious knowledge.

A science specialist is defined as one with at least one Advanced Level pass from the science group and, possibly, in 'other subjects' but *no* A level pass from the arts group. Similarly an arts specialist is defined negatively as one who has a pass in an arts subject but not in a science subject at advanced level. On the basis of this rather limited definition they show that the number of school leavers in that year with at least one A level pass was made up as follows:

TABLE 50. *A level 'specialists'.*

Science specialists	25,090
Arts specialists	26,300
Those with at least one A level pass from both the science and the arts group	3,000
Those with passes at A level only in 'other subjects'	3,800

Any definition of a specialist, and especially of an arts specialist, in school terms tends to be somewhat artificial. Equally any attempt to define a broad, or non-specialist, curriculum in terms of school examination subjects is bound to be artificial if not completely arbitrary. One might take as an example the three combinations of G.C.E. subjects set out below. These have been chosen to show the passes at ordinary and advanced level which, limited as they are in number, represent the minimum undertaking which an English grammar school pupil might plan in order to meet the minimum 'general' and 'course' requirements of as many English universities as possible with the intention of going on to take a degree in geography, classics and chemistry respectively:

Example A	Ordinary level	English language
		Mathematics
		French
	Advanced level	English literature
		History
		Geography
Example B	Ordinary level	English Language
		Mathematics
	Advanced level	Latin
		Greek
		Ancient History
Example C	Ordinary level	English Language
		French
	Advanced level	Mathematics
		Physics
		Chemistry

It would be difficult to maintain that the first example really represents a narrow specialization at the Advanced level. The other two examples are clearly specialist in that the three A level subjects are closely interrelated. Yet, if the three pupils represented by these examples failed to gain a place at an English university and decided to try their luck in Scotland, the third would, as one might expect, be refused a Certificate of Attestation of Fitness on the grounds that his A level subjects were all drawn from one group: the second, however, in spite of having taken an equally – if not more – specialized sixth form course, would be granted his attestation for the reason that linguistic studies in Latin and Greek fall into a different group in the Scottish University Entrance Board regulations from any kind of history – even ancient history. The pupil in the first example would on the other hand, be refused an attestation because his three A level subjects do not include either a foreign language or maths or science.

The general requirements of most English universities are similar to those of the Scottish Universities Entrance Board in their insistence upon a study of English, of a language other than English, and of mathematics or science. They differ in that a pupil is only required to take all three up to the age of about sixteen whereas in Scotland he has to do so up to the age of seventeen. Beyond that stage the English system differs not merely in allowing the exclusive study of either languages or scientific and mathematical subjects, but in allowing the 'English' group of subjects equal status with linguistic and scientific subjects.

A UNIFYING ELEMENT

But, although sixth form work and specialization are regarded as being virtually synonymous, the idea of some special bias has been inherent in English thinking about the secondary school curriculum at earlier stages than the sixth. Up to the middle of the nineteenth century the teaching of the classics dominated the Public Schools no less than the University of Oxford. The Clarendon Commission recommended in 1864 that rather more attention should be paid to mathematics, science, modern languages and music or drawing. Nevertheless they felt that some 'unifying element' was necessary and considered that in the classics this was still to be found. 'Among the services which the schools have rendered is undoubtedly to be reckoned the maintenance of classical literature as the staple of English education, a service which far outweighs the error of having clung to these studies too exclusively.'[1] The move at the end of the century to broaden the school curriculum even further, however, and the increasing importance attached to science and technology, finally succeeded in reducing the classics to but one among many disciplines. It was at least admitted that the classicist who had been badly taught might be ill-educated, even if the classics well taught remained a sufficient basis for a sound education.

'We are aware [said the Bryce Report] that there are some who would limit the term education to the discipline of faculty and the culture of character by means of the more humane and generous studies, and who would deny the name to instruction in those practical arts and sciences by means of which man becomes a craftsman or a breadwinner. But this is an impossible limitation as things now stand. We have just seen that the training in classics may have as little liberal culture in it as instruction in a practical art; modern literature may be made a field for as narrow and technical a drill as the most formal science.'[2]

The Bryce Report expounded the proposition that there were three elements in all secondary education – 'which we may call the literary, the scientific and the technical', and suggested that all three elements ought to be present in every curriculum. But there was no question of requiring that equal weight should be given to all three:

'They may be combined in a great variety of forms and proportions. Experience alone can show which forms and which proportions are most likely to be absolutely best, we will not say as a scheme of intellectual training but even as fitted to the needs of particular classes of persons inhabiting particular areas and engaged in particular kinds of industry.'[3]

The notion that all these elements must be included in a liberal secondary education was enshrined in Morant's *Secondary School Regulations* in 1904. The regulations prescribed a 'general education, physical, mental and moral' which must include (i) English, history and geography, (ii) at least one language other than English, (iii) mathematics and science, (iv) drawing and (v) physical

[1] Clarendon Report, 1864, p. 56. [2] Bryce Report, 1895, pp. 132–5.
[3] Ibid., p. 284.

exercises, and some provision had to be made for teaching manual work to boys and housewifery to girls. With the introduction of these regulations south of the border the extent to which England and Scotland diverged in their interpretation of what was meant by a liberal education at the secondary school level was reduced to the fact that music was compulsory in Scottish secondary schools but not in English, and that the Board of Education insisted on some provision being made for the teaching of manual work and housewifery, whereas the Scotch Education Department did not. The Scottish regulations were in fact more explicit in allowing some variation in emphasis: they required English (with literature and history) and, 'as a rule', a language other than English, to be studied throughout the secondary course but all other subjects need only 'find a place in every curriculum although they need not always be studied throughout'. The organization of the Leaving Certificate also allowed examination subjects to be taken at two different levels whereas the School Certificate required that all subjects taken for the examination must be given equal emphasis up to the age of about sixteen. The School Certificate was more directly responsible than the 1904 regulations for imposing, for a time, a more rigid pattern on the schools than the Bryce Commission would have wished.

Morant's regulations were mainly concerned with the establishment of a four-year secondary course, and the School Certificate, together with the matriculation requirements of the universities helped to formalize the curriculum of the secondary schools up to the fifth form. The fact that the sixth forms were at the same time rapidly developing and that the schools were unable to decide whether their main task lay in the provision of academic courses for those preparing for university entrance, or whether they should take cognizance of the growing numbers of their pupils who entered directly into industry and commerce meant, however, that the basic course for the first four years was constantly open to reassessment. Underlying this was the conflict between the feeling that the school course needed some 'unifying element' and the belief that various different elements were necessary to an all-round liberal education. At this period there was very little question of the downward pressures from the sixth forms which have been blamed more recently for the practice of pre-specialization lower down the school. The first assault in fact on Morant's conception of a general and liberal education up to at least the age of sixteen came on behalf of those who would introduce technical and vocational studies into the secondary schools. It was the Board of Education which opened the breach by writing, in their report for 1912–13, that,

'while it would clearly be improper to allow pupils to concentrate their attention upon a single subject or group of subjects before a good foundation of general education has been laid, or to carry specialization so far as to encroach on the sphere of the Technical School . . . the Board are prepared in suitable cases to approve schemes of instruction which vary considerably from that of the normal secondary school. The variation may take the form of specialised work in the higher classes alone, or the school course may be given a certain bias throughout with the object of developing interest in and capacity for the occupations, whether rural, industrial or commercial, which the majority of pupils are likely to take up.'

By 1922 the Board were giving a rather different reason for each school having a particular bias: 'a general curriculum is only justified in so far as it is a nucleus curriculum and leaves sufficient margin in time for the individual tendencies of schools and staffs to operate.' The Spens Committee seemed to agree. They produced every possible reason for disagreeing with the fundamental ideas incorporated in Morant's regulations: 'Educational values' inhere, not in particular subjects, but in the spirit of study. *To obtain these values it is not necessary to study a wide range of subjects.*' There should be some unifying element in the curriculum – for which purpose English should take over the function previously performed by the classics. Some pre-vocational training would be in the interests of many grammar school pupils. Yet, in the end, the Committee believed so implicitly that certain natural groups of subjects (or rather 'activities' as they preferred to call them) each had an important contribution to make to the education of the adolescent – which could not be made by any other activity – that they concluded by recommending a curriculum which, in its broad outline, was no different from that contained in the regulations of Morant which they had so strongly criticized. They concluded that the curriculum of every grammar school should include:

I English, religious knowledge (scripture), history, geography, literature.
II Languages.
III Mathematics, science.
IV Music, art, handicraft, domestic science.
V Physical education.

The only respect in which their recommendations differed from existing practice was that they thought that the subjects in groups IV and V should receive a more prominent place in the curriculum and that although the schools should provide opportunities for the study of all the subjects in the first three groups, this did not mean that all pupils must study all these subjects at the same time or for the whole of their school life.[1] This was only a return to the position taken by the Bryce Commission.

The Norwood Report, concerned as it was with academic standards in the grammar schools, was much more in favour of specialization:

'The phrases "the balance of the curriculum" and "breadth of curriculum" seem to be misleading and indeed to have misled. The phrase "the balance of the curriculum" throws the emphasis in the wrong place; subjects are not in themselves complementary or antithetic or even antidotic to one another, as they sometimes seem to be regarded. . . . The curriculum cannot be balanced by opposing, say, Art or Music to the study of Languages or Mathematics. A broad education might be based on very few subjects handled by a teacher with a breadth of outlook.'[2]

[1] Spens Report, 1938, pp. 164–89. [2] Norwood Report, 1943, p. 60.

The report deplored a 'certain sameness' which results from all schools trying to find place for too many subjects. It is part of the thesis of the tripartite system that secondary schools should cater for the variety of interests and aptitudes as well as abilities of their pupils and therefore the Norwood Report advocated freedom to the schools to devise curricula suited to their pupils and to local conditions. From thirteen plus onwards, therefore, the report considered some differentiation of the curriculum to be legitimate, and its authors were apparently not at all concerned by the fact that 'such differentiation generally follows two main lines of interest, namely, "humanities" and natural science and mathematics.' In the years fourteen plus and fifteen plus it was felt that differentiation was probably best shown in increased emphasis on suitable subjects rather than in widely different choice of subjects. From fifteen plus onwards the load of subjects should be made lighter:

'Part of the criticism, we believe, of the Secondary School pupil arises from his study of too many subjects with the same degree of intensity; and we should recommend that in the last year or even the last two years of the Main school course, four subjects should be studied as chief subjects, and that contact with some should be maintained and opportunity be given to make acquaintance with others.' 'The compromise which in education must always cause thought and anxiety is the compromise between breadth and depth. At the moment, speaking generally, a broad area of ground is dug and it is dug all to the same depth; we should prefer that much the same area should be partly trenched deep and partly dug over.'[1]

If that was the attitude of the Norwood Committee to the curriculum of the grammar school up to the fifth form it goes without saying that, although they made no detailed recommendations about the sixth form, they hoped that the number of subjects would not be too numerous. At the same time they hoped that sixth form specialists would have opportunity, as they had lower down the school, of maintaining contact or 'making acquaintance' with subjects outside their main field of study. They suggested, for example, that lectures on the development of scientific theory would be of value to those who were not giving special attention to science. And this gives us a clue to the main difference in attitude between the schools in England and those in Scotland when it comes to the planning of the curriculum. The English schools start from the basis of specialization and of the particular interests of the pupil. They may plead that the pupil on the arts side should be 'numerate' and that the science specialist should be 'literate', but the assumption is that the knowledge of the specialist in his own field shall be thorough and that his knowledge of other fields must necessarily be that of the amateur. The idea of integrating the curriculum, or of giving it a unifying element has in practice amounted to this, that other topics must be in some way related or complementary, to the one subject, or group of subjects, which forms the core of any given courses of study.

The Crowther Committee devoted a considerable amount of attention to the

[1] Ibid., p. 74.

criticism that the sixth forms of English grammar schools had carried specialization too far, and strongly recommended that humanists should be made to be 'numerate' and that scientists should be trained to be 'literate'. They considered, however, and rejected, a suggestion that three advanced level subjects should normally form the sixth form programme, but that for the arts specialist one of his three subjects should normally be a science and for the scientist one should be taken from the arts side. The result of this they said would perhaps be something like the continental system [or the Scottish] but on a less broadly extended front. But they disliked the suggestion for three reasons: first, that it would reduce the number of A level subjects a sixth former could take within his chosen discipline, and would thereby forfeit the advantages which accrue from the interlocking of related specialist studies. Secondly they felt that the 'subject-minded' pupil ('as the best are at this age') would resent being forced to study a subject in which he was not very interested: 'It seems to us clear that, although this plan may command the interest of those pupils whose interests are diffuse, it would not solve the problems of most of the intellectually better Sixth Formers.' Thirdly they felt that the curriculum in any subject, if it was designed for the specialist, would be so very different from the type of curriculum required to meet the needs of the non-specialist that the scheme was impracticable. Moreover the value of the teaching in most subjects would be considerably lessened by the presence of two groups of pupils with widely differing interest in, and knowledge of, the subject and its background.[1]

SCOTLAND

It is sufficient to set beside this reasoning of the Crowther Report a quotation describing the Scottish universities before 1892:

'There is nothing anywhere quite like a Scottish University class as it was then. It was a heterogeneous but united body from first to last. One entered and, allowing for wear and tear, one left college, with the same body of students. But that united body included students of all degrees of excellence and variety of capacity, from the candidate for honours in all subjects in which honours could be taken – classics, mathematics, philosophy and the sciences – to the humblest aspirant of a pass degree. The fact that one was a candidate for honours did not separate him from the class. The work for honours was something additional, done entirely by private reading. . . . The mathematical student contended for a good place in the Latin and Greek class; the classical student for a good place in mathematics and physics: both for distinction in philosophy and literature. . . . Such a system was, one may suppose, simply an extension of the school, and so it was, but under new conditions of ever-increasing freedom, self-determination, and responsibility.'[2]

If there is one thing on which most Scottish teachers are quite clear, it is that

[1] Crowther Report, 1959, pp. 272, 273.
[2] Burnet, Grierson and others. *Problem of National Education* (1919), quoted in Davie, op. cit., p. 101.

they do not wish to adopt the English system of specialization. The Advisory Council on Education in Scotland in their Report on Secondary Education published in 1947 recommended that the Leaving Certificate should be reorganized to conform to the English pattern of a school certificate at age sixteen and a higher school certificate at age eighteen. They felt that the new school certificate might be awarded on a subject, not a group, basis. But they did not suggest

'that the curriculum leading up to the School Certificate should be determined by the immature notions of the pupil or the predilections of the headmaster. On the contrary we hold that the Scottish Education Department must continue to lay down the broad lines on which secondary education is to proceed, ensuring a proper balance of studies and due attention to those subjects which enlightened opinion deems essential.'

The new higher school certificate, which should be awarded on examinations at both the principal and the subsidiary level, should allow considerable flexibility. Many pupils would study more intensively some of the subjects they had taken up to school certificate level and others would break new ground – for example 'much of the best work in foreign languages will fall within the VIth Form period, the Classical pupil turning to Russian, Spanish or Italian', but,

'even at the VIth Form stage, the curriculum should, in our view, still be subject to the general approval of the Scottish Education Department, in order to ensure two essential conditions – (1) that every pupil continue till the end of the school course the systematic study of the understanding and use of English, and (2) that no course be unduly narrow or over-specialized. In regard to (2), however, we are satisfied that a VIth Form course can be both wide and liberal without necessarily conforming to a stern doctrine of "compulsions".'

The Council were in fact confident that the evils of premature specialization would be avoided partly because the Scottish universities could be relied upon not to exert the kind of pressures on the schools of which Oxford and Cambridge were guilty and partly because the Scottish Education Department would be stout champions of the Scottish tradition. But it was on this second safeguard that they placed greatest reliance.[1]

In their enthusiasm for their own proposals they would have been prepared to ignore the question of university entrance requirements: 'We realise that the proposed School Certificate could not stand related to university entrance requirements as the Leaving Certificate has long done. So far from deploring this, we welcome it, for we are convinced that the effects of the existing arrangements on the Leaving Certificate and through it on Scottish secondary education have been bad.' Yet they did call in aid the fact that the universities themselves were at the time reconsidering their admissions policy.

'We have not discussed the matter with the universities or their Entrance Board, but it is common knowledge that from their end also the existing practice is not

[1] *Report on Secondary Education*, pp. 56, 57.

free from difficulties and that the provision of Ordinance LXX that there must be one set of entrance regulations applicable to all faculties becomes increasingly hard to defend. Indeed there are many who have come to think that instead the universities should make two quite distinct demands on their entrants (1) as to their general education, and (2) as to their progress in those special studies germane to what they propose to do in the university itself.'[1]

If, in fact, those who thought this had carried the day, then the Scottish universities' entrance system would have been exactly parallel with that of the English universities, and the schools would probably perforce have adopted something much more like the English G.C.E. As it is the universities still base their admission requirements on the higher grade. The 1960 working party which also recommended the introduction of an advanced grade did consult the universities and reported that

'The Entrance Board and the four Senates are agreed that the university entrance requirements should be so framed as to make it possible, and normal, for a secondary school pupil to fulfil them in the fifth year. This implies that passes on the Higher grade, or some combination of passes on the Higher and the Ordinary grades, would qualify for university entrance, and the attainment of Advanced grade passes would be unnecessary for this purpose.'[2]

With the abolition of the lower grade when the Scottish Certificate of Education was introduced the Scottish Universities Entrance Board recast their requirements almost entirely in terms of the higher grade, rather than in terms of combinations of the higher and the ordinary grades, thus attempting to preserve to a considerable extent the position that all subjects qualifying for their attestation of fitness must be studied up to the fifth year.

PREMATURE SPECIALIZATION

Most of the misgivings which have been expressed in England have been on the score of 'premature' specialization or of 'excessive' specialization. It is the adjectives which are important. Premature specialization affects the fourth and fifth years of the grammar schools, although it is downward pressures from the sixth forms and, through them, the universities which have been blamed for the phenomenon. There are two aspects to it. First, a pupil may be confronted with a choice of curriculum which channels his future education along one particular line and makes it impossible for him to change his mind at a later date without some difficulty and loss of time. It might be better to distinguish this aspect of the problem by calling it 'canalization' rather than premature specialization. The universities have been blamed for the canalization of sixth form studies by their insistence on faculty or 'course' requirements in terms of the A level passes they require a student to hold in a subject before he can read it at the university. If higher education is to be based at all on the student's

[1] Ibid., p. 58.
[2] *The Post-Fourth Year Examination Structure in Scotland* (Cmnd. 1068), 1960, p. 13.

S

previously acquired knowledge, it is difficult to see how this can be avoided altogether. It is, however, worth pointing out that there are certain university disciplines for which it is impossible to demand a course requirement simply because the subjects are not offered by secondary schools – law, philosophy, psychology and the social sciences are obvious examples. It should also be mentioned that it is the Oxford and Cambridge open scholarships (and not the universities themselves) which have been blamed for their influence on special-ization in the sixth form. At these two universities there are no specific course requirements laid down at all.

In turn it is downward pressures from the sixth form which have been blamed for the canalization of the curriculum in the lower school. The Crowther Report attributes the overloading of the fifth form timetable firstly to the 'habit of finishing off with a pass in the G.C.E. all the subjects that the pupil will not be continuing in the Sixth Form, and secondly to 'the desire to start the job of the Sixth Form in the Fifth and to ask for more periods for this purpose – or at least to meet the entrance requirements of the Sixth Form'.[1] Historically this is quite inaccurate. The complaint boils down to two features of the grammar school course: the stage at which a second modern language is introduced for some pupils, and the choice which has to be made between taking either general science or two separate science subjects (e.g. physics and chemistry) as distinct ordinary level subjects. To go no further back than the Spens Report, specimen timetables were then suggested which included opportunities for pupils who would be learning a second foreign language from the second year onwards and for those who would take up a third foreign language in their third year. There was also provision for pupils who would specialize in science or mathematics from their fourth year onwards. This is precisely the same situation as the Crowther Committee found in the grammar schools in 1956–7, that what they termed 'door-closing options' had to be made, for those who wished to take up a second language, in the third year of most schools, and, for the future science specialists, in the fourth year.

But it is not merely that the pre-specialization which the Crowther Report condemned had been the practice of the schools for at least twenty years. The Spens Report had strongly approved of an innovation which had recently been made in the School Certificate whereby general science had been introduced as a less demanding alternative to physics and chemistry as separate subjects. The Committee thought that this would help to lighten the load for some pupils, who would not be pursuing their scientific studies beyond the fifth form. They were quite satisfied that in the last year, and possibly in the last two years, before the School Certificate, the practice should be continued of giving to pupils who were going on to the sixth form and the university such systematic instruction in the subjects in which they proposed to specialize as would lay a firm foundation for their sixth form studies. But they wanted to lighten the curriculum by allowing pupils in the main school to reduce the attention they gave to subjects which they would not be taking any further. In short canaliza-

[1] Ibid., p. 216.

tion was clearly not only an existing element in the organization of the grammar schools – and one which was approved by the Spens and Norwood Reports – the choice between general science and separate science subjects, which is now seen as part of the pre-specialization process, was, far from being the result of any extra pressures from the sixth form, a device to afford relief.

The more recent practice of the schools, which was condemned by Crowther, depends on smaller differences in the allocation of time than had been recommended in the Spens Report. Having scrutinized some typical school timetables the Crowther Committee pointed out that the need for making the decision between general science and separate science subjects

'turns frequently on the difference between six and eight periods a week for two years [in the Spens recommendations it turned on the choice between six and ten] and it is a little absurd to ask boys aged fourteen to make a decision of life-long importance for the sake of two periods a week. It is reasonable to ask whether a revision of syllabuses, especially perhaps in Chemistry, could not be devised which would enable all pupils to follow basic courses covering sufficient ground to make sixth form work possible.'[1]

The second objection to premature specialization is that the choice which has to be made too early is usually based on preferences which are only half formulated and may reflect all sorts of immature and inadequate motives – by likes and dislikes for certain teachers rather than for particular subjects. In this sense, of course, it can be premature even if it does not close any doors. Coupled with this is the feeling that, even if educational benefits are to be gained from specialization, they are more than counterbalanced by the loss of giving up other subjects before they can be brought to the stage at which any lasting benefit is derived from having studied them. As the Crowther Report puts it: 'To abandon French under the first shadow of the subjunctive is probably to condemn oneself to the tourist phrase book, to be shut out of one of the great literatures of Europe, and to sacrifice half the value of the investment already made in French lessons.' In this respect there is an interesting difference between the Consultative Committee in 1938 and the Central Advisory Council in 1959 in the estimate they made of what the schools can achieve in language teaching by the age of sixteen. The Spens Committee recommended that all grammar school pupils should study at least one language other than their own, and that all those whose taste and aptitude for it was sufficient should take up a second foreign language one year after the first. They felt that the study of a modern and a classical language would be of benefit even to those who were not going to take languages in the sixth form:

'Many boys and girls who will never write a prose in a modern foreign language can learn to read a book or newspaper in that language intelligently and to understand and speak on simple topics, and may acquire some understanding of the people who use that language and of their contribution to civilisation';

[1] Ibid., p. 217.

and it was possible 'to give Latin a value and an interest that the pupil can appreciate even if he leaves school at 16'.[1]

The Crowther Report, on the other hand, mentioned 'a very widespread complaint, which we believe to be justified, about the average standard of competence in the use of language among the boys and girls who leave the schools'. The implication was that an adequate command of a foreign language could not be achieved by the age of sixteen, and that the inclusion of languages in the curriculum in the main school was mainly to be justified by the contribution it made to the acquisition of a mastery of English. The Council were unanimous in regarding a complete command of the mother tongue as the most important element in general education, and in suggesting that the teaching of linguistics in the schools needed radical rethinking. They were divided in their attitude to compulsory Latin, but a majority thought that 'the schools should be free to devise their own means of teaching a mastery of language, and if they think they can do so by revising the methods of teaching English or by modern languages, they should be free to do so'. They all believed that, even if both Latin and one modern foreign language were retained in a school's curriculum from the second or third year, the introduction of a third language was never justified until a much later stage.[2] One wonders whether the schools have lost the art of language teaching or whether expectations have changed.

EXCESSIVE SPECIALIZATION

The Scottish determination not to surrender to the English malpractice of specialization is frequently supported by pointing to the supposed fact that the English themselves are unhappy about it. It is certainly true that many English teachers are uneasy about the pressures on their pupils associated with specialization, though one doubts whether they would be happy to see their sixth formers remain as 'uncommitted' as Scottish pupils are supposed to be. For there is no evidence in the official reports that the fundamental basis of specialization in school has been seriously questioned. The Crowther Report, for example, 'after considering the matter most carefully', were 'agreed in accepting and endorsing the English principle of specialization, or intensive study, as it would be better described'. That report, the Committee of Vice-Chancellors and Principals a few years earlier, and the Secondary School Examinations Council a year or two later, all considered some of the criticisms that had been made of the sixth form, and recommended that these objections could largely be met if the normal commitment of the sixth former were to be reduced from three A level subjects to two. That does not sound like a disapproval of specialization.

The pressure of competition for university places is strong. But, if one is to judge by the amount of time set aside by the schools for A level courses in the sixth forms there is, historically, no case for blaming the universities for imposing excessive specialization on them. The Board of Education pamphlet on the work of the sixth form published in 1938 mentioned that the Board had in the

[1] Spens Report, 1938, p. 176.   [2] Crowther Report, 1959, pp. 211–13.

past recommended that not less than two-thirds nor more than three-quarters of a sixth form pupil's time should be devoted to his main subjects, and repeated this recommendation. The Crowther Report recorded that the actual practice of most grammar schools in 1959 was in fact to give between two-thirds and three-quarters of the available time to advanced level studies, and recommended that they should continue to do so. The report wanted A level syllabuses to be pruned so that more attention might be given to quality than to mere quantity of factual knowledge, but was not in favour of any reduction in the time or attention devoted to specialist studies. It expressed the hope that sixth formers could be encouraged to take their 'minority time' rather more seriously than some of them appeared to do, and made some new suggestions about the use of that time, but clearly did not want it to encroach on the time available for study in depth of the pupils' main studies. The Secondary School Examinations Council in their third report in 1960 took the same view on the reduction of the content of A level syllabuses in order to achieve a better quality of work, and recommended the introduction of five different grades of pass mark with the intention of emphasizing the different quality of thought displayed by candidates in the examination. It must be debatable whether this has had the effect of relieving pressures in the sixth form or merely of adding to the pupils' anxiety by stressing the need to earn a good grade. A deplorable result of this step has in fact been that some pupils return to school to take the same A levels again merely to improve their grade. But in terms of the allocation of time the main pattern of sixth form studies for the ablest appears to have changed very little since the nineteen-twenties. The differences are, firstly, that subsidiary subjects are no longer examinable in the sense that they are no longer essential to the award of a certificate, and secondly, that competition for university places tinges specialist studies with that extra anxiety which comes from striving not merely to attain a fixed standard but to do better than everybody else. To that extent it is true that the remedy for such defects as are admitted in the sixth form rests outside the schools themselves.

MINORITY TIME

But there is obviously another reason for the schools' doubts about the extent of specialization. Previously it was thought to be a quite sufficient guarantee of general education that a reasonable spread of subjects should be undertaken up to the age of sixteen. Five passes in the appropriate subjects in the G.C.E. at ordinary level correspond to the standard which was originally fixed for matriculation into a university. The reason for some of the dissatisfaction with narrow specialists from the sixth forms at the present time is quite simply that the ordinary level is no longer felt to be an adequate level at which to drop the study of complementary subjects. Some members of the Crowther Committee thought that the present examinations in English and French did not offer satisfactory safeguards of linguistic teaching in the lower school, or satisfactory training in logical thought and the disciplined use of words. The teaching and the examination of English have, above all, caused concern. In their eighth report (1964) the Secondary School Examinations Council wrote: 'We have considered most seriously whether we should advise the cessation [of ordinary level examinations in English] for educational reasons, as well as for reasons related to the changing demand for qualifications in English language. We have come very near to that conclusion.'[1] They in fact recommended that the ordinary level should be allowed a respite of a few years in the hope that the new Certificate of Secondary Education would offer a more appropriate assessment of the linguistic capabilities of children who left school at about the age of sixteen – since the entry for O level English had been 'swollen to well-nigh unmanageable size because of the many purposes the test is called upon to serve'. And, as regards those who stayed at school longer, they pointed to the fact that some universities had already discarded O level English as a part of their matriculation requirements and others might do so: this was a reference to the recommendation of a sub-committee on university entrance requirements of the Committee of Vice-Chancellors and Principals that 'a paper in the use of English, designed to encourage the serious study of the use of English in the sixth form, and demanding more than the kind of competence now required for passing the paper in English Language in the G.C.E. at ordinary level' should in future form part of the 'general requirement' for matriculation. The Secondary School Examinations Council also considered whether such a 'use of English' paper should be included in the G.C.E. They came to the conclusion that, for the time being, it should not. The Council also considered a suggestion put to the Vice-Chancellors and Principals that sixth formers should take a general paper (which might include questions on general topics for all candidates, together with questions on literature, history, art and the like, appropriate to the needs of those offering science subjects at advanced level; and, for those offering non-science subjects at advanced level, questions calling for an elementary insight into science and some understanding of simple mathematical processes, of logical problems and of quantitative reasoning). The Council disapproved of the immediate introduction of a general paper. Finally they also looked at the suggestion that university entrants might be required to take an examination in the use of a foreign language, and expressed doubts about this. This may seem a rather negative attitude to the problem of assessing the use made by sixth formers of their minority time. The hesitation is, however, attributable to a suspicion of the effect of examinations on the work of the schools. The S.S.E.C. concluded their sixth report by saying:

'We consider that a fully satisfactory relationship between sixth form studies and university entrance requirements is unlikely to be achieved while competition for university entry remains as severe as it is today and we believe that the proposal to examine an additional area of sixth form work can, at best, provide only a palliative for the difficulties felt by the universities, and may in the process inhibit far more promising developments in the sixth form curriculum.'[2]

[1] *The Examining of English Language*, p. 14.
[2] *Sixth Form Studies and University Entrance Requirements*, 1962, p. 8.

One way in which minority time in the sixth could be used is, of course, to embark on the study of some entirely fresh subject. This is in fact done by some pupils who take up a new foreign language. But, with that exception, it seems that English grammar schools make far less use of the possibility of pupils taking a new O level subject between the ages of sixteen and eighteen than Scottish senior secondary schools already show signs of making of the opportunity presented to them to do the same thing now that the ordinary grade of the S.C.E. can be taken in any year from the fourth to the sixth. The English attitude suggests a reluctance to lose the benefits of the investment in time spent on the study of subjects up to the ordinary level, a desire to avoid presenting their sixth formers with the prospect of acquiring many more new facts outside the area of their advanced level subjects, and a belief that the proper function of minority time in the sixth form is to encourage the pupils to think in a more mature way about the facts they have already assimilated in the lower school, or about facts and problems which may be assumed to be matters of common experience.

MAJOR AND MINOR?

The most intricate attempt so far to design a more flexible programme of sixth form studies is contained in a Working Paper on *Sixth Form Curriculum and Examinations* published by the Schools Council. This suggests that twenty-four periods in a thirty-five period school week should be devoted to examinable subjects. (Shades of the time-honoured 'two-thirds to three-quarters' rule!) Little is said in detail about the use of the remaining eleven periods (the 'minority time' of the Crowther Report), but the implication is that the schools have made some progress in the development of general studies for sixth formers and, for that reason, the Council would not like to see this time encroached upon. The main proposal is that examinable subjects should be taught both in 'major' courses, requiring eight periods a week, and in 'minor' courses requiring four – over two years in both cases. Eight periods per week is already the normal allocation for advanced level courses so that the proposed 'major' subjects would clearly be as demanding as the present A level.

The scheme would obviously make it possible for a sixth former still to take three A levels, but the Council gloss over this possibility in the hope that the universities may be persuaded to reduce their normal demands from three A levels to two. They are obviously comforted by the knowledge that their scheme will still be workable even if the universities are unsympathetic, but place their greatest emphasis on the needs of the non-university sixth former. For him the options would range from two 'majors' and two 'minors' through one 'major' and several supporting 'minors' to a genuine 'sixth form with a difference' in which the course would consist of a whole string of 'minor' courses. A common pattern would, however, be a curriculum consisting of two 'major' courses in related subjects, and two 'minor' courses, of which one would be in a supporting subject and the other in a contrasting subject.

But the most interesting feature of the Council's scheme is not so much its championship of a new kind of subsidiary course. Rather is it this: the possibility is mentioned that any given subject could be treated in a 'minor' course in a variety of different ways, the implication being that 'minor' English, for example, might need to have a different syllabus for arts specialists, for modern linguists and for scientists. But the whole proposal would make much greater demands on sixth-form staffing than does the present organization of G.C.E. courses. For that reason, and that reason alone, therefore, the Council come to the conclusion that the range of syllabuses in any given subject in any particular school would have to be restricted. So the traditional English assumption that a sixth former's subsidiary subjects should be coloured by his specialism might have to be abandoned, not mainly on grounds of principle, but chiefly for administrative reasons.

WHAT IS A SUBJECT?

No consideration of specialization in the secondary schools would be complete without some reference to the definition of what is meant by a 'subject'. At first sight it might appear that the pupil of an English grammar school had in fact had a wider education than his Scottish counterpart, even though he had concentrated on two or three advanced level subjects from the age of sixteen to eighteen, when it could be shown that he had passed no less than nine subjects at the ordinary level before he began to specialize: the Scottish pupil before 1961, on the other hand, might have taken only five subjects in all in the Leaving Certificate. The Scottish pupil, however, would almost certainly have taken 'English', whereas the pupil south of the border would probably have taken 'English language' and 'English literature' as separate subjects. The Scottish pupil might have taken 'science' rather than 'physics' and 'chemistry'; 'mathematics' instead of 'mathematics' plus 'applied mathematics' or 'additional mathematics'; 'technical subjects' instead of 'handicraft' and 'technical drawing'. Until very recently the Scottish Education Department showed a considerable predilection for composite or portmanteau subjects, and their syllabuses have been cast wider than those of the English examining boards. For example, 'English' for examination purposes has always meant both language and literature. The requirements for the literature part of the Scottish examination have remained virtually unchanged for at least fifty years:

'candidates will be expected to have some acquaintance with the authorship and period of the leading masterpieces of our literature. . . . Knowledge of literary history should in all cases be based on a first hand acquaintance with literature itself, acquired by the careful study of a few well-chosen masterpieces supplemented by more cursory reading in a wider but no less carefully selected range of English classics. Answers which show that the study of English literature has been interpreted to mean the committing to memory of lists of authors and their books – and the answers of candidates so trained seldom fail by an occasional absurdity to give evidence of such training – will be treated with the utmost rigour, and will not be held to compensate for deficiency in the essential parts of the examination. On the other hand, such answers as show independent reading, careful and methodical instruction, or intelligent criticism, will be accorded full weight in the adjudgement of marks'

– even the detailed wording of this regulation has remained the same for fifty years. There has been no need to change it because it is couched in such general terms. In England practice has differed at different periods: suffice it to say that in the Cambridge local examinations in the early eighteen-sixties language and literature were taken separately and in the literature paper there were questions on set books. That is the practice of all the examining boards at the present. During the nineteen-twenties and the first half of the thirties, on the other hand, 'English' was a single subject.[1]

On the science side England started by treating the several science subjects separately and only introduced later a subject called 'general science'. The history of examinations in science subjects is slightly complicated in that botany was a fairly popular subject but zoology was hardly taken at all until the composite subject of biology began to be taken by so many candidates that it ultimately replaced the separate biological subjects altogether. Physics and chemistry were even more popular as separate subjects and have continued to hold their own, although a composite paper in physics-with-chemistry and the examination in general science are now taken by approximately equal numbers of candidates. Nevertheless the figures in Table 51 show that there has been a general trend toward broader examination curricula:

TABLE 51. *Numbers of candidates presented in the School Certificate and the Ordinary level of the G.C.E.*

	1926	1938	1950	1955	1962
Botany	13,627	6,828	1,280	658	—
Zoology	—	—	—	56	—
BIOLOGY	86	15,852	31,070	46,952	113,108
Physics	13,255	19,042	23,240	37,157	91,015
Heat, Light and Sound	2,980	2,533	—	—	—
Electricity and Magnetism	1,729	2,326	—	—	—
Chemistry	21,527	27,246	22,949	34,954	76,561
PHYSICS WITH CHEMISTRY	3,042	6,913	8,663	11,837	27,374
GENERAL SCIENCE	1,340	8,784	25,889	25,207	27,891
ADDITIONAL GENERAL SCIENCE	—	—	4,435	2,740	1,591

[1] And most of the English panels for the C.S.E. have decided to treat literature and language together.

In Scotland conversely the arrangement up to 1963 was that all the science subjects were treated as 'half subjects'. It was necessary to pass in two of them in order to obtain a pass in science. Now, however, there is the alternative of taking either two half subjects as before, or of taking any one science subject as a full subject.

The most sweeping of the recent changes in the Scottish Certificate of Education has been in the field of technical subjects. Previously it was only possible to take a group of subjects which must include either woodwork or metalwork together with technical drawing and mechanics. Now, woodwork, metalwork, engineering drawing, building drawing and applied mechanics are all treated as separate subjects.

These and similar changes in other subjects are a direct consequence of the introduction of the ordinary grade in the S.C.E. The working party on the Curriculum of the Senior Secondary School which was charged with the task of considering the effects of the new ordinary grade made two recommendations. The first was that the requirement in the regulations for the certificate that certain subjects should be studied throughout the secondary school course should be dropped:

'If our recommendation that no subject should by regulation be made compulsory is accepted, the obligation to include these subjects in every course will no longer exist. While it is, in our opinion, unlikely in these circumstances that any of the subjects concerned would be entirely omitted, it is probable that some pupils would discontinue them after two years.'[1]

Secondly, the working party recommended the splitting up of composite examination subjects:

'This proposed separation of branches is justified on various counts. In general each of the branches is educationally of sufficient value to rank as a distinct unit, and as such it could be given more adequate treatment than it can at present receive as one part of a composite subject. Again, this division of composite subjects should make it possible to lighten a course by restricting the study either to one branch instead of two, or to two branches instead of three or four. It would also allow a pupil who in the third and later years had not sufficient time to include all branches of a subject to continue the study of at least one branch. New and interesting combinations of subjects would become possible.'[2]

Thus the decision to make subjects examinable at the age of sixteen instead of at seventeen has brought in its train a somewhat different conception of what is meant by a subject, and Scottish schools, although keeping well clear of what they conceive to be the English error of specialization, have moved one step away from the comprehensive treatment of school subjects to which they were accustomed.

It may be that, with the growth of knowledge, school syllabuses must neces-

---

[1] *Report of the Working Party on the Curriculum of the Senior Secondary School*, 1959, p. 19.
[2] Ibid., p. 20.

sarily confine themselves to the illumination of certain carefully chosen aspects of a subject: this has long been the practice in English literature on both sides of the border, even though the Scottish practice leaves more freedom to the schools than does the English habit of prescribing set books and also pays more attention to putting each work in its historical context. Similarly in history, examination syllabuses in England soon began to prescribe particular periods for intensive study, and the Scottish Education Department adopted the same practice in 1930.[1] If, in the science subjects, English examining boards have abandoned such restricted subjects as 'heat, light and sound' or 'electricity and magnetism' they have begun on the arts side to experiment with such subjects as 'English economic history' or 'British constitution'.

SUMMARY

In Scotland, no less than in England, there must be a divergence between courses from the age of twelve or thirteen, and there is usually a difference between the one-language and the two-language course from the beginning of the secondary stage. What distinguishes this from English practice is that it is not a selection of future specialisms, but a selection of the ablest for the typical pre-university course and an exclusion of the rest from that particular opportunity. Given the ability to attempt to qualify for a degree course it is possible to postpone the choice of course until one enters the university, and, in many cases until as late as the end of the second year at the university. In fact the Scottish system sometimes seems to fall into the opposite error of not pressing the student to commit himself enough: it has not been unknown for undergraduates to wait for examination results before deciding which subjects offer the best prospects of steering a successful route through the complexities of the M.A. regulations.

In spite of slight differences in school organization and in the content of examination syllabuses, the basic pattern of the academic secondary course in the 'main school' of both the English grammar school and the Scottish senior secondary school is not very dissimilar. The difference lies in the reasons behind the choices that have to be made. And this, if it does not lead to a different organization, does have its effect on the pupils' attitudes. Whether or not the requirements of the sixth form have an undesirable effect on the actual teaching programme of the lower forms of the English grammar school, it cannot be denied that the very existence of the sixth form does condition the thinking of the younger pupils and leads them to consider the choice between subjects in a different light. If a pupil who intends to stay at school until he is eighteen knows from the age of eleven that in the end he will be required to study two or three subjects intensively, then he inevitably starts to make up his mind about which subjects interest him most, or at least which he is best at, and, by the time he has reached the fifth form he will probably have begun to think of himself as a scientist or a linguist or a historian or whatever it may be. Specialization may have first been introduced into English schools because subject-mindedness is a

[1] And the 'patch' method of teaching history is now becoming popular in Scotland.

fact of life. Or subject-mindedness may be so common among pupils of this age simply because specialization is an established fact of educational life. For this reason the assertion in the Crowther Report that subject-mindedness is a factor to be reckoned with, whether we like it or not, is a questionable one. Rather more reliable support for the statement comes from those Scottish headmasters who claim to discern some subject-mindedness in their ablest pupils by the time that they reach their fifth or sixth year – though even they may be the pupils who have already decided that they will be capable of taking a (specialist) honours degree at the university. The Crowther Report advanced four arguments in favour of the unique English system: first, that able boys and girls are eager by the time they are sixteen – the ablest by fifteen – to get down to the serious study of some one aspect of human knowledge which, with the one-sided enthusiasm of the young, they allow for a time to obscure all other fields of endeavour. Secondly, that concentration on a limited field leads naturally to study in depth. 'The boy embarks on a chain of discovery; he finds that ultimately each new fact he encounters fits into the jigsaw. . . . Most of what he does has a bearing, which gradually becomes apparent to him, on the rest of his work. In a word he begins to assume responsibility for his own education.' Thirdly 'through this discipline, a boy can be introduced into one or two areas which throw light on the achievement of man and the nature of the world he lives in'. And fourthly 'given the right teaching, a boy will by the end of his school days, begin to come out on the further side of "subject mindedness" '[1]. The questions which have to be asked are (i) whether these arguments are valid: (ii) whether they are valid in respect of all children who stay at school until the age of seventeen or eighteen, or only of the most able among such children, and (iii) whether the right place to cater for this phase of subject-mindedness is in the secondary schools. Coupled with the last question, of course, is the extent to which the atmosphere of the schools is more paternal than that of the universities and the degree of maturity needed to pass successfully from one to the other. The English answers to these questions are quite emphatically that the claim made by the Crowther Report is true of the majority of children who remain at school between the ages of sixteen and eighteen in the sixth form, and that eighteen is the minimum age at which school-boys and school-girls become mature enough to go away to (predominantly residential) universities.

That the English way of doing things needs modification to meet modern conditions is not overlooked, but it would appear to be improved standards in the schools which are largely responsible for any changes that are needed. Premature specialization is now frowned upon, but it is only quite recently that choices made at thirteen have been felt to be made at too young an age. Both the Spens and the Norwood Reports were perfectly content that a pupil's future studies should have been determined by them. Thirteen was seen to be the appropriate age, not solely from consideration of grammar school organization and the supposed needs of the future university student, but after having looked at secondary education as a whole. But the raising of standards and the lengthening

[1] Crowther Report, 1959, pp. 262–4.

of the average school career of grammar school pupils have contributed to the more recent feeling that thirteen is too young for door-closing options. The raising of standards in other secondary schools, and the lengthening of school life for all to fifteen, and, in due course, to sixteen, together with the growing practice of presenting secondary modern school pupils for the G.C.E., have contributed to the feeling that doors ought not to be closed. Above all, the grammar schools believe that it is the raising of their own standards in the sixth forms which calls for modifications in their past practice. They are proud of their record in specialist studies. A pass at the advanced level represents as creditable an achievement as can be shown by any school pupil anywhere in the world. What worries the schools is that progress has been uneven. General studies in the sixth have not kept pace with specialist. The equivalent of a credit pass in school certificate is no longer good enough as a testimony of general education. But the problem of how best the sixth former can maintain acquaintance with complementary subjects is one which they prefer, with some cooperation from the universities, to solve in their own way.

The Scots, having long since reconciled themselves to the innovation of the English-style honours degree in the universities, believe that subject-mindedness is a factor to be reckoned with, but that it comes later and is confined to the out-standingly able. For those of the second order of ability the compromise of the present ordinary M.A. represents a suitable balance between general education and specialization.

PART VII

The Teachers

Graduation for the nation?
Ilka teacher-quine – M.A.?

CHAPTER TWENTY-THREE

A Graduate Profession?

SCOTLAND

The ideal of a 'graduate profession' is shared by teachers in England and in Scotland. But the phrase means different things to them. The policy of the Educational Institute of Scotland can be traced back at least to the resolution of their Annual General Meeting in 1865 to the effect that 'after 1870 no teacher entering the profession be appointed without having attended at least two sessions at a university'. By the time of the A.G.M. in 1938 the policy had reached the stage of a fully graduate and trained profession: 'No teacher should be admitted to the profession who has not completed a recognised course of training and who is not a graduate of a Scottish or other approved university.' The Report of the National Union of Teachers on Educational Reconstruction in 1939, on the other hand, recommended that 'in the interests of a unified educational system and a united profession, it is essential that every teacher should be of graduate status', and that every training college should become an integral part of a university and should provide an alternative, but equivalent, form of training to that followed by a student working for a degree. The English attitude immediately pre-Robbins is fairly summed up by Professor M. V. C. Jeffreys:

'The dream of the N.U.T. very naturally, is of a fully unified and equalized profession. This ideal is sometimes expressed in the claim that teaching should be a "graduate profession". What this usually means, however, is not that every teacher should have a university degree (which is certainly impossible and probably undesirable) but that all qualified teachers should be recognized as having the equivalent of graduate status for salary purposes, and should have a four-year course of training or its equivalent.'[1]

The association of the teaching profession in Scotland with the universities is an historic one. Not that every teacher had necessarily completed a degree or that graduates were attracted into teaching as a lifelong career. 'The financial inducements to teach were so poor that graduates would not have entered the profession unless in the hope of leaving it in a few years for the Church.'[2] The older schoolmaster would often be a 'stickit Minister' – one whose ambition to enter the church had not been realized. The younger schoolmaster would often be a youth who was still prosecuting his studies at the university. In either case

[1] M. V. C. Jeffreys, *Revolution in Teacher Training*, 1961, p. 73.
[2] I. J. Simpson, *Education in Aberdeenshire before 1872*, 1947, p. 76.

T

attendance at the university did not necessarily mean the acquisition of a degree: the Argyll Commission found in 1867 that over seventy per cent of teachers in the burgh and middle class schools had studied at some university and that half of these were in fact graduates. Certain areas of the country were in a more favoured position than others. Ayrshire had a close connection with the University of Glasgow: 'a good many of the parish schoolmasters had been to College in Glasgow and a few of these had graduated.'[1] The north-east had an even closer connection with the two universities of Aberdeen: from 1828 onwards the counties of Aberdeenshire, Moray and Banff benefited from the funds of the Dick Bequest which were used to pay a supplement to the salary of any teacher who passed a stiff written examination, success in which presupposed study at a university. These payments have been discontinued since the adoption of nationally negotiated salary scales. But, in 1933 as an example, eighty-seven per cent of all men teachers in Aberdeenshire were graduates compared with 65.5 per cent in Scotland as a whole (and less than 16 per cent in England).

But the introduction of courses of professional training for teachers in the eighteen-forties had caused a fundamental change in the methods of preparing to become a teacher. In particular the pupil-teacher system was devised to meet the needs of the situation in England, but was extended to Scotland too. In teacher training, as in other aspects of education, government intervention in the mid-nineteenth century was a mixed blessing. Moreover the pupil-teacher system had been intended as a temporary expedient to meet the huge demand for teachers in England, but in both countries it remained in existence much longer than had been expected (though it was eventually abolished in Scotland earlier than south of the border). Boyd describes the effect of the system in Ayrshire:

'Many parish dominies came straight from the university to their school – a number of them with the ministry as a further goal – and they learned to teach by teaching. The other way into a school of standing was to make a success of teaching in a private school or to act as tutor in a county family and commend oneself to a minister or patron and through them to the appointing heritors. The coming of the pupil-teacher system gradually changed all that. Not only had the teacher-to-be to serve his apprenticeship like any other craftsman, but to obtain government recognition he had to learn the business under a teacher who had been trained himself and had his own teaching skill properly certified. In this way the first move had been taken to make teaching a real profession. But, as it happened, the very training that was to fit the teacher for his job had the unfortunate effect of lowering the educational standard of the Scottish dominies. The elementary teachers no longer needed to go to the university but combined a smattering of general education with their training in the Normal School in the teaching art. Even with the universities conferring their certificates, as they did under the 1861 Act, most of the certificated teachers of the new generation fell below the academic level of their predecessors. Scotland had to bring its educa-

---

[1] W. Boyd., *Education in Ayrshire through Seven Centuries*, 1961, p. 56.

tional system under its own control before that could be rectified by a restoration of the university connection.'[1]

The 1861 Act had relieved the presbyteries of the right to approve the appointment of schoolmasters to the parochial schools, and had empowered the universities to award teaching certificates to teachers (in any school) who sought recognition by the state. But in fact when Scotland did begin to bring its educational system under its own control this formal connection with the universities was severed, and the right of granting teaching certificates was transferred to the Scottish Education Department. After the 1870–72 legislation there was a second enormous increase in the number of teachers required and in the proportion of women entering the profession. Women teachers had been slowly catching up on their male colleagues throughout the nineteenth century, but between 1870 and 1900 the proportion of teachers who were women increased in England from fifty-three to seventy-four per cent and in Scotland from thirty-one to sixty-four per cent. Women were at first, of course, debarred from taking university degrees: they were first permitted to do so at the University of London in 1880, and at the Scottish universities in 1892. The large influx of women into teaching therefore served to reduce the percentage of graduates. In Scotland the male tradition of attendance at the university soon enabled the men to recover from the changes in the method of entry to the profession and to retrieve the situation. But the number of women who sought a degree even when it became open to them to do so on equal terms was much smaller. The following table gives a comparison of the proportions of graduates teaching in the schools: it includes all graduates, whether trained or not: a comparison based only on trained graduates would be even less favourable to England.

TABLE 52. *Percentage of teachers who were graduates: Maintained Schools*

	England Elementary		Secondary	England All schools	Scotland All schools
1920					
Men	3.3		66.0	15.5	49.0
Women	0.6		54.0	5.3	12.0
1938					
Men	14.4		80.0	16.0	70.0
Women	4.3		70.0	14.0	32.0
	Primary	Secondary Modern	Grammar		
1960					
Men	7.7	20.4	82.6	30.0	66.0
Women	2.6	13.6	73.3	12.4	34.0

It is impossible to separate the figures for primary and secondary schools in Scotland because of the large number of all-age schools. Most of the non-

[1] Ibid., p. 160.

graduate men are in fact employed in teaching secondary pupils, since they are the teachers who are qualified to teach such subjects as physical education, art, music and technical subjects. Of the men who are qualified to teach in primary classes at present ninety per cent are graduates.

Coincidentally with alterations in the scheme of teacher training, the pattern of Scottish degree courses was altered in such a way that graduation of itself came to be regarded as a less suitable preparation for teaching than it had been in the past. One of the Assistant Commissioners reporting to the Schools Inquiry Commission in 1868 on schools he had visited in Scotland had seen

'some features in the Scotch course which render an Ordinary Scotch graduate more likely to succeed as a teacher than an English graduate. For example the psychological reading of Scotch students seems to me an undoubted advantage to them as teachers, and supplies to some extent the place of technical training in the art of instruction. Thus the Scotch teachers who are graduates in arts do not appear to me to show the same obvious want of training as that shown by English graduates.'

Logic and moral philosophy were retained after 1889 in the curriculum for the ordinary degree, but were no longer compulsory subjects in the honours course. But alterations in the spread of other subjects taken for the ordinary M.A. made that degree a less satisfactory qualification for the teacher of general subjects. H.M.I. Mr A. King, the inspector for the Glasgow area in 1933, saw disadvantages in the practice of specialist teaching at the post-primary stage, and regretted the passing of the old degree course. By a 'main' subject, leading to a qualification to teach that subject in the advanced divisions, he means a subject in which a 'double' course had been taken at the university:

'From the point of view of a boy's education, for example, it would have been a distinct gain if . . . English, history, geography, mathematics, etc., could have been taken by one and the same teacher. This was the procedure in the older supplementary classes and led to a better understanding between teacher and taught. The older teacher, however, usually had a degree which covered the subjects of English and mathematics at least. Under modern conditions the tale is quite different. The variety of courses leading to a degree and, therefore, to a qualification to teach in an advanced division, has resulted in a comparatively small number having two main subjects. A very few manage to take the academic qualification in English and mathematics . . . a slightly larger number have a qualification in either English or mathematics with the other subject included in the degree: the great majority have the qualification in English or mathematics while the other subject is absent. Those teachers who are in either of the first two categories fit in quite well in a school which is organised on a class system. The others are misfits in such a system.'[1]

But measures had been taken both to remedy the deficiencies of university training and to restore the connection with the universities in a much more real

[1] General Reports for the Years 1930–33, p. 42.

sense than simply delegating to them the responsibility of awarding teaching qualifications. As early as 1906 it was made obligatory on all university graduates to take a course of professional training in which they were not only given instruction in education and psychology, and in the methods of teaching the subjects in which they had qualified for a degree, but an attempt was also made to supplement the knowledge of those who were intending to teach in primary schools in subjects which they had not taken at the university. And earlier, in 1873, the first step had been taken to get the new generation of teachers back into the universities for their higher education. The first Scottish Code introduced a provision whereby 'Queen's Scholars' might, with the approval of their training colleges, attend one or two, but not more, of the classes in a Scottish university prescribed for graduation in arts or science. Both the restriction on the number of classes and the fact that the training college course was only of two years' duration prevented the Queen's scholars from graduating, but the Code of 1893 established a system of 'Queen's studentships' which entitled the holders to receive their academic education at the university, while a local committee in each university town was responsible for the supervision of their professional training.

This idea of a committee in each university town which would supervise the training of teachers was extended in 1906. The Provincial Committees which were established in that year and reorganized as the regional organs of a National Committee for the Training of Teachers in 1920, were in practice responsible for the management of a 'training centre' in which much of the work of professional training was conducted. But the Provincial Committees' duties were expressed as being to provide 'whether by facilitating attendance at university classes or otherwise, courses of instruction suitable for the training or further instruction of teachers'. The *Regulations for the Preliminary Education, Training and Certification of Teachers*, 1924 and 1931, were quite explicit in their separation of professional training from general education. The curriculum of the non-graduate training course, for example, had to include the principles and methods of teaching the several subjects of the primary school curriculum; psychology, ethics and logic in their direct application to teaching, and adequate practice in teaching, under proper supervision, each of the subjects of the primary school curriculum. These requirements being met, the training course might provide for 'the revisal or the development of the students' knowledge of the subjects of general education'. For this latter purpose students might attend classes at a university or central institution (the Provincial Committee would decide which classes were suitable for the purpose), and it was only in 'subjects where instruction cannot conveniently be arranged for in connection with a University or Central Institution' that the Committee might, with the approval of the Scottish Education Department, provide instruction themselves. The training centres were closely, if indirectly, connected with the universities in the sense that they were controlled by the Provincial Committees on which the universities were represented, and in Edinburgh and St Andrews the professor of education at the University and the director of the training centre were the same person. But the centres were in no way under the academic control of the university as such: they were not seen as doing the same sort of job as the universities. They were specialist institutions concerned exclusively with the professional training of future teachers, except in so far as they performed a simple residual function of providing courses which were not otherwise available.

The training regulations of 1924, although they followed the essential framework of the organization of teacher training established in 1906, introduced important measures to improve the standard of education of future teachers. It is worth quoting the Department's own words:

'The Regulations of 1906 gave every encouragement to those who were willing to undertake a course of study at a University or Central Institution either during their period of training or before it had begun. In the case of men, this policy has been so successful that there has been a steady and a rapid fall in the number of male entrants who elect to restrict their training to the minimum of two years. Last year the total had dwindled to 35. It was therefore decided that after 1926 every man wishing to train for the Teacher's General Certificate must obtain a degree or the diploma of a central institution. In the case of women the hard facts of the situation are such as meanwhile to preclude the application of a similar compulsion. Of those who entered upon training for the Teacher's General Certificate last October as many as 646 (nearly half) deliberately chose the two years' course, despite the fact that the longer alternatives were open to them on exactly the same terms as to men. It would plainly be rash to assume that a compulsory extension of the period of training from two years to four would not act as a deterrent and divert a considerable number from the teaching profession altogether.'

Nevertheless the entrance qualifications for the non-graduate course for women were tightened up. The Leaving Certificate was in future to be required of all entrants, the training centres were asked to give preference to women who chose to take at least a three-years' course. And the promise was made that, as soon as it seemed practicable to do so, the non-graduate course would be extended to three years. This, in effect, was done in 1931.

The hope that compulsory graduation would be extended to women as well as to men was never realized. The total number of non-graduates admitted to training dropped during the 'thirties to about one-quarter of the total of students (men and women) admitted to courses leading to the Teacher's General Certificate, but the need for teachers was still such that the source of non-graduate women could not be allowed to dry up. Since then, the proportion of non-graduate women has steadily risen again. Scotland did have, thirty years before England, a three-year non-graduate course, but, were it not for the fact that the qualifications for entrance to that course were expressed in terms of an examination normally taken at the age of seventeen, the claim that this was a great advance over England would have been fraudulent. Compared with the English girl who took a full sixth form course and then went on to a training college for two years, the Scottish girl merely spent one less year at school in order to spend one more year at the training centre. Of course, many English students were able to gain admission to college on the basis of only a School Certificate, but they had to be over the age of eighteen on admission, whereas Scottish students could enter training before they were seventeen.

As a result of the changes introduced in 1924 and 1931 the main varieties of training course offered in Scotland up to the end of the second world war were as follows:

(a) Men and women who graduated at the university, without having committed themselves to teaching from the start of their course, would proceed to the training centre for a four-term course of postgraduate professional training.

(b) A four-year concurrent course of training was offered for prospective graduate teachers. They would be enrolled at the training centre and attend certain classes there in subjects not offered at the university (in many cases simply classes in physical education and art) as well as undertaking some teaching practice at times which did not interrupt their university studies. The course was concurrent in name more than in practice, but it did offer the attraction that it could be completed in four years, whereas a student needed four years and one term if he did not enrol at the training centre from the beginning of his degree course.

(c) Non-graduate women might take a three-year course, which could include attendance at as many as five university classes. Although falling short of the requirements for graduation, this could give them a qualification to teach in secondary schools.

(d) Non-graduate women intending to teach in primary schools might during their three-year course, be permitted to take a limited number of classes at the university – usually not more than two.

(e) Arrangements similar to those for graduates were in force for prospective teachers of such subjects as art, music or domestic science: tuition in the specialist subject was given at a central institution and led to the diploma of that institution. The training centres provided professional training. In some cases the specialist course and the professional training were concurrent and in others 'end-on'.

The Scottish Advisory Council in 1946 asked themselves the question: 'Should all students desiring to become teachers of general subjects in primary schools be required to take a university degree in arts or science?' They reached the conclusion that they should not. They rejected the idea of a special kind of degree for teachers on the grounds that it would not carry as much prestige as the traditional university degrees. They considered that the traditional degree courses were not always suitable in content and treatment for future teachers, and they thought that the principle of graduation for all 'deprives us of the opportunity of making full use of the resources of institutions of higher education other than the universities. . . . We recommend that much fuller use be made of the rich and varied resources of these institutions.'[1] By this they did not mean that more use should be made of the facilities of the training centres. Their suggestion was that the non-graduate course should include instruction in the subjects of the primary school curriculum: English, history, geography, general science and mathematics. As regards courses in these subjects the training centres should be free either to arrange attendance at the university or to provide comparable courses themselves. The training course should also include at least one subject studied for purely cultural interest. This should normally be taken at a university or central institution.

Since the war the reduction of the 'end-on' postgraduate course from four terms to three has meant that the concurrent four-year course no longer has any attraction, and has fallen into disuse. The practice of non-graduate students attending a limited number of university classes has also fallen into abeyance, with the result that teachers in secondary schools normally need to have a degree or the diploma of a central institution. As regards primary schools the enormous increase in the numbers of non-graduate women students – far greater than the increase after 1870 – meant that the training centres were forced to provide a three-year course which, if it were not to be devoted entirely to professional training, would include 'cultural' courses given by their own staff. In 1958 the training centres became colleges. They were renamed Colleges of Education. The Provincial Committees were disbanded and replaced by independent governing bodies responsible for the management of each college. The regulations under which they operate still provide for cooperation with the universities and other educational establishments but there is a considerable change of emphasis.

'Subject to the provisions of the Training Regulations, each governing body shall provide in, or in connection with, the college of education under their administration, such of the courses required by the said Regulations as they consider necessary to enable candidates to obtain qualifications for which provision is made in the said Regulations.'

The regulations in question are those of 1931 which continued in force until 1 April, 1965, and to that extent the powers given to governing bodies were perhaps slightly ambiguous: since they might only provide such courses as were *required* by those regulations it could be argued that they were not strictly empowered thereby to provide courses for the development of a student's general education which were only a permissive part of the old Provincial Committees' functions. Nevertheless that is precisely what they began to do (though more than a decade had passed since the Advisory Council had suggested changes in the courses). Another clause in the 1958 regulations, however, is sufficiently widely worded to stand a new interpretation since the publication of the Robbins Report. It reads:

'Each governing body shall negotiate with the university in their vicinity with a view to securing that attendance at appropriate courses in the university and in

[1] *Training of Teachers* (Cmd. 6723), 1948, p. 27.

the college may be recognised for the purposes of qualifications awarded by the governing body and the university respectively.'

This covers the provision of courses in the colleges of education leading to the award of a university degree, as the Robbins Committee recommended.

The fact that the training centres only performed a residual function, together with the dominance of the universities in Scotland, might be thought likely to have led to a situation in which the colleges of education would lack status or prestige. In practice the differentiation of function – the very fact that they were seen not to be emulating the universities – has probably helped them. Since 1958 they have been completely independent institutions. Even before that they were under no kind of tutelage by bodies outside the field of teacher training: they were subject only to the National Committee for the Training of Teachers. Their autonomy can be judged to have been due largely to the strict definition of their functions in the past. Now, the limitations on the types of course they may provide are being broken down.

The Robbins Report made two main recommendations affecting the Scottish colleges of education. First, that they should offer courses leading to a degree awarded by the universities. In effect this meant that the colleges would remain independent institutions preparing some of their students for what would virtually be an external degree (although the courses would be planned and assessed by a joint board of studies). It is rather different from the recommendations for England which would have led to the incorporation of the training colleges into 'schools of education' which would be part of the university. In Scotland the universities will not be concerned at all with non-graduate teacher-trainees whereas in England they may.

The other Robbins recommendation for Scotland was that all graduates training for teaching should take a university diploma in education. This needs some explanation for those familiar only with the English system. In England most graduates take their year of professional training in a university department of education, and receive their diploma (or whatever their teaching qualification may be called) from the university. In Scotland the post-graduate professional training is undertaken entirely by the colleges of education. But the Scottish universities do offer a degree in education, the Ed.B. or B.Ed., which can only be taken by those who already hold a first degree. The first part of the Ed.B. course leads to a university diploma in education, and the diploma can be taken concurrently with the college of education course. Students are usually excused certain parts of the theoretical study of education and psychology which would otherwise have formed part of their college course. The result is that they undergo, in the college of education, a course of 'technical training in the art of instruction', but take, at the university, a more demanding course in education and psychology than they would otherwise be expected to do, and this helps them on the way towards a second degree. It is a curious compromise by which the colleges lose their ablest students in theoretical subjects which should be closely related to their practical training, and the university departments of education and psychology are confined to a strictly academic study of education which leaves them little or no influence on the practice of teaching. It is, of course, based on a deployment of lecturers' responsibilities in the colleges of education which differs from that in university departments of education in England. The recommendation in the Robbins Report would have produced an even wider split between the theoretical and practical aspects of teacher training (and a gulf between graduate and non-graduate courses of training such as is well established in England), in that all post-graduate trainees would have taken this concurrent course and all would have been required to take the diploma in education. The indications are that the Robbins recommendation will not be accepted by any of the institutions concerned.

Since the degree course which the colleges of education will in future be providing over four years will lead to a first degree to be known as a B.Ed., the former Ed.B. will be renamed M.Ed. to make clear its status as a second degree.

ENGLAND

The English universities have been much less concerned with the higher education of prospective teachers than have the universities of Scotland, but for those whom they have trained they have been almost exclusively responsible. The training colleges, likewise, have been almost exclusively responsible for the higher education as well as the training of non-graduate teachers. The training colleges were first on the scene. They were founded in the first half of the nineteenth century, not only to provide some training in the art of teaching but also to make good the lack of people of sufficient education to staff the schools.

The association of the universities with the education and training of teachers in England dates from 1890 with the founding of the so-called 'day training colleges in association with the universities and university colleges'. These day training colleges were to provide both the normal two-year course for non-graduates and a three-year course for those who wished to proceed to a degree. By 1900 a majority of their students were in fact taking degree courses but

'educationally the combination of degree work and professional training, even when the course extended over three years, had been found in many cases to overwork the student or prejudice one or both of the essential elements of the course. It became clear that each part, to be done well, required the student's whole mind, and that he could not be expected to do justice to both unless he had time for each of them and had completed one before beginning the other.'[1]

Regulations made in 1918 therefore made provision for a four-year course (which had in practice been introduced in 1911); students taking this course spent three years as normal undergraduates, though under some general supervision by the university training department, and a fourth year undergoing professional training. The day training college thus became neither a day college, since many of the students were resident, nor a training college. It developed

[1] *Training of Teachers for Public Elementary Schools* (Cmd. 2809), 1925, p. 17.

into the university department of education (although one two-year non-graduate course at a university continued up to 1951). This change of direction to the experiment of the day training college was given a push by the Education Act, 1902. Although the new venture had so far stimulated the universities that twenty day training colleges were established, the fact that, after 1902, the local education authorities also had power to establish their own training colleges (and contributed between them a score of new colleges) meant that those attached to the universities became a less significant part of the total teacher training provision than had been intended. Secondly, the opening of new municipal Secondary schools created a demand for graduate teachers which the university training departments were called upon to meet. The four-year course within a university came to be regarded as the normal source of supply of grammar school teachers and the training colleges proper remained responsible for the rest. Admittedly, and particularly during the period of over-supply of qualified teachers in the 'thirties, many of the products of the university training departments found their way into elementary schools. For example the McNair committee in 1944 pointed out that 'these institutions are commonly regarded as preparing teachers particularly for the secondary schools, though in fact sixty per cent of their students become teachers in elementary schools'. But the elementary schools to which they went are those which we now call secondary: they taught in the senior elementary schools. This is made clear by a comparison of the percentages of teachers in the elementary schools in 1938 who were graduates with the percentage of graduate teachers in the primary and secondary modern schools in 1962:

TABLE 53. *Percentage of all teachers who were graduates: England.*

	1938	1962		
	Elementary schools	Primary and Secondary modern together	Primary	Secondary modern
Men	14.4	15.7	7.4	20.2
Women	4.3	5.1	2.5	13.0

Much fewer than ten per cent of all graduate teachers are now teaching in primary schools and the presumption is that the same was true of infants and junior departments just before the war.

The recruitment of graduates to the teaching profession before the war was, of course, affected by economic considerations. Those who were accustomed to the standard of living which could be provided for them by parents able to afford to pay for them to go to Oxford or Cambridge were unlikely to be attracted by teachers' salaries. If their degree enabled them to get a better paid job (as it was likely to do) they would not go into teaching. Or, if they did teach, it would be in an independent school. At the other end of the social scale many who might have had the ability to take a degree went instead to a teachers' training college because it was cheaper and the course was shorter. A Departmental Committee on the Training of Teachers in 1925 said that 'the career of elementary school teaching remains one of the few professional careers within the ordinary reach of capable children of the less well-to-do classes'.[1] At the same time, to commit oneself to teaching was one way of obtaining some financial assistance for a university course provided that one's parents could afford to pay part of the cost. Nearly half the undergraduates in 1930 who were in receipt of some kind of financial help from public funds were receiving a four-year grant to cover part of the cost of a degree course followed by the one-year post-graduate training course. (They accounted for 19 per cent of all university students; 40.6 per cent of all students were being given some financial assistance.) The standard rate of grant at this time, however, was £43 a year plus tuition fees. The cost of attending a provincial university was reckoned to be about £130 a year and the annual cost at Oxford and Cambridge at between £200 and £275. Some local education authorities were prepared to add to the grants from the Board of Education by a supplementary grant or by a loan: others were not. The inevitable result of these financial facts is given in Table 54.

TABLE 54. *University students: England* 1930

	Percentage who had previously attended a public elementary school	Percentage receiving assistance from public funds
Oxford and Cambridge	10.8	38
London University	15.6	34
Other English universities	36.1	54

The number of Oxford and Cambridge graduates who found their way into the schools via the university departments of education as trained graduates was very small compared with the numbers from other universities:

TABLE 55. *'Four-year' students: England*

	Total number completing the four year course 1936–38	As a percentage of the total number graduating in the years 1935–37
Oxford and Cambridge	407	4
London University	653	5
Other English universities	2,763	21

Of those who did complete the four-year course the Oxford and Cambridge graduates had a much better chance of appointment to the staff of a Secondary

[1] Cmd. 2409, p. 34.

school, forcing the graduates of other universities to look for jobs in the senior departments of elementary schools:

TABLE 56. *Percentage of students from Departments of Education completing training in 1936–38 who obtained posts in schools.*

	Secondary schools	Elementary schools	Not known	Total
Oxford and Cambridge	56	7	37	100
London University	50	18	32	100
Other English universities	23	50	27	100

Students at Oxford and Cambridge are still less interested in the teaching profession as a career than the students of other universities. Table 57 gives the percentages of undergraduates in 1955—56 who said that they intended to take up teaching after they had graduated. Their answers were related to teaching of all types, including teaching in independent as well as maintained schools.

TABLE 57. *Percentage of university students intending to teach*

	Cambridge	Oxford	London	Other English universities	Scottish universities
Percentage of all students who intended to teach	9.5	12.0	13.0	24.0	23.8
Percentage of those whose fathers were teachers who intended to teach	13.9	14.4	14.9	25.5	17.8
Percentage of those whose fathers were not teachers who intended to teach	9.1	11.8	12.8	23.9	24.4

It might be inferred that the tendency to follow in father's footsteps is much more marked at Oxford and Cambridge than at the other universities, and that Scottish students appear to be put off the idea of teaching if their father happens to be a teacher. Any such conclusion about the extent of 'self recruitment' to teaching however ignores the influence of teacher-mothers. And there is another interpretation of the figures: the proportion of students with teacher-fathers appears to have been lowest at Oxford and Cambridge and highest at the Scottish universities. This kind of comparison between undergraduates at Scottish and English universities must, however, be treated with caution. The very much larger proportion of Scottish students who are taking an ordinary, rather than an honours, degree must affect their career prospects.

In 1925 some attempt was made to bridge the gulf between the universities, with their responsibility for graduates intending to teach in grammar schools, and the training colleges, who looked after all the rest. In a sense the universities were brought into a closer relationship with the whole field of teacher training by being given the role which the Scottish universities had played for a brief period in the eighteen-sixties. Up to 1925 the Board of Education had been solely responsible for examining training college students, but the Board then set up Joint Examining Boards, on which the universities were represented, to relieve them of this task. Following up this small beginning, the McNair Committee, reporting in 1944, offered two alternative suggestions for the future organization of teacher training in England. The first, the School of Education proposal, involved the affiliation of training colleges to the universities. It contemplated considerable flexibility of organization in that students enrolled in one college might attend courses provided at some other institution within the School (though not, apparently, other schools or faculties in the university); there would also be interchange of staff. The university would decide which lecturers in the affiliated colleges should be granted the title of recognized teacher within the school of education, and whether courses taken in an affiliated institution could be accepted as qualifying for part of the requirements of a degree course. The second proposal, for the establishment of Institutes of Education, was more limited. It was to provide for the coordination of the 'training work' of colleges associated with each institute, and also of the departments of education (which would remain separate from the training colleges). The broad outlines of the second proposal were in the event adopted, though the precise pattern differed from one institute to another. Most of the institutes, through joint academic boards, achieve some coordination of the academic as well as of the strictly professional part of the training college courses.

The Robbins Committee revived the idea of something much more like the McNair school of education scheme. The report was adamant on the importance of academic and administrative control going together, and recommended that the training colleges should draw their funds from a revised University Grants Committee. The Secretary of State has, however, decided that the colleges shall remain administratively separate, even though they may be more closely associated academically with the universities and prepare some of their students for a degree.

The present position, therefore, is: secondary teachers in Scotland, but not in England, must normally hold graduate or graduate-equivalent qualifications: in primary schools Scottish men, but not women, must also hold a degree or equivalent qualification.

In Scotland all graduates must also take a course of professional training. Without exception they train in a college of education, though some of them may concurrently take part of the university course leading to a second degree. In England graduates do not need to take a course of professional training. Most of those who train do so in a university department of education, but a few take a one-year course in a college of education.

Colleges of education in both countries will in future offer a four-year concurrent course leading to a degree awarded by a university, but their precise relationships with the university will differ. Scottish colleges of education will be solely responsible for their non-graduate courses, as they have been for several years. English colleges of education will continue to be affiliated to an institute of education, or may, in spite of the Government's 'binary system', be incorporated into a university school of education.

CHAPTER TWENTY-FOUR

Non-graduate Courses

ENGLAND

The most noteworthy point about the Robbins Report is that it includes teacher training colleges, with universities and colleges of advanced technology, in the sphere of higher education. Up to about forty years ago the function of the teacher-training system was partly to give instruction in the art of teaching and partly to ensure that the prospective teacher had at least received a reasonably satisfactory education of secondary standard. By the nineteen-twenties the end of the pupil-teacher and junior student schemes (which had provided for those who had not completed a full secondary course) was in sight, and the colleges asked themselves afresh what their aim should be with their non-graduate students. In England a departmental committee in 1925 said that:

'The more the Training Colleges' function can approximate to the reality indicated by the word "Training", the less the Colleges should need to concern themselves with supplementing the future teacher's general education, or carrying his knowledge of the essential subjects of the Elementary School curriculum up to the necessary pitch. This point, we think, should usually have been reached before the teacher leaves the secondary school.'[1]

A few years earlier H.M.I. Mr J. C. Smith, the Chief Inspector in charge of teacher training in Scotland had written: 'The Scottish system proceeds on the assumption that the general education of the students is, in the main complete on entry, so that the college course can be devoted in the main to professional training.'[2]

What was meant by 'training' in these two quotations was, however, rather different. Originally the English colleges had had to do far more in the way of general education than those in Scotland: 'The Battersea Normal School, like the institutions of the two great educational societies and unlike Stow's Glasgow Normal Seminary in its early days, set out to teach the subjects of school instruction as well as to give training in the technique of teaching method'.[3] Gradually, however, they came to limit the number of school subjects in which they attempted to carry their students' knowledge up to the necessary pitch. To some extent they were influenced in this by the fact that they were training non-graduate teachers for the senior departments of the elementary schools as well as for younger children. As the teacher of senior children needed greater know-

[1] *Training of Teachers for Public Elementary Schools*, p. 71.
[2] *Report and Statistics on the Training of Teachers 1920–21*, p. 13.
[3] A. W. Rich, *The Training of Teachers*, 1933, p. 76.

ledge of the subjects he would be called upon to teach, so it was necessary to reduce the range of subjects he could study to any satisfactory level in two years. But there would have been no need to match the course for primary teachers to that for the teachers of seniors had the colleges not been predisposed to the idea of some degree of specialization. The Board of Education's *Regulations for the Training of Teachers*, 1913, laid down that the two-year course should provide '(i) a course of professional training giving a suitable preparation for the work of teaching in Public Elementary Schools, and (ii) continue the students' general education by making a special study of selected subjects'. The professional part of the course was to include the principles and practice of teaching, hygiene and physical education: students might specialize in the teaching of pupils in junior and infant schools or in senior departments. (This has since further been refined in that students at some colleges may now specialize either for infants or for juniors, as well as specializing for teaching in secondary modern schools, whereas in Scotland the Teacher's General Certificate up to 1965 was, technically, and largely in practice, a qualification to teach any age group from five to fifteen, and, even now, the Teacher's Primary Certificate covers the age-range five to twelve.) The other subjects of the training college curriculum prescribed in 1913 were divided into two groups:

Group A. English, history, geography, mathematics, elementary science (or alternatively physics, chemistry, botany or biology as advanced subjects), Welsh and French (advanced level only).

Group B: Music, drawing, handwork, gardening, needlework, housecraft.

Students training to teach in the senior departments usually took four courses, one at least being at advanced level. Other students usually took five subjects of which two must be from Group A and two from Group B. What the 1925 Departmental Committee meant by the reality of the word 'training' becomes clearer when one reads how emphatically they felt that 'we cannot approve any reversion to a Training College course which includes the academic study of all the ordinary school subjects', and recommended that 'in the course of every student there should be one subject selected and studied at least as much for itself as for the purposes of Elementary School teaching, and carried to as high a pitch as can be attained in the two years'. This became the common practice. A 'main course' – or in some cases, two courses – in a subject of the student's choice became a regular feature of the training. In 1957 the National Advisory Council recorded that 'there are different views about the number of main courses which a student should be expected or required to take, and about the types of subject which are suitable for study as main courses'. But they added not only that 'the choice . . . will, generally speaking, lie between one and two, as indeed it does at present', but also that, with a three-year course and better quality of student, 'the attainment in one or more subjects of a standard nationally acceptable and of a quality comparable with that in the universities becomes a reasonable objective'.[1]

In their attempt to do everything – a bit of practical training, some child

---

[1] *Scope and Content of the Three-Year Course of Teacher Training*, p. 3.

study and education, and one or two 'main' subjects[1] – in two years, there is no doubt that the English colleges grossly over-crowded their curriculum and, quite often, their reach exceeded their grasp.

Practice and theory in English training colleges are difficult to reconcile. Their two-year students had very little time to themselves, and yet the assumption seems to be that, in the matter of the development of the kind of personality and character suitable for teaching, living in the right environment is important, and even that simply living may be enough. For the past fifty years or more it has been impossible to qualify as a teacher in England before one's twentieth birthday, because, even while the colleges had only a two-year course, the minimum age for admission was fixed at eighteen. The McNair Report recommended an extension of the course to three years, not primarily to give the students an opportunity to acquire more knowledge or skill, but because 'students in general have not, by twenty years of age, reached a maturity equal to the responsibility of educating children'.[2] The intention was that the additional year should be used to some extent merely to spread out the content of the course over a longer period. The two-year course was overcrowded: 'Many students in training colleges do not mature by living: they survive by hurrying.' Thirteen years later, when a decision had finally been made to implement the McNair recommendation, the sixth report of the National Advisory Council on the Training and Supply of Teachers took much the same view in its recommendations about the scope and content of the three-year course. The sentence from the McNair Report about maturing by living was quoted, and the word 'mature' or 'maturity' appears no less than eight times in the first five pages of the report. Maturity it is suggested, is best achieved by simply leaving the students to themselves. 'One of the chief needs is to give the students more time at their own disposal.' Too much instruction 'can make learning a barren experience'.[3]

However, the colleges do now have three years beyond the age of eighteen at their disposal, and the Robbins recommendation that they should offer degree courses for their ablest students is a more logical development from what they have been trying to do in the past than it is in Scotland.

SCOTLAND

H.M. Chief Inspector Mr Smith had meant something quite different by 'training' in his report for 1921: 'It is conceived in the belief that Education is a science, though as yet an imperfect one, with the corollary that professional training should be grounded in the scientific study of child nature.' When the Scottish course for non-graduates was extended from two years to three, the training centres were very much specialist institutions for providing theoretical and practical training in the techniques of teaching. General education was pro-

[1] The Robbins Committee found that in 1961/2 six per cent of women on a three year general course were taking three main subjects, thirty-four per cent two and fifty-one per cent one main subject.   [2] McNair Report, *Teachers and Youth Leaders*, 1944, p. 65.
[3] *Scope and Content of the Three Year Course of Teacher Training*, 1957, p. 2.

vided elsewhere, and the expectation was that the universities would increasingly become the places where future teachers received their own education. The two-year course was confined to courses in educational science and the methods of teaching all the subjects of the primary school curriculum. The course was the same for all students: there was no element of choice or of specialization. When the course was extended to three years it simply did the same job, but did it more thoroughly.

In Scotland there is no feeling that twenty is too young to be a teacher. In spite of the three-year course it always has been possible to qualify before reaching one's twentieth birthday. The minimum age for admission is normally seventeen, but the principals of the colleges have discretion to accept girls at the age of sixteen and nine months, and the practice has usually been to do so, except when, as in the years 1963 to 1965, the pressure on places has been such that it seemed desirable to insist on the minimum of seventeen in order slightly to restrict the number of applicants. In the conditions of over-supply of teachers between the wars, however, it had been thought more important to introduce a general raising of academic standards for admission rather than raise the minimum age. There is, even yet, no suggestion that the age should be raised above seventeen.

It is only since they began to enjoy the autonomy granted them in 1958 that the Scottish colleges of education have begun to try to find time in their curriculum for courses which are not rigorously directed towards the needs of teachers in the classroom situation. They have mostly done it by compressing back into two years the matter that they had become accustomed to spread over three. This will be made clear by a comparison of the allocation of time at one Scottish college in the two-year course in 1920–21, in the three-year course as recently as 1959–60, and the allocation for professional and basic curriculum studies in 1962–63, which left some time free again in the third year for the students' personal education. (See Table 58).

These timetables are set out in terms of forty-five-minute classes, with a total of thirty-five such classes available in the week. A 'double' period for practical subjects means an hour and a half. The college terms are slightly shorter in Scotland than in England so that the academic year usually totals only thirty to thirty-three weeks instead of the thirty-four to thirty-six common in England.

This is, however, a time of rapid change in teacher training, and especially in Scotland. The college in question adopted a new curriculum, as shown, in 1962. Only three years later it abandoned it in favour of a course which allows eight hours per week for 'cultural' studies in all three years.

THE TRAINING COURSE

The most obvious consequence of the difference in the conception of what is meant by 'training' is that Scottish students spend much more time on teaching practice than do English trainees. Since the English course was extended from

TABLE 58. *Timetable of a Scottish college of education.*

	1920–21		1959–60			1962–63		
year	1	2	1	2	3	1	2	3
1. Hygiene and physical exercises	3	1½	3	4	3	2	3	2
2. Education (including psychology, ethics, logic, history and theory)	2	5	1	2	2	3	6	5
3. Methods and blackboard practice together with teaching practice	5	5	7	9	9	1*	2*	3*
4. English	2	2 or 4	4	2	2	5	—	—
5. Arithmetic	—†	—†	2	—	—	1	2	1
6. Nature study	4	—	2	2	2	2	2	—
7. Geography	1	—	2	1	—	4	—	—
8. History	1	1	2	—	1	—	4	—
9. Religious instruction	1	1	1	1	1	2	2	—
10. Singing	3	3	2 ⎫			2 ⎫		
11. Drawing	2	2	2 ⎬ 2 2			2 ⎪ 4		
12. Needlework	2	2	2 ⎭			2 ⎬		
13. Handwork	2	2	—	2	4	2 ⎭		
14. Phonetics and voice training	1	1	1	1	1	2	2	—
'Cultural' studies	—	—	—	—	—	—	—	12
	29	25½–27½	31	26	27	30	29	24

* The time allocation for earlier years includes one-day-a-week practice throughout the course. In 1962–63 teaching practice was rearranged to include more block practice.

† Classes in arithmetic were only arranged for those who had not had a satisfactory training in the subject before entering training.

two years to three, most of the colleges have increased the amount of teaching practice so that the average allotment has risen from about twelve weeks in all to about fifteen. The Scottish colleges of education, conversely, have recently shown a tendency to make a reduction in the amount of teaching practice their non-graduate women undertake. At some colleges, until a year or two ago, teaching practice might amount in total to the equivalent of as much as twenty-six weeks during the three years; about twenty-one or twenty-two is now more usual.

For the English student, teaching practice usually means a block of at least two or three weeks which are spent entirely in the school. Visits for observational purposes may be paid at other time. Scottish students have their periods of block practice (and the move has been to increase the importance attached to these), but it has been much more common than in England to assign a student to teach in a particular school throughout a term or more; she will spend one or more days a week in that school, and the other days in college. Although this makes for genuine 'concurrent' training it clearly limits the kind of teaching which a student can undertake: it is based on the assumption that she will take such 'lessons' as the class teacher asks of her. The English colleges adopted the block practice method because few of them are situated in large towns in which it would be easy for the students to spend part of the week in school and the rest in college, but they would probably also argue that the valuable aspect of teaching practice is the continuous observation of a class over an unbroken period, and that primary schools do not have 'lessons'.

In their survey of students the Robbins Committee found that, during a week in 1961–62, about sixty per cent of three-year students in Scottish colleges of education had done some teaching practice compared with about forty per cent of women on three-year general courses in English training colleges, and that the average time spent in the schools by the Scottish students was exactly double the average for English students. Teaching practice was defined to include observational visits.

TABLE 59. *Students on teaching practice.*

	SCOTLAND	ENGLAND	
No teaching practice	41	59	
Whole or part of one day	34	31	Average number of days per week in schools:
More than one day, but less than 5	19	4	
Five days	5	5	England 0.6
			Scotland 1.2
All students	100	100	

The Report makes the point that the figures cannot be taken to indicate the distribution of teaching practice over the courses as a whole, since there is no guarantee that the week chosen for the survey was completely typical. This is a disadvantage common to all the information which was collected in the survey of teacher training students.

When it comes to an analysis of the amount of time spent by training college students in different kinds of study the Report is even less satisfactory. The figures given are in Table 60.

To present the figures as simple averages in this way is open to several objections. As the Report itself says: 'Hours of teaching appear from the table to be lower in Scotland than in England and Wales, but if an allowance were made for the higher proportion of Scottish students engaged in teaching practice during the week of the survey there would be little difference.' And there is another difficulty of comparison. The English course was only extended to three years in 1960. In 1961–62 there were no third-year students. But third-year students in the Scottish colleges of education were included in the survey, and it is a common practice in both countries gradually to reduce the amount of formal teaching given to students as they proceed through the course: the survey itself showed that the average hours of teaching received (all types of course) dropped

TABLE 60. *Average hours of teaching received by three-year women students on general courses of training* 1961–62.

	SCOTLAND	ENGLAND AND WALES
Lectures	7.4	9.2
Large seminars	1.1	1.6
Small seminars	—	0.2
Tutorials	—	0.1
Practicals	4.5	4.2
Other periods	0.1	0.5
Total teaching	13.3	15.9
Private Study	9.8	17.0
Teaching practice	5.8	2.9
	28.9	35.8

from 17.6 hours in the first year to 15.1 in the second: the drop in the third year, had there been one in England, would probably have been at least as great. Perhaps there is, in fact, little difference in the amount of formal teaching received by teachers in training in the two countries.

The fact that the timetables of Scottish colleges appear to be more over-crowded than the Robbins survey suggests may simply be a subjective impression due to the fact that the colleges are non-residential. For example, the Robbins survey shows that four per cent of students claimed to have attended classes of one sort or another for twenty-six or more hours in the week in question. This was in England. In Scotland no student had attended more than twenty-five hours. A twenty-six hour week, though heavy, is not exceptionally so in a residential college: in at least one Scottish college, however, the total working week only adds up to twenty-six and a quarter hours in college because the timetable has to allow for students to travel by bus and train from consider-able distances to reach the college from their homes.[1]

[1] When the Robbins survey of training college students is set beside the survey of university students it can be seen that teacher-trainees spend slightly more time at lectures, etc., or on teaching practice, but considerably less time on private study.

	Average hours per week spent by students on:				
	Teaching received		Teaching practice		Private study
Training colleges:					
England (women on general courses)	15.9	+	2.9	= 18.8	17.0
Scotland (non-graduate women)	13.3	+	5.8	= 19.1	9.8
Universities:					
Oxford and Cambridge	11.0		—		25.4
London	15.7		—		24.4
Larger Civic	15.8		—		21.2
Smaller Civic	12.9		—		23.9
Scotland	17.0		—		23.1

Unsatisfactory as the Robbins survey figures are, it is difficult to make any other general comparisons because the English colleges differ so much in the organization of their courses. In Table 61 an outline is given of the allocation of time in two Scottish colleges (and shows how much they resemble each other) and three English colleges (and shows how much they vary). The table refers to the academic year 1963–64 and gives the time allocations in hours (by the clock) although the actual length adopted for classes is sometimes forty-five minutes, sometimes sixty minutes and sometimes longer. It shows the time-table when students are in college for five days in the week and ignores day-a-week teaching practice which is not undertaken for the whole academic year.

Only one of the three English colleges has significantly fewer class contact hours (to use the jargon) than the two Scottish colleges, but all three devote considerably less time to curriculum courses. Some of the differences between the English colleges are accounted for by the fact that two offer only one main course (and a subsidiary) whereas the third offers two main courses. It will be noticed that, having cut down curriculum courses in order to find time in the third year for study in greater depth of subjects of the students' own choice, the Scottish colleges have not been able to resist the temptation of making them do no less than three subjects.

TABLE 61. *Timetables of five colleges of education.*

	Scottish college A			Scottish college B			English college C			English college D			English college E		
Year	1	2	3	1	2	3	1	2	3	1	2	3	1	2	3
Professional															
Education	2	5	8	2	5	7	6	6	6	3	4½	12	3	3	3
One-day-a-week teaching practice				4											
	2	5	8	6	5	7	6	6	6	3	4½	12	3	3	3
Curriculum courses															
English (including speech)	6	2	2	3	3	—	1½	1½	—	2¼	1	1	1	1	—
Mathematics	1	2	1	2	—	—	1½	1½	—	2¼	1	1	1	1	—
Religious education	2	2	—	2	—	—	¾	—	—	2¼	1	1	1	1	—
Geography	3	—	—	2	—	—	—	—	—	1½	1	—	} 1 hour each of either one or two of these		
History	—	3	—	—	3	—	—	—	—	—	—	—			
Science	2	2	—	—	5	—	—	—	—	1½	1	—			
Physical education (including health educ.)	2	4	2	3	3	—	2¼	1½	—	2¼	1½	—	1	1	—
Music	2 }	4 (Music, Art, Craft)	—	2 }	4 (Music, Art, Craft)	—	—	—	—	1½	1½	—	} 2 hours each of either two or one of these		
Art	2		—	2		—	—	—	—	1½	1	—			
Craft	4		—	4		—	—	—	—	—	—	—			
	24	19	5	20	18	—	6	4½	—	15	9	4	8–9	8–9	—
'Personal education'															
'Main' subject (a)	—	—	3	—	—	6	4½	4½	4½	3	4½	6	3	3	3
'Main' subject (b)	—	—	4	—	—	5	—	—	—	—	—	—	3	3	3
Subsidiary subject	—	—	—	—	—	—	1½	1½	1½	3	4½	—	—	—	—
Other 'cultural' studies	—	—	2	—	—	3	3	1½	—	—	—	—	—	—	—
	—	—	9	—	—	14	9	7½	6	6	9	6	6	6	6
Total weekly lectures	26	24	22	26	23	21	21	18	12	24	22½	22	17–18	17–18	9

CHAPTER TWENTY-FIVE

Qualifications and Salaries

SCOTLAND

Until 1965 there were three different kinds of teacher's certificate in Scottish schools, and teachers were supposed to be restricted to the type of teaching covered by their qualifications. The Teacher's General Certificate was the basic qualification for teaching in primary schools. It could be obtained by non-graduate women after a three-year course or by a graduate after a one-year course. Originally it was the qualification required for teaching in the elementary schools, and covered the whole age-range from five to thirteen, and, later, fourteen. Even after the introduction of the 1939 Code, and the recognition of all post-primary education as 'secondary', it still technically covered the teaching of all children of compulsory school age. When the elementary schools began to develop advanced divisions, provision had been made for an additional qualification for holders of the General Certificate by way of endorsement on the certificate of a particular qualification to teach a specific subject or subjects to senior pupils. To be precise, the endorsement conferred a qualification to teach specific subjects to pupils in the first three years of any post-primary course, and could therefore entitle the holder to teach in the lower part of the Secondary schools as well as in the advanced divisions. The academic requirement for the endorsement was normally that the teacher should have taken a double course at the university in the subject he wished to teach, and it was open to a non-graduate teacher who had attended university classes without graduating as well as to a graduate to obtain the endorsement. This was more common before the war than after 1945. Even before the war the form of the certificate was out of date. As the work of the advanced divisions became established, many teachers found themselves teaching only senior pupils. Some of the advanced divisions had been centralized either in a school providing only that type of course or in a Secondary school with no primary department. After the war the certificate became even further out of date with more and more teachers concentrating on teaching in secondary departments. With the introduction of the ordinary grade in the Scottish Certificate of Education, the Teacher's General Certificate with endorsement came to be commonly regarded as a qualification to teach up to the ordinary grade. What had originally been intended as an extra qualification to spend some time teaching a particular subject in the first three years of a secondary course came to be used as the basic qualification to teach it full time over a four-year secondary course. Yet, in order to obtain this qualification teachers had to train to teach in primary schools. There was no teaching qualification at all for teaching general subjects in secondary schools.

Apart from the Teacher's General Certificate, Scottish qualifications entitled the teachers holding them to teach particular subjects rather than particular groups of children. The Teacher's Special Certificate was originally granted only to graduates with a first- or second-class honours degree in a subject which forms a normal part of the school curriculum. In 1959 it was thrown open to those with a third-class degree, but it could still only be obtained by honours graduates in a school subject. An honours graduate in, for example, psychology could not acquire a qualification to teach in a senior secondary school. The Teacher's Technical Certificate was similar to the Special Certificate in that it related to the teaching of a particular subject at any level. It covered the practical, as distinct from the academic, subjects. Music, art and physical education were described as 'technical' subjects. The use to which the Technical Certificate was put differed only in this respect, that as a qualification to teach the subject at any level it was literally used for that purpose. The Special Certificate, which conferred a qualification to teach, for example, classics at any level in the schools was naturally only used to teach the subject to pupils in a senior secondary school course. But the Technical Certificate might be used by teachers of, for example, art either to teach pupils studying art for the Scottish Certificate of Education or by a visiting specialist teacher of art to teach primary school pupils. For many teachers of art, music and physical education their first job might well be as visiting specialist in primary schools until they are able to work their way up to a full time job in a secondary school.

On 1 April 1965 new regulations were introduced which brought matters up to date in so far as they recognized the fact that all post-primary education is now classed as 'secondary'. There are now two forms of teacher's certificate, the Teacher's Certificate (Primary Education) and the Teacher's Certificate (Secondary Education) – as well as a Further Education Certificate. The Teacher's Certificate (Primary Education) is, like the former General Certificate, open to graduates (both men and women) after a one-year course at a college of education, and is a qualification to teach in a primary school or department. It is also open to non-graduate women after a three-year course. The Teacher's Certificate (Secondary Education), however, follows the practice of the former endorsements and of the Special and the Technical Certificates in that it only confers a qualification to teach a specified subject or specified subjects in a secondary school or department. The Scottish Education Department pre-scribes in considerable detail the qualifications in each subject of the secondary school curriculum which are regarded as an adequate basis for the award of a secondary certificate to teach that subject. The only innovation which has been made is that a graduate in some non-school subject may now acquire a qualifica-tion to teach in a secondary school by taking a supplementary course in a recognized school subject which is within the general field covered by his degree. The intention of the supplementary course is to give him enough basic information about some subject which is commonly taught in schools to permit of his being given a secondary certificate to teach that subject. The Secretary of State has ruled that the standards to be achieved on completion of a supplementary course will be those achieved on the completion of either one or two graduating courses in the subject concerned.[1]

The former Special and Technical Certificates were, and the new Secondary Certificate will continue to be, a source of considerable difficulty in the assessment of teachers who have graduated outside Scotland and apply for recognition as certificated teachers in Scotland. The rules for 'exceptional recognition' require that they shall not only possess a degree which is regarded as being of a standard equivalent to that of a Scottish university, but, if they are to be recognized as qualified to teach a subject in a secondary school, their course of study must be shown to have been equally relevant to the teaching of that subject. Even the degree courses of Scottish universities come under scrutiny in this respect, and it is an interesting sidelight on the relations between the state system of education and the universities that, at a time when the English universities (particularly the new foundations) are experimenting with new types of degree course, the Scottish universities are under this difficulty in introducing courses with unorthodox studies or unusual combinations of study. Such new courses are likely to be most attractive to undergraduates who are thinking of teaching, and it is a wise precaution for a university to seek the reactions of the Scottish Council for the Training of Teachers before offering a new course. If this body should hesitate to grant its immediate approval to the proposal for the purposes of recognition for teaching (as has by no means been unknown) it could strike a blow at the university's scheme which, while not necessarily mortal, could be fairly serious in its effect. Anyone who might wish to teach in Scotland would be ill advised to graduate at some of the new English universities: graduates of the University of Keele have already experienced difficulty. And, coming nearer home, there has been some hesitation about agreeing that some degrees of the new University of Strathclyde should be recognized for the purposes of teaching qualifications in Scotland.[2]

The rigidity of this system of qualification has had its effect on the course in colleges of education. No one would seek to defend a situation in which they were forced to give the holder of an ordinary degree who firmly intended to teach in secondary schools some training in primary school teaching simply because he could only qualify for a Teacher's General Certificate. Nevertheless the colleges felt constrained to observe the letter of the law. More particularly, the requirements for the endorsement on the General Certificate and for the award of the Special and Technical Certificate required that the student should not only hold the requisite academic qualifications but also have undertaken teaching practice and a course in the methods of teaching the particular subject he wished to be qualified to teach. Not only, therefore, did the type of qualification conferred influence the schools towards specialist subject teaching in their

[1] See Scottish Education Department *Memorandum on Entry Requirements and Courses*, 1965, p. 4.
[2] Ibid., p. 4.

organization, but it also forced a strong specialist bias into the training of teachers. This position continues under the new regulations.

ENGLAND

If the Scottish system was a tidy one in years past, was made untidy by a failure to keep the requirements of the regulations up to date with the changing conditions in the schools, and is still very inflexible, the English system was never very tidy, and, in an attempt to remove some of the anomalies, was made even more illogical, even though it is very flexible. Before the war the regulations prescribed the qualifications required by various types of teacher employed in the elementary schools. They included Certificated Teachers, Uncertificated Teachers (for whom, oddly enough certain qualifications were prescribed), Supplementary Teachers (uncertificated teachers who were not qualified to rank as Uncertificated Teachers) and Teachers of Special Subjects (that is teachers qualified to teach such subjects as handicraft and domestic subjects but not qualified to be classed as Certificated Teachers). For Secondary schools, on the other hand, no qualifications were laid down, although graduates received a higher rate of pay than non-graduates. The teaching staff merely had to be 'suitable and sufficient in number and qualifications for providing adequate instruction'. The McNair Committee described the result as follows:

'It is broadly true to say that the certificated teacher is to the elementary school what the graduate teacher is to the secondary school. The certificated teacher who has had the minimum of two years training has no status in the secondary school as a trained teacher; he is classified for salary purposes merely as a non-graduate: and the graduate who is not trained has no academic status in the elementary school. He is graded merely as an uncertificated teacher, or, rather, he would be so graded if he were self-sacrificing enough to take a post in an elementary school.'[1]

There were anomalies in this system even when the elementary and secondary schools formed two quite separate, but occasionally overlapping, types of school. When the 1944 Act produced a more coherent school system, and, in particular, 'promoted' the senior elementary schools to be secondary modern schools, it was felt impossible to do otherwise than to grant 'qualified teacher' status to all who would previously have been qualified to teach in either type of school. In short it was possible to become a qualified teacher either by taking the two-year course of training or by the simple possession of a university degree, with or without professional training. This has produced the illogical position that a graduate who does not even attempt to take a course of professional training is automatically recognized as a qualified teacher, but, since failure on the post-graduate training course cannot be ignored altogether, a graduate who does take the course and fails it cannot become a qualified teacher. Although different

[1] McNair Report, 1944, p. 11.

teaching qualifications attract different salaries under the Burnham scale, in terms of the actual entitlement to teach there is only one class of qualified teacher in England. There may be different routes into the profession, but, however he may have achieved qualified status, a teacher is permitted, as far as the regulations are concerned, to teach any subject in any type of school except a special school for the blind, the partially sighted, the deaf or the partially deaf. (For these schools a special, or an additional, qualification is required. On the other hand such a highly specialized course as the Manchester University Diploma in the Teaching of the Deaf does confer 'qualified status', and therefore entitlement to teach in any type of school.)

There is always the danger in the English system that the gap between the graduate and the non-graduate sections of the teaching profession will open up again. The training colleges reacted sharply when the Minister of Education pointed out to them that the greatest shortage of teachers in the late nineteen-sixties would probably be in the primary schools and tried to persuade them to concentrate on courses for primary teachers, at the same time revealing that he relied on the larger output of the universities to staff the secondary schools, without taking any steps to make the professional training of graduate entrants compulsory. It is not perhaps the difference between graduates and non-graduate to which objections are raised so much as the difference between untrained graduates and trained non-graduates. But graduate teachers are already finding their way more than in the past into secondary modern schools and the split which formerly existed between the staffs of Secondary and elementary schools could become a split between secondary and primary. In spite of encouragement to do so as the needs of the schools dictate, there are few teachers who spend part of their career in a primary school and part in a secondary school.

SALARIES

In Scotland the fact that the teaching profession is more clearly identifiable means that perhaps the difference between the graduate and the non-graduate is less marked. The difference is rather a sex difference. Men have to be graduates: the profession is male-dominated in comparison with England, headships of all but the smallest schools go to men, and it is very common for a man, particularly an ordinary graduate, to spend his first years in teaching in a secondary school, but to find his best chance of promotion in the headship of a primary school. There is a danger that the primary schools will find themselves predominantly staffed by (non-graduate) women whose total time in teaching is limited, but under the control of men who come in from the secondary schools to take the headships.

In a country in which academic distinction is so highly regarded as it is in Scotland, graduates are in a strong bargaining position. The principle of equal pay for men and women could be accepted without in fact paying the majority of women teachers the same as men simply because their qualifications are different. The differential between graduate and non-graduate teachers is much greater than in England:

TABLE 62. *Teachers' salaries* 1963

Three year non-graduate teacher	
England ..	.. £630 rising to £1,250 in fifteen years
Scotland ..	.. £600 ,, ,, £1,190 in fourteen years
Trained graduate teaching in secondary schools with three years for degree and one year training	
England ..	.. £760 rising to £1,380 in fifteen years
Scotland ..	.. £820 ,, ,, £1,470 in twelve years
Good honours graduate teaching in secondary schools with four years for degree and one year training	
England ..	.. £880 rising to £1,500 in fifteen years
Scotland ..	.. £900 ,, £1,750 in ten years

UNQUALIFIED TEACHERS

The attempt to achieve an entirely graduate profession has, for the time being, not only been shown to be impossible of realization in present conditions of shortage (there is even talk that Scotland may be forced to swallow the pill of non-graduate men), it has also been pushed into the background by the more immediate aim of the teachers' organizations to eliminate uncertificated teachers from the schools.

Because of the different basis of teaching qualifications it is not easy to make an exact comparison between the qualifications held by English and by Scottish teachers. The following table, however, attempts to give an approximate picture. It suggests that, although the number of teachers who are regarded as uncertificated in Scotland is much larger than the number who are unqualified in England, the number who hold lower qualifications than unqualified teachers in England is smaller. This does not mean that the teachers' organizations are any less anxious to persuade the authorities to replace (or simply dismiss without replacing) those who do not meet the requirements for certification in Scotland.

TABLE 63. *Qualifications of Teachers.*

ENGLAND

		QUALIFIED									UNQUALIFIED
TRAINED				Trained outside England and Wales, but qualified		UNTRAINED but holding some qualification					Holding no qualification
Trained Graduates	Graduate Equiv.	Others		Graduates	Others	Graduates	Graduate Equiv.	Others	Qualified by long service		
35,728	2,638	179,104		942	1,767	13,969	1,558	12,637	4,190		6,229
13.4%	1.0%	70.0%		0.3%	0.6%	5.4%	0.6%	4.7%	1.6%		2.4%

Total trained: 220,179 = 85.3%

Total untrained: 32,354 = 12.3%
Total qualified: 252,533 = 97.6%

Unqualified 2.4%

SCOTLAND

		CERTIFICATED					UNTRAINED but holding some qualification		UNQUALIFIED
Graduates	Technical	Others		Trained outside Scotland but uncertificated			Graduates	Others	Holding no qualification
Certificate				Graduates	Others				
16,914	6,650	13,402		56	294		225	1,183	588
43.0%	17.0%	34.0%		0.1%	0.7%		0.6%	3.0%	1.5%

Total certificated: 36,966 = 94%

Total uncertificated: 2,346 = 6.0%

PART VIII

Some Conclusions

Fae Monday morn till Friday nicht I'd yark the learnin in,
Though I widna touch the fancy frills, for that wid be a sin!
Nae drawin, singin, dancin – they're the cantrips o' the De'il!
Na, I widna hae sic ongauns in my couthy country skweel.

CHAPTER TWENTY-SIX

Moral Training

The danger of making comparisons is that one easily falls into the trap of exaggerating differences. Examiners, with their fondness for the 'compare and contrast' type of question, know only too well what ingenuity can be used in discovering distinctions where none exist. Similarities can be overlooked perhaps because they are too obvious. English and Scottish schools have been responsive to the same changes in educational fashion, subject to the same fluctuations in government policy and have suffered from much the same economic difficulties. They share approximately the same language. And, of course, it is impossible to generalize about the schools of two countries in which, even though the balance of power between government and local authority, headmaster and class teachers may not be quite the same, considerable freedom is given to individual members of the teaching profession. The differences in beliefs and practice between particular schools in England, and between particular schools in Scotland, are probably at least as great as the differences which have been described between the official doctrines of the Scottish Education Department and the Department of Education and Science (and its predecessors, the Ministry and the Board of Education).

Nevertheless it is suggested that the official documents quoted, however stoutly individual teachers may ignore them, would not reveal quite so many contrasts unless they were indicative of important divergences in national policy and national attitudes. The range of variety which may be found in British schools is considerable, but the gulf between north and south is, in spite of all the pressures towards uniformity which have been felt over the past fifty years (if not before), significantly wide.

The temptation is not merely to describe the differences which exist but to try to explain them. The longer history of public education in Scotland is still relevant to an understanding of present-day differences. But that it is so relevant raises the suspicion that Scots are essentially conservative in educational matters. State education in England is more recent, is still benefiting from the impetus given by the 1944 Act, and appears to be more dynamic. But the experience of the nineteen-thirties suggests that perhaps English schools, with their pragmatic approach, are more easily affected by external circumstances and have been thriving recently only because the economy has demanded it. Geography, the distribution of population, and some historical accidents account for many of the differences in school organization, yet it has been argued that the ways in which the schools are organized also betray some more basic educational assumptions. Observed differences lead one to generalize about the educational philosophy underlying them. In turn one is led to suggest, rather than assert, differences in the climate of national opinion, differences in religious beliefs and in social structure, which may in part account for this philosophic divergence. The educational commentator cannot, however, go much beyond hinting at the more obvious of these factors. The schools partly reflect the assumptions of the society they serve, and partly help to form the attitudes of that society. The limitation of a discussion which focuses only on the work of the schools is that it is bound to give some account of the first half of this process, but is likely to ignore the second altogether: the result is to exaggerate the effect of 'outside' influences on the schools, and perhaps to draw rather facile conclusions. It seems necessary in these concluding chapters, therefore, to correct the balance by examining some aspects of the difference between Scottish and English schools which are based on the practice of the schools themselves.

CORPORAL PUNISHMENT

The question of corporal punishment may be taken as an example. There can be little doubt that there are some teachers in England who use corporal punishment just as frequently as some Scottish teachers, and some teachers in Scotland who abhor its use just as much as some English teachers. Yet there is equally little doubt that the tawse is used in Scotland much more frequently than the cane in England. The Board of Education said in 1937 that the practice of the best elementary schools was to dispense with corporal punishment altogether, though they were not prepared to state officially that teachers should be denied the right to inflict physical pain as an ultimate sanction. In 1959 the Ministry of Education were quite emphatic in their view that corporal punishment should be unnecessary in primary schools. The London School Board had introduced its first regulations governing corporal punishment in 1871, and first prohibited in 1907 the use of any physical punishment, other than a slap with the open hand, on children under the age of seven. The views of teachers who wished to keep the cane were much the same then as now. But before the second world war most local education authorities in England had forbidden the use of corporal punishment for certain categories of pupils (all children below a given age, all girls of whatever age, etc.), and had imposed clear conditions for its exercise, which considerably restricted its use in primary schools. The result is that, whatever the position may be with older children, the number of eight- and nine-year-olds in England who are ever beaten by their teachers is almost certainly negligible. The Scottish Education Department, on the other hand, actually thought in 1950 that the use of corporal punishment might have a salutary effect. By 1965 they had so far changed their view that they made approximately the same statement as had appeared in the English *Handbook* for 1937. But only seven Scottish education authorities have made rules governing the use of corporal punishment by the teachers in their employment. Although few infants get the strap, the number of eight- and nine-year-olds who do is probably appreciable.

But the rules made by authority are relatively unimportant. If Scottish teachers have been accustomed to use the strap it must imply either that the majority of Scottish parents have approved of corporal punishment for their children, or that they have acquiesced in its use by the teaching profession, or at the very least that traditional habits have been slower to change in Scotland than in England. The strong position of a Calvinistic church in Scotland does not 'explain' a harsher attitude towards discipline in many Scottish schools, still less the fact that it is imposed by physical means. Examples of a belief in a strict separation of function in some spheres of Scottish education do not explain whether parents have a more acquiescent attitude towards the authority of the teacher. The more closely knit organization of the teaching profession does not necessarily mean that its members are more conservative. On the contrary, it is unfair to teachers to assume that they do exactly what society expects them to do, or are content to continue to behave as society permits them to behave. In fact, as the Educational Institute of Scotland has complained, 'the teacher's position is made still more invidious by the ambivalent attitude of society towards corporal punishment'. And any comparison between England and Scotland which is based on what people say rather than what they do is bound to run into difficulty: the E.I.S., many of whose members certainly use corporal punishment quite frequently, have recently recommended that it be progressively banished entirely from Scottish schools, whereas the National Union of Teachers, whose members probably resort to its use less frequently, have recently asserted that teachers should not be deprived of the right to do so.

The theory and practice of education is changing rapidly in both England and Scotland – though whether it is changing any more rapidly than at other times during the past fifty years is by no means certain. Nevertheless, to trace the development of the ideas propounded in the official reports regarding the schools' part in the moral training of their pupils may help to explain differences of emphasis in a question which is controversial in both countries.

THE SCHOOLS' PART

There appear to be two main respects in which the English view differs from the Scottish. First, the schools south of the border have been accustomed to take more upon themselves. 'English educators have always professed to regard character training as the chief of their responsibilities', says the 1927 *Handbook*, and sets the parents firmly in their place by saying that 'by far the most important of the potential allies of the schools is, of course, the home'.[1] Allowance is of course made in England for the rights of the parents and their religious beliefs, but phrases can be found in the reports which suggest a readiness to usurp the functions of the home, and the schools have been forced by past controversies to be suspicious of the churches. The schools in Scotland have been content to take their place, but no more than their place in a scheme of things in which appropriate responsibility has been apportioned between the

[1] *Handbook*, 1927, p. 10.

schools, the parents and the church. In 1950 the Department seemed to make a very grudging admission that the schools should accept responsibility for the moral upbringing of their pupils:

'For the child's intellectual education the school is mainly responsible; for his moral education the responsibility lies partly with the school, but principally with his parents, who may or may not bring him within the range of religious influence. Home life now often differs very greatly from what it was a generation or two ago, and not a few parents are neglectful of the moral training of their children. Consequently there is a tendency to expect the school to make good the omissions of the home in this respect.'[1]

Secondly, both England and Scotland are sufficiently within the tradition of western European Christianity to assume a dichotomy between man's sinful nature and his spiritual aspirations, yet in the manipulation of the child's emotions and sentiments for the purpose of moral training English schools have been accustomed to pay far less attention to his intellect: the Scots have been more ready to give the intellect at least equal place, and the schools have, if anything, concentrated on the intellectual aspects of moral training as being within their proper sphere of influence.

CHARACTER FORMATION IN ENGLAND

It may be that the English attitude is a result of the influence of the Victorian Public School, whose overwhelming effect on the educational system is no more marked than in the field of character training. Certainly the Public School took its boys away from their homes for a quarter of a year at a time. It created an artificial environment designed to foster a special brand of *esprit de corps*, made up of loyalty to a small group, the house, and the larger institution, the school. The emphasis was on tradition, and in this considerable use was made of the natural conservatism of the young. New boys were initiated into the 'done thing'. The older boys returned an exercise of responsibility for the enjoyment of privileges. But community service was limited to the life of the school itself; it did not look beyond the school boundaries. The school Chapel was part of the tradition of the institution, and a part of 'good form'. The doctrine of muscular Christianity combined with a belief in the moral virtues of team games and led to a separation between religious knowledge (as a classroom subject, which in England is examinable and a soft option at that) and general Christian teaching (which was part of the out-of-class activities of the school). The actual classroom work was, in fact, something set apart from the moral training offered by the school. To be sure, a certain amount of gerund grinding was thought – like cold showers before breakfast – to instil some moral virtue in the younger pupils. But the aim with the older sixth formers was to cultivate the easy confidence of the amateur and the gentleman. Scholarship might be one of the more virtuous pleasures open to man, but this did not mean that it was a virtue in

[1] *Memorandum*, 1950, p. 110.

itself. Individuality, and even a mild eccentricity, could be tolerated within the limits set by 'good form' but it was in matters of the mind that freedom of thought and self-expression were more readily accepted than in matters of behaviour.

The extent to which English secondary schools have in the past borrowed many of the techniques of the Public Schools is well known: the prefect system, the house system, team games, the school spirit: all are as much part of the maintained secondary school as of the independent school, even though some of them are far less appropriate or effective in a day school than in a boarding school. But the primary schools have copied the Public Schools too. The 1905 *Handbook* stressed the importance of developing the corporate life of the elementary school, suggested that 'the most direct means of fostering school traditions is to organize schools games' and that 'the practice of giving some of the older boys and girls responsible duties as monitors is an excellent one'. There were also references to the direct teaching of moral virtues by the use of 'impressive examples' of the lives of great men and women,[1] and this aspect of training received rather more emphasis in later editions of the *Handbooks* up to 1937 after which, although still given passing mention, the explicit teaching of a code of behaviour tended to be played down in favour of simply creating the kind of environment in which children would be led to form the right attitudes naturally. The modern infants school, as described in the 1959 *Handbook*, does not use the more obvious techniques suitable for older children (the earlier *Handbooks* were probably referring to the senior departments when they advocated team games and monitors), but it nevertheless uses methods which can be traced back to the Public Schools. By helping the children to develop their own individuality, the schools help them to free themselves from the ties of home, and the implication is that teachers should have a proper suspicion of the over-protective mother. As the Ministry put it: 'When they come to school at five, many are barely loosed from their mother's apron strings; when they leave at seven most of them are self-reliant, able to hold their own with other children, and well established as school boys and school girls.' The process of initiation into the school community is all-important:

'When he begins school each newcomer needs the teacher's special help and attention, and ideally he is received into a small group. . . . Children who are still settling down need the steady companionship of the teacher whom they are getting to know and the familiar environment of their own class and classroom. They need also to feel the steadying effects of the regular life in school, which, if disrupted, may for some lead to set-backs. . . . There has in recent years grown up in a few infant schools a practice of organizing the schools so that each class contains children of different ages – five to over seven. This is to carry into the large school the kind of classification that is automatic in the small school, and it is an attempt to reproduce a kind of family atmosphere in which older and younger children live together, the younger ones emulating and imitating the

---

[1] *Handbook*, 1905, pp. 9, 10.

older ones.[1] Where schools are so organized the initiation of the five-year-olds is comparatively easy.'

The justification of the English infant school is that it 'sets out to provide for the children a fuller life than their homes can do', and that 'it should offer good upbringing in personal behaviour and in attitudes to other people, though these do not appear as part of the curriculum or in schemes of work.'[2] When the children move up at the age of seven to the junior school,

'the change from being the big boys and girls in one school to being the little ones in another comes at a time when children have in fact already shown that they are capable of being self-reliant and responsible. From the beginning therefore, the children should be given the chance to exercise resourcefulness and to undertake responsible duties. At this time the children also recognize more clearly that each is one of a group; they are beginning to give more weight to the opinion of their fellows and to appeal less to the authority of the teacher against them'.

The criteria of good behaviour are not established by talking about them. The teacher achieves his purpose by establishing the right environment and the right spirit within the (or rather 'his') class. There is a grudging admission that 'admittedly, the school must share the responsibility for the outcome of education in this broad sense with the children's families and other influences in the environment; but even so, the teachers' responsibilities remain great', and there is, above all, the suggestion that children do what the teacher asks from a sense of personal loyalty 'because it is he who asks'.[3]

TRAINING FOR CITIZENSHIP IN SCOTLAND: PRIMARY SCHOOLS

In Scotland the first of the series of reports published by the Advisory Council just after the war was on Training for Citizenship.[4] Its recommendations were incorporated in a circular issued by the Scottish Education Department. Although the circular says that 'at the secondary stage, as at the primary, training should be less a matter of formal instruction than of providing opportunities of practising citizenship', nevertheless at least as much weight is put on the contribution which all subjects in the curriculum can make – at any rate in an indirect way – as on the other devices usual in schools to encourage the virtues of good behaviour and good citizenship. Indeed there is a warning that extracurricular activities 'must not be allowed to distract the pupil's attention unduly from his studies. While everything possible should be done to make his school life full and interesting, his training will fail in a main point if it does not bring home to him the fundamental importance of well-directed industry and per-

---

[1] This is not in fact such a very recent idea. The 1933 *Report of the Consultative Committee on Infant and Nursery Schools* (also under the Chairmanship of W. H. Hadow) records that 'many schools have experimented with what is known as a "vertical" classification' (p. 138).

[2] *Handbook*, 1959, p. 42.   [3] Ibid., p. 83.

[4] *Training for Citizenship* (Cmd. 6495) 1945.

severance'.[1] The warning is one which was added by the Department: it does not appear in the original report.

When they went on to produce their separate reports on primary and on secondary education the Advisory Council became even more interested in the ways in which children develop their own powers – of action as well as of thought. In the primary report they spoke of

'the shifting of emphasis from merely intellectual training to the development of the whole personality, with new emphasis on physical and emotional training, and from passive reception and the memorizing of facts to the encouragement of each child to develop by his own activity all those gifts he possesses and those virtues to which he is capable of attaining'.[2]

But it was the Scottish Education Department's *Memorandum on the Primary School in Scotland*, published in 1950, that ran to six impressions over the next ten years, was a textbook in the colleges of education, and, as references to it in the annual reports confirm, represented the official view over that period. The many quotations from the *Memorandum* in Chapter 8 show that, however tentatively the Department may have been working towards the educational principles they finally adopted in 1965, and whatever may have been said in the earlier document about the value of activity by the pupils, in the 'fifties both education and morality were things which were handed down by the teacher as the representative of adult standards, and the children had to learn to conform. No further quotations are necessary except to reiterate the point that, in contrast with the family atmosphere recommended for English primary schools, the contribution which the Scottish school was thought best able to make to the moral training of young children was that 'as it is a larger unit than the family, it resembles more closely the still larger community of which the pupil will in due time become a member. It is thus in a favourable position to instil those qualities which make for good relations between the individual and his fellows'.[3] It is only in the 1965 *Memorandum* that the conversion to a developmental approach is so wholehearted that it is applied without reservation to the formation of moral concepts as much as to intellectual growth. The Scottish primary school is now also advised to imitate the family and to be content with merely setting the scene in which children can develop the notions of good behaviour which they already nourish within themselves. 'The cultivation of desirable habits, attitudes, qualities, of character and modes of behaviour cannot be reduced to the level of items on a timetable; it is nevertheless an essential part of education, which is achieved, not through explicit instruction, but as a result of the tone of the school.' So completely is this new approach adopted that the Scottish *Memorandum* goes far beyond most English primary schools in taking over the techniques developed in another age for another age group by the Public Schools: the young child

'should learn to belong to his school, and take pride in its beauty, its equipment,

---

[1] *Training for Citizenship* (Circular 23), 1945, p. 6.
[2] *Primary Report*, p. 3.   [3] *Memorandum*, 1950, p. 110.

its surroundings and its achievements. There are many ways of fostering a desirable school spirit. Opportunities of meeting regularly as a unit, and of taking part in school activities such as concerts, services, parties, excursions, clubs and inter-school sport, enlarge the child's understanding of what a school is and encourage his urge to share in its larger identity. A school badge, or song, or dance, can also contribute to this end. A house system may be another useful way of providing the child with a cause towards which he can make his own effort individually and in co-operation with others.'[1]

Gone are the children – 'all normal children' – who have days when they 'appear unusually aggressive, self-centred, nervous, acquisitive, capricious or deceitful': now behaviour problems in the primary school are limited to a few five-year-olds who may be quite lacking in self-control. Even that will be attributable to faults in nurture rather than in nature: 'If they have been accustomed at home to receive a rational explanation for any controls which were necessary, they will generally respond well to a similarly reasoned approach in school. On the other hand, if discipline at home has been dictatorial, the school may find itself with pupils whose reactions vary from apathetically submissive to openly rebellious or destructive.' The school can however easily manipulate children's feelings of loyalty, their need for affection and their capacity for imitation: 'Finding themselves as members of a small group, with common interests, needs and desires, and wishing to stand well with the community, they assimilate enough of the manners and customs of those around them to be accepted, and concepts of desirable social attitudes and actions begin to develop.'[2] The Scottish Education Department does not go quite so far as the Ministry of Education had done in suggesting that good behaviour might be a matter of personal loyalty to one well-loved teacher, still less that children may even be more moral than their teachers but, from now on, precept is out, punishment is kept in the background as the ultimate sanction, and the tone of the school and the general atmosphere of security engendered by a teacher who is unfailingly optimistic and cheerful, are enough in themselves to set most children on the paths of virtue.

TRAINING FOR CITIZENSHIP IN SCOTLAND: SECONDARY SCHOOLS

Both the primary and the secondary reports of the Scottish Advisory Council were in many ways an embarrassment to the Department in the years immediately after the war. In their report on *Secondary Education* they took the same humanistic view as they had done when writing about primary schools, but they were much more passionate in pleading it:

'The adolescent pupil requires the encompassing presence of mature and balanced personalities, disinterestedly regardful of the child as a person and manifesting toward him a consistent and active good will. In the genial warmth of such an atmosphere the growing life will respond with trust and self-expression not

[1] *Memorandum*, 1965, p. 23. [2] Ibid., p. 7.

disturbed by fears or spoiled by concealment. The aspirations of adolescence are nourished, its instinct to imitate finds a worthy pattern, and its whole impulsive life is controlled without violence and directed along healthy and creative channels. Thus environed, the developing personality has fair prospects of attaining an adult selfhood that is at once finely social and fully individual.'[1]

But whereas an older tradition survived in the primary schools for another twenty years, most of the recommendations of the Advisory Council found an echo in the Department's own *Memorandum on Junior Secondary Education* when it came to be published in 1955. To be sure the Department expressed one or two interesting reservations: for example the Advisory Council had advocated the abolition of prizes because they led to an 'unlovely concentration on marks and class places, singling out for approbation one form of superiority alone and neglecting many another excellence'. In the Department's view 'the objections to giving prizes to individual pupils are possibly exaggerated by the Council'.[2] Nevertheless English readers will find much that is familiar in the following passage:

'The school itself should be a community of which each pupil can feel himself to be an active and responsible member. The pupils should feel that it is *their* school, that it exists for their benefit, and that they, in turn, owe it service. The creation of a good community spirit is a major responsibility of the Headmaster, and the example of the staff as a whole is an important contributory factor. If the pupils see that their teachers regard the school as a unity in which all the members are serving together for the common good, they will themselves more readily acquire the same attitude. Young people have a natural instinct for service and loyalty, and the school should enlist these qualities on its own behalf and give them an outlet within its own sphere. Through many of the general activities of the schools – morning assembly, organised games, prefect system, meals, clubs of various kinds – the pupils may practice the art of living and working together, may learn respect for the rights and feelings of others, and may thus make their contribution to the creation of a good community spirit.'[3]

In their annual report for 1961 the Department described the main developments in junior secondary education since the publication of their *Memorandum* five years earlier. 'Among the most encouraging features of junior secondary education today are the fruitful developments that have taken place in the corporate life of the schools, as shown both in the activities which form part of the communal life of the school as a whole and in those of different groups which are more of an extra-curricula nature.' The report went on to comment that

'The natural leaders in all school activities tend to be found among the older and abler pupils, and this tends to be reflected in the general level of the activities pursued. As a result, the fifteen-year-old leavers from junior secondary schools which provide only non-certificate courses appear in general to have derived

---

[1] *Secondary Report*, p. 11. [2] Circular 206, 1951.
[3] *Memorandum on Junior Secondary Education*, p. 9.

greater benefit from the communal and extra-curricular activities of their schools than have those who leave at the same age from comprehensive schools'.[1]

MORAL TEACHING IN ENGLAND

But, just when the Scottish Education Department were congratulating the schools on the fostering of a communal spirit, urging them to develop the 'house' system to induce loyalty, discipline and other social qualities, and suggesting how they might make the prefect system one of real value, schools south of the border seem to have been having second thoughts, and the Newsom Report seems to have been encouraging them to do so.

'The majority of schools make use of House systems, with awards for good work and behaviour as well as for competitive sport. A few large, new schools exist whose buildings have been designed on a House basis, and in which the House units can operate as small communities in themselves, with a physical identity. But this is exceptional, and the typical day school operates its Houses despite, rather than aided by its buildings. Most schools still clearly feel that this is an effective way of developing group loyalties or providing opportunities for service; just a few have doubts as to how far older pupils who are within sight of leaving may really feel involved in what are inevitably somewhat artificial institutions.

'Most schools see value in creating a corps of prefects and monitors, which sets an example of service and provides opportunities to exercise leadership at many levels. The non-prefects are not always impressed:

"The school was over-run with prefects and monitors who could not control the rest of us and were wasting their time."

"Prefects were mostly fake."

'A few heads suggest that a less authoritarian organisation may be more appropriate to present day concepts, and are anxious to find ways in which all the older pupils can be given personal responsibility. . . .

'We recognise the value many schools continue to find in traditional forms of social organisation, but think they would be wise to seek also other ways of distributing responsibility. "Training for Leadership", except in very limited spheres, becomes an increasingly difficult principle to apply to the education of large numbers of boys and girls who almost by definition are not outstanding, and who are generally much less likely to become members of an élite at school or afterwards. It may be that learning to become a reliable member of a group of equals is, for many, a better general preparation for life. . . . As larger numbers of older pupils remain longer at school, more subtle systems of sharing responsibility and developing initiative may have to be found. Community service projects appear to offer particularly satisfying possibilities.'[2]

It is not completely true to say that the idea of public service in the Public Schools was entirely an inward-looking thing. Some distinguished contributions

[1] *Education in Scotland in 1961* (Cmnd. 1673). pp. 39 and 41.
[2] Newsom Report, 1963, pp. 67–9.

to social service – missions and dockland settlements – have been associated with the Public Schools, but generally speaking their isolation and their residential character made it difficult for them to organize projects of help to the local community. Since the work of Gordonstoun became well known, of course, the idea of public service as an integral part of the schools' day to day programme has become more widely accepted. The Spens Report, too, had one short paragraph in which it was suggested that 'further activities take the form of adventures in altruism and social service by which the school transcends the confines of its normal life', and the Scottish Education Department have suggested that community service projects might be linked with local studies in which – again combining moral with intellectual training – pupils might be of some use to the neighbourhood at the same time as they learned more about it. But the emphasis on community service as an element in the moral training of children not in the first flight of ability which is given in the Newsom Report is something new in British education.

In the strictly English context the biggest innovation in the Newsom Report is not even the suggestions for community service but the emphasis which is placed on moral training, not through example and through the tone of the school, but by explicit instruction. The Spens Report had stated the traditional view: the behavioural aspects of good citizenship should certainly be discussed with the older pupils, but the teacher should quite clearly be seen to step out from behind his desk and talk with his pupils on equal terms:

'There should be definite periods in the time-table in which no formal teaching is undertaken, in which all kinds of questions, at times relating to the formal work in hand, but more often to other matters of general interest – and among these we include many of the problems of citizenship – may be informally discussed by the pupils themselves. In these discussions the teacher, divesting himself for the moment of his authority, will, as opportunity offers, join, but always on "level" terms with his pupils and with no attempt to over-ride the opinions of his pupils except by fair argument.'[1]

The Newsom Report, by recommending that the last year or two of school life should be positively 'outgoing', calls for something more, and for something rather different from this kind of man-to-man discussion. It states explicitly that civics, current affairs, modern history, social studies, whether under those names or not, ought to feature in the programme of every school: positive guidance to boys and girls on sexual morals is essential: there is a need for teachers whose training has included some realistic sociological study. Simple moral teaching is not the plain straight-forward thing that it may have been in the past, because there is no universally accepted code of behaviour or of religious beliefs in contemporary society, but

'however diverse the staff may be in their philosophical alignment, all will approve of positive well-doing; there is much common ground which Christian

[1] Spens Report, 1935, p. 189.

and agnostic may travel together. Christian ethics after all owe much to Aristotle as well as to Judaism. Orthodoxy finds no difficulty, but rather support in the concept of a natural law. History and geography, literature, civics, science, all play their part in forming the moral outlook of boys and girls, and through all these subjects the whole staff, irrespective of their religious affiliations, can make a united contribution to both the spiritual and moral development of the pupils.'

The situation has changed so much that the danger is no longer of authoritarianism but of too much doubt. Whilst, therefore, children expect their teachers to discuss problems in a straightforward way, without shirking awkward questions, this is not in itself enough: boys and girls, we are told, 'are the first to demand that teachers should know what they are talking about'; they demand from them the authoritative guidance which comes both from superior knowledge and from superior experience.[1]

[1] Newsom Report, 1963, pp. 2–59.

CHAPTER TWENTY-SEVEN

Teacher and Taught

There are two factors in the design of education which may have a profound effect on the relationship between the teacher and his pupils. First there is the choice between a broad education and a more specialist course. Whatever the theoretical merits of a wide curriculum, it may well be that the organizational problems involved – and in particular the fact that the student may have many teachers none of whom feels any close responsibility for his welfare – go far to outweigh the advantages claimed. Secondly, there is the matter of assessment: are the teachers themselves responsible for examining their students or are examinations completely external?

THE UNIVERSITIES: TUTOR AND STUDENT

In support of the thesis that it has traditionally been the English practice to separate personal guidance from academic teaching it may not be too far-fetched to point to the division of tutorial responsibility at Cambridge (if not at Oxford). It is well known that the teaching at the two ancient universities is organized quite differently from the teaching at any other British university. Elsewhere the lecture course provides the basic framework of the instruction: tutorials and seminars are used to supplement the lectures with a more intimate type of instruction in which the student is able, as he cannot be in large lectures, to participate actively. At Oxford and Cambridge it is the tutorial which is the basic form of instruction: the tutor guides the student's reading, sets him written work to do, and advises him which lectures he should attend: but the lectures are ancillary to the course of study determined by the tutor. This being so, and since most students are taking only one subject, it might have been thought that the obvious way of providing for the personal welfare of undergraduates would have been to make the man responsible for his education also responsible for giving personal guidance. But at Cambridge the tutorials are given by a 'supervisor' of studies: the 'tutor' to whom the undergraduates can turn for personal advice is usually a different member of his college. This division of responsibility is probably unavoidable at the present time when increasing numbers have made it necessary to appoint research students and others outside the college as supervisors, but this was not always so.

In the Scottish universities the position of the 'regent' was originally somewhat similar to that of the supervisor at Cambridge. In spite of the encyclopaedic nature of the curriculum, teaching was undertaken by regents who rotated with their classes throughout their courses and were responsible for the whole of their instruction. During the eighteenth century a system of specialist teaching replaced teaching by the regents. But the role of the regents has been revived more recently in some Scottish universities: they now act as personal mentors to a group of students. All the Scottish universities also have advisers of studies who are responsible for guiding students through the complexities of the degree regulations. Neither the regent nor the adviser of studies will necessarily teach any of the students assigned to him, but this is dictated by the nature of the courses: a student taking the ordinary M.A. at a Scottish university will be following courses of study in two or three different departments each year, all of equal importance, so that he does not 'belong' to any one department in preference to the others. The Robbins Committee found that a far higher percentage of ordinary degree students at Scottish universities had been allotted to an individual adviser of studies than at any English university other than Oxford and Cambridge: more of them claimed to have received advice on the planning of their course, but only two per cent of them said that they had seen their adviser more than once or twice a term.

THE SCHOOLS: FORM MASTER AND PUPIL

This problem of appointing one member of the teaching staff to be responsible for the oversight of the progress made, and the personal problems met, by an individual pupil following a course conducted by a number of different specialists is, of course, one which preoccupies the secondary schools. As English secondary schools adopted a broader curriculum the institutions of both the form master and the housemaster lay to hand as a means of meeting the problem. The senior departments of the elementary schools were slow to adopt specialist teaching and, when they did, the long tradition of class teaching led naturally to the continuance of the form master as the teacher who carried particular responsibility for his class, even if he saw less of them than he had when he had worked as a teacher of general subjects. The Hadow Report, however, uses the word specialist only to describe teachers of handicraft, domestic subjects, art as applied to industrial processes and other practical subjects, although it goes on to recommend that the training colleges should pay heed to the demand for a large body of teachers with special qualifications to teach the various branches of the curriculum. The Board of Education's 1927 *Handbook* suggests that the schools should make fuller use of the diversity of tastes and abilities 'which is almost sure to exist among the staff' and says that

'Specialisation of this kind has been attempted too seldom in the Elementary Schools, and, in consequence, much talent in teaching has run to waste. Its adoption, especially in senior classes, would often be greatly to the advantage of both teacher and taught; and if it is judiciously used, it is quite compatible with the exercise of the strong influence which the class teacher should have on the characters of his scholars.'[1]

[1] *Handbook*, 1927, p. 39.

The 1927 recommendation is repeated almost word for word in the 1937 edition of the *Handbook*, but a note of caution is added: the possible disadvantages of specialization are spelled out and 'it will obviously be the duty of the head teacher to watch carefully the operation of specialised teaching to avoid these dangers, and to take steps to see that someone is responsible for the well-being and progress of each individual child, either the class teacher or a person whose functions are akin to those of a tutor or housemaster'.[1]

At least up to 1944, when they became secondary modern schools, it would seem that most English senior schools entrusted the teaching of the 'class' subjects – English, mathematics, geography and history – to the class teacher. In Scotland it would seem that the already more rapid adoption of specialist teaching was accelerated by the system of qualification by way of endorsement on the teachers' certificate of an additional qualification to teach only a specified subject or subjects to the senior classes, coupled with a change in the pattern of the ordinary M.A. course. It was in 1933 that one of H.M. Inspectors in Scotland mentioned some of the weaknesses of specialist teaching and expressed the hope that at least English, history, geography and mathematics might be taken by one teacher. The Scottish Advisory Council, in their report on the training of teachers in 1946, made the same point but, as they considered that the same standard as that already required for the endorsement was necessary in each subject for teachers who would teach several subjects in a secondary school, they were forced into the position of recommending that the training course for graduate teachers in secondary schools should extend to five years. Needless to say their recommendation has not been adopted.

There is one piece of evidence that the form master system in Scottish schools was an import from England. One of the Chief Inspectors in his Report for 1925–26 not only referred to it as an English idea but felt it necessary to explain for the benefit of Scottish readers what the system was: 'In the secondary schools it is generally admitted that the sudden change at the qualifying stage from one teacher to several is not entirely advantageous. . . . A remedy is sometimes found in the English form master system, the selection for each class of one of the specialist teachers whose business it is. . . .'[2] Since that date the official reports give little clue as to whether form masters play a more important part in one country than the other: the Scottish Education Department and the Ministry of Education alike have been in the habit of referring to their role from time to time invariably in order to exhort form masters to take their responsibilities more seriously and to suggest to headteachers that they organize their schools in such a way that they can do so. The Newsom Report, however, considered that 'a return to a general practitioner basis in the "classroom subjects" as a whole seems equally undesirable and indeed impracticable if the kind of work sketched out in the last few chapters is to be attempted'. The Report described the present situation in English secondary modern schools as follows:

'Some of the teachers will have been students in teachers' training colleges before

---

[1] *Handbook*, 1937, p. 40.   [2] *General Reports for the Year 1925–26*, p. 44.
Y

the last war. They are the professional general practitioners: they provide the most stable and the most flexible part of the staff, but promotion has carried many of them on to more specialised duties. They will have been accustomed to take their own form for both English and arithmetic but their training and most of their experience in their more formative years was with younger boys and girls than those with whom we are mostly concerned. Another group will have come from the general teachers' training colleges since the war. They will have made a deeper study of one, or sometimes two, subjects than their pre-war colleagues did, but this often means that they feel unfitted, certainly in their earlier years of teaching, to teach other subjects.'[1]

Thus the extent of specialist teaching, and the problems it presents of treating each pupil as an individual, are now much the same in England as in Scotland.

JOURNEYMAN AND APPRENTICE

One solution to the problem which has been put forward in both countries is also similar. The Newsom Report says:

'The more points of contact teachers have with their pupils, the better the chance they have of establishing successful personal relations. All that we have said earlier in relation to the value of extra-curricular activities applies here, and the suggestion that more teachers should be able to make some contribution in the field of art, crafts, music and physical education has added force in that these are subjects particularly likely to lead to informal, recreative activities outside the lesson programme.'[2]

The Scottish Education Department in their Report for 1961 say:

'Some teachers contrive to talk to their pupils both inside and outside the class-room in such a way as to convey the implication that they are more grown up than they used to be. In the atmosphere of craftsmanship which is natural in art rooms and in technical workshops there is frequently found a relationship between pupil and teacher akin to the traditional relationship of the apprentice to the journeyman, and such a relationship is wholly admirable.'[3]

The interesting thing about this model of the apprentice and the master craftsman is that it seeks to impose a responsibility for tutorial care on those teachers who are responsible for subjects which, of their very nature, are least susceptible to examination and external assessment, and in respect of those children who are least likely ever to enter as candidates in an examination. Part of the intention, of course, is that teachers should be induced to show rather more respect for the individuality of pupils whom, in the past, they have been accustomed to treat very much as children, both because of their limited intellectual accomplishments and because they have left school at such an early age:

---

[1] Newsom Report, 1963, p. 176. [2] Ibid., p. 102.
[3] *Education in Scotland in 1961*, p. 51.

but it will also help both sides if the teachers are those who, by the nature of the subjects they teach, have less easily measurable norms by which to judge the children's efforts, and if the children have never been made to feel a sense of failure in these particular subjects other than the sense of one's own short-comings which is a spur to greater effort.

THE MAINTENANCE OF STANDARDS

The relationship between teachers and their other pupils – the upper forty per cent who are expected to take public examinations – must, however, be expected to change in England, if not in Scotland as a result of the enormous increase in the amount of examining which will follow the introduction of the Certificate of Secondary Education and the increased participation of teachers in the examining process which will be necessary. The teacher who is responsible for both training his pupils and assessing the results of that training must neces-sarily maintain a more detached attitude towards them than the teacher who is simply preparing children for an external examination. The teacher who has no responsibility for the final assessment of his own pupils can become much more personally involved with them. If it is an external examination for which he is preparing them, he is, in a very real sense, on their side against the examiners.

In England internal assessment and teacher-participation in examinations are currently favoured as a means of giving the schools more freedom to determine their own curricula. The change that this will bring about in the relationship between teacher and pupil is a side effect which seems not to have been discussed. In Scotland the past record of teacher-participation in examinations is a proud one. The reduction in this since the introduction of the Scottish Certificate of Education is a side effect of administrative changes in the conduct of the exam-inations. The teaching profession will be compensated by being represented on the new Examination Board, but that is not at all the same thing.

Up to the present teachers have had very little choice in the manner in which their pupils shall be examined. The fact that the examining boards for the Cer-tificate of Secondary Education will arrange three different methods – external examination on the board's own syllabus; external examination but on a syllabus proposed by the school; and external moderation of internal school examina-tions – will in due course provide evidence of which mode the profession prefers.

At university level the Hale Report does supply some statement of opinions by university teachers. Only half the teachers at Oxford and Cambridge covered by a sample survey expected to be participating in university examinations, but eighty-two per cent of them thought that the present method of written degree examinations was satisfactory. Nearly all the teachers in the Scottish universities expected to take part in examinations but a smaller proportion (seventy-one per cent) thought that written examinations were a satisfactory form of assessment. This could simply mean that those who have had opportunity of knowing their students and of marking their papers have most reason to doubt the validity of the examinations. But it could imply that there is something incompatible between the tutorial relationship and the examining function. Perhaps tutors at Oxford and Cambridge were complacent about written examinations because they wanted to have no hand in any alternative.

Be that as it may, there is surely some significance in the paradox that, under the English system of specialization, where the teacher is better placed to have an intimate knowledge of his pupils' capabilities, importance is attached to the quality of performance (and who better could award credits and distinctions than the teachers?), yet examinations are external. In Scotland, on the other hand, because of the broad nature of the curriculum, teachers see more pupils for less time, examinations have in the past been an affair of pass or fail, with no nonsense about credits, yet the teachers have had a hand in examining.

Whatever its effect on the relationship between teacher and taught, the active participation of teachers in examining calls for something more than a high standard of integrity and a sense of professional standards; it also presupposes a certain minimum experience by those members of the profession who are responsible for the final assessment of their pupils. The newly qualified teacher, able as he may be in other respects, simply does not have that familiarity with the standards achieved by large numbers of children on which he can base his norms, whether for the purposes of submitting estimates for an examination set externally or for establishing the standards for an internal examination. As might be expected, therefore, the practice in Scottish schools is to insist that only experienced teachers shall be charged with presenting pupils for the Scottish Certificate of Education. There is an importance attached not only to professional training for admission to the profession but also to seniority within the profession which is not found in England. There are other reasons for this, but one of the most important factors must be that teachers are felt to be responsible for setting standards. It is not simply that children who are facing an important examination deserve the best teachers in order to enhance their chances of success – the brilliant young teacher would in that case have his part to play – it is that the teaching of examination candidates must be securely based on a familiarity with the standards expected. This is not to overlook that examinations are taken so seriously that headmasters are reluctant to entrust their senior classes with a teacher who is untried.

CHAPTER TWENTY-EIGHT

The Transmission of Culture

THE PROFESSION OF WORK

The fact that Scottish teachers in the past played an active part in the examining of their pupils does not mean that they were either given, or – apparently – desired any more freedom to determine their own curricula than did English teachers under a system of external examinations. The subjects to be taught were laid down in the Codes, the content of each subject was determined for the secondary schools by the examination regulations, and the teaching in primary schools was governed by the concept of a profession of work judged appropriate for each stage. The very fact that educational provision was more generous in Scotland meant that curriculum planning was more structured. The primary schools were, for many years, charged with bringing all, or nearly all, their children up to a level of attainment at the age of about twelve which would serve as an adequate starting point for secondary education. Compared with England a high proportion of the children did in fact go on to a secondary school. The secondary schools are now criticized for having concentrated too much on the type of course which led to university entrance but, again, compared with England a high proportion of their pupils did go on to a university. Because the system was so comprehensive, and because each stage could be regarded as preparatory for the next, the profession of work at each stage could be regarded as an integral part of the total body of knowledge which alone could fit a person for his place in civilized society.

In the English elementary schools the few who won a scholarship to the secondary school could be looked upon as rather exceptional: they owed their success to their own innate abilities. The same was true of the few who won scholarships to the universities from the maintained grammar schools. In the independent secondary schools and at the universities, the attitude was rather more that, having succeeded in obtaining a place at the favoured institution, the student was assured of some minimum success. The precise degree of that success was up to him: his teacher would help him as much as he could and then leave him to his fate in the examination room, knowing that a bare pass was easily gained, but confident that, wherever that extra ability lay to gain a credit or a 'first', it had been carefully nurtured. The English system leads naturally to the feeling that each stage of education is worth while for itself, and that the function of the curriculum is to give to the individual opportunity for self-development: the Scottish system tends to concentrate more on the curriculum as the vehicle for the transmission of the national culture. These are, of course, two aspects of education which are so closely interwoven as to be inseparable, though there is room for a difference of emphasis.

The Spens Report made the point clearly. The chapter on the Principles of the Curriculum started by discussing the various influences which help to determine what the schools shall teach:

'Of these the first and foremost is the community, acting either formally through its organ, the State, or less explicitly but none the less effectively by imposing its "form and pressure" upon schools that are not subject to State regulations as well as upon those that are. Speaking broadly, the interest of the State is to see that the schools provide the means by which the nation's life may be maintained in its integrity from generation to generation; to make sure that the young are prepared to preserve – and some to advance – its standards in all modes of activity which are important to the common weal. In a democratic community it must "educate its masters"; in communities of other types it must see that the citizens are trained for obedient and willing service. Underneath this explicit, overt educational activity of the State, working through laws and regulations, there is the unformulated but very real demand of the community that the young shall grow up in conformity with the national ethos.'

This is the most important influence on the planning of courses. But in their execution, according to Spens, the State has 'everything to gain from the free growth of individuality among its potential citizens. In our view a school fulfils its proper purposes in so far as it fosters that growth, helping every boy and girl to achieve the highest degree of individual development of which he or she is capable.'[1]

This article of faith was echoed in very similar phrases by the Advisory Council on Education in Scotland and, more recently, by the Scottish Education Department. It is in their interpretation of this very general statement of aims that English schools differ in emphasis from those in Scotland. In the balance which they are constantly striving to achieve between general and more special-ized studies, English schools are clearly concerned to bring their pupils into at least some superficial contact with many of the facets of a nationally transmitted culture and into rather closer contact with some aspects of it. Nevertheless the main justification for specialization in the secondary schools, and of the con-centrated nature of the syllabuses in some subjects, is in the exercise it gives to the pupils for the development of their own powers: they use the material of the national culture for their own ends. The Scottish distrust of specialization, and the fact that many of the syllabuses are more in the nature of a broad general survey of the subject than a concentrated study of selected topics, suggests a greater concern to see that the rising generation is made familiar with the main features of the cultural tradition.

[1] Spens Report, 1938, pp. 149–52.

TEACHING AND LEARNING

If there is this difference in emphasis, then it is to be expected that in England there should be more insistence on active learning by the pupils and less concern if the quality of the teaching they receive is rather variable. In Scotland it is to be expected that the accent should be on the imparting of information and on ensuring that the average competence of the teaching profession should be as high as possible.

The difference in attitude is most marked in the doubts expressed by Scottish schools about the introduction of an advanced grade. Opposition to it is partly based on a fear that the evil of specialization will follow in its train, though this seems unlikely as long as the universities base their entrance requirements on the higher grade, since the amount of specialization which it is possible to graft on to the present pattern in one year after the highers must be minimal. Opposition is no doubt partly attributable to a desire not to tackle a job unless it can be done well: many Scottish teachers would probably object to the kind of makeshift arrangements which went by the name of sixth forms in English grammar schools before the war; and the number of very small rural secondary schools in Scotland presents a very real problem. But there is also a reluctance to embark on what is now regarded as work proper to the universities. This is not because the teachers of the fifth and sixth years in Scottish schools are any less well qualified than their opposite numbers in England, or because they are any less willing to face an intellectual challenge. It is simply that traditions of teaching are different.

The grammar school teacher in England, particularly if he is a graduate of Oxford or Cambridge, will have received much of his tuition at the university in a small tutorial group – perhaps even alone with his tutor, so that he will have been made to feel that he was contributing almost as much to his own education as his teacher. At Oxford and Cambridge his tutor will not have been a professor since those who hold a university chair are forbidden by statute from taking part in college teaching: his tutor may have been a university reader or lecturer, but it is just as likely that he will have been a junior fellow of the college holding no university appointment, or a research student, or even someone employed part-time to give tutorials who had no other connection with the university at all. He will have attended at least some of the lectures he went to (chosen because they were given by some of the more famous names of the academic world) purely for inspirational purposes, or for entertainment, and not for the sake of acquiring information. Although therefore, the senior members of a grammar school staff keep some of the sixth form work to themselves because it is more pleasant, their own experience may well suggest that there is no objection to their sharing it with an untrained graduate straight from the university.

At the Scottish universities no undergraduate, from the most able candidate for honours to the humblest aspirant to an ordinary degree, can have avoided being taught by a senior member of the departments in which he took graduating subjects – usually by the professor in person. In the Scottish universities a student cannot sit a degree examination without a 'class certificate' from the head of the department concerned to the effect that he has 'regularly attended and duly performed' the work of the class, and such a certificate may be refused if he has put in less than seventy-five per cent of the possible attendances. A strict check on attendances is being increasingly dropped, but the fact remains that the lecture is the normal way of covering the work of the course. The Scottish tradition requires that as much of the lecturing as possible should be given by the professor himself, and that it is particularly important that the professor should try to give at least one of the lecture courses in his department attended by first-year students. The whole point of the universities is that students should be brought into contact with the very best minds.

For much the same reasons undergraduates in Scotland spend more time receiving instruction than at other British universities. The Hale Report gave figures based on a 'standardised average' for each university in an attempt to exclude differences in the distribution between faculties and departments: the actual hours spent on each form of instruction by the students in the survey was then expressed in relation to the standardized average for each group of universities:

TABLE 64. *Hours of instruction related to a standardized average*

University	Lectures	Written Exercise Classes	Practicals	Tutorials	Seminars	Private Study
Oxford and Cambridge	−1.26	−0.18	−0.77	+0.89	−0.82	+1.91
London	−0.23	+0.32	−0.22	−0.12	+0.44	+0.84
Larger civic	−0.22	+0.02	+0.19	−0.17	+0.20	−1.35
Smaller civic	+0.21	−0.14	−0.33	−0.18	+0.09	+0.28
Scotland	+1.58	+0.04	+0.52	−0.33	+0.11	+0.36

The comparison is not entirely a fair one because the Scottish universities take a much higher proportion of ordinary degree students than any English university. Unfortunately separate figures are not given for honours and pass degree students. The only evidence for the difference is in the figures given in the Robbins Report of the frequency with which discussion periods with their academic supervisor were attended by Scottish students and undergraduates at the larger civic universities in England, which between them account for the majority of pass degree students:

TABLE 65. *Percentage of students who met their academic supervisor*

	Once a fort-night or more frequently	Twice a term or less frequently	No academic supervision
LARGER CIVIC UNIVERSITIES IN ENGLAND			
Honours	45	29	25
Pass	23	46	31
SCOTTISH UNIVERSITIES			
Honours	18	52	29
Pass	2	82	16

Whatever the reason, most Scottish teachers have been accustomed, during their own education, to receiving more formal tuition than English teachers. The reason, almost certainly, is to be found in the nature and organization of the general degree: nearly two-thirds of Scottish graduate teachers are in fact ordinary graduates. This must predispose them to place greater emphasis than do their English colleagues on the imparting of knowledge to their pupils and less on the pupils' own contribution to the learning process.

In the schools there is no such simple measure of the balance between formal instruction and private study as there is at the universities. Even in England, below the sixth forms pupils spend very little time at school in private study. The main difference in practice between England and Scotland in the main part of the secondary school course is that, whereas the typical timetable of a Scottish school provides for forty periods of forty minutes each in the week, it is more common in England to find thirty-five periods of forty-five minutes. In the primary schools there is a more marked contrast between the insistence on a feeling of leisureliness in the Ministry of Education's 1959 *Handbook* and the obsession of the Scottish 1950 *Memorandum* with the importance of avoiding any waste of time.

SUMMARY

On the whole each aspect of the educational systems of England and Scotland in which differences of emphasis are to be found, whether it be in the primary school, the secondary school or those institutions in which the teachers receive their education and training, reinforces every other aspect: in England, the importance attached to individuality and self-expression, the relationship between teacher and taught, the belief in specialization, examination practice and the separation of moral from intellectual training; in Scotland, the emphasis on the transmission of adult standards and ideals, the broadness of the curriculum, more attention devoted to teaching than to learning and a different view of examinations.

English practice requires the creation of an environment in which the child can develop naturally: that this will be an artificial environment is acknowledged. The aim is to create a situation in which childhood nature can be relied upon to produce a reasonably well-adjusted young person: it is then up to each individual to make the necessary adjustment to adult life after he has left school. English administrators spend all their time considering the schools as organizations. English teachers are not required to place any particular *expertise* in the forefront of their professional equipment: they are called upon to understand children and to 'be themselves'.

The aristocratic nature of English society, perhaps also a distrust of the intellect, have produced a school system which is essentially democratic because it depreciates the authority of the adult and emphasizes the individual worth of every single child who is not completely unresponsive or actively anti-social. It appears to take an extremely optimistic view of human nature: this may involve a certain amount of self-deception since it is part of the technique to encourage good behaviour by simply assuming that good behaviour is axiomatic and perhaps teachers (or at least the lucky ones) live in a fool's paradise created by the *Handbook of Suggestions*. Nevertheless the English attitude towards the young is an essentially generous one.

Scottish practice is much more to regard children as miniature adults and the schools as society writ small. The harmony which existed in the eighteenth century between intellectual accomplishments and moral values was the basis on which the schools came to regard it as their function to concentrate on only one aspect of the training of the young to fit into the community. The particular brand of democratic society which is Scotland's pride has produced an essentially authoritarian attitude in the schools. That which is valued most is precisely that which it takes the young the most effort and the longest period of training to acquire. The teacher therefore sets the standards to which the pupils must learn to conform. This calls for considerable skill on their part: they must not only be fully qualified in the subjects they teach but also have a complete grasp of the best method of imparting their knowledge. The whole approach is one which inevitably leads to a somewhat ungenerous assessment of the nature of childhood.

At the same time there is sufficient common ground between the two countries to ensure that the education they offer to children between the ages of about eleven and sixteen or seventeen, though it may differ in detail, conforms basically to the same pattern. At least the same problems of providing suitably for the whole range of abilities and interests of children between these ages have had to be tackled, even if they have been approached from a somewhat different direction because of the very different backgrounds from which the schools started some fifty years ago. The main contrasts are to be found in the primary schools, in the English sixth form and in the ordinary degree courses of the Scottish universities. In these three fields recent developments suggest that, here too, England and Scotland are becoming less dissimilar.

In England it is probably social and economic factors which are most important in current rethinking of the schools' way of doing their job. Educational developments during the first half of the twentieth century followed a fairly logical progression. Opportunities were increased, but the methods used in the schools were largely the working out in practice of ideas which were already half formed: on the whole the movement of theoretical ideas about education confirmed the direction in which the schools were set. Now the stage has been reached when England might cease to be an aristocracy and become more a technocracy. The demand is for skilled manpower in industry and commerce: the demand in administration is for the expert rather than the all-round amateur. At the same time the questioning of traditional beliefs has put an end to comfortable assumptions and seems to demand a more authoritarian approach to moral training. The schools are being called upon to shoulder a responsibility they are well accustomed to accept, but they will have to carry it out in a different way. English educationalists are responding in the way they know best by debating about school organization, but there are signs that the content and methods of the school syllabus may be altered too.

Scotland, on the other hand, has reached a point at which the country's economy can no longer assume the export of all her best talent. But she is not so much worried about the supply of the top level of professional people and technologists as of technicians and craftsmen: it is the second stratum of education which most needs to be developed. At the same time the challenge to traditional beliefs serves to call in question a traditional authoritarianism without substituting a new one. At least in the primary schools, however, it is as much an educational-philosophic development as any influence from outside the schools which is responsible for changed ideas.

It would be an interesting study to trace how far the same psychological theories, equally accessible to both English and Scottish educators, has met with a different reception in the two parts of the Kingdom simply because the climate of educational thought was, in the one country, favourable, and in the other unreceptive. Unfortunately the official reports are not the most rewarding fields in which to find statements of abstract principle: they are severely practical in purpose and extremely eclectic in character. In the curious blend which they present of practical advice and the distillation of currently popular beliefs it is difficult to isolate with any certainty the influence of any particular theorist. There is, however, one notable exception to this: the Scottish *Memorandum on Primary Education in Scotland* of 1965 represents a complete reversal of most of what the Department had been saying fifteen years earlier: it was obviously written very much under the influence of the teachings of Piaget. That the general tenor of a memorandum of this type can so clearly be traced to one specific influence has all the signs of a sudden conversion.

As for the children themselves, they are not aware of the niceties of their teachers' attitudes towards education. They do pick up, and exaggerate in their own way, the more obvious outward and visible signs of the values near to their teachers' hearts. English schools have long looked upon character building as one of their important aims, and some of the means they have used towards this end grew out of the very defects of the schools and universities at the beginning of the nineteenth century. The prefect system in the Public Schools was first introduced as a way of harnessing the tyranny of the older boys over the younger:

'Even at Rugby and in the days of Arnold such practices as tossing in blankets and roasting of small boys before an open fire were not unknown – as readers of *Tom Brown's School Days* will remember. But Arnold never acquiesced in evils such as these, and it was in order to deal with them that he developed the prefect system, the origin of which is often associated with his name and with Rugby. In an article in the *Quarterly Journal of Education* he speaks of the "power given by the supreme authorities of the school to the Sixth Form, to be exercised by them over the lower boys, for the sake of securing a regular government amongst the boys themselves, and avoiding the evils of anarchy; in other words of the lawless tyranny of physical strength".'[1]

In the universities, rowing, rugby and cricket took the place of less desirable sports. To quote Barnard again:

'There is no doubt that extravagance became less fashionable at Oxford and Cambridge as the second half of the nineteenth century progressed. This was largely due to the development of secondary education and the throwing open of scholarships so as to widen the field from which candidates were drawn. It is also probable, as Professor Archer suggests, that the development of sports at the universities put an end to the exclusiveness of the hunting, shooting and racing type of undergraduates. The Oxford and Cambridge boat race, as an annual event, dates from 1856; inter-collegiate boat races started about 1815 and were properly organised from about 1837. Cricket (in top hats) also developed in the forties. All these activities gave prominence in college to the undergraduate who could *do* things – and not to the man with the greatest wealth or the "best family" or the most extravagant tastes; and this characteristic *fortunately* has remained true of both Oxford and Cambridge.'[2]

For the casual visitor to English schools the most obvious sign of the things that have been held in the highest esteem are the boards of varnished oak bearing in gold letters the names of those pupils who have been appointed prefect or Captain of the School, Captain of the Eleven or of the Fifteen. There may in addition be public evidence of academic distinction, but usually in the form which is thought to bring most honour to the school as well as to the individual – the names may also be recorded of those who have won open scholarships to Oxford or Cambridge.

Amongst the pupils themselves the boy who draws attention to himself by regularly coming top of his class has been likely to earn the nickname of 'swot' and could only enjoy the regard of his fellows if he compensated for his intellectual difference from the common crowd by also being good at games or a

---

[1] H. C. Barnard, *A History of English Education* ,1947, p. 77.
[2] Ibid., p. 125, (my italics).

more than usually unassuming person. The distrust of the intellectual may be only a form of self-reassurance, and most boys do enjoy games, but it is probably no accident that the recent growth of interest in the less formal and more individual types of physical activity coincides with a suggestion that, in their upper classes schools should be deliberately outgoing, and also with the moves towards a reorganization of secondary schools which would produce a more adult atmosphere in those which cater for later adolescence. At the same time the expansion of higher education is bound to have its effect on the attitudes of school children themselves to academic achievements.

One of the reports on Scottish schools brought back to the Schools Inquiry Commission in 1868 mentioned 'the dux, seated at the head of the class, wearing perhaps a medal.' The dux is the scholar who sits at the top of the senior class. Dux medals are still awarded (just as prizes are awarded in English schools), though they are nowadays not worn in class. It is still common practice for the pupils in a class to be seated in their order of merit as determined by school examinations. Some colour is given to the suggestion that moral and intellectual merit have in the past been confused in Scottish schools by the fact that it was not uncommon for children to be punished to check mistakes in their work as well as for bad behaviour. This was still sufficiently common for the Department to feel it necessary in 1950 to tell primary school teachers that the practice should be abandoned. Even in 1965 they felt it necessary to say that children should not be seated in an order determined by their intellectual ability.

The casual visitor to a Scottish school will see the same varnished oak boards with gold lettering. He may see the names of the Head Prefects or of the Captain of Cricket or Football, but the place of honour, on the walls of the school itself, in the esteem of the staff, and also of the pupils, is reserved for the Dux of the school. The essential difference between the schools of north and south is undoubtedly that, whereas these same oak boards are not to be found in English primary schools, a Dux board is by no means uncommon in primary schools in Scotland. All the indications are that, sooner or later, they will disappear. Meantime they are a more permanent reminder of an attitude which is changing than the mark made across the palm of one's hand by the tawse.

Glossary

Maintained school (England)

One which is maintained by the local education authority, i.e. the authority pays the salaries of the teachers and other employees, pays for heating, lighting, etc. and provides the equipment. The building does not necessarily belong to the Authority since maintained schools are either County (originally 'Board schools'; later known as 'provided' schools) or Voluntary ('non-provided') schools.

County school

One which was provided by the school board or local education authority and is wholly the responsibility of the authority.

Voluntary school

One which was provided by some other body and is normally vested in trustees. Voluntary schools are of two types: the Voluntary Controlled School, although not originally built by the authority and not legally vested in them is wholly their financial responsibility: this includes not only maintenance of the building but also the cost of any necessary improvements. The Voluntary Aided school is 'maintained' by the local education authority in every respect except that they are not responsible for repairs to the exterior of the building (they *are* responsible for maintenance of the interior of the building). Any capital improvement of an Aided school is the responsibility of the trustees, though they may apply to the Department of Education and Science for a grant or loan towards the cost.

Public school (Scotland)

Any school under the management of an education authority and is the rough equivalent of the English maintained school. It may have originally been either a 'provided' or a 'transferred' school.

Transferred school

One which was built by somebody other than the education authority but has been transferred to them either by sale or by lease. They are, of course, fully responsible for its maintenance and improvement

A new Voluntary school in England may be built by promoters who can then (subject to directions by the Secretary of State) expect the local education authority to maintain it. New schools may similarly be built in Scotland and then transferred to the education authority or representations may be made to the Secretary of State that a new denominational school is necessary and he may empower (but not compel) the education authority to build one.

Primary Education

England. Full-time education suitable to the requirements of pupils under the age of ten years sixth months, and other pupils under the age of twelve whom it is expedient to educate with them. The Education Act permits the Secretary of State to approve schools which retain pupils beyond the prescribed age by way of experiment.

Scotland. Progressive elementary education in such subjects as may be prescribed in the Code regard being had to the age, ability and aptitude of the pupils concerned. The 1965 Code requires that, in each year of attendance at a primary school, pupils shall be given instruction in reading, writing and arithmetic; in the use and understanding of written and spoken English; in music; in art and handwork; in nature study; and in physical education. They shall also, from such stage as is appropriate having regard to their age, ability and aptitude, be given instruction in geography, history, written composition and, in the case of girls, needlework.

Secondary Education

England. Full-time education suitable to the requirements of pupils between the ages of twelve and nineteen together with those over the age of ten years six months, whom it is expedient to educate with them, but excluding the education provided in establishments of further education.

Scotland. Progressive courses of instruction of such length and in such subjects as may be approved and appropriate to the age, ability and aptitude of pupils who have been transferred from primary schools and departments. The provision of secondary education shall be deemed adequate if a reasonable variety of courses is provided from which the parent of a pupil may select a course from which, in the opinion of the education authority he shows reasonable promise of profiting.

Primary school

England. A school for providing primary education, and also, until the section of the Act requiring that primary and secondary education shall be provided in separate schools shall have been implemented, a school which provides both both primary and secondary education.

Scotland. Not defined in the Act, but in fact a school which only provides primary education.

Secondary school

England. A school for providing secondary education (and nothing else).

Scotland. Not defined in the Act, but in fact a school which provides secondary education (whether or not it also provides primary education).

Department

England. A part of a school which is under the control of its own headteacher. In practice the distinction between (a) a primary 'school' with an infants 'department' and a junior 'department' each under a different headteacher, and (b) two adjacent, but separate 'schools' is so slight as to be meaningless. The former will have one body of managers: the latter will, more often than not, have a single body of managers to control the two 'schools' (though they could in theory be different).

Scotland. 'Department' is not defined, although 'primary department' and 'secondary department' are used in the Code as if the meaning were self-evident. Occasionally the term may be used to describe the infants or the junior or senior division of a primary school or department. Whatever the usage, a department is always part of a school all of which is under the control of the same head-teacher.

Infants

England. Children between the age at which they start school (other than in nursery schools or classes) and the age of seven plus.

Scotland. The classes designated as Primary I and Primary II.

Juniors

England. Children between the ages of seven plus and eleven plus.

Scotland. Children in the classes designated as Primary III, IV and V (i.e. seven plus to nine plus).

Seniors

England (pre-1945 usage). Children attending a Senior department, i.e. one catering for children from the age of seven, eight or nine or – increasingly after the Hadow Report – eleven up to the age of fourteen or fifteen.

Scotland. Children in the classes designated Primary VI and VII.

All-age school (England only)

A school which meantime provides both primary and secondary education. The term is not used in Scotland.

Reorganization (England)

The separation of primary and secondary education. Most frequently by 'decapitating' a number of all-age schools, i.e. transferring all their senior pupils to a new secondary modern school.

Religious Instruction

England (all schools). Religious instruction must be given in every maintained school (both Country and Voluntary). Any pupil may be excused from the religious instruction given in the school at his parents' request – and may be withdrawn from school on certain conditions in order to receive some form of religious instruction different from that provided in the school: this other religious instruction must be given off the school premises except in a county secondary school, where it *may* be arranged to be given on the school premises. It may not be made a condition of attendance at any maintained school that a pupil attends, or does not attend, a particular Sunday school or place of worship.

England (County schools). The religious instruction must be given in accordance with the '*agreed syllabus*', which is drawn up for each authority's area by an advisory committee representative of the churches and the teachers.

England (Voluntary Controlled schools). The religious instruction is given in accordance with the agreed syllabus. But arrangements have to be made for the children whose parents so request to receive religious instruction in accordance with the trust deed or the established practice of the school during not more than two periods a week.

England (Voluntary Aided schools). The religious instruction is given in accordance with the trust deed or the established practice of the school. But if any parents so request, their children may, subject to certain conditions, be given religious instruction in accordance with the agreed syllabus.

Scotland (all schools). The education authority may continue to provide religious instruction in accordance with the established custom of the school. The times devoted to religious instruction must be specified by the Secretary of State for each school. No pupil may be placed at a disadvantage by reason of the denomination he or his parents belong to, or by reason of his being withdrawn from the religious instruction provided in the school. An education authority may cease to provide religious instruction in a school if their proposal to do so is approved by a majority of local government electors in the area.

Scotland (Transferred schools). For each Transferred school the education authority must appoint an unpaid supervisor of religious instruction approved by the church or denominational body in whose interest the school was formerly conducted to report to the authority on the efficiency of the religious instruction provided.

Teachers: Tenure of office

England (County schools). Teachers can only be appointed and dismissed by the local education authority.

England (Controlled schools). Teachers can only be appointed and dismissed by the local education authority except that a certain proportion of the staff may be selected as '*reserved teachers*' for their fitness and competence to give religious instruction in accordance with the practice of the school and they then become

z

liable to be dismissed by the foundation managers or governors if they do not give such instruction efficiently and suitably. The headteacher may not be a 'reserved teacher'.

England (Aided schools). A teacher appointed to give religious instruction (other than in accordance with the agreed syllabus) who fails to do so efficiently and suitably may be dismissed by the foundation managers or governors without the consent of the local education authority. The appointment and dismissal of all other teachers in Aided schools is governed by the rules of management or articles of government of the school, but no teacher may be dismissed without the approval of the local education authority.

Scotland (all schools). All teachers are appointed by the education authority. Teachers appointed to a transferred school must also be approved as regards religious belief and character by the church or denominational body in whose interest the school was formerly conducted. Before the setting up of the Teachers' General Council no teacher could be dismissed except after a resolution of a two-thirds majority of the members present at an education committee meeting: the teacher could then appeal to the Secretary of State who might hold a public enquiry.

Episcopal Church. The Scottish Province of the Church of England.

Direct Grant Schools

The category of direct grant schools in England was established more or less by accident. In 1919 independent grammar schools were given the option of receiving financial assistance from public funds either from the local education authority or by means of a capitation grant direct from the Board of Education. By 1943 there were 232 which had adopted the latter course. After the 1944 Act came into force the direct grant list was reviewed and a large number of independent schools and schools which had up to them been aided by the local education authorities applied for admission to the list. The Minister of Education of the time enumerated four principles on which the new direct grant list was to be compiled: they included the financial stability of the school, its non-local character, the nature of the education provided and the views of the L.E.A. for the area in which it was situated. In the event the number of schools on the list fell from 232 in 1943 to 164 in 1952. Pressure was however exerted on the Ministry from time to time to re-open the list, and in 1957 this was done. There were in 1964, 179 schools on the direct grant list. Of these 83 were boys' schools, 94 girls' and two mixed schools: 57 of the direct grant boys' schools in England and Wales were in membership of the Headmasters' Conference and just over half of these were boarding schools.

Direct grant schools have come to be regarded as a half-way stage between the maintained school and the completely independent school. At least 25 per cent of their places have to be offered as free places to pupils who have spent at least two years in a maintained primary school and any local education authority which takes up free places in the school can in addition apply to the governors of the school to take up reserved places up to a normal maximum of a further 25 per cent of the places available. Up to half the places in the schools may therefore be at the disposal of the L.E.A. The remaining places – the residuary places – are allocated on the basis of an entrance examination set by the school. But the tuition fees for the residuary places are fixed by the Department of Education and Science. The fees are scaled according to the parents' income, and the maximum fee is also fixed.

The income of the Direct Grant schools therefore comes from (a) endowments, (b) the L.E.A. which pays the full fees of free and reserved place holders, (c) the parents of residuary place holders who pay according to their income, (d) a fixed capitation grant from the central government and (e) the balance of the graded fees for residuary place holders (which is also paid by the Department).

The category of grant-aided schools in Scotland only includes 29 schools. They receive from the Scottish Education Department 60 per cent of their approved expenditure or of their approved deficit, whichever is the lower. Their fees are fixed by the managers subject to the Department's approval but there is no parental income scale laid down by the Department. They are not required to reserve any fixed proportion of their places for education authority pupils and many of them reserve no places at all, though some, because of local circumstances have agreed to special arrangements under which the education authority can take up some places in the school.

List of Tables

Bibliography

Text references are given in square brackets

ADAMSON, J. W. *A Short History of Education.* Cambridge University Press, 1922. [4]

BALFOUR, G. *The Educational Systems of Great Britain and Ireland.* Oxford University Press, 1903. [210, Tables 3 & 4]

BANKS, O. *Parity and Prestige in English Secondary Education.* Routledge & Kegan Paul, 1955. [146, 194]

BARNARD, H. C. *A History of English Education from 1760.* 2nd edn. University of London Press, 1961. [20, 332]

BOYD, W. *Education in Ayrshire through Seven Centuries.* University of London Press, 1961. [6, 274, 275]

BRAMWELL, R. D. *Elementary School Work 1900–1925.* University of Durham, 1961. [103,]

DAVIE, G. E. *The Democratic Intellect.* Edinburgh University Press, 1961. [4, 5, 22, 242] Quoting Burnet, Grierson and Others, Problems of National Education, 1919. [15, 255] Quoting Edinburgh Review. [23]

DIXON, N. 'Comprehensive Education and the Small Burgh School', in *Education in the North,* Spring 1965. [72–73]

DOUGLAS, J. W. B. *The Home and the School.* MacGibbon & Kee, 1964. [221]

EDWARDS, R. *The Secondary Technical School.* University of London Press, 1960. [164]

JEFFREYS, M. V. C. *Revolution in Teacher Training.* Pitman, 1961. [273]

GRAVES, J. *Policy and Progress in Secondary Education 1902–1942.* Nelson, 1943. [12]

KELSALL, R. K. *Applications for Admission to Universities.* Association of Universities of the British Commonwealth, 1957. [Table 57]

KNOX, H. M. *Two Hundred and Fifty Years of Scottish Education.* Oliver & Boyd, 1953. [7, 16, 20, 65, 237]

LEWIS, R. and MAUDE, A. *The English Middle Classes,* Penguin, 1949 [213, 214]

MACKINTOSH, M. *Education in Scotland,* Robert Gibson, 1962. [218]

MCCLELLAND, W. *Selection for Secondary Education.* University of London Press, 1942. [217]

MORGAN, A. *The Rise and Progress of Scottish Education.* Oliver & Boyd, 1927. [6, 18]

National Foundation for Educational Research. *A Survey of Rewards and Punishments in Schools.* Newnes, 1952. [308]

RICH, R. W. *The Training of Teachers during the Nineteenth Century.* Cambridge University Press, 1933. [234, 288]

SAMPSON, A. *Anatomy of Britain Today.* Hodder & Stoughton, 1965. [214, 234]

SAUNDERS, L. J. *Scottish Democracy 1815–1840.* Oliver & Boyd, 1950. [8, 211]

SCOTLAND, J. 'The Quality of Student Teachers', in *Scottish Educational Journal,* Vol 47, pp. 115–17 and 133–4. [232, Table 47]

SCOTTISH COUNCIL FOR RESEARCH IN EDUCATION. *Curriculum for Pupils of Twelve to Fifteen Years.* University of London Press, 1931. [96]

The Prognostic Value of University Entrance Examinations in Scotland. University of London Press, 1936. [231, Table 46]

Scottish Primary School Organisation. University of London Press, 1939. [89]

See also McClelland, *Selection for Secondary Education,* Boyd, *Education in Ayrshire* and Simpson *Education in Aberdeenshire.*

Scottish Educational Journal (Leader) Vol. 6, p. 375. [47]

SIMPSON, I. J. *Education in Aberdeenshire before 1872.* University of London Press, 1947. [273]

TREVELYAN, G. M. *English Social History*. Longmans, 1942. [213]

TROPP, A. *The School Teachers*. Heinemann, 1957. [39]

VINCENT, W. A. L. *The State and School Education 1640–1660*. S.P.C.K., 1950. [3, 4, 8]

WADE, N. A. *Post-Primary Education in the Primary Schools of Scotland 1872–1936*. University of London Press, 1939. [45, 46, Table 32]

WHITELEY, L. D. *The Poor Student and the University*. Allen & Unwin, 1933. [Table 54]

WISEMAN, Ed. *Examinations and English Education*. Manchester University Press, 1961. [54]

OFFICIAL PUBLICATIONS

Nineteenth Century Reports

1826–30. *Scottish Universities* (Rosebery Commission). [22, 210, 242]

1861. *Elementary Education* (Newcastle Commission). [14, 83]

1864. *Public Schools* (Clarendon Commission). [14, 251]

1867. *Scottish Education* (Argyll Commission). [14, 16, 210, 212,]

1868. *Endowed Schools* (School Inquiry or Taunton Commission). [14, 54, 210, 212, 276, 333]

1875. *Endowed Schools and Hospitals – Scotland* (Colebrooke). [18]

1876. *Scottish Universities* (Inglis Commission). [22, 243]

1880. *Endowed Institutions – Scotland* (Moncrieff Commission). [19, 66]

1888. *Elementary Education* (Cross Commission). [50]

1895. *Secondary Education* (Bryce Commission). [20, 35, 50, 140, 251]

ENGLAND

Reports of the Consultative Committee

1926. *The Education of the Adolescent* (Hadow Report, 1926). [10, 25, 51, 52, 99, 145, 147, 150, 157]

1931. *The Primary School* (Hadow Report, 1931). [83, 97, 99]

1933. *Infant and Nursery Schools* (Hadow Report, 1933). [83, 312]

1938. *Secondary Education with special reference to Grammar Schools and Technical High Schools* (Spens Report). [53, 77, 127, 138–44, 151, 162, 169, 175, 193, 247, 253, 259, 317, 326, Tables 16, 51]

Reports of the Central Advisory Council (England)

1954. *Early Leaving*. [152, Tables 21 and 24]

1959. *15 to 18* (Crowther Report). [28, 155, 159, 199, 255, 257–60, 262, 268, Table 23]

1963. *Half Our Future* (Newsom Report). [161, 162, 189–92, 316–18, 322]

Reports of the Secondary School Examinations Council and Schools Council

1943. *Committee on Curriculum and Examinations in Secondary Schools* (Norwood Report). [53, 129, 142–4, 148, 151, 163, 194, 253]

1958. *Committee on Secondary School Examinations other than the G.C.E.* (Beloe Report). [158, Table 25]

1960. Third Report: *The General Certificate of Education and Sixth Form Studies* [226]

1961. Fourth Report: *The Certificate of Secondary Education*. [160, Table 26]

1963. Sixth Report: *Sixth Form Studies and University Entrance Requirements*. [262]

1963. Eighth Report: *Examining English Language*. [262]

1963. Examinations Bulletin No. 1. [223]

1966. Working Paper No. 5: Sixth Form Curriculum and Examinations. [263]

Reports of Departmental Committees, Working Parties, etc.

1925. *Training of Teachers for Public Elementary Schools* (Cmd. 2409). [282, 284, 288]

1944. *Teachers and Youth Leaders* (McNair Report). [283, 286, 290, 300]

1957. *The Scope and Content of the Three Year Course of Teacher Training* (Sixth Report of the National Advisory Council for the Training and Supply of Teachers). [289, 290]

Handbooks, Pamphlets and Memoranda

1905. Board of Education, *Handbook of Suggestions.* [57, 61, 101–22, 311]

1927. Board of Education, *Handbook of Suggestions.* [61, 84, 87, 98, 101–22, 309, 320]

1937. Board of Education, *Handbook of Suggestions.* [62, 84, 88, 90, 101–22, 140, 308, 321]

1959. Ministry of Education, *Primary Education.* [62, 64, 101–22, 312]

1928. *The New Prospect in Education.* [84]

1938. *The Organisation and Curriculum of Sixth Forms in Secondary Schools* (Pamphlet 114). [142, 260, Table 19]

1945. *The Nation's Schools* (Pamphlet 1). [151, 165, 166]

1947. *The New Secondary Education* (Pamphlet 9). [148, 150]

Circulars

1912. Circular 826. [140]

1925.   ,,   1350. [84]

1946.   ,,   113. [55]

1955.   ,,   289. [158]

1965.   ,,   10/65. [75, 201–4]

SCOTLAND

Reports of the Advisory Council

1944. *Training for Citizenship* (Cmd. 6495). [312]

1946. *Training of Teachers* (Cmd. 6723). [280, 321]

1946. *Primary Education* (Cmd. 6973). [62, 64, 217, 313]

1947. *Secondary Education* (Cmd. 7005). [40, 57, 174–6, 178, 256, 315]

1960. *Committee on the Post Fourth Year Examination Structure in Scotland* (Cmnd. 1068). [134, 257]

1961. *Committee on Transfer from Primary to Secondary Education* (Cmnd. 1538). [217]

Reports of Departmental Committees, Working Parties, etc.

1959. *Working Party on the Curriculum of the Senior Secondary School* (Introduction of the Ordinary Grade of the Scottish Leaving Certificate). [133, 178, 200, 266]

1962. *Working Party on Consultation on Educational Matters*

1962. *Working Party on the Appointment of Teachers to Education Committees.* [42]

1962. *Working Party on Relations between Education Authorities and Teachers.* [41, 60]

1963. *The Teaching Profession in Scotland* (Wheatley Report) (Cmnd. 2066). [43]

1963. *From School to Further Education* (Brunton Report). [27, 189–92]

Handbooks, Pamphlets and Memoranda

1950. *The Primary School in Scotland.* [62, 63, 87, 101–22, 310, 313, 315]

1955. *Junior Secondary Education.* [177, 315]

1965. *Primary Education in Scotland.* [60, 63, 64, 87, 93, 105, 120–2, 308, 314, 331]

1939. *Educational Pamphlet No. 4.* [109]

1939. *Memorandum Explanatory of the Day School Code.* [50, 90, 172]

1965. *Memorandum on Entry Requirements and Courses.* [299]

Circulars

1903. Circular 374. [46, 47]

1921.   ,,   44. [47, 95, 96]

1936.   ,,   103. [49]

GREAT BRITAIN

1958. *Grants to Students* (Anderson Report) (Cmnd. 1051). [236]

1963. *Higher Education* (Robbins Report) (Cmnd. 2154). [21, 28, 38, 235, 244, 246, 281, 286 294, 320, Tables 7, 39, 40, 41, 44, 45, 59, 60, 65]

1964. *University Teaching Methods* (Hale Report). [231, 233, 244, 246, 323, 328, Table 64]

Index